REACHING
FOR A
NEW DEAL

REACHING FOR A NEW DEAL

Ambitious Governance, Economic Meltdown, and Polarized Politics in Obama's First Two Years

Theda Skocpol and
Lawrence R. Jacobs,
editors

Russell Sage Foundation
New York

The Russell Sage Foundation

The Russell Sage Foundation, one of the oldest of America's general purpose foundations, was established in 1907 by Mrs. Margaret Olivia Sage for "the improvement of social and living conditions in the United States." The Foundation seeks to fulfill this mandate by fostering the development and dissemination of knowledge about the country's political, social, and economic problems. While the Foundation endeavors to assure the accuracy and objectivity of each book it publishes, the conclusions and interpretations in Russell Sage Foundation publications are those of the authors and not of the Foundation, its Trustees, or its staff. Publication by Russell Sage, therefore, does not imply Foundation endorsement.

Library of Congress Cataloging-in-Publication Data

Reaching for a new deal : ambitious governance, economic meltdown, and polarized politics in Obama's first two years / Theda Skocpol and Lawrence R. Jacobs, editors.
    p. cm.
    Includes bibliographical references and index.
    ISBN 978-0-87154-855-9 (pbk. : alk. paper) — ISBN 978-1-61044-711-9 (ebook)
    1. United States—Economic policy—2009– 2. United States—Politics and government—2009– 3. Polarization (Social sciences)—United States—History—21st century. 4. Recessions—United States—History—21st century.
I. Skocpol, Theda. II. Jacobs, Lawrence R.
    HC106.84.R43 2011
    330.973'0932—dc22   2011002140

Text design by Genna Patacsil.

RUSSELL SAGE FOUNDATION
112 East 64th Street, New York, New York 10065
10 9 8 7 6 5 4 3 2 1

Contents

Contributors |

THEDA SKOCPOL is the Victor S. Thomas Professor of Government and Sociology at Harvard University.

LAWRENCE R. JACOBS is the Walter F. and Joan Mondale Chair for Political Studies and director of the Center for the Study of Politics and Governance in the Hubert H. Humphrey Institute and Department of Political Science at the University of Minnesota.

ANDREA LOUISE CAMPBELL is associate professor of political science at MIT.

DANIEL CARPENTER is the Freed Professor of Government at Harvard University.

JUDITH A. LAYZER is associate professor of environmental policy in the Department of Urban Studies and Planning at MIT

LORRAINE M. McDONNELL is professor of political science at the University of California, Santa Barbara.

SUZANNE METTLER is the Clinton Rossiter Professor of American Institutions in the Department of Government at Cornell University.

JOHN D. SKRENTNY is director of the Center for Comparative Immigration Studies and professor of sociology at the University of California, San Diego.

DORIAN T. WARREN is assistant professor in the Department of Political Science and the School of International and Public Affairs at Columbia University.

Chapter 1 | Reaching for a New Deal: Ambitious Governance, Economic Meltdown, and Polarized Politics

Theda Skocpol and
Lawrence R. Jacobs

"THE NEW NEW DEAL—What Barack Obama can learn from F.D.R.—and what Democrats need to do" was the feature story in the *Time* magazine of November 24, 2008, which hit the newsstands soon after the historic 2008 elections. The striking cover portrayed a grinning Obama wearing a fedora and riding in an open car, a cigarette in a long silver holder jutting from his lips. The image nicely suggested that the newly elected president might be able to propel a shift in U.S. governance and politics comparable to that of Franklin Delano Roosevelt's first New Deal in the 1930s. Put another way, it seemed that the Obama administration, working with Democrats in control of both chambers of Congress, might be able to fashion public programs and tax measures to mitigate and reverse trends toward greater social inequality that have marked American society in recent decades—and to do so in a way that could build majority support and electoral momentum for the future (Beinart 2008). Not just *Time* magazine writers, but many pundits reacting to the 2008 election as well, speculated that Obama's presidency could be pivotal in the same way as FDR and Ronald Reagan before him, shifting the role of government in U.S. life.

By two years after Obama took the oath of office, the jaunty image was long gone—even though the record of accomplishments was impressive. President Obama and the Democrats of the 111th Congress fashioned

1

landmark legislation during 2009 and 2010—comprehensive health care reform, revamped higher educational loans, and regulation of Wall Street financial practices vital to the health of the U.S. and world economy. Morale and degrees of effectiveness were restored or established in many parts of federal administration that had languished or abandoned key missions, and the Obama administration made assiduous use of cabinet powers to spur school reforms, improve health and safety enforcement, enforce immigration laws, and tackle environmental threats. What is more, economists of various persuasions and the nonpartisan Congressional Budget Office agree that the fledgling Obama administration and congressional majorities took the basic steps necessary in 2009 to cut short a financial crisis, prevent a sudden disappearance of the U.S. auto industry, and forestall overall economic collapse into a second Great Depression. After a few months, America's beleaguered economy turned from nearly unprecedented contraction to growth (Geithner 2010).

All this happened as the White House also pulled the nation back from the protracted bloodletting in Iraq, redefined and intensified the previously faltering war in Afghanistan, and reengaged global negotiations over environmental, security, and financial issues. Few new presidents have been greeted with so many crises at once, and few have tackled so much so fast, whatever missed opportunities, political controversies, and maladroit steps there have been along the way. The Obama administration made progress during 2009 and 2010 despite a solid wall of opposition from congressional Republicans, whose obstruction of remedial steps to prevent the collapse of the financial system and national economy may be without parallel in a juncture of true national emergency. Years from now, when current political passions calm and historians look back, the first two years of the Obama presidency and the 111th Congress are bound to stand out as one of the most active and consequential junctures in modern U.S. history, a moment when, amidst popular dismay, partisan polarization, and clashing movements, the White House and Congress tackled extraordinary challenges, averted catastrophe, and put policies in place to foster a healthier, better educated, and more equal American society.

But as of 2011, with a brash, Republican-led House of Representatives driving much of the agenda in Washington, D.C., in the wake of massive November 2010 electoral losses for Democrats, Obama's presidency has been declared a failure by opponents and a disappointment by some initial supporters (for a sample of ongoing debates, see Alterman 2010; Hirsh 2010; Judis 2010a, 2010b; Klein 2010; Kuttner 2010; Krauthammer 2010; Krugman 2010a). According to official reports, the U.S. economy pulled out of recession during 2010, but growth remained sluggish and the creation of jobs, especially in the private sector, did not keep up with the needs of a growing population or counter the desperation of millions who lost employment or hours of work in the Great Recession (Krugman 2010b). The crisis of 2008 and 2009 in the United States was triggered by financial shenanigans and a real-estate bubble, so even as overall growth stumbles back to life, retirees and near-retirees have seen lifetime savings shrink, and millions of American families are saddled with mortgaged homes they cannot sell for enough to cover what they owe. In many parts of the country, communities are blighted by depressed real estate markets and dotted with abandoned shopping malls and storefronts. As tax revenues have fallen, state and local governments struggle to maintain services needed more than ever and have boosted unemployment by laying off state employees. Overall, state cutbacks have counteracted much of the boost from federal stimulus spending in 2009 and 2010. On the federal level, as stimulus spending wound down, Obama struck a postelection deal with congressional Republicans in December 2010 to temporarily sustain unemployment benefits and middle-class tax breaks in exchange for extending tax cuts for the affluent for two more years, even though experts rate such cuts for the affluent as one of the least effective ways to boost economic growth.

The story is also one of stubbornly divergent economic fortunes (Reich 2010). As overall economic growth returned in 2010, things seemed to have recovered in the upper-middle-class enclaves where managers and professionals live and work, but the economic doldrums persisted in most other urban, suburban, and rural areas—places where, no matter how much prices are reduced, most consumers cannot afford to buy enough to jumpstart robust growth and new hiring. Going into the Great Recession, the United States had developed glaring gaps of income and wealth, divergences that reached the highest point since the late 1920s. Long gone is the postwar U.S. economy in which a rising tide lifted all boats. Since the late 1970s, the U.S. rich, super-rich, and super-super-rich have seen their wealth and incomes soar, but the upper middle class has experienced a modest rise in fortunes, and everyone else has treaded water—in what Jacob Hacker and Paul Pierson (2010, chap. 1) aptly call a winner-take-all economy. Americans of modest means tried to keep up by taking on debt with credit cards and second mortgages, which fed the financial meltdown in 2008 and has made it hard for families to resume consumer purchases since then. The struggling recovery has intensified the unequal fortunes of Americans, as the rich and the upper middle class regain footing first and other Americans slip further behind and struggle to afford the basics of life. The nonpartisan U.S. Census Bureau reported the highest number of Americans and children living in poverty since it began collecting these data half a century ago, and community groups placed the need for food assistance at a quarter-century peak.

By any standard, massive suffering and uncertainty continue for workers and communities facing a lack of jobs, home foreclosures, and lost wealth in pensions and home equity; and entire cohorts of young adults are finding it nearly impossible to launch stable careers and build families. Yet since the initial recovery steps taken in early 2009, the Obama administration has proved unable to persuade Congress to do much more to save or create new jobs, especially not through additional federal spending (Montgomery and Irwin 2010). Some would argue that it has not even tried very hard to get Congress to accept such steps. For Americans primarily worried about jobs, the major reforms Obama and congressional Democrats delivered during 2009 and 2010—reconfiguring the health insurance system, regulating Wall Street—have not seemed directly relevant to their daily lives.

The political tsunami in November 2010 resulted, in part, from deep divisions among Americans about the realities and prospects of the economy, with many voters questioning the effectiveness of federal government efforts to cope with economic stagnation, immigration dilemmas, and environmental threats (Silverleib 2010). Jobs were the top concern, but many people also worried about taxes and looming federal debts, because even before Obama arrived at the White House, unpaid wars and upward-tilted tax cuts had run up considerable federal red ink, and the federal government had spent still more to avert another Great Depression. Americans were upset to see significant new spending and federal indebtedness without tangible robust recovery for ordinary workers and families. Voters experiencing the bad could not readily grasp that things could have been far worse. Because Democrats were the incumbent party, they bore the brunt of public doubts: in the U.S. House of Representatives they lost the majority and gave up a post–World War II record sixty-three seats; in the Senate they were reduced to fifty-three seats, well short of the sixty-vote majority necessary to overcome a filibuster; and in governorships and state legislatures they also saw major losses, especially in the Midwest. Whether or not most Americans had confidence that Republicans would make things better—and polls in late 2010 and early 2011 suggested that they did not have it—the voters expressed their dismay about government ineffectiveness by voting against the incumbent party.

At least, that was the case for voters who actually appeared at the polls. As is typical in a midterm election, only about 40 percent of those eligible actually voted, and they were skewed toward older, richer, whiter voters—the very groups that had been least supportive of Obama in the

2008 election. Political science models tell us that when the presidency and both chambers of Congress are held by one party, the next election almost always brings a shift back toward the opposition under any economic and governing scenario. Republicans made outsized gains in the 2010 state and federal elections because of a double whammy: the natural swing against the in-party, exacerbated by voter anger at the continuing economic downturn and polarization and ineffectiveness in Washington.

MAKING SENSE OF THE OBAMA PRESIDENCY SO FAR

Postmortems on Obama's presidency did not wait for the official results of the November 2010 election. Even before the votes were in, many analysts—both partisans and ostensibly neutral pundits—declared that Republican gains amounted to a repudiation of President Obama and his ideas for using federal government powers to expand economic opportunity and security. Sweeping aside the complex set of factors at work in this election, many have equated Republican gains with an embrace of small-government, low-tax prescriptions. Just as pundits had mistakenly declared Obama the second coming of Franklin Delano Roosevelt in the fall of 2008, they began portraying him as a less successful version of Jimmy Carter. Democrats once touted as the inevitable new majority in a demographically changing nation, where youth and minorities seemed to own the future, were dismissed after November 2010 as has-beens in cable news segments dominated by crowing Republican "analysts."

Extreme and simplified interpretive swings keep producers swirling in a 24/7 media world, but they are misleading. They don't prepare us for what may happen from election to election, especially because the ranks of voters will again expand in 2012 to include more of the young, nonwhite, and less well-to-do citizens who more typically show up in presidential contests. Even less do extreme and simplified interpretations tell us about actual governmental accomplishments and what citizens think about them—or may come to think about them over time. The 2010 election principally hinged on frustration with high unemployment and the ongoing adverse consequences of policy choices and a financial crisis not of Obama's making. Contrary to claims that voters are repudiating the use of government for reformist purposes, polls repeatedly show that voters want concrete measures to help the economy, create jobs, improve health care, and expand access to education, as well as measures to tighten regulation of the financial sector.

The 2010 election was not a referendum on so-called government takeovers—for the obvious reason that none were attempted in the early

Obama presidency. As this volume explains, in one major policy area after another, the Obama administration accommodated established stakeholders and sought significant but circumscribed reforms to surmount obstacles in the legislative process and avoid unified opposition from businesses and regional interests. The Obama White House never acceded to calls from leftists to break up the banks or bypass private health insurers. Legislative blueprints that might have reworked the energy economy or empowered labor unions were stymied in Congress and never pushed very hard by the White House. This does not mean that Obama and the Democrats did nothing or entirely deferred to corporate interests; on the contrary, significant steps have been taken to help the majority of Americans. But the legislative and administrative reforms that moved forward did so with many accommodations to market realities, fashioned by Obama officials and advocates of business interests within both parties in Congress.

Our project offers the first rigorous investigation of the first two years of the Obama presidency and draws an interim balance sheet—one that shows remarkable policy accomplishments in key realms, tempered by legislative defeats and gridlock, intense political opposition, and heightened public anxiety during a persistent national economic crisis. We do not arrive at interpretations breathlessly at the last minute. From the fall of 2008 through the fall of 2010, as the early Obama era took shape and the president and others set agendas and pushed for redirected policies, we tracked happenings in and beyond Washington, D.C. We have tracked data, collected key documents, interviewed key players, and analyzed public opinion, interest group maneuvers, popular outbursts, and congressional votes. We have developed big-picture assessments, and offer real-time analysis and predictions based on in-depth understanding of what has transpired at a dramatic juncture in U.S. politics. Pointed analyses of the policy successes, partial successes, backfired efforts, and outright shortfalls of Obama's reach for another New Deal offer a remarkable window into U.S. politics—and give us telling insights into where clashing partisans, maneuvering interest groups, and ambitious politicians may take America next.

What happens when a youthful president, backed by substantial but not overwhelming congressional majorities, takes office during a gathering economic storm and tries to turn the titanic U.S. ship of state amidst the choppy seas of partisan clamor and nonstop interest group lobbying? How much change do existing political institutions allow—and why more in some policy areas than others? Can ambitious presidential initiatives make headway in an acute economic crisis that arouses widespread popular anxieties and shifts calculations for businesses large and small?

Even with large congressional majorities from the same party, what can a change-oriented president do to help Americans who are not rich and well connected in a political system that favors big contributors and insiders? Which presidential attempts to ask more from the rich to create budgetary room for policies on behalf of the majority make headway; and which are partially or entirely thwarted?

Of course, answering the sorts of big questions that motivate this project, not to mention attempting to draw an interim bottom line after the first two years of a change-oriented presidency, are in some ways premature endeavors. Only the fullness of time and the longer perspective of history will allow final answers to the questions we pose. But, in another sense, grappling with these big questions is a much better way to probe Obama's ambitious presidency and its political consequences than trucking in simpleminded oppositions of success versus failure or more government versus rejection of government. Grappling with these big questions is also a better way to analyze the early Obama era than highly specialized social science that latches on to one narrow strand of a complex real-world dynamic. The contributors to this collection are all scholars who know how to synthesize findings about various aspects of politics that other scholars treat in isolation. We track and consider the intersections of presidential and bureaucratic initiatives, congressional coalition-building, social movements, interest group bargaining, and shifts in electoral behavior and public opinion. All of these have combined and played out in real time in the fulcrum of individual policy areas.

Another key feature of our Reaching for a New Deal project is its focus on what government actually does—and what battling political actors are trying to get government to do, or stop doing. Too much punditry and social science today discuss everything in politics except the programs and government actions that really matter. By contrast, we start with those actions. We probe the economic steps taken, and not taken, by the Obama White House, and investigate in detail eight major realms of government endeavor where Obama and his allies have attempted major redirections in the scope and content of domestic public policy. We look at health care, higher education, financial reform, labor law, elementary and secondary education, immigration regulation, energy and climate-change policy, and—last but not least—taxes and government revenues (how to pay for it all).

In each area, we describe what Obama and his allies set out to change, spelling out how agendas were set during the election campaign and the early months of this presidency. We then probe the priorities set in Congress and the cabinet and analyze the fate of major domestic policy initiatives. Our analyses go beyond what President Obama himself and his administration decided to do or avoid doing at various junctures, because American politics is not solely or even primarily a story of presidential choices, style, or personality—even if a good many pundits and some academics remained overly obsessed with such personality-oriented accounts (Jacobs and King 2010). Our challenge is to develop a real-time holistic approach that looks at all of the maneuvering actors, and the opportunities and constraints they have faced within evolving institutional and political contexts.

In the remainder of this chapter, we look first at why circumstances seemed so ripe for another New Deal following the 2008 elections, and then probe how critical events and inherited conditions in government, politics, and the media have profoundly shaped what the Obama presidency attempted and achieved in 2009 and 2010—as well as what allies and opponents have done in response, giving rise to surprising political twists. We put our cards on the table about why an ambitious presidency that seemed to have strong winds at its back ran into fierce blowback, and why an American citizenry that seemed so hopeful about change in 2008 voted against the change president's party in the November 2010 election—putting the breaks on much of Obama's reform agenda and throwing him onto the political defensive leading into 2011 and 2012. Obama's early presidency did indeed reach for another New Deal, and much of the ambitious agenda was furthered—indeed much more than is yet visible to many citizens and analysts. But the immediate political results, certainly, were not what anyone could have anticipated when that November 24 issue of *Time* magazine appeared on the newsstands in 2008. Instead, a resurgent Republican right, fueled by Tea Party activism, has upended political equations once again, raising the stakes at what will remain for some time a dramatic, uncertain, and pivotal moment in American democracy and governance.

WHY DID ANOTHER NEW DEAL SEEM POSSIBLE?

As the 2008 elections wrapped up and the newly elected president and Congress moved toward taking office, there were a number of reasons to believe that the November election had opened the door to more than incremental or routine shifts in U.S. public policy and politics. First, the election outcomes themselves were remarkable (Todd and Gawiser 2009). Most presidential elections from 1992 to 2004 had ended up in plurality victories, such as Bill Clinton by 43 percent in the three-way 1992 contest, or in very close outcomes, virtually tied between the Democratic and Republican contestants, such as Clinton with 49.2 percent of the vote in 1996 and Bush with 47.9 percent in 2000 and 50.7 percent in 2004. But Barack Obama won decisively, especially for a Democrat in recent memory—and amazingly decisively for an African American with a foreign parent. Obama's margin over John McCain was 53 percent to 46 percent in the total popular vote, and 365 to 173 in the electoral college. At the same time, congressional Democrats strengthened their majorities in both the House and the Senate—carrying forward a partisan shift that started in 2006. The Democratic margin kept growing in the Senate, and eventually, midway through 2009, when the protracted court battles in Minnesota were finally settled, the fifty-eight Democrats plus two Independents in the Senate Democratic caucus ended up with what the media trumpeted as a filibuster-proof supermajority.

The U.S. elections of 2006 and 2008 were also marked by the mobilization of new blocs of voters into greater participation, as well as enhanced support for the Democratic Party. Younger voters raised their level of engagement; African Americans turned out in droves to vote for the first black presidential candidate; and Latino voters increased their participation and shifted toward greater support for Democrats. After the 2008 election, commentators especially noted the age-gradient of partisan divisions, and trumpeted the Democratic Party, preferred by under-forty-five-year-olds, as the party of the future (see, for example, Runyan 2008).

Obama also won election at a juncture when most Americans of all political persuasions were disillusioned with his predecessor, George W. Bush, and had soured on the economic and foreign policy directions the country had taken when the Republican Party controlled both Congress and the presidency from 2000 through 2006. To reach the White House backed by congressional party majorities after the country has repudiated the predecessors is an excellent situation for an ambitious president determined to change policy direction (Skowronek 1993).

In addition, some analysts would say that it is good for a president who wants to use federal power vigorously to come to office during a deep economic downturn, when businesses and average citizens want and need government help (Kuttner 2009). During the original New Deal, certainly, President Franklin Roosevelt and the Democratic Party were able to do a great deal amidst the massive Great Depression. Similarly, Obama took office just as an epochal financial meltdown was plunging the country into the deepest economic downturn since the 1930s. Obama's chief of staff, Rahm Emanuel, famously quipped, "You don't ever want a crisis to go to waste" (quoted in Krugman 2008). In fact, the advent of the financial and subsequent economic crises helped Obama and the Democrats build their margins of electoral victory against McCain and the Republicans in the 2008 election. Racial prejudices that many electoral analysts expected to hurt Obama in competition with McCain were mitigated in many parts of the country by the overriding desire of white working-class voters to elect a Democrat rather than a Republican to guide the economy.

Obama assumed the presidency after being unusually straightforward with the voting public that he would seek to change the direction of federal social and fiscal policies. During the 2008 general election and, before that, during the interminable Democratic Party primaries, Obama had vividly spoken about redistributive issues in a way highly unusual for any Democratic presidential nominee in recent memory. He talked quite frankly about the need to do more to help average Americans, and didn't back off from the proposition that rich families, making more than $250,000 a year, should pay higher taxes. No Democratic presidential candidate since the ill-fated Walter Mondale, during the 1984 campaign, had been as unambiguously willing to talk about raising taxes for anyone. What is more, Obama called for promoting growth and economic renewal from the bottom up rather than the top down to reinvigorate the American middle class and broaden its ranks (2008). This amounted to more than empty talk following years of federal policies that had actually redistributed wealth upward across the country (Jacobs and Skocpol 2005; Bartels 2008, chaps. 1, 2; Hacker and Pierson 2010, chap. 1).

Finally, politics is a team sport that calls for allies, coordination, and advance planning. Democrats and their allies had started making preparations in 2006 and earlier to take control of lawmaking when the party next elected a president. The Center for American Progress and other Washington think tanks developed detailed policies for an incoming administration to consider. Progressives had developed a strongly networked set of activists and funders to lobby for reform in Washington, and had learned to use the Internet to mobilize supporters across the country. Allies in government had started to develop the capacity to move large-scale legislation. Thus Peter Orszag, the future director of Obama's budget office, ran the Congressional Budget Office between January 2007 and November 2008, restocking its staff and developing sophisticated cost-estimating protocols in anticipation of the likelihood that a new Democratic president and Congress would need to move forward efficiently with many ambitious legislative proposals (Lizza 2009).

A decisive election, a public responsive to a new president's calls for change, strong congressional majorities, and experts and movement allies ready to go—it all looked like a promising opening for the second coming of FDR.

CAVEATS: THE USUAL OBSTACLES
TO POLICY CHANGE

Yet even at the height of the hoopla over a possible New New Deal, many political analysts sounded notes of caution. It is a well-known regularity that electoral outcomes tend to swing back and forth, especially in midterm congressional elections held when one party has control of the presidency and both Houses of Congress. FDR's 1936 landslide was followed by midterm losses of seventy-one seats in the House and half a dozen in the Senate; Lyndon Johnson's Democratic Party lost forty-seven House seats two years after their landslide win in 1964. In general, the party in power has lost twenty-five seats in the House since World War II, and the losses have been higher when presidential approval ratings have slipped below 50 percent, as was the case for Obama during 2010. In general, older, richer, and whiter voters are the ones most likely to turn out in midterm elections—and according to exit polling for the 2008 election, these were the demographics least enamored of Barack Obama (Todd and Gawiser 2009, 30–31).

Analysts knew from the start—and so did Democratic Party strategists—that the president and his congressional copartisans would likely face electoral setbacks in 2010. Even as they sought to manage an overall national economic recovery, the White House and Democrats in Congress tried to deal with the looming 2010 electoral moment of truth by delivering benefits and reassurance to older voters. But the probability of midterm losses animated Obama and other Democratic leaders as they raced against the clock to accomplish major legislative breakthroughs before their congressional majorities were thinned or lost.

Beyond normal electoral swings, it has long been well documented in survey research that Americans are ideologically cautious about strong government or governmental activism. Since the very beginning of mass surveys, researchers have noted that if you ask Americans abstract questions—such as "do you agree that people in government waste a lot of money we pay in taxes?"—they favor the free market and oppose government intervention. If you ask about specifics, however—such as "do you support Social Security?" or "would you be willing to pay more taxes for early childhood education?"—they tend to support liberal positions about active government (Free and Cantril 1968; Page and Jacobs 2009). Americans are, in short, philosophical conservatives and operational liberals. This means that even if Americans approve many specific measures furthered by President Obama and the Democrats, their reflexive antigovernment worries can be evoked by political opponents—all the more readily in a period of economic anxiety and uncertain progress in creating jobs. As a young, change-oriented president, Obama would have faced such worries under any circumstances. But the spreading economic distress of 2009 and 2010 generated genuine fear that was readily exploited by political foes who equated even mild government activism with radicalism.

Another obstacle that was clear to many analysts from the start lay in the divisions inherent in a large congressional majority. Substantial Democratic majorities in Congress created opportunities for Obama, which he would exploit. Apparent openings to pass new legislation, however, were compromised by significant intraparty divisions that prevented the consensus in certain policy areas that would be necessary to overcome the filibuster. Partisan polarization has created the impression that America's two major parties are similarly unified teams, that Democrats should be expected to support Obama's full agenda, much as a British parliamentary party would back the prime minister. In truth, Republican legislative coalitions do often approximate the bloc voting seen in a parliamentary system; this has been especially true in recent years, when Republicans held slim congressional margins and when right-wing interest groups made it clear that they would punish defectors with primary election challenges (Hacker and Pierson 2005). But congressional Democrats have long been fractured by ideology and regional and economic concerns. Many of them harbor deep suspicion and opposition about tightening government regulations or raising taxes even for the very wealthy.

Ideological splits within the Democratic Party are reinforced on certain issues by regional divisions. For example, Obama's call for energy reform was haunted by the split between Democratic lawmakers from coal-producing states and those from regions with businesses focused on developing other sources of energy; and health care reform was slowed, in part, because of tensions between legislators from the (mostly midwestern) states that provide health care at lower cost and the (eastern and western) states where costs are higher (even taking account of the overall cost of living). In many specific policy areas, Republicans opposed to Obama's agenda could find allies—or at least foot-draggers—within the Democratic Party.

Despite the usual obstacles, during the first few months of the Obama presidency it appeared that major changes were afoot and might prove enduringly popular. Obama started out with sky-high public approval ratings, and quickly persuaded Congress to pass the American Recovery and Reinvestment Act (the so-called stimulus), which was not as large as progressives wanted to see but nevertheless injected nearly a trillion dollars into the economy and included initial resources for new policy initiatives in education, clean energy production, and health care (Alter 2010,

135–37). The fledgling Obama administration quickly signed legislation about fair pay and children's health insurance that had been vetoed under President Bush.

What is more, the first Obama budget was a bold and readable document, not the usual snoozy bureaucratic treatise. *A New Era of Responsibility: Renewing America's Promise* outlined a very broad vision of how the new president planned to address major issues in education, health care, and energy and the environment (Office of Management and Budget 2009). The budget called for regulatory shifts and new directions in taxing and spending—for movement away from providing subsidies to favored private industries and tax cuts for the very wealthy; and toward broadening access to higher education, stimulating K-12 school reform, paying for health insurance for all Americans, and encouraging new environmentally friendly programs. In contrast to the Republican legislative strategy of relentlessly cutting taxes and talking about spending cuts without delivering them, Obama candidly proposed a fiscal policy that would expand social benefits for middle- and lower-income Americans and pay for them with specific spending cuts and tax increases on the privileged. Countering long-term efforts to arouse ideological opposition to big government in general, Obama and his allies aimed to stir the operational liberal aspirations of many Americans by pushing for specific measures to help key groups.

Big trouble started brewing from the start of Obama's term in 2009. Changing directions in federal policies in so many realms ran into more than the garden-variety difficulties we have already surveyed. Nearly two years after Obama's inauguration, we can highlight a series of happenstances and obdurate contextual realities that have profoundly limited and deflected Obama's reach for another New Deal, or obstructed change altogether.

As we look at key limiting factors in greater depth, it often helps to draw contrasts to the first New Deal of the 1930s—not because the nature and timing of events, let alone the structure of government and society, are the same between the 1930s and now, but because they are indeed different in telling ways (on this historical-institutional approach, see Pierson and Skocpol 2002; Soss, Hacker, and Mettler 2007). Comparisons across historical periods highlight major shifts in societal institutions and the overall U.S. political system, as well as flashpoints of conflict and sequences of change. Taken together, the factors we are about to analyze have limited Obama's ambitious reach for another New Deal. They also help us understand why fierce political backlashes greeted his partially successful and sometimes thwarted efforts to redirect federal policies on behalf of regular Americans in 2009 and 2010.

REFORMIST PRESIDENTS AND ECONOMIC CRISES

Although both Franklin Delano Roosevelt and Barack Obama came into office as change-oriented Democrats, the timing, nature, and severity of economic crises explain critical differences between Obama's debut in 2009 and 2010 and FDR's launch of the New Deal in 1933 and 1934. Roosevelt took office several years into the Great Depression, when the U.S. economy was at a nadir; some 25 percent of Americans were unemployed and the nation was begging for strong federal action. Congressional Republicans and Democrats alike were ready to vote for the bills FDR sent them; and citizens battered by the Great Depression were open to the direct federal creation of jobs. By contrast, Obama took office amidst a sudden financial seizure that was just beginning to push the national economy into a downturn of as-yet undetermined proportions.

Because FDR took charge at a moment of despair following a predecessor Republican president who had been unable to counter several years of deepening economic disaster, Roosevelt and his advisors knew they had to create jobs almost any way they could, and the president's emergency proposals were voted through by legislators of both parties before they even saw the written texts (Patterson 1967, chap. 1). In contrast, Obama's steps to spur recovery met from the start with a nearly universal wall of partisan opposition, because Republicans knew, as all experts did, that the country would plunge into deeper recession with unemployment ballooning for many months. Obama would end up being associated with steep economic decline and severe job losses, as Hoover once was. In addition, because the American people had yet to experience much of what was to come in the Great Recession, they could not know what to demand or expect from initial federal recovery efforts.

Fixing the Economy from the Top Down

It is worth tarrying a bit on this last point. Because Obama took office without the full effects of the financial crisis hitting the supply of jobs and the operation of the Main Street economy, he arguably lacked FDR's clear-cut opening to dramatize a full-blown national economic emergency and to pursue a full range of policies, including direct federal creation of large numbers of jobs. From the start, the new president, a cautious lawyer by training, heard key options taken off the table not just by Republicans and conservative Democrats in Congress and the Beltway media, but also by his own economic advisors, who were leery of disrupting existing business practices and hesitant to embrace policies outside conventional boundaries (Alter 2010, chaps. 11, 12; Hirsh 2010).

The nature as well as the phasing of the crisis affected Obama's economic leadership, real and perceived. His strong election victory over McCain was spurred by the Wall Street crisis that broke in September 2008, as conventional wisdom has long recognized. But looking deeper, we can see that candidate Obama was drawn into cooperation with the outgoing Bush administration starting well before the November election, as well as during the transition. Decades earlier, FDR had deliberately avoided Hoover's invitations to work together, but with the economic meltdown of late 2008 and 2009 just getting started, Obama could not avoid transitional efforts to prevent the initial Wall Street crisis from spiraling out of control, a catastrophe that would have taken down the world financial system and plunged the United States into a massive and prolonged depression. In short, FDR came in when the patient was near death, whereas Obama wanted to keep the patient's raging fever from turning into pneumonia.

Cooperation to deal with Wall Street woes started in earnest during the campaign in mid-September, when GOP candidate McCain tried to call off the first presidential debate and hold a summit at the Bush White House. As Jonathan Alter reminds us in *The Promise: President Obama, Year One*, this campaign stunt backfired on McCain because Obama was the one who looked cool, calm, wise, and in charge (2010, 9–14). What also mattered about this episode was that soon-to-be president-elect Obama became engaged with Bush administration efforts to mitigate the financial crisis through the politically unpopular decision to build congressional support for a massive financial rescue plan, the Troubled Asset Relief Program (TARP). Starting at that misguided September 2008 session at the White House, Obama gained confidence that he could master complex issues and work with financial experts—yet, as we can now see, he was also drawn into a save-Wall-Street-first approach to economic recovery that was highly unpopular and fabulously expensive.

This was inevitable in a sense, but also ironic. The insurgent Democratic candidate who campaigned by promising a bottom-up approach to economic growth and renewal in America started his presidential economic efforts amidst a bipartisan scramble to help Wall Street first. A couple of months later, President-Elect Obama would also urge President Bush as his term wound down to support legislation to rescue collapsing U.S. auto companies. To millions of Americans beginning to face the realities of declining family fortunes, underwater mortgages, and looming pink slips, all this looked like helping the big guys float free and leaving ordinary Americans to drown.

Assembling a Team and Planning for Recovery

Obama's initial economic efforts also limited his purview going forward. After his victory at the polls, the president-elect quickly decided that two Wall Street–connected experts, Timothy Geithner and Lawrence Summers, would lead his White House economic advisory team (Alter 2010, 49–53). In a financially induced crisis, Obama believed they were uniquely qualified to figure out where reforms were needed—and perhaps persuade bankers to help the larger economy going forward. But building this kind of economic team—especially given the well-known proclivity of Summers for taking control of the process of generating policy alternatives—also meant that Obama was not going to hear day-to-day from other kinds of economic experts who thought of jobs first, or who saw U.S. economic recovery over the longer term as requiring commitments to structural transformation and seeding innovative new industries. Paul Volcker joined the administration, but was sidelined for much of the first year (Hirsh 2010). Nor would prominent noneconomists be involved in economic policy design, as social worker Harry Hopkins was in FDR's brain trust.

Drawing on established macroeconomic wisdom and the purported common sense of the financial community to which they were connected, Summers and Geithner advised Obama to counter the Wall Street crisis with bank bailouts that imposed minimal penalties, hoping to cajole and soothe bankers into resuming lending. They urged Obama to avoid nationalizing banks and other aggressive steps out of fear that such undertakings could cause "a disastrous run on those banks" (Alter 2010, 206). Beyond that, Obama's team, joined by other orthodox economic advisors, urged spending a lot of federal money as quickly as possible—which necessarily meant spending on established programs that could be expanded without new planning or protracted negotiations. Tax cuts would also be added into the Recovery Act, accounting for a third of the overall stimulus package even though most economists knew they would deliver less bang for the buck than direct spending. Calm the bankers, cut taxes, and quickly spend as much as Congress would enact for projects that could be implemented without a lot of corruption, and then be patient as the economy slowly recovered over the course of 2010 and 2011. That was the prescription.

An energetic push to boost employment through massive infrastructure construction or industrial innovation—let alone any New Deal–style public employment programs—was not earnestly recommended to Obama. There were certainly outside economic mavericks like Paul Krugman who said from the start that Obama was proposing to spend too little and do too much to accommodate banks and businesses. Members of Congress like Jim Oberstar pressed for large investments in transportation infrastructure. But, for the most part, Obama seemed to cleave to orthodox experts. "When he brought in Summers and Geithner he just thought he was getting the best of the best" (Michael Greenberger as quoted in Hirsh 2010). Obama hoped to use the stimulus to seed significant green energy projects, a move that would have injected more innovative industrial policy into the emergency recovery effort. But according to Alter (2010, 85–86), Obama backed off when it was pointed out that legal wrangling over environmental regulations could slow spending; he also retreated when Summers pushed back against the idea of featuring large infrastructure efforts as part of the recovery effort.

Endorsing the bold yet orthodox recovery steps his advisors urged upon him, Obama's White House tried to hit the middle on the overall price tag. Some economists, such as Paul Krugman, argued from the get-go that he needed to get Congress to spend more than a trillion, to make up for the drop in consumer demand, and to keep the proportion devoted to tax cuts to a minimum. But such advice did not seem realistic to the Obama White House, which felt it had to stay under a trillion to get Congress to pass any stimulus (Krugman 2010a). Furthermore, perhaps naively, the newly installed Obama hoped to woo congressional Republicans with substantial up-front tax cuts of the sorts they had claimed to support in the past. Because Obama offered Republicans policy concessions and got less than a handful of votes for his outreach, most postmortems on what went wrong with the stimulus focus on his unnecessary concessions about taxes (instead of more stimulative direct spending) as well as on the inadequate size of the stimulus package given the collapse of consumer demand. But his choices were understandable for a brand-new president who had promised the 2008 electorate that he would change the political tone in Washington. Moreover, as we discuss later, it is not at all clear that Congress would have passed a bigger, more spending-heavy Recovery Act, no matter what Obama had proposed.

Missing Jobs

In retrospect, the fact that Obama's economic recovery strategy was not truly a jobs program turns out to matter more (Alter 2010, 85–86; Hirsh 2010). The American Recovery and Reinvestment Act is better understood as a Hail Mary pass to goose aggregate economic growth by 2010, hoping that jobs would come back in tandem with the revival of overall GDP growth, or following soon after growth resumed. The absence of a jobs program stemmed, in part, from the decision of Democratic leaders to push the large stimulus package through Congress very soon after

Obama's inauguration, both to stave off the looming financial and economic disaster as best they could and to conserve time within the president's honeymoon period for the pursuit of long-planned efforts such as
comprehensive health care reform. The idea was to get some of those reforms through in ample time to take effect before the next elections. Yet
this approach meant that the White House largely deferred to congressional appropriators, letting them push money into their long-standing wish
lists. A bold plan for creating new jobs would have taken much longer to
formulate, and would have run into many congressional buzz-saws.

President Obama's quickly devised economic recovery strategy also
confused American citizens, many of whom did not see how heightened
federal spending, funded through a growing deficit, could work. Most
citizens wanted jobs saved or available, which Obama's spending and tax
cuts would, at best, bring about only indirectly and gradually. By the summer of 2010, even aggregate growth was slowing, and unemployment remained near 10 percent. Citizens looked back and believed that Obama—
supported by his Democratic Congress—had first saved Wall Street and
other corporate giants, and then left much of Main Street foundering. During the run-up to the November 2010 election, and afterwards into 2011,
Obama and his party were hampered by too little job growth and the sense
among many Americans that "federal spending does not work" to create
economic recovery (Silverleib 2010)—or, worse, that the usual insiders
were the real beneficiaries of recovery efforts. In one of several piercing
ironies, the winds of populism and change that swept Obama into office
in 2008 turned against him two years later, and threatened to block further
government actions to promote economic recovery and broaden social opportunity.

PARTISAN POLARIZATION AND
REPUBLICAN OBSTRUCTION

As noted, at the start of the first New Deal, President Franklin Roosevelt
enjoyed bipartisan support for recovery efforts launched at an economic
nadir. But even though President-Elect Obama had partnered with Republican officials to handle the 2008 financial crisis during the closing days of
the Bush presidency, his own initial recovery proposal got virtually no
votes from congressional Republicans, even as their home states clamored
for fiscal relief. As the months went by, Republican opposition hardened
and grassroots populist movements arrayed under the Tea Party banner
took to the streets to excoriate the president and any and all new federal
initiatives being debated in the 111th Congress. Both GOP strategic calculations and the birth of a media-driven grassroots movement on the far

right figured into the crystallization of intense opposition to Obama's presidency and policy proposals—despite the fact that the Obama White House was trying to prop up and revive the private sector in the U.S. economy.

GOP Leaders Decide to Oppose Everything

At the elite level, Republican congressional leaders attuned to a dispirited, heavily white-southern voter base—and goosed on by flamboyant right-wing media commentators—decided from the start of Obama's presidency on all-out opposition. This was a cold-blooded political bet, possible in light of the economic down-spiral in the wake of the Wall Street bailout undertaken by the outgoing Bush administration. Two-thirds of House Republicans voted against the unpopular bailout when it first came up under Bush, and only half voted for the final legislation, despite pleas from Bush officials and business leaders after the stock market plunged following the abortive first congressional vote. As the Democrats took charge, congressional Republicans aimed to pin the bailout on Obama and, indeed, succeeded in convincing many voters that the bailout and the American Recovery and Reinvestment Act (the stimulus) were one and the same.

It was all a bunch of expensive federal handouts, congressional Republicans told the public—and that message gained a lot of traction, even if particular GOP representatives and senators regularly went home for ribbon-cutting ceremonies celebrating job-creating stimulus projects they had voted against in Washington. Republicans knew that Americans like the specifics of government spending, even when they doubt the value of higher spending overall. Republican strategists also knew that if unemployment reached a high level, unified Republican opposition to Obama's agenda in Washington would position their party as the only alternative to what they would be able to call a failed presidency and 111th Congress.

In addition to facing partisan efforts to blame him for using emergency federal spending to stave off dire economic troubles that originated during the Bush presidency, Obama also inherited Bush's huge federal budget deficit—bills run up by off-budget wars, tax cuts for the very wealthy, and a new Medicare drug benefit not paid for with future revenue streams. Add the inherited unpaid bills and declining taxes due to the recession to the unavoidable cost of bailouts and the stimulus, and it was easy to see that President Obama started out with deficit problems that would only grow—quite apart from funding for any of the new long-term reform measures he had promised the electorate during 2008. Republicans knew they could take political advantage of the new president's terrible luck, and they decided to do so.

Tea Partiers Erupt

Any chance that any Republicans in Washington might have drifted toward cooperation with the Obama administration—the nation faced an emergency, after all, so it might have seemed logical—dwindled after the Tea Party networks sprang to life early in 2009. Conservative activists in and around the Republican Party were understandably demoralized in the aftermath of the 2008 elections, which left pundits projecting a permanent shift toward the Democrats. But when CNBC commentator Rick Santelli went on a rant against "freeloaders" supposedly taking advantage of federal mortgage-reduction programs and called for a new American "Tea Party" to protest an overweening federal government, conservative activists across the country recognized a great opportunity to regroup and rebrand themselves. Activists in many states warmed up Internet lists and began to convene local meetings and protests, and Fox reporters and commentators helped national organizers and financial backers advertise colorful national protest days—always touting the efforts for weeks and days before any actual happening (see Williamson and Skocpol 2010, figs. 4 and 5). Then, when the Fox-encouraged protests happened, the rest of the media flocked to cover the events and follow up with grassroots networks holding meetings across the country.

For the critical first year of the Obama presidency, and especially at peak moments like the 2009 summertime town meeting outbursts over health care reform, mainstream media outlets found it irresistible to cover outlandish protest actions with older white demonstrators dressed up like Revolutionary War patriots and carrying extremist signs. It made for great television, and constant online buzz, even if most Americans were not involved and had no idea who these folks were. For many months, analysts debated whether this was a grassroots protest of unaffiliated independents disillusioned with Obama. As it gradually became clear through national surveys and ethnographic work, Tea Partiers are mostly previously active conservative Republicans, older, whiter, and more well-to-do on average than other Americans (Williamson and Skocpol 2010). They espouse more stereotypical suspicions of nonwhites than other Republicans, let alone Americans overall, and are deeply angered by the suspicion that unworthy, "freeloading" people—including immigrants, the young, and lower-income minorities—might get benefits from the federal government. They fear that such expenditures, even in a recession, could end up costing people like them higher taxes or could squeeze programs such as Medicare to which they feel entitled.

Tea Party anger is diffuse but intense; it reached a boil among people who turned out disproportionately for the 2010 midterm elections, and remained primed to turn out again for the next presidential contest in 2012. Tea Party organizers are highly skillful and practical in how they contact and motivate voters (Williamson and Skocpol 2010). In key states like Virginia, Tea Partiers have moved from organizing loose local networks to creating an ongoing federation that can affect elections and policy battles at local, state, and national levels. Whatever the long-term electoral effects end up being, Tea Partiers have their greatest initial impact on Republican politicians, pressuring officeholders to oppose or repeal Obama initiatives such as health care reform, and threatening primary challenges against Republicans who show signs of dialogue or compromise with Democrats. Primary defeats in 2010 of established conservatives such as Bob Bennett of Utah struck fear into other Republicans in Congress and made them ever more reluctant to compromise on policy or personnel in 2011 and 2012. For GOP moderates such as Senator Olympia Snowe of Maine, the best hope for staving off a primary challenge from Maine Tea Partiers is to avoid breaks with GOP leaders in Congress, who remain determined to undermine Obama legislative and budgetary priorities.

Polarization Deepens

Among both GOP leaders and conservative grassroots activists, in short, rightward-pulling ideological polarization expressed through party politics has become more intense under Obama, even though he campaigned for office with appeals to widespread public desires for bipartisan cooperation and has repeatedly reached out to Republicans in Washington. We need to keep in mind the longer-term trends that Obama has probably been powerless to counter, especially once his GOP opponents chose obstruction. Decades ago, in the middle of the twentieth century, ideological and party divisions did not entirely overlap in U.S. electoral politics. There were many conservative southern Democrats and a fair number of moderate to slightly liberal northern Republicans. Congress often functioned through old-boy bipartisan deals. All of this started to disappear after the civil rights movement of the 1960s, as the Republican Party turned toward the right and became the home of white southerners.

Polarization, especially at the level of elected representatives and advocacy elites, proceeded apace over the last part of the twentieth century, sorting ideological conservatives into the Republican Party and liberals into the Democratic Party (McCarty, Poole, and Rosenthal 2008). Beyond such sorting, conservative activists used money and grassroots campaigns to pull the Republican Party even further to the right, especially in congressional voting and public debates over social issues and taxes (Hacker and Pierson 2005; Sinclair 2006). Polarization has gone further on the Republican than on the Democratic side, and polarized congressional voting has tended to favor conservative obstruction of social policy initiatives to help lower- or middle-income people (Bartels 2008; McCarty 2007). No wonder, then, that when a new Democratic president arrived in office promising to use federal initiatives actively to favor lower- and middle-income people, long-operating conservative forces were determined to mount all the opposition they could. Such "just say no" strategies failed to stop health care reform and might have backfired more broadly had it not been for continued economic sluggishness. History shows us that democratic publics are open to fearful messages in periods of high unemployment and threatened family fortunes.

POLICY IMPLICATIONS OF CONGRESSIONAL REALITIES

An activist president can move forward on various fronts—from attempting to shape public opinion to making court appointments, from action through regulatory bodies and executive agencies to asking Congress to pass legislation. Obama has of course pushed initiatives across the board; yet many of his choices about when and how to proceed, as well as the issues he has prioritized, have depended on what legislators thinking of their own interests were willing to do, amidst ongoing struggles among lobbyists and social movements.

Herding Democratic Cats

After 2008, the Democrats had substantial margins in both the House and Senate, but only in the House were they truly in control—when they could get their intraparty act together. The Speaker of the House can control through simple majority votes which legislation is voted upon, when the vote occurs, and the handling of amendments. Senate rules, by contrast, slow things down (Binder and Smith 1996). A single senator can object by placing a hold on nominations and bills, often secretly, and by custom the minority can request many delays in committees and on the floor. What is more, the potential exists for the minority to demand a supermajority vote, sixty rather than fifty-one, on virtually all matters—from procedure and presidential nominees to the enactment of legislation. The filibuster—which takes sixty votes to break—used to be reserved for major, controversial issues, but has been invoked more frequently in recent decades (Sinclair 2009; Klein 2009). The filibuster has been invoked especially frequently, indeed unremittingly, when Republicans face Democratic leadership. Under Barack Obama, Republican obstructionists have decided to invoke the supermajority rule on almost every issue small and large; hence they have prevented the president from assembling his administration in normal time, kept much-needed judicial appointments from filling court vacancies, and blocked most reform initiatives. In general, Senate action by filibuster ensures that Americans see a dysfunctional government, with everything slowed to a crawl. The filibuster was invoked more often in 2009, for example, than in the entire decade of the 1950s (Frumin and Reif 2010). As leaders of a party and angry conservative movement that wants to undercut and hobble government when Democrats have any say, GOP leaders have made the calculation that such behavior will help rather than hurt their cause with the American people.

The press emphasized that Obama and the Democrats held a supposedly filibuster-proof sixty-vote majority for many months during the 111th Congress—from the time when Senator Al Franken was seated in July 2009 following Minnesota's contested election, until mid-January 2010, when a Republican, Scott Brown, surprisingly won a special election to fill the seat of the late Senator Ted Kennedy. But in truth, there never was a reliable sixty-vote margin. Senator Joe Lieberman, an Independent, could never be counted on to stick with anyone's team, or even his own previous positions; and various conservative Democrats regularly defected. Obama's Democratic margins in Congress never reached the level enjoyed by previous Democratic presidents (Silver 2010). Throughout his presidential term, Jimmy Carter had a stronger Senate majority than Obama. And FDR, John Kennedy, and Lyndon Johnson had larger majorities to work with when they pushed far-reaching social programs—although in those days, of course, many Democrats were southern conservatives.

Because Republicans in the 111th Congress remained throughout 2009 and 2010 almost entirely opposed to Obama's initiatives, the drama in one policy area after another focused on what sorts of Democratic coalitions could be formed, and whether defections on any given issue would make forward movement impossible. Obviously, legislative action was always precarious in the Senate, where any one or two Democrats could kill all possibility of forward movement. But even in the House, where the Democrats had a seventy-five-vote margin in a majoritarian chamber, various kinds of issues could peel off dozens of Democrats, if ideological or regional concerns were aroused, or businesses connected to particular representatives started pushing back against Democratic proposals. House as well as Senate Democrats remained an incoherent coterie of assorted liberals along with many moderates and conservatives. The nonliberals included highly vulnerable representatives elected in competitive or even Republican-leaning districts: forty-eight House Democrats were elected in 2008 in districts that voted for McCain and many were defeated in the 2010 elections, for example. Some of these endangered Democrats, like Virginia's Tom Perriello, won in 2008 by a few hundred votes in Republican-leaning districts and yet still went on to fully support Obama's agenda in apparent acceptance of what would be their defeat in 2010. But such stoicism was unusual. Many Democrats anticipating tough reelection battles groped for self-preservation by ostentatiously displaying independence from President Obama and their chamber's party leadership even though their prospects in 2010 were in truth primarily tied to the partisan balance in their districts.

In the U.S. political system, neither the president nor party leaders have the power to discipline legislators for disloyalty, as leaders in a parliamentary system would be able to do. Although Democrats in the 111th Congress achieved a measure of unity on some legislation, enormous efforts were required to build supportive coalitions. And majorities simply could not be assembled for certain Obama priorities. Democratic unity was selective and sensitive to what came up when on the calendar, and in what sequence. What is more, as the 2010 midterm election loomed and President Obama's initially high approval ratings fell below the symbolically important 50 percent, many House and Senate Democrats stopped cooperating with Majority Leader Harry Reid and Speaker Nancy Pelosi, as exemplified by the defection of dozens of moderate House Democrats from their leadership's call to vote on extensions of tax cuts before November 2010. Pelosi's plan to extend cuts for the middle class but to allow those on income above $250,000 a year to expire seemed like a logical move for a Democratic House but was blocked by skittish House Democrats who feared nonstop attacks from wealthy interests and Republican opponents. The public saw disarray in the governing party of 2009 and 2010 because, in fact, there was disarray.

ONE WAY OR ANOTHER

Across the various policy areas we study in the book, the avenues open to the White House to move priorities for policy change during the 111th Congress depended on conflicts and coalitions among Democrats. On some issues, such as health care reform, the concerns of more conservative and more liberal Democrats could (with great difficulty) be brokered by patient congressional leaders. Measures meant to address long-term deficits that concerned conservative Blue Dogs could be married to regulations and benefits designed to help lower- and middle-income Americans, as most moderate and liberal Democrats wanted. But in other major issue areas, such as immigration and energy, regional divisions among Democrats were profound and proved unbridgeable. Grand legislative bargains in those areas required some Republican votes, because quite a few Democrats were certain to be lost in any attempted bargain. When even a handful of Republican votes were not forthcoming, given the increasingly lockstep Republican obstructionist strike against Obama, bold legislation proved impossible. In the labor law area, for instance, conservative Democrats in the Senate were never willing to accept any version of the Employee Free Choice Act favored by the labor unions, and Republicans have long been adamantly opposed to it.

White House perceptions of the possibilities in the 111th Congress drove its choice of what issues to pursue when and whether to call for legislation or proceed through administrative and regulatory efforts. When the president's agenda made little headway in Congress given Republican obstruction and too little Democratic unity, the White House turned instead to administrative and regulatory measures—either in anticipation of the dead end in Congress, or after the fact. When labor law changes faltered, for example, Obama circumvented Republican obstruction in the Senate and put a lawyer favored by the labor unions onto the National Labor Relations Board; and Labor Secretary Hilda Solis energetically enforced existing workplace regulations that Bush administration officials had left loosely enforced. Similarly, the Obama administration took regulatory steps to help the environment, even though major legislation had stalled in Congress.

Most commentators focus on the president as a leader who advances legislation in Congress, but Obama built on decades of expansion in the executive branch's institutional capacity to further presidential priorities by rule-making and other administrative means. Initiated by FDR and then substantially strengthened by Republicans, the administrative presidency enabled the Obama White House to circumvent congressional roadblocks and instead use the Office of Management and Budget to monitor and control policymaking in the executive branch, while relying on loyal political appointees in the agencies to follow the White House agenda. Our investigations of eight key policy areas elaborate the specific interplay of political conditions and alternative modalities of presidential action. But the point to stress here is a broader one. Outside observers and critics from the left have excoriated the Obama administration for not leading on major issues—such as environmental or labor legislation. But his room for maneuver was highly constrained for reasons no single president could have controlled. The possibilities—and impossibilities—for assembling Democratic coalitions in the 111th Congress were decisive to how Obama made headway as he pursued an overall agenda for major policy changes during 2009 and 2010. Public pushes for big legislation were not always the best way forward.

When Ideology and Partisanship Overlap

Of course, in the original New Deal of the 1930s, congressional coalitions were often decisive and dispositive as well. A conservative coalition formed in Congress by 1934 and placed limits on FDR's initiatives for the remainder of the domestic New Deal of the 1930s (Patterson 1967). Yet New Deal divisions were not a purely partisan matter, because many of the conservatives in that bloc were southern Democrats—indeed they were chairs of powerful committees. In the 1930s, as now, proposed federal reforms evoked fierce counterpressures, but Obama faced a more partisan division of Democrats against Republicans than FDR did in his day.

Of necessity during 2009 and 2010, Obama's White House repeatedly caucused with Democratic House Speaker Nancy Pelosi and Democratic Senate Majority Leader Harry Reid, looking for ways to coordinate agendas and move key bills through the many hurdles that mark today's legislative process, especially in the Senate. Even though the watching public might not understand why Democrats spent so much time negotiating among themselves, or why the president couldn't just tell Congress to "get it done," the early Obama administration understandably devoted much effort to prodding and cajoling Congress in consultation with key congressional Democrats. This happened not merely because Obama is a former senator and thinks in legislative terms, and not only because his former chief of staff, Rahm Emanuel, is a seasoned wheeler-dealer from the House of Representatives (Bai 2010). More than that, Obama and his White House aides knew that the 111th Congress was their best chance to further big legislative reforms. To take advantage of congressional Democratic majorities, they devoted enormous time to working with the congressional leaders to assemble fragile and shifting coalitions. The congressional sausage-making involving the president was confusing and dispiriting for Americans to watch, but a necessary price for moving big legislative reforms.

But the understandable efforts of the White House to work with Democratic leaders looked purely partisan because liberal versus conservative differences have become closely aligned with the major party labels. Much of the national system of political communication is geared to give extra voice to opposition that comes from the minority party. In the Obama administration, therefore, Republicans enjoyed the regular access to the media that the minority party automatically receives. And they used that access, in part, to cry foul about the very congressional consultations they boycotted and tried to obstruct. On the one hand, GOP leaders refused to enter into legislative bargains or talk about compromises with the White House, and on the other claimed that the Democrats were excluding them in favor of high-handed partisan fiat. Republicans were able to prevent Democratic action, or else force Democrats into elaborate bargaining to hold coalitions together—all the while decrying partisanship and blaming Democrats for delays and special deals, such as the Cornhusker Kickback used during the Senate endgame in health care reform to cajole Ben Nelson of Nebraska to join other Democrats to break the Republican filibuster in late 2009.

Through all of this, Obama and congressional Democrats ended up looking to the larger public both responsible for partisan rancor and incompetent at settling legislative quarrels. The primary problem, though, lay not with Obama or with Democrats as such, but with laborious institutional rules that fostered deadlocks and delay. The price of moving major legislation was to absorb the public punishment and loss of time associated with assembling complex coalitions. There was little choice if Obama and the Democrats wanted to act to save the economy and try to carry through on major campaign promises. Enduring repeated Republican charges about partisanship and deal-making was the price of actually trying to govern in an era when ideology and party identity aligned so closely.

MEDIA CLIMATE AND PRESIDENTIAL COMMUNICATION

When FDR communicated with everyday Americans, he enjoyed a comparatively unfiltered opportunity. Although established newspapers were largely hostile to him during the 1930s, his famous fireside chats broadcast on the radio reached millions, revealing both the scope of that broadly shared communication modality and the eagerness of all Americans to hear from their president in a time of national crisis. The media dynamics surrounding Obama's presidency have been quite different. White House and Democratic messages passed through the refracting filter of commentators, whereas conservatives projected their messages through major media outlets openly aligned with the GOP that in turn influenced agendas for other outlets in a fragmented and competitive media environment.

This assertion may come as a surprise to some, because during the 2007 and 2008 primary and general election campaigns, Barack Obama and the Democratic Party proved extraordinarily adept at shaping public perceptions and using a mesh of old and new media to motivate and activate voters (Wolffe 2009). Part of Obama's appeal to elites within the Democratic Party—the super delegates, the majority of whom ended up swinging his way in the contest with Hillary Rodham Clinton—was his ability as a communicator and the capacities of his political operation to reach and activate millions of voters. Observers within and beyond the Democratic Party expected President Obama to continue to frame public issues successfully in major speeches, and expected his White House and his Democratic National Committee to engage in effective ongoing communication and mobilization on behalf not just of the president's policy agenda and eventual reelection, but also in support of all Democratic candidates.

That it has not worked out that way is an understatement, and this seems puzzling to many. The explanation for weak popular mobilization after Obama took office lies in part in the effort to reorganize Obama for America, the grassroots election operation, into an arm of the Democratic National Committee called Organizing for America. Grassroots activism works better when it is loosely linked to centralizing institutions; and besides, it is much harder to mobilize people for a congressionally centered, year-long legislative battle like the one for health care reform than it is to focus efforts on electing a president on one certain date (Dreier 2010).

The mystery about Obama's media presence and messaging seems deeper. To be sure, President Obama is a new-media user just as FDR was in his day. Just as FDR used radio fireside chats to get very regularly into the ears of ordinary Americans, Obama records weekly YouTube presidential addresses that are watched by millions of Americans at the click of a computer mouse. And Obama does sit-down interviews with journalists, supplemented by appearances on soft-format popular television shows such as *The View* and late-night comedy hours, to reach people without going through formal news conferences or other formats filtered by professional reporters. Obama does quite well in such direct visual formats.

Fragmented Media and Segmented Audiences

But here the cross-era similarities in creative presidential communication end, because Obama's White House faces an institutionally fragmented media environment that segments listening, viewing, and online audiences in ways that make attention fleeting, even as Americans divide into different communicative and reality communities (Prior 2007; Shapiro and Jacobs 2011). All contemporary institutional leaders, including the president of the United States, find it hard to get an overall message through to most Americans at the same time—a situation that is somewhat modified during presidential elections and huge crises like 9/11, but otherwise prevails. What is more, intense commercial competition within the fragmented institutional setting means that issue entrepreneurs pushing controversies from the margins can quickly inject a controversy into intense coverage across channels (Dreier and Martin 2010). Critics of the White House, left and right, but especially right, have a lot of agenda-setting advantages. The Republican Party and right-wing controversy-peddlers have, in particular, been aided by Fox News, a massive, widely watched television network unabashedly aligned with the GOP. Other networks try to compete with Fox either through imitation of formats if not content (CNN, quite often) or through a degree of differentiation (MSNBC), but either way, the premium is placed on magnifying or arguing with highly provocative voices that first appear on Fox (or on right-wing blogs en route to Fox).

In due course, even the proudest old-line media, including newspapers like the *New York Times*, allow some of their agenda to be taken up by topics launched from the right-wing noise and echo machine. More often, the old media splinter the communications by Obama and Democrats by rarely quoting them at length and counterbalancing them with competing interpretations. Republican messages are delivered intact, but Democratic ones are garbled.

Beyond that, news media sponsor incessant polls that reinforce controversial narratives by repeating the same phrases and accusations as questions—often asking the public about simplified stereotypes of complicated matters, such as government takeover of health care or the imposition of so-called death panels, that citizens barely understand—and then reporting the findings and trends as if they were popularly given. Even avowedly leftist or liberal media sources, from print media to radio and television and blogs, end up devoting a lot of their space to arguing with the loudest right-wing provocateurs or reporting polls about simplified choices, superficial controversies, or election horse-races measured months before most voters are paying close attention. When liberal outlets go beyond such back and forth, they often criticize the White House from the left.

Amidst all of the cacophony going on 24/7/365, it is very difficult for the president, let alone congressional leaders trying to push forward with difficult legislative initiatives, to communicate accurate information about what is going on. Thus, during the protracted health care debates, wildly false ideas and information crowded out accurate information and aroused public fears and disgust that far outran the realities of what was in the legislation.

More broadly, the fragmentation of the media and the resulting intensification of divisions and their emotional significance have not only reinforced the sorting of everyday Americans into divergent parties but also affected their perceptions of reality (Taber and Lodge 2006). Mistaken information about Obama's birth, religious status, supposed promotion of nonexistent death panels, and supposedly socialist policies are often the only claims that conservatives hear on these topics as they form their views. Similarly, liberals in the health care battles heard again and again that the public option was all that mattered; to this day, many liberals do not realize that the final Patient Protection and Affordable Care Act empowers states to establish a public option or single-payer system within their border or region as well as create new programs to help ordinary Americans afford access to health insurance coverage and high-quality health care. Although education and attentiveness to public affairs have long had an impact on political and policy knowledge, scholars are now finding that even well-educated, "sophisticated" individuals are particularly prone to misperceptions, given the interaction of segmented media consumption with existing beliefs and values. We hear what we want, and see evidence for what we already know to be true.

Has Obama Projected a Powerful Message?

Acknowledging these facts about current media institutions and dynamics in the United States, many critics have nevertheless questioned the communications strategy of the Obama White House, especially on economic issues. Why has the president never given major nationally televised speeches on the economy and his overall recovery plan? In the priority area of health care reform, Obama did give major speeches and orchestrate theatrically effective issue forums at key intervals, displaying presidential leadership and offering framings that proved influential beyond as well as within the Beltway. U.S. policies in Iraq and Afghanistan have also been addressed by the president in nationally visible settings. But Obama has been curiously silent on the nation's economic crisis.

Why, during his initial honeymoon period in the first half of 2009, did Obama not engage in sustained and nationally televised public explanations about why the stimulus was structured as it was, how it differed from the Bush Wall Street bailouts, and why government spending can function to create millions of jobs? Although Obama traveled the country from Racine, Wisconsin, to Elkhart County, Indiana, highlighting individual initiatives and progress in selected areas (see Obama 2010), these efforts lacked the galvanizing, agenda-setting effect of a major speech or sustained national communications strategy; and their fragmented focus inherently restricted the White House's ability to present a coherent economic plan. Perhaps the president and his advisors believed an overall framing of economic strategy in socially understandable and value-laden terms was too difficult to pull off or was unnecessary—a common mistake of Democratic policy wonks who presume that facts speak for themselves and that sharply pitched communications are inappropriate. If so, President Obama and his White House advisors failed to understand that American citizens have heard for many years a steady stream of arguments about how government spending hurts the economy and that tax cuts are the only way to spur growth and create jobs (Smith 2007a, 2007b). Against that backdrop of public beliefs and misunderstandings, the president needed to invest his time and institutional resources in effectively framing his overall economic recovery strategy if he wanted citizens to understand why he proposed what he did—especially if he wanted citizens to be able to track successes and shortfalls and remain patient through a protracted recovery process.

Even more to the point, as FDR proved back in the 1930s, and as Ronald Reagan demonstrated again when he struggled to preserve presidential power during an economic downturn in the 1980s, citizens in a democracy need and want a sense of strategic presidential leadership in a period of crisis. Whether Larry Summers thought a given measure would pass Ivy League muster, whether Rahm Emanuel thought it would get through Congress, President Obama needed from early 2009 onward to convey to Americans his bold plan for national economic recovery and job creation. Most citizens would probably have accepted setbacks and delays with some patience if they felt certain that the president was leading them to a better place. Obama's failure to engage in effective public leadership on the economy constitutes, in an important sense, democratic political malpractice—he botched a central function of the presidency in a period of economic crisis (Dionne 2010).

There is, of course, another way to look at the situation. The Obama White House may have underestimated the need for public framing, but more likely the president and his advisors, juggling multiple crises abroad and at home, were focused on getting things through Congress beyond the stimulus itself. Obama originally decided to run for the presidency not to handle a sudden Wall Street–induced meltdown, but to further foundational reforms intended to put America's economy and society on a sounder long-term trajectory (Hirsh 2010). Hence the stress on reforming health care, education, labor relations, and energy and environmental issues, with a nod toward the notion of reviving the "grand bargain" on immigration reform that President Bush had tried and failed to move through Congress.

Obama and senior administration officials seem to have hoped that, with Wall Street stabilized and the stimulus unfolding by the spring and summer of 2010, overall economic growth would send its own message and that facts would make their case. They paid attention to implementing the stimulus transparently and efficiently. Surely they knew that job growth would lag—and one suspects they did not want to tell Americans the full truth about that—but they must have hoped that, as months passed, families and communities would see progress on the ground, that they would feel positive effects from unemployment benefits, state aid, construction contracts, and gradually reviving private-sector jobs. Evidence suggests that the overall White House political strategy depended on private-sector economic expansion reviving on its own after the initial push from government (Geithner 2010; Hirsh 2010). Thus no persistent and forceful plan for public framing of the White House's economic and job initiatives was developed to make incomplete success comprehensible to most Americans. White House communications may also have been hobbled by a reluctance to offend the business interests the president's advisors hoped would revive growth within existing structural parameters. Unlike Ronald Reagan, who could keep demonizing government as he attempted to minimize the political costs of the sharp recession heading into the 1982 midterm elections, Obama found it hard to voice any full-throttled attack on the bankers and corporate chieftains he and his advisors depended upon to spark the economy as soon as possible.

Interestingly, during 2009 and 2010 Obama and his White House also seemed unwilling to call for anything beyond what they thought Congress would pass the next month (Bai 2010). This lowered the president's leadership profile at a time of protracted national economic crisis and caused him to seem mired in small-bore maneuvers, closeted with congressional factions. Media structures and dynamics in and of themselves did not force Obama's White House to be so timid. The president and his advisors seem to have chosen that route. Put simply, when it comes to Americans' sustained confusion about what is and is not working for the economy or the federal budget, tepid presidential tactics and framing, not just inescapable constraints, bear part of the responsibility.

DEMONIZING OBAMA

Although the Obama White House pulled its punches, opponents of the president and his policies were never silent or restrained, either in Congress or in the media. A number of right-wing media commentators, especially Glenn Beck and Rush Limbaugh, have stopped at virtually nothing to demonize Obama, to portray him as alien, possibly foreign-born, as a

"Nazi" or a socialist—in short, as the Other, an enemy to America and Americans.

Racial Stereotypes Live On

During the 2008 election, Obama's race and parentage (that his father was a foreign student) receded in importance as the financial crisis exploded, even though independent right-wing groups tried to arouse voter fears based on these characteristics and the Republican ticket of John McCain and Sarah Palin stirred up stories of Obama's so-called otherness—citing supposed friendships with terrorists and controversial preachers and activists. In the end, those charges did not prevent Obama from winning. The election of the nation's first African American president by a large majority of voters seemed to confirm that racial stereotyping had lost out in the face of deeper worries about the economy and a broad disenchantment with GOP leadership.

But any hope that racial and nativist fears were permanently overcome was dashed after Obama assumed the presidency, because millions of Americans found him hard to accept and have remained open to manipulators of hoary stereotypes. Popular anxieties might have remained largely subterranean had not ultra-right agitators and media entrepreneurs been so willing to stir the pot—even as conservative Republicans competed to see who could go the furthest in attacking President Obama. The 2010 political primary season encouraged a rhetorical sprint toward the outrageous right; and the lead-in to the 2012 Republican presidential primaries will keep the pot boiling. There is no established heir apparent as the leading GOP presidential candidate, and the freelancing contenders include willing wielders of racial innuendo such as Sarah Palin and Newt Gingrich. All GOP contenders are trying to appeal to the same heavily white and disproportionately southern base voters, not to mention striving to attract hard-to-predict Tea Partiers, some of whom show open contempt for Obama in ways that often include racist images and over-the-top rhetoric laced with racial innuendo.

Attempts to Revive the Conservative Economic Narrative

Popular racial anxieties stoked by race-baiting leaders are not the only sources of intense opposition to President Obama, his agenda, and his allies. Many wealthy conservatives and powerful stakeholders angry at higher taxes and tighter regulations are also in the field. Ultimately, many of the very same Wall Street and other business interests saved by Obama's emergency economic programs have turned against him too. The Supreme Court's decision in the Citizens United case has taken all fetters off wealthy interests who want to intervene in election contests by giving big money to tarnish Democratic candidates and further demonize Obama as supposedly responsible for big government spending. "Obama's bailouts" are alleged to be "killing jobs" and delaying economic recovery. During the debates over expiring Bush-era tax cuts for the very rich, the U.S. right wing resumed its long-standing public campaigns to convince Americans that huge tax breaks for the super wealthy are the most effective way to create more jobs, even as the same conservatives claim that they want to substantially reduce the budget deficit.

Polls tell us that substantial majorities of Americans oppose tax cuts for the rich, but Democrats did not act to stop such cuts when they could in 2009 and 2010, and did not give citizens a framework in which to understand how huge tax cuts for the very rich increase the deficit but create few jobs and do little for the national economy. Over the course of 2009 and 2010, President Obama's failure to envelop his economic recovery efforts in a persuasive master narrative ceded the public debate, in effect, to long-time conservative nostrums about big government as the enemy of economic growth. That contrasts sharply with other twentieth-century change-oriented presidents, from FDR to Reagan, who constantly offered narratives, vivid metaphors, and value-oriented framings to help the public understand why the other side was to blame for crises, and why they were pushing good solutions—even if it would take a long time for the solutions to work, and even if Congress would not immediately fall into line.

CREATING NEW FEDERAL PROGRAMS
VERSUS RESHAPING ESTABLISHED POLICIES

Finally, we come to the biggest difference between the 1930s and now—and the one that matters most as we move toward analyzing the efforts to achieve policy shifts in realms such as health care, higher education, and energy and the environment. In the 1930s, the New Dealers in Congress and in the FDR administration were advocating new kinds of federal government interventions—new financial regulations, unprecedented national policies like minimum wage and maximum hour rules, Social Security, unemployment insurance, and new rights for labor unions to organize. Previously, apart from setting tariffs and seeding infrastructure and western expansion, the U.S. federal government had intervened actively in economic and social affairs only temporarily during major wars. The New Dealers, amidst a massive Great Depression, were advocating a series of innovative permanent peacetime interventions. They were selling new ideas in a huge economic emergency—and, ultimately, World War II reinforced and helped entrench much of what had begun during the Depression.

Today, by contrast, Obama and his Democratic allies offer revised frameworks for already pervasive federal regulations, benefits, and taxes—but not first-time interventions. As we have seen, they started these efforts just as a big economic downturn was gathering steam, not at its nadir; and in contrast to the impacts of World II on New Deal initiatives, the wars Obama inherited in Afghanistan and Iraq drained rather than reinforced economic resources and presidential attention from domestic reforms.

Obama arrived in office following a half-century of previous accretions of pervasive regulatory and fiscal interventions—and set out to reverse some of those and redirect others. The new president and his allies came to office dogged by federal deficits already run up to high levels: finding new resources for redistributive social benefits—such as more generous college loans for low-income families, or subsidies to help poor and lower-middle-income people afford health insurance—required that they raise new revenues or recapture revenues previously devoted to other federal programs.

Pundits declare nearly every day that Americans in the early twenty-first century are fighting about government versus the market. This is nonsense. Over the past six decades, Democrats and Republicans alike in Washington have presided over more or less steady increases in taxes and tax subsidies, regulatory interventions, and social spending, not to mention rising deficits. Both parties have participated in building up a massive, ramified, expensive, and pervasive subsidy and regulatory state (Pierson 2007). This steady accretion of government activism precipitated the conservative backlash against President George W. Bush as an "impostor," as one book title put it (Bartlett 2006). On the margin, Democrats tilt the tax advantages and subsidies toward working families and the middle class, and Republicans since 1980 have pushed subsidies and advantages toward favored industries and very wealthy taxpayers (Jacobs and Skocpol 2005; Bartels 2008; Hacker and Pierson 2010). Neither party has cut back in any important respect. Consequently, every region of the United States, and every industry and social stratum, has a stake in existing federal interventions into the economy and the society.

In our day and age, therefore, when a change-oriented president like Obama arrives in Washington aiming to transform the forms and redistributive impact of federal government interventions, he is not starting from scratch like FDR was. He is redirecting resources—and at the same time necessarily asking some citizens and interests already enjoying regulatory advantages, governmental subsidies or benefits, and tax breaks to accept less. Social science tells us that those asked to give up something are quite alert to their potential disadvantage and quick to mobilize against change, whereas those who might benefit from rearrangements in some hypothetical future are likely to be skeptical, and certainly not yet concretely accustomed to the new advantages they could enjoy. Potential beneficiaries therefore remain mostly disengaged. The disparity of mobilization only becomes worse when the previously advantaged are wealthier or better organized, and the potential beneficiaries are lower- or lower-middle-income Americans who may not even vote regularly, and have not been previously mobilized by groups advocating their interests, such as AARP, which stepped in to mobilize seniors after Social Security and Medicare became important (see Campbell 2003). Add to this imbalance the demonstrated finding that officeholders pay more heed to the preferences of the rich than to those of the middle class or the poor, and the dilemma of how to leverage equality-enhancing changes in public policy becomes all the more acute (Bartels 2008; Gilens 2005; Jacobs and Page 2005; Hacker and Pierson 2010). The Obama administration's attempts to deal with imbalances in political capacity by bargaining with and dividing powerful stakeholders have outraged liberal supporters, as happened with the White House decision to cut deals with powerful lobbies during the health care reform battles, to forestall united opposition (Jacobs and Skocpol 2010, chap. 2).

Overall, the knotty dilemma of how to shift policies in redistributive directions in ways that cut against current political inequalities has bedeviled the Obama project from the beginning. Health insurance coverage for lower- and middle-income insured Americans could be financed only through hard-fought steps to place new charges on businesses and the well-to-do. Enhanced Pell Grants for lower-income college students and better loan terms for middle-class students required a battle with private bankers accustomed to receiving guaranteed profits for administering federally backed loans without risk. Proposals for new energy policies aroused resistance from the coal and oil and gas industries, some of which were located in regions represented by congressional Democrats—illustrating but one source of Obama's difficulty in assembling durable legislative coalitions.

What is more, as we see in ongoing tax and budge battles fought at fever pitch, Obama's 2008 campaign promise to allow the expiration of George W. Bush's tax breaks for the very highest income earners faced fierce pushback and was undermined by Democratic skittishness, even when the president's party enjoyed congressional majorities in 2009 and 2010. After Republicans took over the House in the 112th Congress, they put in place rules that favor additional tax cuts and are pledged to slash public spending on programs that benefit ordinary Americans. This sets up confrontations through 2012 between congressional Republicans and President Obama, who must begin to sustain and raise revenues to reduce looming long-term deficits and support existing and newly promised benefits for the majority of Americans. As we document in every policy area considered in this collection, at this point in U.S. history, any second New Deal involving redirection of federal interventions in an equality-enhancing direction is a much more fraught undertaking than the original New Deal—not least because there are no slack federal revenues available. Taxes and the budget will be at the center of domestic political conflicts for months and years to come.

Fighting for a second New Deal in the current U.S. policy and political landscape is also bound to be a more confusing and opaque undertaking, because accretions of previous federal spending, regulations, and tax breaks crowd every major policy area—and large bureaucracies, multiple congressional committees, and hundreds of interest groups have a hand in ongoing policymaking in every realm. In the 1930s, American citizens could see that big, new things were being proposed and debated in Washington. Social Security at its inception was hard to miss: it enjoyed support from two-thirds or more beginning in the mid-1930s. As it was implemented and expanded from the 1930s to the 1970s, its supporters could offer simple metaphors to try to make it popularly understandable.

In contrast, America's contemporary public policies include many complex regulations and publicly invisible tax credits and tax breaks (Mettler 2007; Soss, Hacker, and Mettler 2007). Furthermore, as exemplified by the Patient Protection and Affordable Care Act of 2010, major reforms affecting already mind-bogglingly complex sets of institutional arrangements necessarily turn into massive compilations of regulatory, tax, and spending provisions running to thousands of pages. Such complex measures are difficult for Congress people to master, and virtually impossible to explain to citizens who know that something big is being endlessly and bitterly argued about—but what is it, and how can it be good, or workable? In the case of Affordable Care, citizens remain divided and puzzled long after the reform passes into law.

In short, already huge, pervasive, and complex government undertakings are a challenge to rework—and the politics involved makes it even more challenging for citizen majorities to appreciate what is going on. Obama's agendas for policy change progressed quite remarkably during 2009 and 2010—in health care reform, education loans, financial regulation, and many other realms of law and regulation. But much of what happened was either invisible or ominously incomprehensible to most

citizens. This agenda remains big, worrisome, and easily caricatured—
especially at a time of economic stress when Americans know one thing
for a certainty: the national economy is not getting stronger fast enough to
ensure that a rising tide will lift all boats.

The End of Change?

Our project is called Reaching for a New Deal with a deliberate embrace
of ambiguity. The word *reach* suggests, at times, arrival at a desired desti-
nation, yet likewise connotes an aspiration to get someplace at the edge of
likely attainment, such as when college applicants apply to reach schools.
What happens when a desired goal is reached, but at high political cost?
What happens when the effort to get somewhere falls short? And what
about the possibility of misdirected reach? Have Obama and his allies
pushed in the right directions; and what are the consequences of falling
short, or arriving at interim destinations only to face backlash or incom-
prehension or repudiation?

The New Political Reality

Democrats suffered massive losses in November 2010, losing control of
the House of Representatives, losing seats in the Senate, and losing control
of many governorships and statehouses. Not only that, but the Republican
Party has moved further to the right than at any time in decades. The GOP
"pledge" issued as a 2010 election manifesto called openly for huge tax
cuts for the rich accompanied by rollbacks of all of President Obama's
achievements so far (Republican Party 2010). In all likelihood, there will
be vociferous blocs in both the 112th House and Senate who call not just
for an end to all current federal initiatives to promote economic renewal
and social equity, but also for the rollback of long-established New Deal
and Great Society programs and the undoing of the Affordable Care Act,
the landmark achieved during Obama's first two years. Seemingly rewarded by electoral victories in 2010, sheer obstruction and delay as a
Republican strategy worked in the political short term—and extremist
forces within the GOP will continue to cow others who want to take any
other course. That some Obama priorities succeeded in the lame-duck
congressional session at the very end of 2010 does not gainsay that, on the
big issues of taxes and budgets, the GOP started to get its way even in the
waning days of the Democrat-controlled 111th Congress. During 2011 and
2012, the GOP will demand ever more concessions, and will balk at any
action whenever they do not get all or virtually all of what they want.
Deadlock and shouting will likely reach new crescendos in the 112th Con-

gress even if, occasionally, bipartisan deals are finally struck to avoid immobility on vital issues.

The immediate prospects for congressional Republicans to work with Obama and Democrats to solve major national problems are poor, above all because GOP incumbents face continuing scrutiny from Tea Party activists who hate Obama and might mount primary challenges should signs of cooperation appear. Some pundits blame Obama for such polarization and deadlock, but the logic is puzzling, given the severity of the problems the president has had to tackle and his repeated efforts to find compromises. The recent intense polarization is the by-product, not just of Obama's change-oriented agenda, but also of the strategic choices of Obama's opponents and the media dynamics and institutional advantages for obstruction we have discussed—interacting with the profound social demoralization caused by a deep and prolonged economic downturn.

Economic troubles, especially long-term unemployment, remain the true elephant in the room. Financially induced crises lead to slow recovery, and all the more so when, as in the concurrent housing downturn, families and individuals as well as businesses lose equity. Many analysts also argue that increasing inequalities in the United States have undercut the capacity of the middle strata to consume what the economy can produce—hence reinforcing business caution about investments (Rajan 2010; Reich 2010; Story 2010). If so, the country needs more, not fewer, efforts to bolster middle-class families in consumer and labor markets. Arguments that Obama has not tried to do enough, or has been unable to do enough, have just as much justification as claims that he has overreached toward the left and thus provoked conservative anger (Hirsh 2010).

No one can predict the future, and the frenzies of punditry that followed the 2008 and 2010 elections were overwrought. All we can do here is suggest possibilities. The most clear-cut is that the time of big presidential legislative initiatives ended with the 2010 elections. Even with large Democratic majorities during 2009 and 2010, Congress could only process some of Obama's agenda items, as we have discussed, and the enacting coalitions added up to bare majorities. Republican gains in 2010 cut off legislative possibilities except in the rare instances where bipartisan deals can be put together. In pending unresolved areas such as energy and immigration, this is likely to mean that piecemeal steps, at most, will occur and those steps may be restricted to administrative actions by Obama's departments and agencies. Until the presidential election of 2012 brings a kind of public judgment on GOP obstruction and Obama's performance, there will be more sound and fury in American politics than genuine policy movement.

Will Obama's Early Legislative Accomplishments Be Rolled Back?

More interesting is the question of whether massive Democratic losses in November 2010 will open the door to repealing the major legislative accomplishments of the 111th Congress: health care reform, financial reform, and higher education reform. Republicans are loudly proclaiming their will to repeal health care reform, above all, and House Speaker John Boehner was locked by his own election-time rhetoric into introducing a repeal bill immediately after taking office (Hooper 2010; Republican Party 2010). Obama must spend 2011 and 2012 defending his landmark legislative accomplishments and tending to their administrative implementation in a highly contentious environment. Republican congressional committees are harassing his executive appointees and lugging them into hearing after hearing, looking for scandals and hot-button issues to dramatize. Republican budget-makers seek to de-fund administrative agencies involved in implementing health, education, and financial reforms, forcing huge budget crises (and risking government defaults and shut-downs, which may not be popular). The president is not powerless, though. He can veto outright repeal bills, even if they can make it through the Senate, and his cabinet officers are finding ways to move forward with implementation amidst hearings and budgetary roadblocks.

Chances are that the Obama administration will succeed in moving forward. In the key areas where breakthrough legislation occurred during 2009 and 2010, as well as in areas where action has been primarily by administrative means all along, change in federal regulations and subsidies will proceed through 2012 at least. Obama will keep pushing for redirections of federal efforts through administrative action—and as the communicator-in-chief, will be freed from the need and temptation to closet himself with congressional leaders. Quite possibly, he will regain his voice as a national political leader. And in key areas, such as health care reform, he can already highlight the concrete benefits of his achievements, including the landmark Affordable Care law that Republicans are trying to undo, such as regulations protecting health insurance customers, tax credits for small businesses, new benefits for Medicare recipients, and fiscal controls on Medicare spending. Quite likely, financial reform will survive, with the new Consumer Financial Products Agency launched under the leadership of Elizabeth Warren working directly for the president. The Affordable Care framework will almost certainly survive, too (Jacobs and Skocpol 2010, chap. 5; Skocpol 2010).

The overall thrust of comprehensive health care reform will move forward even if Congress manages to modify many specific regulations and benefits at the behest of businesses and high-end taxpayers—possibly to the detriment of subsidies promised after 2014 to help less-privileged Americans afford insurance. The same kind of quiet evisceration of equality-enhancing measures may occur in a range of policy areas—in congressional committee chambers as well as in regulatory agencies that need to carry out complicated agendas under pressure from lobbyists and hostile legislators.

One reason to expect some backtracking from legislative reforms achieved on paper during 2009 and 2010 is that virtually everything that has passed requires capable, tough, and persistent administrative implementation through a maze of federal agencies, in the case of financial reform, and through state as well as federal agencies, in the case of health care reform. Contentious politics will not only undercut administrative consistency. Contention may also embolden powerful interest groups to maneuver behind the scenes to undercut effective administration of policy changes they do not like. This is where much of the real action will be in coming months, far from the spotlight of shouting partisan politicians and media pundits. Does the U. S. federal government have the administrative capacity to carry through complicated reforms? We will see.

The Political Prospect

Moving beyond what may happen to legislation or rule shifts that Obama and his congressional supporters pushed onto the books in 2009 and 2010, we must ponder what happens to the United States if the immediate political future brings gridlock and enhanced leverage for highly ideological, antigovernment politicians. Whatever one may think of the reforms the Obama administration has pursued, the president has asked Congress and the country to grapple with truly pressing challenges—of economic renewal, environmental degradation, declining educational performance and uneven access to postsecondary institutions, a broken immigration system, and a costly and inefficient health care system, as well as other festering dilemmas. All these are very real problems not likely to go away. Many are epochal challenges that affect the nation's international competitiveness as well as its ability to expand the economy and marshal all available human talents. What does it mean if the U.S. federal government is further weakened in its capacity to deal with major issues, both politically and administratively?

This question becomes all the more pointed when growing federal deficits are brought into the picture—in a polity where powerful partisan and movement forces prefer rhetorically vapid proposals to genuine steps to address the most expensive items in the government's portfolio of existing commitments. Republicans on Capitol Hill and their allies rigidly oppose tax increases even if they are part of a grand bargain that might include trims of entitlements as well as reforms of the tax code. The unresolved challenges covered in the third part of this volume—immigration, energy and climate change, and revenue—cannot be wished away. Furthermore, the political forces now at work are contradictory and toxic, especially in the midst of an economic and employment slowdown that neither the Obama administration nor congressional Republicans are likely to be able to pull the country out of very quickly.

The looming political dangers for both major parties are obvious: Democrats may continue to be undercut by slow economic recovery and may lose the presidency and the Senate in 2012, punished by voters who are frustrated that Obama and congressional Democrats seem to have focused on debating big, future-oriented reforms as the economy continues to lag. But how will Republicans fare with the same public if Republican governors increase unemployment in their states by slashing public infrastructure projects and throwing teachers, police, and firefighters out of work? Of if House Republicans endlessly relitigate health care reform and push investigations and government shutdowns—following the same script that did not work so well for the GOP after 1994?

Public disgust with both major parties seems likely to persist, even deepen. Before long, some analysts speculate, the doors will open to independent or third-party candidacies. But the institutional obstacles in America's federated electoral system are great, likely to prevent sustained third-party capacity from emerging on a national scale. Lone-wolf independents, like Ross Perot in 1992 and 1996, are more likely, but most serve as little more than electoral spoilers and, should an independent actually win major office, would find it hard to make government work. Pounding the desk and shouting will not be enough. More likely than the rise of a viable third party, or the sudden appearance of effective independent executives, will be a continual roiling, as voters throw first one and then another party incumbent out of office. This, too, might lead to a degradation of public capacities, not to mention deepening voter disillusionment.

Looking back at the first New Deal, it is telling that Franklin Delano Roosevelt got many of his early proposals enacted with lightning speed and considerable bipartisan support during 1933 and 1934—but his first efforts did not prove durable or economically adequate. The Supreme Court invalidated much of his initial National Recovery Act, and the economy struggled to revive, and eventually went into another tailspin after Roosevelt, in his second term, cut back federal spending under conservative pressure. Many of the enduring legislative reforms of the New Deal—the ones that laid the basis for postwar prosperity in a middle-class society—came from progressive movements and congressional liberals pressing forward somewhat independently from FDR, or took force during World War II.

History will not simply repeat itself; the phases and dynamics of the Obama reformist presidency have been and will remain different, above all because of the interplay of different political and institutional dynamics with a deep economic crisis whose arrival coincided with the start of the Obama presidency. But the past should remind us that the entire unfolding of politics in a period of crisis does not happen at once, and surprising turns are possible. Obama has time through 2012, certainly, and perhaps for four more years after that, to cement and propel his renovations of U.S. policies. He will succeed or fail at mastering international challenges that will affect his popularity and governing capacity at home in ways still to be determined. Even in domestic politics, despite all of the decay in his popularity, Obama's standing with the U.S. public remains as strong as that of previous U.S. presidents dealing with economic troubles, including Reagan, and his standing in his own party, among declared Democratic identifiers, is much stronger than Bill Clinton's was in the middle of his first term (Klein 2010). Congressional chambers may well change direction more than once in what remains of Obama's presidency, and Democrats and associated grassroots movements may find new voices as they take up the role of criticizing House Republicans and GOP governors, who will face even deeper budget woes as federal stimulus funds from 2009 and 2010 dry up.

The euphoria that accompanied Barack Obama's election and inauguration is long gone, as is the sense that most Americans had in early 2009 that Obama knew how to save the national economy quickly. Nothing can gainsay the fact that Obama's White House has fallen short of facing the full challenge of leading the nation to a confident economic recovery— and presidents are measured not just against each other in some timeless statistical space, but against the depth of national challenges they are called to address as well (Judis 2010a, 2010b). Much depends in the immediate future on whether the currently struggling economic recovery continues, and whether Obama and his administration project more compelling narratives and effective renewal plans for the future. Jobs are what Americans care about, and right now neither party seems to be offering ideas that experts believe will boost employment to meet the supply of job seekers. Reforms in revenues, health care, energy policy, education, labor relations, and immigration are all inextricably tied up with economic policy and national economic trends, and with what the president is able to convince Americans the economy needs. U.S. political and governing capacity may also hinge on economic effectiveness, because the federal government could devolve into permanent shouting and deadlock if people remain angry and distrustful.

As hard as Obama's first two years turned out to be, his future captaincy is likely to be much more difficult. The only thing certain is that U.S. politics is navigating very rough waters. Whether the U.S. ship of state will founder, or come through it, remains to be seen. And if the ship comes through the storm, will it have all Americans still on board, or just the comfortable and the well-connected? That, too, remains to be seen.

LOOKING AHEAD: THE PLAN OF THE COLLECTION

The chapters to come in this book build on the critical overview of Obama's presidency we have offered in this chapter. Leading scholars have delved in detail into what was attempted and achieved or stymied—and with what political effects. Investigations of eight major areas of U.S. domestic policy are grouped into three major sections.

In the first part, contributors focus on landmark pieces of reform legislation fashioned and enacted during 2009 and 2010. The first three chapters probe, in turn, the hard-fought enactment of comprehensive health care reform through legislative bargains and interest group struggles that took up much of the oxygen in the first year of Obama's presidency; the achievement of a sharp change of direction in federal higher education policy, reducing the role of bankers and enhancing funding for low- and middle-income students; and the enactment of a new framework for federal regulation of the powerful financial services sectors in the U.S. economy. Action in all three of these areas occurred through the legislative process with backing from Democratic majority coalitions in Congress and very little Republican support or acquiescence.

In part two, the focus shifts to policy realms where the federal government has less direct leverage because comprehensive labor law reform remains obstructed in Congress by many Democratic as well as Republican senators, and because states and localities matter more in primary and secondary education even though the federal role has increased in recent times. In distinct ways, Obama cabinet officials and administrative agencies have taken the lead, using regulations to help workers and unions, and using modest funding and an administratively orchestrated "race to the top" competition to spur ongoing educational reforms in the states even as existing teaching positions were maintained through stop-gap federal funding.

Finally, part three looks at festering national challenges—immigration regulation, energy and climate change, and taxes—where Obama has called for large-scale bargains backed by bipartisan congressional coalitions, but to little positive effect. The battles over health care reform took longer to reach resolution than the White House originally anticipated, tightening the window for any other major efforts. Even more to the point, fault lines by region or ideology left Democrats in Congress struggling to muster majorities for other major reforms beyond health care and financial regulation, and Republicans were unwilling to sign on to compromises. Yet the challenges about immigration, energy and climate change, and taxes are inescapable, setting the stage for future battles as Republicans gain ground. Each analyst not only explains the stalemates that have taken shape so far, but also probes where things might go next.

REFERENCES

Alter, Jonathan. 2010. *The Promise: President Obama, Year One.* New York: Simon and Schuster.

Alterman, Eric. 2010. "Kabuki Democracy: Why a Progressive Presidency Is Impossible, for Now." *The Nation*, July 7, 2010, pp. 11–14.

Bai, Matt. 2010. "The Paradox of a Legislative President." *New York Times*, August 18, 2010.

Bartels, Larry M. 2008. *Unequal Democracy: The Political Economy of the New Gilded Age.* New York: Russell Sage Foundation; Princeton, N.J.: Princeton University Press.

Bartlett, Bruce. 2006. *Impostor: How George W. Bush Bankrupted America and Betrayed the Reagan Legacy.* New York: Doubleday.

Beinart, Peter. 2008. "The New Liberal Order." *Time*, November 24, 2008, pp. 30–32.

Binder, Sarah A., and Steven S. Smith. 1996. *Politics or Principle: Filibustering in the United States Senate.* Washington, D.C.: Brookings Institution Press.

Campbell, Andrea Louise. 2003. *How Policies Make Citizens: Senior Political Activism and the American Welfare State.* Princeton, N.J.: Princeton University Press.

Dionne, E. J., Jr. 2010. "It's the Politicking, Stupid!" *The New Republic*, August 30, 2010.

Dreier, Peter. 2010. "Lessons from the Health-Care Wars." *The American Prospect* 21(4): 29–34.

Dreier, Peter, and Christopher R. Martin. 2010. "How ACORN Was Framed: Political Controversy and Media Agenda Setting." *Perspectives on Politics* 8(3): 76–92.

Free, Lloyd A., and Hadley Cantril. 1968. *The Political Beliefs of Americans: A Study of Public Opinion.* New York: Simon and Schuster.

Frumin, Ben, and Jason Reif. 2010. "The Rise of Cloture: How GOP Filibuster Threats Have Changed the Senate." *Talking Points Memo DC*, January 27, 2010. Available at: http://tpmdc.talkingpointsmemo.com/2010/01/the-rise-of

-cloture-how-gop-filibuster-threats-have-changed-the-senate.php (accessed September 20, 2010).

Geithner, Timothy F. 2010. "Welcome to the Recovery." *New York Times*, August 2, 2010.

Gilens, Martin. 2005. "Inequality and Democratic Responsiveness." *Public Opinion Quarterly* 69(5): 77–76.

Hacker, Jacob S., and Paul Pierson. 2005. *Off Center: The Republican Revolution and the Erosion of American Democracy.* New Haven, Conn.: Yale University Press.

———. 2010. *Winner-Take-All Politics: How Washington Made the Rich Richer—and Turned Its Back on the Middle Class.* New York: Simon and Schuster.

Hirsh, Michael. 2010. "Obama's Old Deal: Why the 44th President Is No FDR—and the Economy Is Still in the Doldrums." *Newsweek*, August 29, 2010.

Hooper, Molly K. 2010. "GOP Moves to Repeal Health Care Law." *The Hill*, May 27, 2010. Available at: http://thehill.com/homenews/house/100369-gop-moves-to-repeal-healthcare-law (accessed September 20, 2010).

Jacobs, Lawrence R., and Desmond S. King. 2010. "Varieties of Obamaism: Structure, Agency and the Obama Presidency." *Perspectives on Politics* 8(3): 793–802.

Jacobs, Lawrence R., and Benjamin I. Page. 2005. "Who Influences U.S. Foreign Policy?" *American Political Science Review* 99(February): 10–24.

Jacobs, Lawrence R., and Theda Skocpol, eds. 2005. *Inequality and American Democracy: What We Know and What We Need to Learn.* New York: Russell Sage Foundation.

———. 2010. *Health Reform and American Politics: What Everyone Needs to Know.* New York: Oxford University Press.

Judis, John B. 2010a. "The Unnecessary Fall: A Counter-History of the Obama Presidency." *The New Republic*, August 12, 2010. Available at: http://www.tnr.com/article/politics/magazine/76972/obama-failure-polls-populism-recession-health-care (accessed September 20, 2010).

———. 2010b. "Defending 'The Unnecessary Fall of Barack Obama.'" *The New Republic*, August 25, 2010. Available at: http://www.tnr.com/article/politics/77204/unnecessary-fall-barack-obama-response (accessed September 20, 2010).

Klein, Ezra. 2009. "The Rise of the Filibuster: An Interview with Barbara Sinclair." *Washington Post*, September 26, 2009.

———. 2010. "If Only Obama Had. . . ." *Washington Post*, August 25, 2010. Available at: http://voices.washingtonpost.com/ezra-klein/2010/08/if_only_obama_had.html (accessed September 20, 2010).

Krauthammer, Charles. 2010. "Obama's Next Act." *Washington Post*, July 16, 2010, p. A19.

Krugman, Paul. 2008. "Franklin Delano Obama?" *New York Times*, November 10, 2008, p. A29.

———. 2010a. "The Pundit Delusion." *New York Times*, July 19, 2010.

———. 2010b. "This Is Not a Recovery." *New York Times*, August 26, 2010.

Kuttner, Robert. 2009. "Obama's Economic Opportunity." *The American Prospect* 20(1): 1–4.

———. 2010. *A Presidency in Peril: The Inside Story of Obama's Promise, Wall Street's Power, and the Struggle to Control Our Economic Future.* New York: Chelsea Green Publishing.

Lizza, Ryan. 2009. "Money Talks." *The New Yorker*, May 4, 2009.

McCarty, Nolan. 2007. "The Policy Effects of Political Polarization." In *The Transformation of American Politics: Activist Government and the Rise of Conservatism*, edited by Paul Pierson and Theda Skocpol. Princeton, N.J.: Princeton University Press.

McCarty, Nolan, Keith T. Poole, and Howard Rosenthal. 2008. *Polarized Politics: The Dance of Ideology and Unequal Riches.* Cambridge, Mass.: MIT Press.

Mettler, Suzanne. 2007. "The Transformed Welfare State and the Redistribution of Political Voice." In *The Transformation of American Politics: Activist Government and the Rise of Conservatism*, edited by Paul Pierson and Theda Skocpol. Princeton, N.J.: Princeton University Press.

Montgomery, Lori, and Neil Irwin. 2010. "As Midterms Loom, Democrats Work to Shore Up Faltering Recovery." *Washington Post*, August 25, 2010, p. A15.

Obama, Barack. 2008. "Transcript: Barack Obama's Acceptance Speech." *New York Times*, August 28, 2008. Available at: http://www.nytimes.com/2008/08/28/us/politics/28text-obama.html (accessed September 20, 2010).

———. 2010. "Remarks by the President at a Town Hall Meeting on the Economy in Racine, Wisconsin, June 30, 2010." Washington: The White House, Office of the Press Secretary. Available at: http://www.whitehouse.gov/the-press-office/remarks-president-a-town-hall-meeting-economy-racine-wisconsin (accessed September 20, 2010).

Office of Management and Budget. 2009. *A New Era of Responsibility: Renewing America's Promise.* Washington: The White House. Available at: http://www.gpoaccess.gov/usbudget/fy10/pdf/fy10-newera.pdf (accessed January 30, 2011).

Page, Benjamin I., and Lawrence R. Jacobs. 2009. *Class War? What Americans Really Think about Economic Inequality.* Chicago: University of Chicago Press.

Patterson, James T. 1967. *Congressional Conservatism and the New Deal: The Growth of the Conservative Coalition in Congress, 1933–1939.* Lexington: University of Kentucky Press.

Pierson, Paul. 2007. "The Rise and Reconfiguration of Activist Government." In *The Transformation of American Politics: Activist Government and the Rise of Conservatism*, edited by Paul Pierson and Theda Skocpol. Princeton, N.J.: Princeton University Press.

Pierson, Paul, and Theda Skocpol. 2002. "Historical Institutionalism in Contemporary Political Science." In *Political Science: State of the Discipline*, edited by Ira Katznelson and Helen V. Milner. New York: W. W. Norton.

Prior, Markus. 2007. *Post-Broadcast Democracy: How Media Choice Increases Inequality in Political Involvement and Polarizes Elections*. Cambridge and New York: Cambridge University Press.

Rajan, Raghuram G. 2010. "Let Them Eat Credit: How Inequality Is at the Root of the Great Recession." *The New Republic*, August 27, 2010.

Reich, Robert B. 2010. *After Shock: The Next Economy and America's Future*. New York: Alfred A. Knopf.

Republican Party. 2010. "A Pledge to America: The Republican Agenda." *GOP.gov*, August 23, 2010. Available at: http://pledge.gop.gov (accessed Feburary 2, 2011).

Runyan, Rob. 2008. "Vote Might Widen Divide between Children, Parents." *USA Today*, November 1, 2008. Available at: http://www.usatoday.com/news/politics/2008–11–01–1879376114_x.htm (accessed September 20, 2010).

Shapiro, Robert, and Lawrence R. Jacobs. 2011. *The Oxford Handbook of American Public Opinion and the Media*. Oxford: Oxford University Press.

Silver, Nate. 2010. "Obama's No F.D.R.—Nor Does He Have F.D.R.'s Majority." *Five Thirty Eight*, March 1, 2010. Available at: http://www.fivethirtyeight.com/2010/03/obamas-no-fdr-nor-does-he-have-fdrs.html (accessed September 20, 2010).

Silverleib, Alan. 2010. "Recession Not Over, Public Says." *CNN.com*, September 26, 2010.

Sinclair, Barbara. 2006. *Party Wars: Polarization and the Politics of National Policy Making*. Norman: University of Oklahoma Press.

———. 2009. "The New World of U.S. Senators." In *Congress Reconsidered*, edited by Lawrence Dodd and Bruce Oppenheimer. Washington, D.C.: Congressional Quarterly Press.

Skocpol, Theda. 2010. "The Political Challenges That May Undermine Health Reform." *Health Affairs* 29(7): 1288–92.

Skowronek, Stephen. 1993. *The Politics Presidents Make: Leadership from John Adams to Bill Clinton*. Cambridge, Mass.: Belknap Press of Harvard University Press.

Smith, Mark A. 2007a. "Economic Insecurity, Party Reputations, and the Republican Ascendance." In *The Transformation of American Politics: Activist Government and the Rise of Conservatism*, edited by Paul Pierson and Theda Skocpol. Princeton, N.J.: Princeton University Press.

———. 2007b. *The Right Talk: How Conservatives Transformed the Great Society into the Economic Society*. Princeton, N.J.: Princeton University Press.

Soss, Joe, Jacob S. Hacker, and Suzanne Mettler, eds. 2007. *Remaking America: Democracy and Public Policy in an Age of Inequality*. New York: Russell Sage Foundation.

Story, Louise. 2010. "Income Inequality and Financial Crises." *New York Times*, August 22, 2010, p. WK5.

Taber, Charles S., and Milton Lodge. 2006. "Motivated Skepticism in the Evaluation of Political Beliefs." *American Journal of Political Science* 50(3): 755–69.

Todd, Chuck, and Sheldon Gawiser. 2009. *How Barack Obama Won: A State-by-State Guide to the Historic 2008 Presidential Election.* New York: Vintage.

Williamson, Vanessa, and Theda Skocpol. 2010. "The Tea Party and the Rebirth of Republican Conservatism." Unpublished article, Harvard University, August 2010.

Wolffe, Richard. 2009. *Renegade: The Making of a President.* New York: Crown Publishers.

PART I | Legislative Landmarks

Chapter 2 | Hard-Fought Legacy: Obama, Congressional Democrats, and the Struggle for Comprehensive Health Care Reform

Lawrence R. Jacobs and
Theda Skocpol

"I will judge my first term as president based on . . . whether we have delivered the kind of health care that every American deserves and that our system can afford."

THE WORDS WERE those of Barack Obama, junior senator from Illinois, delivered at a Las Vegas issues forum early in the prolonged Democratic Party primary process of the 2008 presidential election (Obama 2007, 18). The forum was cosponsored by the Service Employees International Union, a key blue-collar organization, and the Center for American Progress, a Washington think tank preparing plans for the next Democratic president—underlining that health care reform is a long-running Democratic priority for elites and grass roots alike.

Starting with Harry Truman's crusade for "compulsory" universal health insurance at the end of World War II, Democratic presidents and Congresses repeatedly championed the cause. Bill Clinton, the last Democrat to hold the presidency in the twentieth century, started his term of office with an ultimately abortive push for comprehensive health care reform (Skocpol 1996). In the wake of the Clinton failure, calls for reform did not go away, because mounting millions of Americans lost health coverage even as costs to families and businesses continued to rise. By 2007, with the U.S. citizenry disillusioned about Republican governance, the Democrats assembled in Las Vegas knew their party had an excellent shot to win both the presidency and additional congressional seats in 2008. If that happened, another crack at comprehensive health care reform was sure to be at the top of the to-do list if core Democratic constituencies had anything to say about it.

Ironically, observers agree that candidate Obama performed poorly at the 2007 Las Vegas forum. He was "vague and platitudinous," outclassed by Hillary Rodham Clinton and John Edwards, rival candidates who issued detailed health care reform plans months before Obama issued his proposal (Heilemann and Halperin 2010, 207; Obama 2008). Indeed, throughout the primaries and the 2008 presidential campaign, candidate Obama remained cautious and evasive on reform specifics. He never promised to extend insurance coverage to all adults as well as children; he remained fuzzy on whether Americans should be required to obtain coverage if government help could make it affordable; and he assiduously avoided advocating specific cost-control measures that might irritate unions, health care providers, and employers.

But flash-forward three years. On March 23, 2010, we witness President Obama surrounded by cheering supporters in the East Room of the White House as he signs into law the remarkably comprehensive Patient Protection and Affordable Health Care Act. This law, modified and supplemented by the Health Care and Education Reconciliation Act signed on March 30, amounts to a landmark in modern U.S. social legislation, comparable to Social Security, Medicare, and the Civil Rights Act.

Affordable Care, as we call the set of health care reform laws, includes many provisions that candidate Obama had originally fudged—and, overall, it promises the comprehensive marriage of near-universal health coverage with improved cost controls that was long sought, without success, by so many of Obama's presidential predecessors.

Affordable Care mandates major expansions in Medicaid for lower-income families, and couples this mode of expanding coverage with federally guaranteed subsidies to enable lower-middle-income people to buy private health insurance plans on regulated state-level exchanges (for a full overview of the law's provisions, including who benefits and who pays, see Jacobs and Skocpol 2010, chap. 4; Kaiser Family Foundation 2010a). Overall, the law promises to expand health insurance coverage to nearly all U.S. citizens and legal residents, an additional 32 million people by 2014. In addition, Affordable Care includes an array of measures designed to reduce the future rate of cost increases in Medicare and promote more cost-effective practices by physicians, hospitals, private insurance companies, and businesses in the health care sector. According to the Congressional Budget Office, Affordable Care will not only greatly expand insurance coverage, it will slightly reduce the overall federal budget deficit over the next ten years and bring major deficit reduction in the second decade (2010).

The enactment of such a bold health care reform just fifteen months after Barack Obama took office as the forty-fourth president of the United States was doubly remarkable. For many months before any presidential signing ceremony, bills had to wend their way through a formidable obstacle course of partisan attacks, interest group pressures, tenuous legislative coalition-building, and efforts at delay and obstruction enabled by the creative invocation of established congressional rules, customs, and budget procedures. As other chapters in this book explain, many other parts of Obama's ambitious reform agenda fell victim to these obstacles over the course of 2009 and 2010. But Affordable Care ultimately squeaked through—with bare margins of Democratic votes and every single Republican finally voting no in both the House and the Senate.

In addition to its near-miss, Perils-of-Pauline genesis, the Affordable Care Act stands out for its extraordinary economic scope and bold ambition to make America a more equal society. The law calls for revisions of business and governmental practices in one-sixth of the national economy: the insurance market will be remade as health care providers and manufacturers of pharmaceutical drugs and medical devices adjust to new rules and serve many additional patients. Additionally, it offers new consumer protections for Americans who currently have health insurance and makes coverage newly affordable for those who remain uninsured. Remarkably, Affordable Care asks the well-heeled to pay much of the bill for these benefits. As the *New York Times* columnist David Leonhardt noted, this landmark law amounts to "the federal government's biggest attack on economic inequality since inequality began rising more than three decades ago," because it taxes the wealthy and trims tax breaks and business subsidies in the current health economy to pay for new benefits that "flow mostly to households making less than four times the poverty level—$88,200 for a family of four people" (2010).

President Obama not only ended up championing a tougher and more comprehensive health care reform measure than he had suggested in the primaries and general election that brought him to office, he also spent most of his early political capital on the health care reform cause. His campaign for health care reform during the first year and a third of his presidency ignited fierce struggles among legislators, interest groups, and ideological movements that dominated press coverage, and sparked considerable public disillusionment with the political system and worries about the new law. At a time of financial crisis and deep recession, not to mention festering problems in immigration and the environment, the prolonged battle for comprehensive health care reform became one of only a few presidentially encouraged efforts to reach a legislative breakthrough. The Affordable Care Act may well turn out to be the Obama accomplishment with the most wide-ranging consequences for all Americans. Whether he serves one term or two in office, history may end up judging Obama just as he suggested in that brave throwaway line at the March 2007 Las Vegas forum. Early twenty-first century congressional Democrats may likewise be measured by it, underlining the arduous leadership required from House Speaker Nancy Pelosi and Senate Majority Leader Harry Reid.

Historic legacy it may turn out to be, but hard fights over Affordable Care are not over. Legal challenges are wending their way up the hierarchy of federal courts, and core provisions (namely, the mandate for all Americans to purchase insurance once it becomes affordable) could in the end be invalidated by the Supreme Court, even as other seminal changes (from Medicaid expansion to cost controls) are implemented. Beyond the dramas in the courts, complex provisions have to be carried into full effect over the next four years in an ideologically divided polity where conservative Republican opponents and privileged interests have growing clout, especially in the wake of the major victories scored by the GOP in the November 2010 election. Led by Speaker John Boehner, the 112th House has a strong GOP majority gunning to undo the Affordable Care Act. Funding cutbacks, symbolic oppositional votes, and endless investigatory hearings will harry Obama administration officials charged with implementing health care reform during 2011 and 2012. More likely than not, Affordable Care will survive, though with what specific modifications or eviscerations remains to be seen (Skocpol 2010).

The rest of this chapter probes how it came to be that the early Obama administration and Democrats in the 111th Congress gave priority to the drive for bold health care reform and managed to enact legislative breakthroughs in 2010. What do the choices made and the shape of the battles tell us about the narrow window for major, economically redistributive reforms in contemporary U.S. politics? And what may happen now that a new legislative framework is in place? Legislative breakthroughs do not bring politics to an end; they reset the stakes and redirect struggles. Especially when major transfers of wealth and income across strata, age groups, regions, and industries are at issue, the ongoing battles over implementation can be just as fierce and consequential as the initial fights over enabling legislation. How it all shakes out over the next several critical years will profoundly influence the delivery and social distribution of health care in the United States for generations to come.

THE REFORM CHALLENGE

Before 2010, powerful interests had blocked comprehensive health care reform in the United States for almost one hundred years. The first attempts to champion health insurance for working families occurred in the 1910s, when campaigns by the American Association for Labor Legislation and the progressives involved in Teddy Roosevelt's Bull Moose campaign were decried as German-style autocracy and blocked by the American Medical Association (AMA) and insurance companies (Numbers 1978). The next opportunity came in the 1930s, when President Franklin Delano Roosevelt's advisors recommended including health insurance in the Social Security legislation, but he decided to exclude it for fear that the entire legislation would be defeated by AMA opposition (Hirshfield 1970). Immediately after World War II, President Truman's effort to pass "compulsory health insurance" was derided as socialism and blocked in Congress (Poen 1979). The next critical junctures came in 1965, when reformers decided to take what they thought would be a step toward universal health insurance by supporting the enactment of coverage for the elderly through Medicare and for the very poor through Medicaid (Jacobs 1993; Marmor 1973). Yet Medicare, once in place, did not lead to insurance for everyone, because the previously unified senior voting bloc was divided and momentum for broader reforms stalled (Jacobs 2007). In the 1970s, under Republican President Richard Nixon and Democratic President Jimmy Carter, congressional Democrats refused to accept public-private versions of health insurance reform, creating deadlock by holding out for more liberal approaches (Starr 1982, bk. 2, chap. 4). Last was the failed attempt launched in 1993 under Bill and Hillary Clinton, which led to a Republican takeover of the Congress in the fall of 1994 (Skocpol 1996).

After a century of failed efforts to achieve universal health coverage, with partial public programs established instead, the United States was left by the early twenty-first century with a system that is bizarre by international standards. Between the late 1800s and the end of World War II, most other advanced, industrial nations created systems of universal health insurance coverage. In America, a patchwork of policies left tens of millions of citizens and residents uninsured as of 2010—most of them working-age men and women and their children who work for low or modest wages, often in smaller business enterprises (Garrett 2004). Most working-age people, especially those in big business or government jobs, get their health insurance through their employers, and federal and state-level programs provide coverage for the elderly, for military veterans, for discrete categories of medically needy, and for some of the poor and near-poor. This piecemeal system has not only left big gaps, it has been extra-ordinarily costly and inefficient, because a lot of bureaucracy is involved and opportunities are numerous for making profits or saving money by avoiding very sick people or charging extra to categories of businesses or patients with poor options.

As Washington began to debate health care reform, the United States spent about twice as much per person as other industrial countries do on average, and more than 50 percent more than the next-biggest spender, France (Pearson 2009). U.S. businesses that contribute to health insurance for their employees face escalating costs and find themselves at a disad-vantage compared with foreign competitors and other U.S. companies that choose not to provide it (Nichols and Axeen 2008). U.S. workers, in turn, find that money for increased wages has been siphoned into paying for premiums, and workers are often locked into jobs or careers not opti-mal for their talents because they fear losing access to health coverage (Leonhardt 2009).

The complex system that prompted repeated efforts at health care re-form has also disguised high risks. For doctors, getting paid requires fill-ing out thousands of forms, without the certainty that an insurer will agree to pay. Hospitals have to cope with an unpredictable influx of unin-sured people who appear in their emergency rooms (Unland 2004). And many Americans, even those who are insured, face the risk that an illness can wipe out the family savings. In fact, catastrophic health care costs have recently been the leading cause of bankruptcy in the United States (Himmelstein et al. 2009).

Many advocates of health care reform prefer to tackle the broken sys-tem head on by uprooting it in favor of a single-payer system like Cana-da's, where the government handles all payments for health services de-livered by private doctors and hospitals. The Canadian system eliminates a lot of administrative overhead and puts provincial governments in a position to bargain for good prices for physician and hospital services and for pharmaceuticals and medical devices. This system is also conceptually straightforward: hundreds of private insurance companies are out of the picture and public agencies pay for everyone's medical care.

But most U.S. politicians in public office or running for the presidency and Congress, including the preponderance of Democrats, have been committed to modifying the current mixed system rather than replacing it root and branch. Some Democratic elected officials understand that a Canadian-style system might be more efficient and less confusing in prin-ciple, but they fear counterpressures from interests with a powerful stake in the U.S. system. Insurance companies, pharmaceutical manufacturers, medical specialists, and hospital systems have all found aspects of the inherited health system profitable; and Medicare beneficiaries and unions have been intent on retaining the health coverage they struggled to obtain over many years (Gottschalk 2007; Oberlander 2003). If provoked by the threat of sudden, root-and-branch change, such stakeholders could use their huge advantages in organization and money to defeat reformers—especially because the U.S. constituents who stand to benefit most from comprehensive health care reform tend to be less well organized and not likely to vote at high rates. Finally, large numbers of jobs are also at stake—because, after all, insurance companies employ many white-collar workers, as do the benefits departments of private companies that purchase insurance for their employees. Pushing for wholesale disruptions in such arrangements would have provoked an impenetrable firestorm of opposition, politicians concluded.

Calculations of political feasibility thus created a disjuncture between well-documented systemic breakdown and reforms entertained by elected Democrats determined to modify rather than wholly replace the broken system. Since the 1960s, reformers in elected office have started with the premise that the existing set of stakeholders will survive. Their challenge is thus to use a mixture of new regulations and additional public subsidies to fill in the gaps of existing arrangements (Jacobs 1993, 2007; Oberlander 2003). Pragmatic reformers have aimed to devise incremental though significant measures to make health insurance affordable for all businesses and families and the most vulnerable, while prodding current providers and suppliers to operate more efficiently and lower costs.

But approaching reform as an exercise in stretching and reworking the existing health care system has not been a recipe for pain-free consensus, either. In addition to the glaring partisan differences discussed, even reforms that take off from what is already in place have run into fierce opposition from America's wealthiest individuals and families, people who remain ever-vigilant about being asked to help pay for benefits for other citizens. This has been true, and remains true, even though the wealthy and super-wealthy in the United States have in recent decades seen their incomes rise far faster than all other Americans, and have repeatedly benefited from federal tax cuts and write-offs (Bartels 2008, 162–222; Hacker and Pierson 2010). The super-rich have been winners over the past several decades, but are still demanding to retain and improve their economic advantages. During the 2009 and 2010 health care reform battles, President Obama and many congressional Democrats advocated provisions that ask a bit more in taxes from the very wealthy (Calmes and Pear 2009); some proposals were incorporated into legislation, but many also fell by the wayside in the face of fierce resistance from privileged groups.

Beyond stepping on powerful toes, an approach to health care reform that requires squeezing resources and waste out of the current system, not to mention taxing the privileged to help the less privileged, entails complex legislation hard for politicians to devise, challenging to implement, and nearly impossible for the general public to understand. Reform proposals run to thousands of pages and are easily demonized by opponents who can run costly media campaigns aimed at stoking anxiety or anger among people who currently have health insurance, or encouraging blowback from businesses and employees whose livelihoods are intertwined with current arrangements. Intricate new regulations must also be devised by experts, and their long-term effectiveness will depend on the skill and persistence of public administrators.

In sum, even the apparently moderate approach to comprehensive reform—the fill-in-the-gaps approach favored by reformers skeptical of the political feasibility of single-payer or other root-in-branch approaches—has daunting requirements. Fill-in-the-gaps demands policy expertise, determined political leadership, painstakingly brokered compromises, and persistent administrative follow-through. Not many analysts of early twenty-first century U.S. politics would say that any of these are strong suits for today's federal government. Yet when it came to pushing forward with comprehensive health care reform in Obama's fledgling presidency, the stars finally aligned unusually well.

A NEW PRESIDENT WHO DECIDED TO GO BIG

Perhaps the most critical decision in the entire health care reform saga was the least heralded: the White House decision in February and March 2009 to use much of Obama's early political capital on the pursuit of truly comprehensive reform, marrying vastly expanded access to insurance with the imposition of new cost controls. This was by no means an obvious decision and it was made behind closed doors (Alter 2010, chap. 15).

True, even though candidate Obama had been somewhat vague and always cautious about policy specifics during 2007 and 2008, he did emphasize the need for comprehensive health care reform as he campaigned for election (for a full timeline of health care reform events, see appendix table 2A.1). The prolonged competition with Hillary Clinton for the Democratic nomination honed Obama's understanding of the issues, and taught him that Democratic Party constituencies, working people and women above all, cared intensely about health care reform (Blendon et al. 2008). What is more, promises to pursue universal health coverage helped Obama differentiate himself from McCain in the general election, because McCain essentially renewed long-standing Republican calls for less public regulation and more tax subsidies, ideas that few experts believed would greatly expand coverage or control rapidly rising health care costs. But, electioneering aside, there were powerful reasons why Obama, once in office, might have delayed or watered down his campaign pledge to pursue comprehensive health care reform. Washington insiders do not really expect newly installed presidents to keep campaign promises; they expect them to reassess and become more "realistic" about what established interests and arrangements allow. In this instance a massive financial crisis and deepening economic recession provided plenty of excuse to back off from bold reforms of all kinds.

The Obama administration and congressional leaders hit the ground running with a vigorous response to the contracting economy, proposing right after the inauguration a bill that became the American Recovery and Reinvestment Act (the so-called stimulus) featuring $787 billion in spending and tax cuts to spur the economy and make down payments on policy shifts in numerous key areas, including expansions in health insurance coverage for children and the unemployed. But there were also early signs of gathering political troubles. Not a single House Republican voted in favor of the stimulus, and in the Senate only three Republicans (Susan Collins and Olympia Snowe of Maine and Arlen Specter of Pennsylvania) could be attracted to let a watered-down version of the legislation eke through their chamber.

Frightened by the extent of their losses in 2006 and 2008, and dealing with a shrunken popular base that intensely disliked Obama, Republican leaders decided to gamble on total opposition. If they supported Obama initiatives that ended up working, would Republicans get any credit? But if they opposed recovery legislation and any subsequent big initiatives such as health care reform, maybe they could both please their core conservative base and position themselves to be the only alternative if voters remained unhappy in a sluggish economy during the 2010 and 2012 elections. The Republican turn to obstruction could not make much difference in the House of Representatives, where the majority controls the agenda and decides; in the Senate, however, energetic use could be made of the filibuster and other delaying tactics, which in principle allow any forty-one senators to stall legislation.

Over the course of 2009, Republicans would go on to use the filibuster to block even routine nominations and legislative steps as well as major reforms, deploying this blocking maneuver dozens of times, more often in a single year than it was used during all of the 1950s and 1960s (Frumin and Reif 2010). They hoped that splits among Democrats, or chance events such as the death or incapacitation of a Democratic lawmaker, would trip up the drive to pass health care reform. In addition to positioning themselves to slow or block legislation, Republicans and their allies relied on what had become standard procedure in Washington—investing tens of millions into polling to craft deceptive talking points and ads that misled Americans, leaving them with little accurate information about legislative maneuvers in Washington and suspicious about the consequences for themselves and their families (for analysis of how this process works, see Hacker and Pierson 2005; Jacobs and Shapiro 2000). Republican leaders hoped that turning Americans sour about reforms would enhance the gains expected for an out-party in the midterm 2010 election, and maybe even lead to a presidential win in 2012.

Just weeks into Obama's presidency, not only was partisan obstruction taking hold in Washington, the national economy was also spiraling downward and health care reform was far from the public's top priority. Indeed, health care had not been the leading worry when Americans were asked to rank their priorities as of election day back in November 2008. To be sure, 66 percent of Americans told exit pollsters that they were worried about being able to afford health care, and three in five of these worriers supported Obama over McCain. But when asked to name the most important issue that the country needed to address, led by the new president, only 9 percent of voters said health care (about the same for Iraq or terrorism), whereas 63 percent named the economy. This was hardly surprising given that, long before the job market bottomed out in early 2009, 93 percent of voting Americans labeled the state of the economy as poor or not good, and 85 percent said they were worried about it. This overwhelming majority concerned about the economy was substantially higher than the 66 percent who said they were worried about health care (Todd and Gawiser 2009, 43–44).

Debate raged inside the White House about how to use precious months of the president's first year (Alter 2010, 244–46). Should they prioritize what would surely be a tough fight for comprehensive health care reform in a deteriorating economy? Heavy hitters, including Vice President Joe Biden, the top political advisor David Axelrod, Chief of Staff Rahm Emanuel, and Treasury Secretary Timothy Geithner, argued that the administration should concentrate on correcting the country's worst economic crisis since the 1930s and reforming the financial industry to prevent future bankruptcies and financial trickery (Baker 2010, 36). These heavyweights worried that Obama's presidency could be at risk if they failed to get priorities right. Emanuel, in particular, feared a repeat of Clinton's failed effort.

But the advice of senior White House officials to delay health care reform was countered by strong pressure from campaign supporters and leading congressional Democrats already invested in moving forward. After the November election, Senator Ted Kennedy and the powerful chair of the Senate Finance Committee, Max Baucus, met with Obama to insist that health care reform be his top domestic priority after stabilizing the financial and economic systems. Baucus also wrote Obama and publicly released a white paper on health care reform to up the ante. Kennedy's losing battle with brain cancer, his lifelong campaign for health care reform, and his decisive endorsement of Obama during the Democratic primaries made his appeal to move ahead "incredibly emotionally freighted," in the words of a Kennedy aide (confidential interview, January 2010), instilling in Obama a sense that he "needed to do this for Kennedy."

Warnings about overloading Congress did not impress Obama, who believed that separate committees could work simultaneously on an ambitious agenda, with the possibility of legislative successes building on one another. Obama envisaged 2009 as an extraordinary moment, and he saw health care reform as critical to economic recovery and fiscal responsibility (Alter 2010, 248). The economic crisis might make people more wary of change, but it also underlined the need to help citizens and businesses obtain or hold on to vital health coverage. And though Republicans and some congressional Democrats argued that health care reform would explode an already overextended budget and add to the government's debt, Obama's Office of Management and the Budget, led by the influential Peter Orszag, argued that well-designed health legislation was necessary to control medical care costs in the short term and reduce them over time (Lizza 2009). Health care reform that emphasized cost controls along with universal access could free businesses and government budgets from excessive costs, argued Obama's budget gurus, who firmly believed that federal deficits would balloon uncontrollably until there were reforms in health care spending. Marry the fear of future deficits with Obama's realization, honed in the long election campaigns, that his Democratic Party base was expecting bold reforms to cover millions in need of affordable care, and it becomes understandable why Obama decided not to let an unexpected economic crisis divert him from attempting comprehensive rather than piecemeal health care reform.

THE NATURE OF WHITE HOUSE LEADERSHIP

Once Obama chose comprehensive health care reform as a top priority in year one, his White House team forged ahead with a three-part strategy. First, the White House outlined broad principles to define the objectives of health care reform, and left the exact details of how to get there to Congress. Second, the administration tried to blunt the opposition of powerful economic interests by protecting or replacing some of the profits threatened by reform. Finally, the administration focused on the public costs of health care reform, actively promoting specific proposals about how (and how much) to pay for reform, but saying less about exactly how to guarantee broader citizen access to health coverage. Each of these strategies was designed to further congressional legislative progress for comprehensive reform in an environment of entrenched opposition.

Let Congress Legislate and Bargain with Stakeholders

Featuring broad principles was an attempt to avoid the mistakes of "the last war." When President Clinton sought health care reform in 1993, his administration assembled a 500-person presidential commission headed by Hillary Rodham Clinton, and presented a 1,342-page document to Congress in the fall of his first year in the presidency. The plan was so complex that nobody could understand it—except the interests that were going to lose out under the new system, and they mobilized very effectively against it. Not only did the entire reform stall—neither the House nor the Senate voted on legislation—the debacle helped sweep Republicans into Congress in the fall of 1994 and closed the window for another attempt at comprehensive reform for fifteen years. Determined not to repeat the perceived Clinton missteps, Obama decided instead to give speeches outlining broad, popular principles—health care for most Americans, insurance that is more reliable and free from abusive industry practices, cost containment for business, lower prices for families, and improved benefits for the uninsured and the elderly. When it came to specific provisions—such as an individual mandate requiring everyone to purchase insurance; expansions of Medicare; or the so-called public option to set up competition between public and private insurance plans for working-age Americans, Obama at most expressed general support and left the fights to congressional Democrats. The idea was to let congressional committees work out compromises that could actually pass the House and the Senate, to avoid the Clinton error of planning big but getting no concrete legislative results.

The Obama administration did, however, intervene to manage and defuse possible all-out opposition from health-sector stakeholders who in the past had obstructed comprehensive reform. On March 5, 2009, the White House held a forum on health care reform that included representatives from insurance companies, doctors and hospital groups, and the pharmaceutical industry. In their talks with health-sector representatives, the White House had some leverage. Health care reform held risks for industry groups to the extent that it aimed to hold down future increases in medical spending; but it also held new opportunities for profits from millions of new patients and customers. Appealing to their self-interest, the Obama administration persuaded representatives of six major health care industries to sign a May 2009 letter nominally supporting reform of health care and volunteering to accept reduced payments and other cost-cutting measures. After the White House first reached out to stakeholders in the spring of 2009, ongoing discussions were carried on in cooperation with leading congressional Democrats, especially Max Baucus, chair of the Senate Finance Committee (for full details of the bargains with major stakeholders, see Jacobs and Skocpol 2010, chap. 2). Over many months of congressional bill-writing, the White House joined with key leaders on the Hill to hold the line on bargains they made with stakeholders, including a bargain to stay away from certain regulations on the pharmaceutical giants in return for their agreement to institute some price cuts and refrain from opposing reform.

Although pharmaceutical and hospital groups and the AMA continued to lobby actively to increase their profits under the new reforms, these major interests did not engage in the sorts of early, united, and sustained public opposition that derailed the Clinton health care reform. Eventually, the private insurance industry abandoned cooperation and became more publicly critical of certain reform bills, but that happened relatively late in the process. When the insurance companies tried to use an actuarial study to derail reform in October 2009, the White House and its allies pushed back with a fierce, all-out media attack to discredit that move—and did so quite successfully. Criticism was so fierce that Karen Ignagni, chief executive of America's Health Insurance Plans (AHIP), which lobbies for the health insurance industry, was obliged to write an editorial defending the report and reiterating AHIP's commitment to health care reform (2009).

Arguably, the White House and its allies in Congress managed to parry, delay, and divide stakeholder opposition sufficiently to allow reform legislation to squeak through. The deal-making frustrated progressive supporters of health care reform outraged by high drug and insurance prices, but it may have been what it took to win legislation that transfers some resources to nonwealthy Americans in the U.S. polity as it actually functions in the early twenty-first century. The White House approach reflected the hardheaded assessment that health care reform could pass only if an in-built organizational imbalance was neutralized. Normally, well-organized and vigilant stakeholders can defeat threats to their interests, even if most Americans would benefit, because citizens in general cannot match the intensity or the resources of mobilized stakeholders. Presidential rhetoric alone cannot change this equation, so parry and bargain are the tactics of necessity.

The Obama administration also had some success getting cooperation from popularly based interest groups. It worked with AARP to ensure that seniors saw benefits from health care reform, including the closure of the gap in Medicare prescription drug coverage known as the doughnut hole. After a great deal of effort and some breakdowns of cooperation along the way, the administration also convinced labor unions to accept some very limited future excise charges on the most expensive health care plans—a policy Obama himself had opposed during the 2008 campaign. The White House insistence on including some kind of Cadillac tax, as this measure was called, was partly about raising revenue to finance reform, and even more about creating credible cost controls for the long-term future. As we have seen, a central reason for President Obama to push comprehensive health care reform was to reduce the rate of future cost increases—for families, businesses, and the federal budget.

When it came to asking for other kinds of financial concessions to help cover the cost of extending insurance, the Obama administration had failures as well as successes. For instance, early in 2009, Obama proposed to equalize the charitable tax deduction for wealthy and less wealthy people, reducing Treasury losses currently incurred when the wealthy are given more generous deductions. This might seem a logical step to take to squeeze out more resources to help provide health insurance for all Americans. But even though the research shows that most wealthy people would give almost as much to charities with or without a special deduction, that didn't matter (Van de Water 2009). Democratic fat cats mobilized supporters in the nonprofit community to nix that possible source of revenue, working through Representative Charlie Rangel, then the chair of the powerful House Ways and Means Committee (Dorning 2009). Along with union resistance to taxes on expensive insurance plans, the revolt of nonprofits was a clear-cut instance of supposedly liberal groups ostensibly committed to the public interest fighting to retain privileges, even if that meant less money to help cover large numbers of currently uninsured lower- and middle-income people. The dilemma of reforming an already established system riddled with special deals and privileges does not just pit liberals against conservatives, or labor against business, but liberals against liberals. Overall, it is a matter of the vigilant and well-organized against the atomized and inattentive.

Follow the Money

So far, we have summarized two strategies used by the Obama administration to guide health care reform: setting forth broad public principles, and working persistently on compromises to defuse determined opposition. A third strategy is also worth highlighting: the Obama administration intervened most consistently and specifically about how to pay for reform. The White House had to make adjustments as congressional committees accepted or rejected various possibilities such as the reduction in charitable tax deductions, but the president's agents closely tracked the total price tag and the sources of savings or revenues to pay the costs. Analysis of the failed Clinton reform effort led White House strategists to emphasize the importance of the Congressional Budget Office (CBO), the nonpartisan federal agency tasked with calculating the budget impact of legislative proposals. A bad (that is to say, high-cost) CBO "score" can be a death knell for bills in Congress, especially when majorities must be assembled that attract fiscal conservatives to accept new social-welfare initiatives. Obama's director of Management and Budget, Peter Orszag, had previously worked in the CBO, and he tried to guide emerging reform proposals so the numbers would add up—and gain credibility as long-term deficit-reducers—when CBO scored congressional bills.

Obama was quite specific in his recommendations for how to fund reform. The first Obama budget, released at the end of February 2009, included more than $600 million both in new taxes and in cost-cutting measures, intended as a down payment on health care reform. In June, Obama sent a letter to Senate committee chairmen Max Baucus and Edward Kennedy, in which he spoke only in general terms about what benefits should be included in health care reform, but explicitly outlined the budget cuts and tax increases he would recommend to pay for the bill. For instance, when it came to whether to include an individual mandate requiring people to have health insurance, Obama told the senators he was open to their ideas. But regarding cuts to Medicare spending, Obama specifically reiterated his budget recommendations and called for "another $200 to $300 billion" in cuts on top of his earlier recommendations (2009).

Obama's handling of finance underscores a significant fiscal strategy—cutting spending on narrowly cast programs in order to shift them toward new programs geared to benefit broader publics. The commitment of Affordable Care to reduce Medicare spending, and subsidies to banks to process student loans and other steps, defies a common mindset in Washington that equates program cutting with spending reductions. Health care reform, by contrast, combined program expansion with targeted budget cuts. Democrats reduced projected spending on existing programs in order to control future budget deficits and pay for new benefits (Adamy 2010a; Horney and Van de Water 2009).

Focusing on the financing of health care reform interacted with other prongs of White House strategy. Cost-cutting provisions that were negotiated with key stakeholders muted their opposition but also helped identify up front which interests were going to have to give ground in order to make health care reform affordable. Obama's advocacy on the funding sources also provided Democrats in Congress with support in the face of heavy industry lobbying, and cleared the way for negotiations. Perhaps more important, setting a benchmark in terms of savings cleared some room for new expenditures, and therefore expanded the scope of possible help for the uninsured.

THE YEAR OF PITCHED BATTLES AND TORTUOUS NEGOTIATIONS

The advantages of White House approaches to health care reform—set forth broad principles and work continuously behind the scenes to defuse potential veto players and keep a firm grip on costs—became apparent once the House and Senate finally cleared bills and the Congress as a whole signed off on the final Affordable Care legislation. During all of 2009, however, as congressional committees made their legislative "sausage"—amidst intense media scrutiny, fierce stakeholder lobbying, and the push and pull of social movements on the right and left—the president's approach sometimes looked overly passive.

To be sure, when congressional efforts appeared to stall in the late summer of 2009, the president eloquently used his bully pulpit to get reform moving again by giving a major speech to Congress on September 9. But again and again over the many months of debates in and around Congress, media pundits and progressives condemned the White House for a "failure of leadership," for not laying out bold plans and setting deadlines and bottom lines for the specific content of health care reform legislation he would sign. When the two authors of this chapter did interviews with key players in Washington, D.C., in late 2009 and very early 2010, we found disappointment all around that the president had not intervened earlier and more specifically and forcefully. Interestingly, each actor wished the president had intervened to take their side in disputes over policy provisions—such as whether, or not, to include a robust public option, a government-run insurance plan that would be available to working-age Americans along with private insurance options. Each set of actors in this and other struggles thought the president was, or should be, on their side, and should tell the other side to back off! Obama's White House could not have satisfied them all, so it left the contending players to work things out among themselves.

Two disadvantages to the president's approach were unavoidable. First, the White House lost control over the pace and timing of developments. The president called upon the House and Senate to pass bills before the August 2009 summer recess, but neither chamber assembled a completed bill prior to the recess—during which Tea Party protests raged even as business interests ran ads demonizing health care reform. The president looked as if he was losing control of a major priority—and the process was certain to stretch into the winter, if it could be moved forward at all in the face of growing public worries stoked by nonstop attack ads.

Second, Obama's insistence on articulating broad principles and letting House and Senate committees haggle over critical provisions left supporters of health care reform in the dark about where things might head on key issues—like the public option, the generosity of subsidies for the uninsured, and whether new insurance exchanges to enforce rules and structure choices among private plans would be organized nationally or at the level of states and regions. Since many supporters of health care reform in and around the progressive wing of the Democratic Party considered such matters to be central to meaningful change, the president's refusal to weigh in meant that it was hard to mobilize grassroots enthusiasm (Dreier 2010). What, exactly, did the president favor? What would people be supporting? This situation was made worse when certain White House officials tried to get unions and progressive activists to stop pressuring centrist and conservative congressional Democrats to support what liberals considered to be optimal reform provisions (Martin 2009). White House aides were worried about getting *any* bills out of Congress, even as progressive activists stewed about what they considered wimpy provisions that threatened to be continually watered down. In particular, progressive groups and unions became angry when the White House signaled that it might acquiesce to congressional bills that omitted any version of the public option (Stolberg 2009).

As grassroots supporters of health care reform found themselves operating on murky terrain, local networks of conservatives were mobilizing with more intensity than progressives to stop any congressional legislative action at all. "Just say NO!" was the outcry from Tea Party protesters—essentially relabeled and reenergized conservative Republicans (Williamson and Skocpol 2010)—who staged colorful, even outrageous protests that started in the spring of 2009 and reached a crescendo during congressional Town Hall meetings in August. Tea Partiers were a minority but they got a lot of media attention as they lampooned representatives and senators returning to their districts after failing to finalize bills before the August 2009 recess. Compared to the many unions and progressive groups working through well-established alliances, the right-wing protesters were older white men and women who wore funny costumes and held up outrageous signs. The media treated them as something new and visually interesting, and Tea Party protests, along with incessant attack ads funded by the Chamber of Commerce and other antireform interest groups, fanned fears about allegedly looming "cuts in Medicare" and nonexistent "death panels" (AARP 2009). Actual reform bills did not really cut Medicare benefits for older Americans; they aimed to trim business subsidies in the Medicare Advantage programs while substantially expanding benefits to all who depended on Medicare. But this distinction was lost in the media translation.

When Congress returned from the summer recess, President Obama managed to refocus Democrats on the need to move ahead. Three committees had already cleared bills in the House, and the Health, Education, and Labor Committee had acted in the Senate. But before the House and Senate leaders could devise full compromises and pass bills out of each chamber, a roadblock remained that had been there for many weeks before the summer recess: the crucial Senate Finance Committee, chaired by Senator Max Baucus of Montana, was still trying to work out a bipartisan compromise bill that would use a relatively conservative version of comprehensive reform to get votes from a few Republicans. Moderate Democrats in the Senate and House favored this approach both to temper reform and its costs and to provide them with political cover against partisan attack.

Throughout the spring and early summer, the White House had worked with Baucus on deals with critical economic stakeholders, and it had accepted his protracted efforts to win some Republican support. Why? For decades Democrats championed health care reform and Republicans opposed it, so why expect any Republican support—especially given that it was clear starting early in 2009 that congressional Republican leaders were orchestrating a strategy of united obstruction to undercut Obama's presidency? The fact is that the White House and centrist Democrats wanted a modicum of bipartisan support if they could get it, not just because this might lead to more popular and durable reforms, but also because Democratic leaders were not sure they had enough votes to clear the sixty-vote filibuster hurdle in the Senate. Not until summer was Al Franken of Minnesota seated, the sixtieth member of the Democratic Senate Caucus that included two Independents along with fifty-eight rambunctious Democrats who were split between liberals and conservatives. Could the White House and Majority Leader Reid count on Ben Nelson of Nebraska or the mercurial Independent Joe Lieberman of Connecticut? Perhaps Republican Olympia Snowe of Maine would be the key to passing any reform legislation at all.

Although presidential power is widely credited with dictating public policy, the truth is that presidential influence over domestic lawmaking is quite limited. Presidential speeches—such as Obama's nationally televised September address to restart health care reform—can influence the agenda of issues for Washington insiders and all Americans. But constitutional checks and balances prevent any president from having his way with Congress—and this situation was exacerbated in 2009 and 2010 by Republican obstructionist tactics. In practice, Obama and his aides were often little more than frustrated witnesses to congressional maneuvers and delays.

Health care happenings—and non-happenings—in the Senate Finance Committee underline these realities. Chairman Max Baucus sidelined most of his twenty-three-member committee and convened a special caucus, called the Gang of Six, to see whether three hand-picked Democrats—himself along with New Mexico Senator Jeff Bingaman and North Dakota Senator Kent Conrad—could find common ground with three Republicans—Wyoming Senator Mike Enzi, Maine Senator Olympia Snowe, and Baucus's long-time personal friend, and the ranking Republican, Iowa Senator Chuck Grassley. If this Gang of Six had been able to write a bill that all were committed to vote for, that would probably have changed the entire dynamic. The Senate Finance Committee and then, perhaps, the Senate as a whole might have been prodded by Baucus and the president to go along with whatever emerged, setting up a tense endgame of negotiations between a more liberal House bill and a Senate bill significantly tilted toward conservative and business preferences by Republicans. More than half a year was devoted to substantive bipartisan discussions and negotiations by the Gang of Six, closeted from time to time with staff from the White House and the CBO. There were several dozen one-on-one in-depth sessions between Baucus and Grassley as well as thirty-one meetings of the Gang of Six. Senators and staff in these meetings confirm Grassley's later description of them on the Senate floor as driven by the shared conviction that "something has to be done . . . [and that] we worked for a long period of time, thinking we could have something bipartisan" (confidential interviews cited in Jacobs and Skocpol 2010, chap. 2).

As it turned out, though, the Gang of Six process failed after repeated delays—which, in retrospect, the White House would regret. By late summer, Senator Grassley started denouncing "Democrat" health care reform, going so far as to suggest that "death panels" might be in the emerging bills, a ridiculous lie popular with angry right-wing activists even though their ire was aimed at a provision for voluntary end-of-life consultations originally championed by a conservative Republican senator (Rutenberg and Calmes 2009). Only one Republican senator, Olympia Snowe, voted for the Senate Finance bill reported out in October—and she soon backed out of further Senate deal-making and joined all other Republicans in supporting a filibuster to prevent final Senate actions and opposing the Christmas Eve Senate enactment of comprehensive reform.

This was the publicly visible, official dynamic: dying possibilities for any cross-party cooperation on health care reform. Yet in the details of reform provisions hashed out by the Gang of Six as well as in other committees and staff deliberations, the story was more complicated. Hundreds of amendments proposed by House or Senate Republicans received enough bipartisan support to make it into advancing legislation; as we discuss below, some created openings for stakeholders to later lobby for lenient rules during the implementation of new programs. Significant elements of the final legislation that the president ended up signing in 2010 were shaped by GOP amendments and negotiations with Republicans.

Republican refusal to formally and publicly support reforms that included many of their own ideas was rooted in overall party polarization and the GOP leadership's electoral strategy. Republicans negotiating in the Gang of Six or other venues were confronted and pressured by party leaders Mitch McConnell and John Boehner, who were "very concerned about . . . the directions the policy discussions were taking" (Grassley 2009), because any compromises would undermine the Republican Party's unequivocal message and its strategy to make big gains in 2010 and 2012. Tea Party protesters were also pressuring Republicans, and GOPers facing reelection in 2010 were especially in peril if they ignored such pressures. Senate Finance principals Republican Grassley and Democrat Baucus were long-time personal friends and—with perhaps a touch of romantic rosy retrospect—both senators and their staffers recalled good old days when the two of them had worked out deals on potentially controversial legislation that the rest of the Finance Committee and the full Senate endorsed. A repeat hurrah was not possible, though, with today's Congress and larger U.S. polity split into intense partisan and ideological camps. Mere interpersonal agreements just cannot hold or formally ratify policy outcomes any longer, at least on highly charged issues that split the parties.

Although progress was painfully slow, the Obama White House pursued a realistic strategy of facilitating the legislative process—setting out principles, striking deals with stakeholders, providing a lot of behind-the-scenes budget advice, and letting congressional committees do their work. Relatively similar bills were passed in November 2009 by the House, and then, finally, just before Christmas, by the Senate. As appendix tables 2A.2 and 2A.3 spell out, there were differences between the House and Senate bills, and departures from what the White House originally outlined. The House bill was generally more liberal—it included a (limited) public option, more generous benefits, more extensive national administration, and higher taxes on the privileged. But both bills fulfilled the general goals Obama had outlined for a fill-in-the-gaps version of comprehensive reform. As of the end of 2009, it looked as if legislation reconciled between the House and Senate would soon appear on the president's desk to be signed into law. Democrats went home for a brief holiday break exhausted but elated.

HOW REFORM ALMOST DIED, AND THEN BECAME MORE HELPFUL TO ORDINARY AMERICANS

Given the past century of failure, it would hardly have been surprising if Obama's effort to win comprehensive reform had fallen short, even this close to victory. That almost happened. In mid-January 2010, an ill-timed special election was held to fill the Senate seat held for decades by the liberal champion of comprehensive health care reform, Ted Kennedy of Massachusetts, who died in the late summer of 2009. The election occurred just after unseemly deals were struck to get sixty votes to break a filibuster in the Senate, and at a time when Americans were increasingly angry about the deep economic downturn. Facing an inept Democratic opponent, little-known Republican and Tea Party darling Scott Brown promised to oppose costly deals in Washington, D.C., and offered to protect Massachusetts—which already has universal health insurance coverage—from having to pay for benefits for people in other states. Brown won amidst low Democratic turnout, and with considerable support from blue-collar workers—whose union leaders had spent the previous month complaining about health care reform provisions that might trim future insurance benefits for unionized workers (Gerard 2010). Ironically, the union leaders had succeeded in getting most of the irksome provisions watered down or dropped, but the word did not get around before the Massachusetts election. Brown's election made him the forty-first Republican, and with all in his party pledged to filibuster against a final vote on adjusted legislation in the Senate, it looked as if comprehensive health care reform would again fail, this time fizzling at the two-yard line.

For a time, Democrats on Capitol Hill seemed paralyzed despite their still sizable majorities in the House and the Senate, even as Democratic base voters and donors and supporters of health care reform expressed dismay that the president and Congress might stop short. The faint heartbeat of reform was kept alive through the determination of House Speaker Nancy Pelosi to push the president, the Senate, and her frightened House majority to find some way forward (Connolly 2010; Drew 2010). In due course, however, the Brown victory in Massachusetts created a paradoxical result—it spurred Democrats to produce a bolder and more comprehensive health care reform than had been possible when Kennedy was still alive. This happened as congressional Democrats regrouped and built cooperation between House and Senate Democrats, and the White House stared defeat in the face and decided it would prefer to risk pushing hard for completion, whatever complex congressional maneuvering might be required to get around Senate Republican obstruction.

Provoked in part by the fortuitously timed announcement of huge insurance rate hikes—which reminded the public of the need for some new legislation to rein in insurance companies (Berry 2010)—the president took the lead at a nationally televised health care summit convened in late February 2010. This event put the spotlight back on health care reform and publicly revealed lock-step Republican opposition to popular changes, obstruction that had previously been obscured in messy and prolonged 2009 legislative process that most Americans barely understood. For the first time, President Obama advocated a fully fleshed out legislative outline—not coincidentally, including the very provisions that the House and Senate bills already agreed upon. In taking responsibility for finishing health care reform, Obama gave the Democrats in Congress the cover they needed to put together a negotiated agreement between the House and Senate Democrats, using special procedures in place of the usual inter-chamber conference followed by final House and Senate votes that typically wraps up legislation. The usual steps could not happen this time, because Republicans in the Senate would block a final vote on any bill produced by the House-Senate conference.

Under the tactical agreement they reached, the House would vote for the Senate's version of the bill, and then pass a second sidecar bill that included a list of agreed-upon fixes and improvements. The House Democrats received a public promise from well more than fifty Senate Democrats to support the sidecar bill, which they could pass by simple majority (less than the usual sixty votes) by a process known as reconciliation. An established procedure by which fiscal bills that do not increase long-term deficits can avoid filibusters, reconciliation has been used repeatedly by Republicans to pass temporary tax cuts and other policy priorities (Breslow 2010). Democrats in the Senate had written budget rules months before in early 2009 that allowed them, theoretically, to use reconciliation to finish health care reform; but throughout 2009 and into early 2010 many moderates balked at doing so. The rest of the caucus stopped deferring to these reluctant members only after the election of Scott Brown forced the realization that the sole alternative to using reconciliation to compromise with the House would be to abort a year-long effort at major health care reform legislation.

Notice how special this circumstance was: Democratic senators were already on the record for their Christmas Eve 2009 votes for comprehensive health care reform, and they backed into majority voting for final adjustments only when Republican obstruction closed off all possibilities for Senate Democrats to use their chamber's super-majority rules to push House Democrats to accepting what marginal Democrats in the Senate wanted—a less economically redistributive and more business-friendly health care reform. When Senate Democrats finally accepted the need to proceed with a majority rather than sixty, conservative senators like Ben Nelson of Nebraska could be bypassed. But it took very special circumstances to get Senate Democrats to bypass their most marginal players— even though Republicans when holding the majority in the Senate had long shown a willingness to bypass their moderates with reconciliation procedures. The truth is that procedural agility comes easier in the U.S. Senate when it is a question of giving pay-offs to the very rich, than when it is a matter of helping ordinary Americans while even slightly increasing taxes on the rich. The Affordable Care endgame is the exception that proves the rule: in today's U.S. polity, given the choke-point role of the nonmajoritarian Senate, it is virtually impossible to use major legislation to help the majority of Americans when privileged interests are opposed.

Before Brown's win and the Senate leadership's turn toward reconciliation procedures, the indispensability of the votes of Ben Nelson, Joseph Lieberman, and a few other conservatives in the Democratic caucus to overcome the filibuster with sixty votes in "regular order" blocked not only certain redistributive aspects of the final health care reform legislation, but also higher education loan reforms. But once Brown was elected, and once all the Senate Republicans refused Obama's final offers to join in helping to pass reform, the ideal point for shaping legislation shifted a bit toward the center-left, and the legislation that eked through proved more equality-enhancing than Republicans or conservative Democrats would have tolerated. The use of reconciliation made it possible for House Democrats to win higher charges on business and the wealthy and more generous subsidies and benefits for lower- and middle-income beneficiaries of health care reform. In addition to removing a number of special deals— such as the Cornhusker Kickback the Senate had used to get Ben Nelson's vote in December 2009—the sidecar bill reduced and delayed the so-called Cadillac tax on generous employee health plans, increased taxes on health care industries, and imposed higher taxes on the wealthiest Medicare beneficiaries. The final bill also folded in the student loan reforms that had been previously stalled by the Senate filibuster. These education-loan reforms had the effect of removing federal subsidies that had previously flowed to banks making student loans (Murray and Montgomery 2010).

Billions of dollars were shifted toward more generous student loans and paying for health care reform. Thanks in part to the new revenues garnered from the fusion of the educational loan and health care reforms, the Congressional Budget Office projected that Affordable Care bills, taken together, would actually cut the federal deficit by about $140 billion over the first decade and by more than a trillion dollars in the second decade (Elmendorf 2010b). This was critical in winning the final votes of Blue Dog conservative Democrats in both the House and the Senate.

Using reconciliation came at a cost, though. According to Senate rules, reconciliation could not be used to change the administrative or regulatory aspects of the health care reform bill passed by the Senate in late 2009. This locked in the Senate's provisions on abortion, which created a tricky endgame in the House. More important for the long run, it forced the House and the Obama administration to accept the provision of the 2009 Senate bill calling for fifty state insurance exchanges to implement regulations and subsidies in health care reform, instead of realizing the hope of many in the White House to manage implementation through a unified national exchange. This administrative outcome will produce competing lines of authority and quite possibly years of confusion, conflict, and widely varying policy choices. On the other hand, despite shifts in the partisan balance in Washington, D.C., the delegation of considerable authority may allow states to proceed with reforms tailored to varied economic and ideological conditions on the ground as well as free up a few states to generate—for future emulation—effective models of public option or single-payer systems.

In March 2010, after some intricate maneuvering by Senate Majority Leader Harry Reid and another round of coalition-building heroics by House Speaker Nancy Pelosi, the House and Senate Democrats finally had the votes to pass health care reform—without the support of a single Republican. The House passed the Senate's health care reform by a vote of 219 to 212, and the sidecar reconciliation bill by a vote of 220 to 211. The Senate, after a week of wrangling and delays, passed the reconciliation bill by a vote of 56 to 43. On Tuesday, March 23, 2010, several hundred people crowded into the East Room of the White House to watch President Obama sign into law the Patient Protection and Affordable Care Act. One week later, the president signed the sidecar bill, finally completing comprehensive health care reform. It was a major victory for Obama, setting his administration on the road to fulfill his March 2007 pledge to "judge my first term as president based on . . . whether we have delivered the kind of health care that every American deserves and that our system can afford."

Two paradoxes of the endgame stand out. First, as we have explained, Scott Brown's apparent knock-out victory in the special Senate contest ended up backfiring, because what had been intended and described by pundits as the death knell for health care reform ended up enabling majoritarian legislation that was substantially more economically redistributive than the Senate legislation passed in 2009. Second and more generally, the culmination of the 2009–2010 health care reform process demonstrates the paradox of partisan obstruction: the effort to block any kind of health care reform ended up unifying Democrats offended by the GOP's obstruction; and it produced more liberal legislation than would have been possible had Republicans taken a formal part in true negotiations for legislation that at least a few of them would vote to enact. Had that happened, the final legislation would have shifted markedly toward the right on issues of redistribution and regulation of business.

The Ongoing Fights about Implementation

Still, the enactment of the new laws in March 2010 marked a beginning, not an end—a promise of accomplishment, not a fait accompli. Social Security and Medicare faced obstacles and redirections long after the enabling laws were passed, respectively, in 1935 and 1965, and Affordable Care will also likely be modified over the next ten to fifteen years. But in the case of Affordable Care, contention over the reform framework itself remains at a political fever pitch, and likely will at least through the 2012 presidential contest.

Unremitting Opposition

Within hours of the passage of Affordable Care, more than a dozen conservative state officials, most of them Republican candidates for office in fall 2010, rushed to court to argue that the new laws were unconstitutional—and the number of challengers in the courts grew in subsequent months. By the end of 2010, two federal district judges had upheld Affordable Care, while Judge Henry Hudson in Virginia invalidated the key provision mandating that all Americans purchase insurance, after public subsidies kick in in 2014. To the disappointment of conservative litigants, Judge Hudson refused to suspend implementation of Affordable Care as appeals wend their way toward the Supreme Court. But additional federal judges may act more aggressively. Even as the constitutionality of components of Affordable Care will remain in doubt until the Supreme Court decides probably sometime in 2012, pathbreaking reforms—including the enormous expansion of Medicaid and new cost controls—will continue to be implemented.

With equal determination and anger, Republicans in Congress vowed to keep up the legislative fight, even after Affordable Care was signed by the president. Even when they were a minority in the 111th Congress, GOP leaders promised their supporters a complete repeal of the new legislation and House Republicans passed one soon after taking over in 2011 (Hooper 2010). The GOP repeal was, in a sense, quixotic, because everyone knew the legislation would die in the 112th Senate, but the House Republicans took this aggressive step to signal all-out opposition to their Tea Party supporters and to put the Obama administration on notice that they intended to come back again and again with efforts to dismantle Affordable Care.

Scholars debate the role of health care reform votes in setting up Democrats to lose sixty-three House seats and forfeit their majority in the November 2010 midterm. There are reasons to think such votes hurt some congressional Democrats, but still conclude that the 2010 results were affected only at the margins. The long-term record of midterm losses for parties that go into such elections controlling the presidency and both chambers of Congress suggests that Democrats were at risk, with or without particular legislative votes. What is more, Americans were generally disgusted with Washington, D.C., in the fall of 2010, and dismayed at the sluggish pace of economic recovery from the deep recession of 2009. The other thing to keep in mind is the distinctive composition of the midterm electorate. Electorates in midterm as opposed to presidential contests are smaller, richer, whiter, and older—all factors that worked to the advantage of Republicans in 2010. What is more, older voters are vigilant about policy questions that affect Medicare and Social Security (Campbell 2003). During the 2009 and 2010 battles over health care reform, seniors were heavily targeted by opponents of reform, who financed a steady drumbeat of lurid attack ads aiming to convince older voters that extensions of benefits to younger Americans could hurt Medicare or make it harder for Medicare recipients to find doctors. The attacks gained considerable traction, so that an already highly motivated Republican base was bolstered in November 2010 by worried older voters (who never liked Obama very much in the first place). In short, although the 2010 election was primarily about typical cycles and the down economy, health care worries helped the GOP to secure control of the House—ensuring new leverage in the divided 112th Congress for politicians and interest groups determined to undermine Affordable Care. Still, the electorate in 2012 will be larger and less tilted toward opponents of Obama, including older voters, so the direction of things in November 2010 may or may not prove permanent.

Ironies and Dynamics of Public Opinion

One of the ironies of health care reform is that its guts—regulation of pernicious insurance practices, help for those without insurance, and new subsidies for Medicare recipients—are quite popular, even as the public remains split on Affordable Care overall (Jacobs 2010). The question is whether the public will continue to worry about Affordable Care as a whole package, or gradually come to rely on specific parts of the 2010 reforms and thus shift toward more acceptance of the law overall, increasingly supporting the reform as a whole. Either scenario could unfold in coming months and years, giving hope both to GOP opponents of ObamaCare and to Democratic defenders of most of what Affordable Care is doing, or promises to do.

According to tracking polls conducted by the Kaiser Family Foundation, overall approval versus disapproval has shifted very little since March 2010 (2010b). About two-fifths of respondents approve, and another two-fifths disapprove, though opposition among older people eased a bit in late 2010. Public evaluations correlate closely with party affiliation, with most Republicans wanting full or partial repeal of Affordable Care, and most Democrats preferring either to keep the law or to enact further reforms to expand it. Indeed, multiple national polls show that a quarter or a third of the opposition to Affordable Care comes from the left, from citizens who want more immediate or sweeping reforms, and not just from people on the right who reject the law as too heavy-handed an exercise of public authority (Alonso-Zaldivar and Agiesta 2010).

Even as Americans are split on Affordable Care as a whole, three-fifths to three-quarters of Americans are quite supportive of its concrete specific programs—new rules to prevent insurance companies from denying care to people with preexisting health problems, or people who become very sick; new subsidies to help families and businesses pay for insurance coverage; new benefits for seniors on Medicare; rules to allow young adults to stay on parental insurance plans until age twenty-six; and so forth. Many Republicans and Independents, not just Democrats, favor these needed reforms. Real-world developments are also bringing popular, specific provisions of Affordable Care steadily into public view. Key provisions went into effect in September 2010, and others at the start of 2011 (Adamy 2010b; Young 2010). The only specific provision of Affordable Care that has lost popularity over time is the mandate that all citizens buy coverage, a provision discussed in the abstract because it does not go into effect until 2014. This provision, of course, has been the focus of nonstop conservative attacks. And many people may not understand how loose the rule will be, or that substantial subsidies will be provided to help even the upper middle class purchase insurance.

Despite the recent political shifts against Democrats, time is not on the side of those who would keep Affordable Care from weaving itself into the expectations and routines of families and businesses. The history of Social Security and Medicare, which also emerged from emotional ideological conflict, suggests that the everyday operation of health care reform will broaden its popularity: ideological and partisan divisions may well be trumped by pragmatism and lived experience with new programs. With each passing month, concrete steps are taken to implement Affordable Care through negotiations among the Obama administration, state-level administrators, and the health insurance companies. As new rules of the game are clarified for the many public and private stakeholders in the health care economy who adapt their operations to them, major groups gain a stake in keeping health care reform on track. Business hates uncertainty; and insurance companies in particular are made nervous by the Republican calls to get rid of the individual mandate—because that could mean that insurance companies are left with a lot of new regulations preventing them from excluding sick patients, even as many citizens are allowed to delay buying health insurance until they get sick.

In this adverse selection scenario, private insurance companies may worry about having to pay for the care of additional very costly sick people without collecting new revenues from many younger, healthier customers. Insurers' determination to avoid this trap will likely fuel tensions between ideologically purist Tea Party Republicans, on the one hand, and pro-business Republicans and their allies, on the other. And if, in the end, Republican politicians or conservative judges manage to get rid of the individual mandate provision, the GOP may find itself in a position of winning a battle but setting up a loss in the overall war over comprehensive health care reform. They would have to explain to voters why not just the individual mandate but also the very popular insurance regulations would have to go. Explaining why private insurance companies should again be able to deny or roll back coverage for sick people would not be a popular task in, say, 2012 or 2014.

In sum, because more and more citizens and businesses are gaining a stake in the unfolding reforms, outright repeal of Affordable Care becomes less likely with every passing month. Nor will the politics of battles over repeal play well for opponents as time moves on. Even with Republicans in control of the 112th House, Senate Democrats can prevent repeal bills or provisions from passing; and President Obama can veto any legislation that presents major threats to ongoing reform implementation. The short-term GOP strategy of holding hearings and symbolic votes to attack Affordable Care leading into the 2012 election may prove less popular during 2011 than some pundits suppose. Americans consistently tell pollsters that they are chiefly worried about the economy. Apart from the hardcore Republican base, voters want Capitol Hill to focus on jobs and bolstering the recovery, and may not like a reopening of endless battles over health care reform. Moving toward the 2012 elections, moreover, President Obama will remain in a position to highlight all the popular features of the reform that Republicans are trying to abolish—and ongoing economic sluggishness may actually make more and more voters anxious about giving up even the smallest gains in health care security. Expect the debate to rage on for at least the next two years at two levels, with Democrats stressing the specifics of health care reform, while Republicans try to highlight threats from "big government."

Presumably, if Republicans can elect a president in 2012, they could finally carry through on promises to repeal Affordable Care; yet even then forty-one senators will be able to stop many rollbacks of the most popular features. By the middle of the coming decade, many Americans may be accustomed to new insurance regulations that protect patients; young Americans will enjoy staying on parental health care plans until age twenty-six; older Americans will enjoy enhanced prescription drug coverage under Medicare; and millions of lower- and lower-middle-income Americans will enjoy, or be on the verge of gaining, health care coverage through Medicaid or by purchasing subsidized plans on the new health insurance exchanges. Some Republican strategists have worried publicly that pushing repeal might increasingly alienate moderate voters, especially following the implementation of popular provisions (Bellatoni 2010). Advocates of repeal should be worried about erosion of their position, because even though Americans resonate with antigovernment arguments when they are broadly posed, they are often very liberal when it comes to the concrete benefits they gain from public programs (Free and Cantril 1967; Page and Jacobs 2009).

Implementation in Washington and the States

Although full repeal may be improbable, gradual chipping away at tax, regulatory, and benefit provisions in Affordable Care is much more likely. Many of the most redistributive policies in the health care reform package do not come into effect until 2014—and conservatives in Congress may be able to modify many relevant provisions in budget bills negotiated in back rooms. Lobbyists will know what is going on, but the general public will remain oblivious, especially given the incapacity of most media reporters to convey anything meaningful about public policymaking. Conceivably, the tax increases on the wealthy and the subsidies for lower-income Americans could shrink before they are ever delivered, if congressional Republicans, perhaps abetted by some Democrats in the Senate, take a series of quiet actions to modify the reform framework enacted in 2010. In addition, businesses will mount one lobbying campaign after another to modify or relax provisions of the law that each sector dislikes—and states with a history of minimal provision for the health care of the poor and the near-poor will continue to protest the fact that, eventually, states will have to join the federal government in paying for broad Medicaid coverage. Businesses and state-level actors disgruntled by regulatory or financial measures in Affordable Care will be able to work through sympathetic congressional representatives to chip away at reform, especially when key budgetary steps have to be taken and Democrats and the president feel compelled to compromise. In the end, Republicans may be able to get some of the sorts of adjustments in Affordable Care that they could have achieved in 2009 by participating in the original legislative process.

Quiet evisceration, far from public view, is the way that redistributive reforms are often undermined in U.S. government, because powerful actors know what to press for and congressional representatives find it useful to their own political careers to make one requested modification after another. Benefits and financial mechanisms helpful to less economically privileged people are often the first to go, because those constituencies may not even know what is happening and congressional politicians know they will pay little price in the press or at the ballot box. What is more, regulations in health care that aspire to control costs also restrict profits, and the stakeholders who want those profits have many ways to influence legislation in nonpublic settings. They have the ear of Republicans and conservative Democrats, and they reward their congressional friends at fundraisers. In our view, quiet, bit-by-bit evisceration—especially because the composition and mood of Congress has shifted toward the right—is the most likely way in which Affordable Care may be undermined (Beutler 2010; Pear 2010). We assume that, in the end, the federal courts will not throw out the laws wholesale, but particular provisions can still be modified in ongoing congressional decisions about funding and adjustments in rules. Each change will seem small, perhaps even to its sponsors, but they will add up.

Equally important to note, much of the fight over implementation will happen in the states. As we noted earlier, Affordable Care ended up calling for state-level health insurance marketplaces, rather than creating a national exchange. In states dominated by conservatives, and where administrative capacity is weak, this will make it relatively easy for lobbyists to undercut Affordable Care's new consumer protections. On the other hand, in states with stronger administrative capacities and more progressive political climates, highly effective health insurance exchanges may be established—and these might even include state or regional public-option plans or single-payer models of health coverage. Some states may establish arrangements that prove unusually good at covering everyone at reasonable cost. The only certainty is that the United States will not have a unitary health-care financing system anytime soon. Health insurance exchanges and their associated rules and subsidies will vary across state lines—and it will be many years before we know whether particular state solutions to widespread problems of access and cost can serve as a model for additional states or the nation as a whole.

The Bottom Line So Far

However future struggles over implementation play out, the passage of Affordable Care in 2010 was a remarkable achievement—enough to make at least a partial case that Barack Obama and the Democrats in Congress during 2009 and 2010 did manage to fashion parts of another New Deal. In a highly partisan atmosphere, in the midst of a burgeoning economic crisis, and with relatively small congressional majorities compared to other Democratic presidents who have pushed through major social reforms, Obama's newly assembled White House thrashed through a forest of entrenched interests and secured a wide-ranging and remarkably progressive health care bill. Truly a landmark in U.S. public social provision, the Affordable Care legislation of 2010 draws resources from the privileged to spread access to affordable health insurance to most of the U.S. citizenry.

But as we have explored, Affordable Care is a blueprint far from fully implemented. The bitter politics of comprehensive health care reform will continue for some time. In the coming months and years, we will see to what extent the promise of Affordable Care can be made a reality in the fifty states and across the nation. Will health care really become affordable for those of lesser means? Will private health care giants truly learn to play by new rules? Will health care providers find ways to improve quality without breaking the bank? Will businesses and the national budget benefit from more cost-effective practices in health care? As written, Affordable Care promises progress on all fronts, and in time we will learn the fate of this hard-fought legacy, fashioned by an embattled Democratic president and Congress during a brief window of political opportunity.

APPENDIX

You will find additional information regarding health reform in this appendix.

Table 2A.1. Timeline of Health Reform Events

The 2008 Election and Obama's Commitment to Health Reform

March 24, 2007	Only weeks into his presidential bid, Obama performs unevenly at a health care forum with other presidential candidates. He remarks, "I will judge my first term as president based on . . . whether we have delivered the kind of health care that every American deserves and that our system can afford."
June 5, 2008	Senator Obama holds Health Care Town Hall in Bristol, Virginia. He discusses cost-cutting measures and preventative care.
August 28, 2008	Senator Obama accepts the Democratic nomination in Denver, Colorado, saying, "Now is the time to finally keep the promise of affordable, accessible health care for every single American."
October 4, 2008	Senator Obama outlines his health care plan in remarks in Newport News, Virginia, opposing a tax on insurance and offering Americans access to private plans comparable to those for federal employees.
February 17, 2009	The president signs the American Recovery and Reinvestment Act, which includes significant health care funding, including $87 billion in additional federal matching funds for Medicaid, $25 billion for COBRA subsidies, and more than $30 billion in other health-related spending (Kaiser Family Foundation 2009).
February 26, 2009	The 2010 fiscal year budget proposal includes a more than $630 billion reserve fund to cover part of the cost of health care reform (Office of Budget and Management 2009).
March 5, 2009	White House holds a forum on health care reform that includes a wide array of administration officials,

prominent members of Congress, and representatives for insurance companies, patients, doctors, hospitals, and the pharmaceutical industry.

Battles over House and Senate Legislation

May 11, 2009	Six major stakeholders in the health care industry—the Advanced Medical Technology Association (AdvaMed), the American Hospital Association (AHA), the Pharmaceutical Research and Manufacturers of America (PhRMA), the American Medical Association (AMA), the association of America's Health Insurance Plans (AHIP), and the Service Employees International Union (SEIU)—sign on to a letter nominally supporting reform of health care and offering some voluntary cost-cutting measures.
June 2009	In a series of speeches, Town Halls, and meetings with congressional leadership, President Obama turns the agenda to health care. Senator Edward Kennedy (D-MA) circulates a plan for a health care reform bill.
June 15, 2009	President Obama addresses the AMA, saying, "One essential step on our journey is to control the spiraling cost of health care in America. And in order to do that, we're going to need the help of the AMA."
July 14, 2009	Three House committees—Energy and Commerce, Ways and Means, and Education and Labor—all agree on a single health care bill, the House Tri-Committee America's Affordable Health Choices Act, HR 3200.
July 15, 2009	The Senate Health, Education, Labor, and Pensions (HELP) Committee passes its version of health care reform legislation, the Affordable Health Choices Act, S 1679.
July 22, 2009	President Obama holds press conference with AARP.
August 2009	During the August recess, members of Congress confront angry constituents at Town Halls. Senator Chuck Grassley (R-IA), who had been a key negotiator in an effort to produce bipartisan health care reform, argues for a much narrower bill (Montgomery and Bacon 2009).

August 16, 2009   The president signals his willingness to drop the public option (Stolberg 2009).

September 9, 2009   President Obama addresses a joint session of Congress urging action on health care reform. He reiterates his priorities for this legislation, including an end to preexisting conditions exclusions and a new insurance exchange. He does not insist on including a public option, and emphasizes the need for deficit reduction.

October 13, 2009   The Senate Finance Committee approves its version of health care reform, the America's Health Future Act, by a vote of 14 to 9.

November 7, 2009   By a vote of 220 to 215, the House passes health care legislation, the Affordable Health Care for America Act, HR 3962. The final bill includes the Stupak Amendment, which restricts abortion coverage.

December 12, 2009   Senator Joseph Lieberman's (I-CT) unexpected opposition to the Senate bill leads Senator Harry Reid (D-NV) to remove both a buy-in to Medicare for those fifty-five and older and the opt-out public option that had previously been included in the legislation.

December 24, 2009   The Senate passes its health care bill, the Patient Protection and Affordable Care Act, HR 3590.

January 15, 2010   The president and top congressional Democrats agree on revisions to legislation, including—after extensive consultation with union officials—a tax on high-cost insurance plans.

Scott Brown Election and the Legislative Endgame

January 19, 2010   Republican Scott Brown defeats Democrat Martha Coakley to fill the Senate seat long held by Senator Edward Kennedy. Progress on final health care reform legislation comes to a halt.

January 27, 2010   President Obama delivers a State of the Union that says little about health care reform.

February 2010	Massive rate increases by Anthem Blue Cross spark national outrage.
February 22, 2010	For the first time, President Obama releases a specific policy proposal for health care reform. His recommendation closely mirrors the Senate legislation, modified as agreed between House and Senate negotiators.
February 25, 2010	President Obama leads the Bipartisan Meeting on Health Care Reform. Interviewed on CNN, White House senior advisor David Axelrod pushes an "up or down vote" on health care reform.
March 3, 2010	President Obama gives a speech calling for action on health care reform. "I, therefore, ask leaders in both houses of Congress to finish their work and schedule a vote in the next few weeks. From now until then, I will do everything in my power to make the case for reform."
March 20, 2010	As Speaker of the House Nancy Pelosi nears the necessary vote total to pass the Senate bill, President Obama rallies the House Democrats.
March 21, 2010	By a vote of 219 to 212, the House of Representatives passes the Senate version of health care reform, the Patient Protection and Affordable Care Act, HR 3590. By a vote of 220 to 211, the House passes the sidecar bill that revises the Senate legislation, the Health Care and Education Reconciliation Act, HR 4872.
March 23, 2010	President Obama signs the first part of the health care legislation, the Patient Protection and Affordable Care Act, into law. Attorneys general in fourteen states sue to block the health care reform law.
March 26, 2010	After numerous delays, the Senate votes for the reconciliation fixes, the Health Care and Education Reconciliation Act, by a vote of 56 to 43. Procedural questions raised by Senate Republicans force the House to vote on the legislation again. It passes a second time, 220 to 207.
March 30, 2010	President Obama signs the Health Care and Education Reconciliation Act into law.

Timeline for Implementation of
Affordable Care Provisions

2010 *An end to rescission*: Insurance companies will no longer be able to rescind coverage when a person gets sick.

      Better coverage for young people: Children can stay on their parents' plans until age twenty-six. Insurance companies will no longer be able to deny coverage to children because of their preexisting conditions.

      Doughnut hole rebate: Provide a $250 rebate to Medicare beneficiaries who reach the Medicare Part D coverage gap, the first step in a process that will gradually close the doughnut hole in seniors' prescription drug coverage.

      Small business tax credits: For small businesses that offer health insurance to their employees, tax credits will offset up to 35 percent percent of the employer contribution.

      Expansion of Medicaid: States are given the option of extending Medicaid to all American citizens and legal residents ineligible for Medicare and earning less than 133 percent of the federal poverty line. Expansion must be complete by 2014; the federal government will offset states' costs.

      Temporary high-risk pool: People with preexisting conditions unable to find insurance are eligible to join the high-risk pool and receive subsidies to make premiums affordable.

2011 *Better coverage for the elderly*: Cost-sharing is eliminated for recommended Medicare-covered preventive services.

2012 *Consumer protections*: New standards will govern how insurers provide information about different plans, allowing consumers to comparison-shop more easily.

2014 *Expansion of coverage*: Credits and subsidies to low- and middle-income families kick in to offset costs of health insurance. Businesses with fifty or more employees are required to offer health insurance or pay a penalty. All U.S. citizens must have qualifying health insurance, with exceptions for those with religious objections or financial hardship (despite public subsidies).

      Health care exchanges: Health care exchanges in all states and regions will allow uninsured people and small businesses to shop for insurance in new marketplaces, providing consumers with better information about competing health plans and different levels of coverage.

Ending annual and lifetime limits: Insurers will no longer be able to cap coverage based on an annual or lifetime limit, protecting patients from losing their coverage when their medical expenses are highest.

Ending preexisting condition exclusions: Insurers can no longer deny coverage to adults because of preexisting conditions.

Shorter waiting periods: Waiting periods for coverage can last no more than ninety days.

2019   An additional 32 million Americans will be insured, according to CBO estimates.

Table 2A.2 The Trajectory of Health Care Reform, Major Benefits

	Strongest Provision ▮ Weakest Provision ▯			
	Obama Principles	House Bill	Senate Bill	Law
		HR 3962: Affordable Health Care for America Act, Passed: November 7, 2009	HR 3590: Patient Protection and Affordable Care Act, Passed: December 24, 2009	PL 111-148: Patient Protection and Affordable Care Act, as amended by the Health Care and Education Reconciliation Act, Signed into law: March 30, 2010
Universal Coverage (Winerman 2010) *Overall increase in coverage from the current rate (83 percent of legal U.S. residents under sixty-five).*	In his campaign, Obama called for a mandate for all children to have coverage. As president, he suggested reform should "aim for universality."	96 percent covered.	94 percent covered.	95 percent covered.
Competition to Make Care More Affordable	Obama supported the creation of a National Health Insurance Exchange and, in general terms, a public insurance program to compete with private insurers.	Sets up a national insurance exchange marketplace.	Sets up state-based insurance exchange marketplaces.	Sets up state-based insurance exchange marketplaces.
		Includes a public option to compete with private health insurance plans.	Does not include a public option or remove the health industry antitrust exemption.	Does not include a public option or remove the health industry antitrust exemption.

| Support for Low- to Middle-Income Americans
The federal poverty line (FPL) was set in 2009 at $10,830 for a single person and $22,050 for a family of four. | Candidate and President Obama called for the expansion of Medicaid and the State Children's Health Insurance Programs (SCHIP). In addition, he supported income-related federal subsidies to make private plans affordable for individuals and families not covered by Medicaid or SCHIP. | Expand Medicaid to all under sixty-five with incomes up to 150 percent of the FPL.

To families with incomes between 133 and 400 percent of the FPL, provide tiered premium credits so families contribute between 3 and 12 percent of income to paying for insurance, and subsidies to cover up to 97 percent of medical costs. | Would remove the health industry exemption from antitrust legislation.

Expand Medicaid to all under sixty-five with incomes up to 133 percent of the FPL.

To families between 133 and 400 percent of the FPL, provide tiered premium credits so families contribute between 2 and 12 percent of income to paying for insurance. To families between 100 and 200 percent of the FPL, provide a sliding scale of credits to cover up to 90 percent of medical costs. | Expand Medicaid to all under sixty-five with incomes up to 133 percent of the FPL.

To families between 133 and 400 percent of the FPL, provide tiered premium credits so families contribute between 2 and 9.5 percent of income to paying for insurance, and subsidies to cover up to 94 percent of medical costs. |

(Table continues on p. 92.)

Table 2A.2 (Continued)

	Strongest Provision		Weakest Provision	
	Obama Principles	House Bill	Senate Bill	Law
Support for Young Adults and the Elderly	Obama supported closing the doughnut hole gap in Medicare prescription drug benefits, and recommended allowing those up to age twenty-five to stay on their parents' health insurance plans.	Over a ten-year period, closes the doughnut hole. Children can stay on their parents' plans until age twenty-seven. Insurance companies cannot charge more than twice as much for older people's premiums as they do for younger people's.	Reduces but does not close the doughnut hole. (Masterson and Carey. 2009) Children can stay on their parents' plans until age twenty-six. Insurance companies cannot charge more than three times as much for older people's premiums as those they offer younger people.	Closes the doughnut hole gap in Medicare prescription drug benefits by 2020. (Winerman 2010) Children can stay on their parents' plans until age twenty-six. Insurance companies cannot charge more than three times as much for older people's premiums as they do for younger people's.

Effective Regulation	Obama's plan declared that "no American will be turned away from any insurance plan because of illness or preexisting conditions."	Effective in 2010, prevents insurance companies from charging women higher premiums than men, excluding customers because of a preexisting condition, rescinding a policy when a person becomes sick.	Prevents insurance companies from charging women higher premiums than men, excluding customers because of a preexisting condition, rescinding a policy when a person becomes sick. Effective in 2010 for children, 2014 for adults.	Prevents insurance companies from charging women higher premiums than men, excluding customers because of a preexisting condition, rescinding a policy when a person becomes sick. Effective in 2010 for children, 2014 for adults.

Source: Author's compilation, unless otherwise noted, based on Kaiser Family Foundation 2010a (summaries of legislative provisions); Obama 2008 (Obama's principles); Office of Management and Budget 2009 (first presidential budget).

Table 2A.3   The Trajectory of Health Care Reform, Major Financing Provisions

	Strongest Provision				Weakest Provision
	Obama Proposals	House Bill	Senate Finance	Senate Bill	Law
		HR 3962: Affordable Health Care for America Act, Passed: November 7, 2009	America's Healthy Future Act (as Amended in Senate Finance Committee), Announced: September 17, 2009	HR 3590: Patient Protection and Affordable Care Act, Passed: December 24, 2009	PL 111-148: Patient Protection and Affordable Care Act, as Amended by the Health Care and Education Reconciliation Act Signed into law: March 30, 2010
High-Earner Tax *Tax increases for the wealthiest Americans.*	Proposes tax increases, including a reduction in the mortgage interest and charitable deductions, for those making over $250,000. Estimated ten-year revenue: $318 billion (Calmes and Pear 2009; Office of Management and Budget 2009).	Institute a 5.4 percent increase in the income tax on individuals earning more than $500,000 or families earning over $1 million. Estimated ten-year revenue: $460 billion (Elmendorf 2009b).	None.	Increase Medicare tax rate from 1.45 to 2.35 percent for individuals earning over $200,000 and couples earning over $250,000. Estimated ten-year revenue: $87 billion (Sahadi 2010).	For individuals earning over $200,000 and couples earning over $250,000, increase Medicare tax rate from 1.45 to 2.35 percent and institute a 3.8 percent tax on unearned income. Estimated ten-year revenue: $210 billion (Sahadi 2010).

Cuts to Government-Guaranteed Corporate Profits *Reductions in overpayments to insurance companies, health care providers, drug companies, and student loan bankers.*				
FY2010 budget proposes health care savings totaling $316 billion, including $177 billion in savings from Medicare Advantage overpayments (Meckler 2009). In June 2009, Obama calls for an additional $309 billion in savings from Medicare and Medicaid (Obama 2009).	Reduce Medicare overspending by $440 billion over ten years, including $170 billion in Medicare Advantage savings (Masterson and Carey 2009).	Reduce Medicare overspending by $404 billion over ten years, including $117 billion from Medicare Advantage (Elmendorf 2009a).	Reduce Medicare overspending by $395 to $400 billion over ten years, including $118 billion in savings from Medicare Advantage.	Reduce Medicare overspending by $390 billion over ten years, including $136 billion in savings from Medicare Advantage (Davis et al. 2010).
				Restructure student loan process, cutting out middle-men bankers, who profit from government-guaranteed student loans, saving $61 billion over ten years (Elmendorf 2010b).

Note: Originally a separate piece of legislation, student loan reform was highlighted by the president in his first State of the Union and passed by the House in September 2009, but stalled in the Senate until a version was included with the final vote on health care reform.

(Table continues on p. 96.)

Table 2A.3 (Continued)

	Strongest Provision				Weakest Provision
	Obama Proposals	House Bill	Senate Finance	Senate Bill	Law
Industry Fees *Annual fees and taxes affecting health-sector companies.*	In May 2009, President Obama meets with health-sector companies, and claims to have secured voluntary pledges from the industry to cut national health care spending by 1.5 percentage points each year, but the plan lacks detail.	2.5 percent tax on medical devices.	Fees include an annual fee of $2.3 billion for drug companies, $4 billion for medical device companies, and $6.7 billion for insurance companies. Estimated ten-year revenue: $88 to $93 billion (Hitt, Adamy, and Weisman 2009).	Fees include an annual fee of $2.3 billion for drug companies, $2 billion for medical device companies, rising to $3 billion after 2017, and a tiered fee system for insurance companies: $2 billion in 2011, $4 billion in 2012, $7 billion in 2013, $9 billion from 2014 through 2016, and $10 billion thereafter. 10 percent tax on tanning salons.	Fees include a 2.3 percent tax on medical devices, and a tiered fee system for drug and insurance companies. Insurance industry payments are delayed until 2014, but are linked to premium growth. These changes are expected to raise about $6 billion more than the Senate bill over ten years, and more thereafter. 10 percent tax on tanning salons.

Cadillac Tax *Tax on the most expensive health plans.*	None.	None. Obama strongly opposes a tax on health care plans during his campaign, attacking Senator McCain for his support of such a proposal.	On most health plans valued at over $8,000 for an individual or $21,000 for a family, there is a tax set at 40 percent of plan value. The provision is effective as of 2013, and linked to inflation. Estimated revenue: $210 billion (Elmendorf 2009a).	On most health plans valued at over $8,500 for an individual or $23,000 for a family, there is a tax set at 40 percent of plan value. The provision is effective as of 2013, and linked to inflation. Estimated revenue: $149 billion (Elmendorf 2010a).	On most health plans valued at over $10,200 for an individual or $27,500 for a family, there is a tax set at 40 percent of plan value. The provision is effective as of 2018, and linked to inflation after 2020. Estimated revenue: $32 billion (Elmendorf 2010b).
Free-Rider Penalty *Penalties on individuals without qualifying coverage and large employers not providing coverage.*	Obama never explicitly endorses an individual or employer mandate, calling only for a "plan that puts the United States on a clear path to cover all Americans" (Office of Management and Budget 2009, 27).	Uninsured would pay 2.5 percent of household adjusted income up to cost of national premium basic plan. Employers must cover 72.5 percent of premium for an individual or	Uninsured would pay a tax of $750 per adult per year. Employers with more than fifty employees not offering coverage pay a fee based on the average national tax credit for each employee	Uninsured would pay a tax equal to the greater of 2 percent of household adjusted income or $750 per person up to $2,250. Employers with more than fifty employees not	Uninsured would pay a tax equal to the greater of 2 percent of household adjusted income or $695 per person up to $2,085. Employers with more than fifty employees not

(Table continues on p. 98.)

Table 2A.3 (Continued)

	Strongest Provision			Weakest Provision	
	Obama Proposals	House Bill	Senate Finance	Senate Bill	Law
Free-Rider Penalty (continued)	Obama also emphasizes the need to make plans affordable to individuals and small businesses.	65 percent for a family, or pay 8 percent of payroll into the Health Insurance Exchange Trust Fund. Employers with payroll less than $500,000 are exempt, and fees are lower than 8 percent for businesses with a payroll less than $750,000. Estimated ten-year revenue: $168 billion (Elmendorf 2009b).	receiving a tax credit, or $400 times the total number of employees in the firm. Estimated ten-year revenue is $27 billion (Elmendorf 2009a).	offering coverage who have at least one employee receiving a tax credit pay $750 per full-time employee. If employer does offer coverage, they must pay the lesser of $3,000 for each tax credit or $750 per employee. Employers offering coverage must offer vouchers for employees below 400 percent of the federal poverty line who buy on the exchange. Additional fees for long waiting periods for coverage. Estimated revenue: $39 billion (Elmendorf 2010a).	offering coverage who have at least one employee receiving a tax credit pay $2,000 times the number of full-time employees minus thirty. If employer does offer coverage, they must pay the lesser of $3,000 for each tax credit or $2,000 times the number of full-time employees minus thirty. Employers offering coverage must offer vouchers for employees below 400 percent FPL who buy on the exchange. Estimated revenue: $65 billion (Elmendorf 2010b).

The timeline and comparisons of bills were prepared by Vanessa Williamson, whose research assistance throughout this project is much appreciated. We are equally grateful for the support of the Russell Sage Foundation, which enabled us to gather data for this project in real time, as the 2009 and 2010 episode in health care reform was unfolding. Our efforts included doing confidential interviews with congressional and White House actors in Washington, D.C., in late 2009 and early 2010, and we thank each person who took the time to speak with us and share information and perspectives on complex processes of policy formulation and legislation.

REFERENCES

AARP. 2009. "AARP, AMA Join Together to Debunk Medicare Myths, Launch National TV Ad." Press release, November 23, 2009. Washington, D.C.: American Association of Retired Persons. Available at: http://share-ws2-md.aarp.org/aarp/presscenter/pressrelease/articles/aarp_ama_national_ad.html (accessed January 28, 2011).

Adamy, Janet. 2010a. "Health Law Augurs Transfer of Funds from Old to Young." *Wall Street Journal*, July 26, 2010.

———. 2010b. "Big Health-Care Changes Arrive in the New Year." *Wall Street Journal*, December 31, 2010, p. A3.

Alonso-Zaldivar, Ricardo, and Jennifer Agiesta. 2010. "AP Poll: Many Think Health Overhaul Should Do More." Associated Press, September 25, 2010. Available at: http://www.chron.com/disp/story.mpl/nation/7218362.html (accessed March 7, 2011).

Alter, Jonathan. 2010. *The Promise: President Obama, Year One*. New York: Simon and Schuster.

Baker, Peter. 2010. "What Happened? The Limits of Rahmism." *New York Times Magazine*, March 14, 2010.

Bartels, Larry M. 2008. *Unequal Democracy: The Political Economy of the New Gilded Age*. New York: Russell Sage Foundation; Princeton, N.J.: Princeton University Press.

Bellatoni, Christina. 2010. "Republicans Back Off Health Care Repeal Pledges." *Talking Points Memo DC*, April 1, 2010. Available at: http://tpmdc.talkingpointsmemo.com/2010/04/republicans-backing-off-health-care-repeal-pledges.php (accessed January 28, 2011).

Berry, Emily. 2010. "Anthem Rate Hike Reignites Health Reform Push." *American Medical News*, March 1, 2010. Available at: http://www.ama-assn.org/amednews/2010/03/01/bil20301.htm (accessed January 28, 2011).

Beutler, Brian. 2010. "Top Republicans Warm to Reconciliation . . . for Repealing Health Reform." *Talking Points Memo*, September 23, 2010. Available at: http://

tpmdc.talkingpointsmemo.com/2010/09/top-republicans-warm-to-reconcil
iationfor-repealing-health-care-reform.php (accessed January 28, 2011).

Blendon, Robert J., Drew E. Altman, John M. Benson, Mollyann Brodie, Tami Buhr, Claudia Deane, and Sasha Buscho. 2008. "Voters and Health Reform in the 2008 Presidential Election." *New England Journal of Medicine* 359(19): 2050–61.

Breslow, Jason M. 2010. "Health Reform's Next Step: 23rd Use of Reconciliation?" *PBS NewsHour,* February 26, 2010.

Calmes, Jackie, and Robert Pear. 2009. "To Pay for Health Care, Obama Looks to Taxes on Affluent." *New York Times,* February 26, 2009, p. A1.

Campbell, Andrea Louise. 2003. *How Policies Make Citizens: Senior Political Activism and the American Welfare State.* Princeton, N.J.: Princeton University Press.

Congressional Budget Office. 2010. H.R. 4872, Reconciliation Act of 2010. March 20, 2010.

Connolly, Ceci. 2010. "How Obama Revived His Health-Care Bill." *Washington Post,* March 23, 2010.

Davis, Patricia A., Paulette C. Morgan, Holly Stockdale, Sibyl Tilson, and Jim Hahn. 2010. "Medicare: Changes Made by the Reconciliation Act of 2010 to Senate-Passed H.R. 3590." CRS report R41124, March 19, 2010. Washington: Congressional Research Service.

Dorning, Mike. 2009. "Obama Defends His Plan to Limit Tax Deductions." *Los Angeles Times,* March 25, 2009.

Dreier, Peter. 2010. "Lessons from the Health-Care Wars." *The American Prospect,* April 5, 2010.

Drew, Elizabeth. 2010. "Is There Life in Health Care Reform?" *New York Review of Books,* March 11, 2010.

Elmendorf, Douglas W. 2009a. Letter to the Honorable Max Baucus, Chairman of the Senate Committee on Finance, October 7, 2009. Washington: Congressional Budget Office. Available at: http://www.cbo.gov/ftpdocs/106xx/doc10642/10-7-Baucus_letter.pdf (accessed January 28, 2011).

———. 2009b. Letter to the Honorable John D. Dingell, U.S. House of Representatives, November 20, 2009. Washington: Congressional Budget Office. Available at: http://www.cbo.gov/ftpdocs/107xx/doc10741/hr3962Revised.pdf (accessed January 28, 2011).

———. 2010a. Letter to the Honorable Harry Reid, Senate Majority Leader, March 11, 2010. Washington: Congressional Budget Office.

———. 2010b. Letter to the Honorable Nancy Pelosi, Speaker of the House of Representatives, March 20, 2010. Washington: Congressional Budget Office. Available at: http://www.cbo.gov/ftpdocs/113xx/doc11379/AmendRecon Prop.pdf (accessed January 28, 2011).

Free, Lloyd, and Hadley Cantril. 1967. *The Political Beliefs of Americans.* New Brunswick, N.J.: Rutgers University Press.

Frumin, Ben, and Jason Reif. 2010. "The Rise of Cloture: How GOP Filibuster Threats Have Changed the Senate." *Talking Points Memo DC*, June 27, 2010. Available at: http://tpmdc.talkingpointsmemo.com/2010/01/the-rise-of-cloture -how-gop-filibuster-threats-have-changed-the-senate.php (accessed January 28, 2011).

Garrett, Bowen. 2004. "Employer-Sponsored Health Insurance Coverage: Sponsorship, Eligibility, and Participation Patterns in 2001." *Kaiser Commission on Medicaid and the Uninsured*, July 2004. Washington, D.C.: Kaiser Family Foundation.

Gerard, Leo. 2010. "USW President on Fox Business Network Opposing 'Cadillac' Health Care Tax." *Fox Business* interview, January 12, 2010. Available at: http:// video.foxbusiness.com/v/3965277/union-president-sounds-off-on-cadillac -tax (accessed January 28, 2011).

Gottschalk, Marie. 2007. "Back to the Future? Health Benefits, Organized Labor, and Universal Health Care." *Journal of Health Politics, Policy, and Law* 32(6): 923–70.

Grassley, Chuck. 2009. Testimony before the U.S. Senate. *Congressional Record* 155(185)(December 10, 2009): S12876–904. Available at: http://www.gpo.gov/ fdsys/pkg/CREC-2009-12-10/html/CREC-2009-12-10-pt1-PgS12876.htm (accessed January 28, 2011).

Hacker, Jacob S., and Paul Pierson. 2005. "Abandoning the Middle." *Perspectives on Politics* 3(1): 33–53.

———. 2010. *Winner-Take-All Politics: How Washington Made the Rich Richer—and Turned Its Back on the Middle Class*. New York: Simon and Schuster.

Heilemann, John, and Mark Halperin. 2010. *Game Change: Obama and the Clintons, McCain and Palin, and the Race of a Lifetime*. New York: HarperCollins.

Himmelstein, David U., Deborah Thorne, Elizabeth Warren, and Steffie Woolhandler. 2009. "Medical Bankruptcy in the United States, 2007: Results of a National Study." *American Journal of Medicine* 122(8): 741–46.

Hirshfield, Daniel S. 1970. *The Lost Reform*. Cambridge, Mass.: Harvard University Press.

Hitt, Greg, Janet Adamy, and Jonathan Weisman. 2009. "Senate Bill Sets Lines for Health Showdown," *Wall Street Journal*, September 17, 2009.

Hooper, Molly K. 2010. "GOP Moves to Repeal Health Care Law." *The Hill.com*, June 2, 2010. Available at: http://thehill.com/homenews/house/100369-gop -moves-to-repeal-healthcare-law (accessed January 28, 2011).

Horney, James R., and Paul N. Van de Water. 2009. "House-Passed and Senate Health Bills Reduce Deficit, Slow Health Care Costs, and Include Realistic Medicare Savings." Washington, D.C.: Center for Budget and Policy Priorities. Available at: http://www.cbpp.org/files/12-4-09health.pdf (accessed January 28, 2011).

Ignagni, Karen. 2009. "About That Health-Reform Cost Study." *Washington Post*, October 20, 2009, p. A19.

Jacobs, Lawrence R. 1993. *The Health of Nations: Public Opinion and the Making of Health Policy in the U.S. and Britain*. Ithaca, N.Y.: Cornell University Press.

———. 2007. "The Implementation and Evolution of Medicare: The Distributional Effects of 'Positive' Policy Feedbacks." In *Remaking America: Democracy and Public Policy in an Age of Inequality,* edited by Joe Soss, Jacob Hacker, and Suzanne Mettler. New York: Russell Sage Foundation.

———. 2010. "The Paradox of Representation: Health Care Reform and De-democratization." Paper prepared for the Rothermere American Institute conference, "The Politics of Ideas and the Politics of Representation: The Case of Health Policy in Rich Democracies." Oxford (November 11–12, 2010).

Jacobs, Lawrence R., and Robert Y. Shapiro. 2000. *Politicians Don't Pander: Political Manipulation and the Loss of Democratic Responsiveness*. Chicago: University of Chicago Press.

Jacobs, Lawrence R., and Theda Skocpol. 2010. *Health Reform and American Politics: What Everyone Needs to Know*. New York: Oxford University Press.

Kaiser Family Foundation. 2009. "American Recovery and Investment Act: Medicaid and Health Care Provisions." Available at: http://www.kff.org/medicaid/upload/7872.pdf (accessed April 22, 2011).

———. 2010a. *Side-by-Side Comparison of Major Health Care Reform Proposals,* June 18, 2010. Washington, D.C.: Kaiser Family Foundation Public Affairs Office. Available at: http://www.kff.org/healthreform/upload/housesenatebill_final .pdf (accessed January 28, 2011).

———. 2010b. "Public Opinion on Health Reform." Washington, D.C.: Kaiser Family Foundation Public Affairs Office. Available at: http://facts.kff.org/results.aspx?view=slides&detail=31 (accessed January 28, 2011).

Leonhardt, David. 2009. "If Health Reform Fails, America's Innovation Gap Will Grow." *New York Times*, December 11, 2009, p. B1.

———. 2010. "In Health Bill, Obama Attacks Wealth Inequality." *New York Times*, March 23, 2010.

Lizza, Ryan. 2009. "Peter Orszag and the Obama Budget." *The New Yorker*, May 4, 2009.

Marmor, Theodore R. 1973. *The Politics of Medicare*. New York: Aldine de Gruyter.

Martin, Jonathan. 2009. "Rahm Emanuel Warns Liberal Groups to Stop Ads." *Politico*, August 6, 2009.

Masterson, Kathleen, and Mary Agnes Carey. 2009. "Charting the Future of the Health Overhaul Bill." *NPR.org*, December 24, 2009. Available at: http://www .npr.org/templates/story/story.php?storyId=120068329 (accessed January 28, 2011).

Meckler, Laura. 2009. "Obama Outlines $313 Billion in New Health Cost Cuts," *Wall Street Journal,* June 13, 2009.

Montgomery, Lori, and Perry Bacon, Jr. 2009. "Key Senator Calls for Narrower Health Reform Measure," *Washington Post*, August 20, 2009.

Murray, Shailagh, and Lori Montgomery. 2010. "Democrats Move Toward Grouping Health Reform with Student-Aid Bill." *Washington Post*, March 12, 2010.

Nichols, Len M., and Sarah Axeen. 2008. "Employer Health Costs in a Global Economy: A Competitive Disadvantage for U.S. Firms." Washington, D.C.: New America Foundation. Available at: http://www.newamerica.net/publications/policy/employer_health_costs_global_economy (accessed January 28, 2011).

Numbers, Ronald L. 1978. *Almost Persuaded: American Physicians and Compulsory Health Insurance, 1912–1920.* Baltimore, Md.: Johns Hopkins University Press.

Obama, Barack. 2007. "New Leadership on Health Care: A Presidential Forum." Speech in Cox Pavilion, Las Vegas, Nevada (March 24, 2007). Available at: http://www.americanprogressaction.org/events/healthforum/files/fulltranscript.pdf (accessed January 30, 2011).

———. 2008. "Barack Obama's Plan for a Healthy America." *Organizing for America.* Available at: http://www.barackobama.com/pdf/HealthPlanFull.pdf (accessed January 28, 2011).

———. 2009. "Text of a Letter from the President to Senator Edward M. Kennedy and Senator Max Baucus." June 3, 2009. Washington: The White House, Office of the Press Secretary. Available at: http://www.whitehouse.gov/the_press_office/Letter-from-President-Obama-to-Chairmen-Edward-M-Kennedy-and-Max-Baucus (accessed January 30, 2011).

Oberlander, Jonathan. 2003. *The Political Life of Medicare.* Chicago: University of Chicago Press.

Office of Management and Budget. 2009. *A New Era of Responsibility: Renewing America's Promise.* Washington: The White House. Available at: http://www.gpoaccess.gov/usbudget/fy10/pdf/fy10-newera.pdf (accessed January 30, 2011).

Page, Benjamin I., and Lawrence R. Jacobs. 2009. *Class War? What Americans Really Think about Economic Inequality.* Chicago: University of Chicago Press.

Pear, Robert. 2010. "Short of Repeal, G.O.P. Will Chip at Health Law." *New York Times*, September 21, 2010, p. A1.

Pearson, Mark. 2009. "Written Statement to Senate Special Committee on Aging." September 30, 2009. Washington, D.C.: Organization for Economic Cooperation and Development, Washington Center. Available at: http://www.oecd.org/dataoecd/5/34/43800977.pdf (accessed January 30, 2011).

Poen, Monte M. 1979. *Harry S. Truman versus the Medical Lobby.* Columbia: University of Missouri Press.

Rutenberg, Jim, and Jackie Calmes. 2009. "False 'Death Panel' Rumor Has Some Familiar Roots." *New York Times*, August 14, 2009, p. A1.

Sahadi, Jeanne. 2010. "Medicare Tax Hikes: What the Rich Will Pay." *CNN Money*,

March 25, 2010. Available at: http://money.cnn.com/2010/03/22/news/economy/medicare_tax_increase/index.htm (accessed January 30, 2011).

Skocpol, Theda. 1996. *Boomerang: Clinton's Health Security Effort and the Turn against Government in U.S. Politics*. New York: W. W. Norton.

———. 2010. "The Political Challenges That May Undermine Health Reform." *Health Affairs* 29(7): 1288–92.

Starr, Paul. 1982. *The Social Transformation of American Medicine*. New York: Basic Books.

Stolberg, Sheryl Gay. 2009. "Public Option in Health Plan May Be Dropped." *New York Times*, August 16, 2009.

Todd, Chuck, and Sheldon Gawiser. 2009. *How Barack Obama Won*. New York: Vintage Books.

Unland, James J. 2004. "Can Community Hospitals Survive without Large Scale Health Reform?" *Journal of Health Care Finance* 30(3): 49–58.

Van de Water, Paul N. 2009. "Proposal to Cap Deductions for High-Income Households Would Reduce Charitable Contributions by Only 1.9 Percent." Washington, D.C.: Center on Budget and Policy Priorities. Available at: http://www.cbpp.org/files/3-3-09bud.pdf (accessed January 30, 2011).

Williamson, Vanessa, and Theda Skocpol. 2010. "The Tea Party and the Rebirth of Republican Conservatism." Unpublished paper, Harvard University, August 2010.

Winerman, Lea. 2010. "Compare the House, Senate, and Reconciliation Bills." *PBS News Hour*, March 19, 2010.

Young, Alison. 2010. "Health Consumers to Start Feeling Effects." *USA Today*, September 22, 2010, p. 8A.

Chapter 3 | Eliminating the Market Middle-Man: Redirecting and Expanding Support for College Students

Suzanne Mettler

"THROUGHOUT OUR HISTORY, education has been at the heart of a bargain this nation has made with its citizens: If you work hard and take responsibility, you'll have a chance for a better life." Writing these words in his book *The Audacity of Hope*, Barack Obama asserted that investments in education offer the most promising way the United States can grow more competitive in the global economy and "modernize and rebuild the social compact that FDR first stitched together in the middle of the last century" (2006, 159). Throughout the 2008 presidential campaign, Obama continually stressed the need to make college more affordable and accessible and to boost graduation rates. Campaigning in Iowa, he announced that an Obama administration would aim to "put a college education within reach of every American" (2007, 4). Once elected, in his first speech to a joint session of Congress he proclaimed, "By 2020, America will once again have the highest proportion of college graduates in the world" (2009a). As some in the higher education policy community in Washington, D.C., noted, never before has a presidential administration placed so much value on education (confidential interviews, 2010).

Yet while the emphasis Obama places on education is new, in stressing the role of national government in promoting higher education he embraces an American tradition with roots as old as the republic itself. Historically, beginning with eighteenth-century land grants and the nineteenth century's Morrill Act, followed by the twentieth century's student aid legislation, the United States used government authority effectively to encourage the development of institutions of higher education and access to college among citizens. In the decades after World War II, the nation led the world in the caliber of its universities and colleges and in its rates of educational attainment: as recently as thirty years ago, 37 percent of Americans age twenty-five through thirty-four held four-year college degrees (OECD 2007).

In recent decades, however, progress flagged: policies no longer continued to expand access to higher education, and policymakers failed to respond accordingly. Over time, student aid policies yielded unintended policy feedback effects. They inadvertently empowered banks and other lenders, which in turn prompted political leaders to curry favor with them to attract campaign contributions. Increasingly, lenders developed strong ties to elected officials as well as to agency staff. In the system that emerged, politicians guarded lenders' subsidies and terms, as programs that could have broadened access were left to languish and few new alternatives received serious consideration. Thus, among today's twenty-five- to thirty-four-year-old Americans, still only 39 percent hold four-year college degrees, barely more than their parents' generation, and ten nations have surpassed the United States in college graduation rates (OECD 2007).

In the middle of the twentieth century, moreover, public policies had promoted equal opportunity by enabling growing percentages of young people from low- to moderate-income backgrounds to go to college. In recent decades, by contrast, they lost their capacity to mitigate inequality. Between 1980 and 2007, the percentage of college graduates from families in the bottom income quartile increased from 6.5 percent to 9.8 percent, a net change of just over 3 percentage points; among those from families in the top quartile, by contrast, the rates soared from 33.6 to 75.9 percent, a 42.3 percentage point increase. Among those in the second and third quartiles, progress was also less than impressive in both absolute and relative terms, growing to 18.3 percent and 33.4 percent, respectively (Mortenson 2007). Increasingly, patterns of college attainment exacerbate economic stratification.

In vowing to set college graduation rates back on course, Obama put forth a highly ambitious goal. To reorient policies, his administration would first need to eradicate the existing system of bank-based student lending, which had itself promulgated an entrenched set of political-economic arrangements, and then to replace it with direct lending. It was a task with parallels to what Stephen Skowronek, describing the political challenges confronting reformers of the Progressive Era, calls "state building as reconstruction" (1982, 167). Only if Obama could accomplish this politically arduous task of destroying student lending in the form that had existed since 1965—a goal Democrats had hoped to achieve for nearly two decades and for which President Clinton had managed to achieve only a modest beginning—would it be possible to pursue innovative policies that might actually boost graduation rates. Obama approached these goals in tandem: he aimed to capture the savings on lender subsidies and to use them both to enhance Pell Grants, making them more generous and endowing the program with entitlement status, and to provide substantial funds to community colleges.

Would President Obama manage to accomplish his goals for higher education policy? As we will see, he achieved a tremendous reorientation in some respects, actually terminating the entrenched system that had privileged lenders and replacing it with loans made directly by government. He also succeeded in his goal of extending generous new tax tuition credits to all but the wealthiest Americans. In other regards, he encountered greater resistance, finding it impossible to make Pell Grants an entitlement or to win the sweeping new programs for community colleges that he had promoted.

The puzzle this paper addresses is why the Obama administration managed to succeed so masterfully in some respects, achieving what seemed unimaginable just a few years ago, yet fell short in others, even in instances when the odds seemed comparable or even less daunting. I combine a historical policy feedback framework with insights about agenda-setting to analyze how existing policies fostered political effects and to explain the circumstances under which change was possible, and to what extent. As noted, student loan policies had long fostered feedback effects that made them deeply entrenched—seemingly indomitable. Yet, as we will see, beginning in 2006 several events signaled that such development had finally become, after decades of strength, substantially weakened. Bank-based student lending had become the victim of both its own self-destruction and the crush of external circumstances, namely the economic collapse. Still, reform was by no means inevitable. As John Kingdon has shown, policy change is possible when the typically independent streams of problem recognition, viable policy alternatives, and political will join and coalesce (1995, 87). In the case of student loan reform, a moment of political opportunity emerged for several reasons. I highlight the ways in which the recession exposed the vulnerabilities of the existing student loan system and reshaped the realm of the possible; the advocacy by administrative agency staff that promoted other goals of the president; and the parallel journey of health care reform, which imperiled student aid policy in some respects but salvaged it in others, particularly with respect to the shift to direct lending. To the extent change actually occurred in Pell

Grants and community college funding, it was because reformers were able to link their fate to the shift to direct lending; to the extent that progress on these programs was curtailed, they suffered a similar fate to other initiatives Obama promoted—becoming the victim of the financial crisis and lack of cohesion within the Democratic Party.

I begin by placing the president's policy objectives in historical context, explaining how policies created in the past have influenced current possibilities. Then I detail the developments that have occurred since January 2009. This section relies especially on interviews conducted in Washington, D.C., during the spring of 2010 with U.S. Department of Education officials, Capitol Hill staffers, lobbyists, and representatives of organizations with a stake in higher education policy.[1]

SETTING THE STAGE: EXISTING POLICIES AND THEIR POLITICS

During the middle of the twentieth century, U.S. policymakers created landmark policies—the GI Bill, the National Defense Education Act of 1958, the Higher Education Act of 1965, and in a 1972 reauthorization of that law, Pell Grants. Early on, these policies not only boosted college degree attainment generally, but they also helped growing numbers of Americans from across the economic spectrum to pursue higher education. Since 1980, however, the distribution of college degrees has become far more heavily skewed to those from the highest income quartile (Mortenson 2007). Although generally young people from higher-income backgrounds are more likely to excel in important prerequisites for college such as grades and scores on standardized tests, controlling for such factors reveals that among individuals with the same academic credentials, those from less advantaged families are less likely to attend college (Kane 2004, 332–35).

A number of factors caused progress to stall, not least the escalation of tuition rates, but it is also true that existing policies failed to perform as successfully as they once did. In part, policymakers simply neglected to update policies, but more important, over the past fifteen years they changed policies in ways that resulted in their being less effective than they had been in expanding access to college.[2] Considering U.S. higher education policy in historical perspective, Obama can be understood as attempting to restore the spirit of equal opportunity that originally flowed from the landmark Higher Education Act of 1965 (HEA), and at the same time to update its core policies to meet contemporary challenges. This is no small feat because, over time, the law developed in unintended ways

that undermined its original aims and fostered the entrenchment and po-
liticization of powerful interests.

The HEA constitutes the contemporary foundation of U.S. higher education policy, governing financial assistance to students as well as incentives for institutional development. When initiated by President Lyndon
B. Johnson, the law's primary goal was to permit Americans equal opportunity in pursuing college degrees. It did so in three major ways: by offering funds to developing institutions, namely historically black and community colleges; by establishing guaranteed student loans (GSL), which
became known as federal family education loans (FFEL); and by offering
grants to low-income students.[3] Because banks had been reluctant to lend
to students who had no credit history and were considered a bad risk,
policymakers created the GSL program to give banks the incentive to lend
to them. As long as lending organizations agreed to low-interest terms, the
government subsidized them by paying half the interest on loans and assuming the risk, promising to pay the balance on defaulted loans. In 1972
amendments to HEA, policymakers bolstered student loans further by
creating the Student Loan Marketing Association (SLM, or Sallie Mae) to
provide a secondary market that would further encourage lending to students. They also enlarged and refashioned the grants program, mandating
that funds be delivered directly to low-income students rather than ad-
ministered to institutions to distribute; these became known as Pell Grants
(Gladieux and Wolanin 1976).

Although the Higher Education Act remained intact—indeed, it has
been reauthorized by Congress eight times, has grown from eight to eleven
titles, and its subsections have mushroomed in number—its ability to foster equal opportunity to higher education has not proven sustainable. Pell
Grants belong to the discretionary part of the federal budget rather than to
mandatory spending; Congress must take action even to maintain benefit
levels as the cost of living rises, but this requires repeated battles over
rates. Amid fiscal worries and partisan conflict, such updating failed to
occur, such that the average Pell Grant deteriorated in real value during
the 1980s and 1990s. Meanwhile, tuition soared at four-year institutions,
outpacing the growth of inflation and median household income. As a
result, overall the value of the maximum Pell diminished from covering
more than 80 percent of the costs of attendance at a public institution in
the mid-1970s to about 40 percent; as a share of private tuition, it shrank
from nearly 40 percent to about 15 percent (College Board 2004; King 2000,
9–10). The demise of these grants left students to rely on loans. Throughout the 1980s, Democrats still promoted student loans in the form in which
they had created them in 1965 and 1972, in effect defending lenders' inter-

ests; Republicans, meanwhile, expressed concern that subsidies amounted to unnecessary government spending. Nonetheless, the two parties found agreement far more readily over student loans, for which they simply needed to ease borrowing limits and restrictions, than over Pell Grants, which led to fractious battles over new spending proposals (Gladieux and Hauptman 1995). As a result, loans replaced grants as the prominent source of student aid; by 2002 the average undergraduate completed her studies $18,900 in debt (Baum and O'Malley 2003). Accordingly, FFEL fostered an increasingly lucrative business for banks and other lenders. Yet such loans failed to expand access to the less well off because they have had greater difficulty in being approved to borrow and been less willing to do so (Price 2004, 82).

As the HEA developed in ways contrary to the vision of its creators, policymakers in both parties began to perceive the problems. In the late 1980s, an official in the George H. W. Bush administration hatched the idea of direct lending by government to avoid paying hefty fees to banks. A bipartisan group began to promote the idea, managing to achieve a pilot program in the 1992 HEA reauthorization. Liberal Democrats that same year had also hoped to make Pell Grants an entitlement, with rates tied to inflation and benefits guaranteed to eligible students as part of mandatory spending. This was deemed necessary not only because of the problem of deteriorating benefit levels but also because the program has repeatedly been subject to budget shortfalls; these occur because more students enroll than appropriators anticipated, requiring legislators to "backfill" billions of dollars midway through the year. Others in the party refused to support the switch to entitlement status, however, citing the large deficit (Mettler 2008).

When Bill Clinton was elected president, he made the pursuit of 100 percent direct lending one of his initial goals. Suddenly, the terms of the battle changed dramatically, and lenders themselves mobilized politically. The Consumer Bankers' Association brought representatives from banks all over the nation to Capitol Hill to lobby, and Sallie Mae launched a public relations campaign. Congress adopted a weakened version of Clinton's plan, permitting the adoption of direct lending on only a limited basis. Perhaps most significant, the fight marked the end of the fragile bipartisanship in higher education policymaking that had survived the Reagan era (Mettler 2009).

Once Republicans took control of both chambers of Congress in 1995, members of both parties became more sharply polarized in their positions on student loans and traded the postures they had each held less than one decade earlier. Most Democrats—with some exceptions—abandoned their prior defense of the lenders. Republicans, by contrast, dropped their concerns about government spending on student loan subsidies and began to work in tandem with lenders, courting them as a source of campaign contributions while seeking rates and terms that boosted their profits (confidential interviews, 2007, 2010).[4]

Over time, student loans generated policy feedback effects, reshaping politics in ways that promoted the interests of powerful banks and lenders rather than equal opportunity for students. Between 1995 and 2005, Sallie Mae's stock returned nearly 2,000 percent, compared with the S&P 500's average 228 percent gain (McLean 2005). In 2006, its CEO was the most highly compensated in the nation, receiving $37 million annually in salary, bonus, and stock awards (*Washington Post* 2006). Lenders proceeded to develop their political capacity to protect the policies that served them so well. They created several new organizations based in Washington, D.C., to represent their interests, and became intensely involved in campaign financing and lobbying. Sallie Mae established its political action committee (PAC) in the late 1990s; by 2006 it emerged as the top donor within the entire finance and credit industry, and fellow donor Nelnet ranked fifth. By 2007, Sallie Mae also outspent all other finance and credit companies—including VISA, MasterCard, and American Express—on lobbying, devoting over $5 million to such activities (Center for Responsive Politics 2010). Through increasingly tight relationships with Republican leaders, the industry gained active support from the party in power.

Late in 2006, however, the political landscape began to change once again. Investigative journalists exposed the stunning profits enjoyed by lenders and the mutually supportive relationship between them and conservative politicians. When young people in 2006 voted at the highest rates in a midterm election in years, helping Democrats to take back control of both chambers of Congress, the victorious party took notice and considered how to respond (confidential interviews, 2007, 2010). In 2007, the newly elected Congress unveiled legislation that put lenders on the defensive. Then–New York Attorney General Andrew Cuomo launched an investigation into the lending practices of Sallie Mae and others, claiming that they maintained improper relationships with institutions of higher education, and that these had been aided by Bush administration appointees in the U.S. Department of Education. The Bush White House began to separate itself from Republicans in Congress by pursuing a course independent from the lenders: it replaced several of its political appointees in the department who had worked in the lending industry for years beforehand, and Bush signed into law the College Cost Reduction and Access Act of 2007, which reduced subsidies to lenders and boosted Pell Grant levels (confidential interviews, 2010; Basken 2007; Shapira 2007). In 2008, when the credit crisis hit and private sources of credit evaporated, Congress intervened and enacted the Ensuring Continued Access to Student Loans Act (ECASLA), authorizing the Department of Education to act as a secondary market, buying FFEL loans from lenders and thus enabling them to stay afloat (Delisle 2009).

As Barack Obama won the presidency, the lenders' star was fading and momentum rising to create and refashion policies to make college more accessible and to elevate completion rates. For years, the FFEL program had fostered feedback effects that promoted its growth, but once circumstances threatened its legitimacy and viability, direct lending emerged as the policy alternative of choice. The fragile foothold reformers had established beginning in 1993, which had survived throughout years when administrators neglected to implement existing law, suddenly gained new credibility as the way reformers might be able to build anew (confidential interviews, 2010). For years, lenders and their allies in Congress had dominated student aid policy, foreclosing new approaches that could expand access to college and boost graduation rates. Now it appeared that their dominance might be over and the way cleared for sweeping changes. Yet, new obstacles to success would arise from within the Democratic Party, emerging both from the limitations of some of its policy alternatives and from stonewalling by some of its own members in Congress.

EARLY ACTION

Once Obama took office, higher education provisions assumed a prominent place in his first major initiative, the economic stimulus bill. The American Recovery and Reinvestment Act of 2009 directed federal dollars toward students and colleges in several ways. Fully 37 percent of the $787 billion stimulus package was allocated in the form of tax credits, and Obama's signature creation for higher education—the American Opportunity Tax Credit—fit into that part of the legislation. The policy, which he had spoken about throughout his campaign, resembled the HOPE Education Tax Credit that Clinton had created in 1997, but differed in some respects: it can be claimed for four years of college rather than only the first two; the benefit maximum is $2,500, representing a $700 increase; whereas the earlier credit was limited to households with earnings up to $48,000 for single earners and $96,000 for couples, the new credit reaches well up into upper-middle-income households earning up to $90,000 and $180,000, respectively; and finally, it is partially refundable, meaning that even those with no tax liability can claim up to $1,000 (Onink 2009).

Yet, although the education tax credit consumed $49 billion, neither advocates for expanded access to higher education nor policy analysts greeted it with much enthusiasm. Such policies have been criticized for doing little more than offsetting the tuition costs of those who would attend college otherwise, and possibly even encouraging institutions to raise tuition (Dynarski 2000; Long 2003; confidential interviews, 2010). Proponents of social tax expenditures in the Obama administration believed that the refundability feature of the new policy would help make it more accessible to low-income people, but the fact that it is obtained only long after tuition is paid makes it unlikely to influence enrollment decisions. Further, Americans seemed little aware of this policy or other tax breaks in the stimulus, which were extended to 95 percent of households with employed members. One year later, when asked whether the Obama administration had increased taxes, decreased taxes, or kept them the same, only 12 percent said that taxes had been decreased, and 24 percent believed they had been increased (CBS News/*New York Times* 2010).

The stimulus bill also devoted $15.6 billion to the Pell Grant program. It improved their availability, with the aim of reaching 7 million low- and moderate-income individuals, and boosted maximum grant levels up from $4,731 to $5,550 (U.S. Congress 2009a; U.S. Department of Education 2009; *CQ Weekly* 2009).[5]

Meanwhile, the president began to fill positions in the U.S. Department of Education, recruiting individuals whose priorities in higher education policy paired well with his own. Although Obama's choice for secretary, Arne Duncan, specialized in K-12 education, he emphasized higher education with his appointments, and put a special focus on access issues. As under secretary he named Martha Kanter, who had worked in the California community college system, the nation's largest, for thirty years, most recently as chancellor of the Foothill–De Anza Community College District in California. Kanter was widely regarded as an innovator in the quest for improved graduation and retention rates, and her appointment constituted an important symbolic victory for the community college sector, typically marginalized in federal policymaking (Keller 2009; confidential interviews, 2010). Obama also named Robert Shireman to be deputy under secretary for the Department of Education, a position that does not require Senate confirmation. Shireman has been regarded as a lightning rod in the higher education arena, having worked for direct lending to replace the FFEL program beginning on the staff of Senator Paul Simon in the late 1980s and then in the Clinton administration during the 1993 battle. Among advocates of expanded access, he has been widely regarded for his cutting-edge ideas and political savvy to match; among defenders of lenders and banks, he has long been despised. Members of both camps agree that he could not have been confirmed given the challenges he presents to existing arrangements (confidential interviews, 2007, 2010).

TOWARD RESTRUCTURED STUDENT FINANCIAL AID

Even after achieving considerable funds for higher education in the stimulus bill, Obama proceeded to place the issue, along with health care reform, at the top of his domestic policy agenda for 2009. The 2010 budget he submitted to Congress at the end of February featured his major goals. First, he aimed to terminate the FFEL student loan program, replacing it entirely with direct lending. Second, he proposed to use the savings—the funds no longer siphoned off to lenders—to make Pell Grants an entitlement, with increases indexed henceforward to the Consumer Price Index (CPI), and to provide funds to states and community colleges to foster student readiness and degree completion.

The plan to end bank-based student lending was viewed in starkly different terms by its proponents and opponents. From Obama's announcement of the initiative through its eventual passage in 2010, critics termed it a "government takeover," warning that 100 percent direct lending would undermine "choice and competition" and would lead to deteriorating customer service for student borrowers and to higher costs for taxpayers (see Consumer Bankers Association 2009; Alarkon 2009). As one Republican staffer put it, "It would make the U.S. Department of Education one of the ten largest banks in the country, but Arne Duncan is not a banker" (confidential interview, 2010). Obama's 2010 budget overview, by contrast, referred to the existing FFEL system as operating "through entitlements for lenders," in terms of both the subsidies government provided to them and the ability that government's guarantee on loans gave them to acquire funds from investors. Department of Education officials emphasized that under direct lending, the private sector would continue to perform several roles, given that the federal government would use "competitive Treasury auctions to acquire capital for student loans from private investors" and the disbursement, servicing, and collection of loans would be carried out through a "competitive contracting process" (Office of Management and Budget 2009; confidential interviews, 2010).

Obama's plan to shift entirely to direct lending received an enormous boost when the Congressional Budget Office released its assessment of the cost savings that would result. Whereas the White House had predicted that replacing FFEL would lower federal spending by $47 billion over ten years, the CBO projected that figure to be nearly twice as large, $87 billion (Lederman 2009b). In the words of the American Council on Education lobbyist Terry Hartle, this announcement was a "game changer" (Gerstein 2009). It diffused the arguments of FFEL advocates who claimed that the system rewarded free enterprise and competition: in fact, that approach was actually costlier. Trade associations within the National Center for Higher Education, some of which had been concerned about their member institutions' capacity to convert to direct lending, quickly dropped their reservations and embraced the change (confidential interviews, 2010).

Emboldened, Obama delivered a fiery speech in April in which he spoke out against the ways that the existing system privileged lenders:

> Under the FFEL program, lenders get a big government subsidy with every loan they make. And these loans are then guaranteed with taxpayer money, which means that if a student defaults, a lender can get back almost all of its money from our government. . . . Taxpayers are paying banks a premium to act as middlemen—a premium that costs the American people billions of dollars each year. . . . Well, that's a premium we cannot afford—not when we could be investing the same money in our students, in our economy, and in our country. (Obama 2009b)

Obama concluded by taking on the lenders directly:

> The banks and the lenders who have reaped a windfall from these subsidies have mobilized an army of lobbyists to try to keep things the way they are. They are gearing up for battle. So am I. They will fight for their special interests. I will fight for . . . American students and their families. And for those who care about America's future, this is a battle we can't afford to lose. (Obama 2009b)

Using language that contrasted with his more muted treatment of the financial sector and health insurance industries, the president expressed confidence that his administration would prevail in its efforts to transform higher education policy.

In an environment in which every legislative initiative requires the support of at least sixty senators to prevent a filibuster, such language might have sounded risky, particularly given that some Democrats had already expressed their opposition to the termination of FFEL. As early as spring of 2009, Nebraska Senator Ben Nelson made clear that he opposed Obama's plan because the lender Nelnet, based in Lincoln, employed 1,000 people in the state. "I think it would be the wrong direction for people to outsource jobs from Lincoln, Nebraska to Washington, D.C.," said Nelson, whose most generous campaign donor over the previous five years had been the student lending organization (Howard 2009). Blanche Lincoln of Arkansas also expressed concerns about potential job losses in her state

(Gerstein 2009). Cognizant that they could not attain sixty supportive votes, in April 2009 Democratic leaders in the budget committees of both chambers planned ahead: they included "reconciliation instructions" in the compromise budget outline that required the committees responsible for education policy to reduce program spending by one billion or more (confidential interviews, 2010). In effect, this would permit the administration's plan for direct lending to be included in a reconciliation bill, thus requiring only fifty-one votes for passage, not the sixty necessary to withstand a filibuster (Field 2009d).

Student loan reform thus appeared to be on track, but Obama's plans for Pell Grants encountered some unexpected early resistance. Advocates both within and outside of government, including representatives of the higher education trade associations, were hopeful that this time—unlike in 1992—the plan could succeed (confidential interviews, 2010). Once again, however, the effort was stymied by Democrats themselves. Senate Budget Committee Chair Kent Conrad (D-ND) and House Appropriations Committee Chair David Obey (D-WI) objected, not wanting to lose authority over the appropriations process (Gerstein 2009). Meanwhile, neither did the chairman of the House Education and Labor Committee, Representative George Miller (D-CA), push for entitlement status, as he considered the pursuit of 100 percent direct lending to be "enough of a fight" already. He also believed that by legislating a formula for regular increases, Congress could produce essentially the same result (confidential interviews, 2010).

As summer began, Obama highlighted the third aspect of his plan for higher education: the strengthening of community colleges. In a July speech at Macomb Community College in Michigan, he emphasized the integral role such institutions play in economic development through job training, and he called on them to produce 5 million new graduates by 2020. He proposed $9 billion for the American Graduation Initiative (AGI), featuring competitive grants to support innovative efforts to improve job training or to strengthen college completion rates; $2.5 billion to back loans for colleges to build and renovate facilities; and $500 million to promote development of online courses (Jaschik 2009). These plans were introduced in the House in legislation that would require states and colleges to meet benchmarks in order to receive the money (Field 2009a). Leaders of community colleges expressed enthusiasm for the programs. Yet, highlighting the different priorities of affluent private institutions, David L. Warren, president of the National Association of Independent Colleges and Universities, expressed concern that the approach could "encroach upon the independence of all institutions" (Field 2009a). Proponents of community colleges, which educate one in three of the nation's college students and do so with meager resources, resented this lack of support. Still, even some of them also voiced reservations privately about the benchmarking approach, leery that it would introduce administrative burdens to colleges and fail to reward true experimentation (confidential interviews, 2010).

ACTION IN THE HOUSE

Over the ensuing months, lenders themselves promoted proposals to re-structure student lending (Field 2009e). A plan spearheaded by Sallie Mae and put forward in conjunction with Nelnet and a few other large-volume, for-profit lenders attracted the most attention because it claimed to offer equivalent savings to the administration's plan. This alternative effec-tively acknowledged that the private lenders themselves lacked access to capital: it would eliminate subsidies to lenders and require the federal government to take ownership of loans—as they did under the present arrangements, known as ECASLA. Yet, the hallmark of the plan was that it would perpetuate a substantial role for the lenders—in loan origination, servicing, and collection—and mandate that government would pay them fees for such activities. The lenders argued that this approach would pre-serve competition, would eliminate the need for campuses to engage in what could be an onerous switch to direct lending, and would avoid job losses.

The plan garnered strikingly little support. In what congressional staff-ers considered a tactical error on the part of Sallie Mae, it failed to repre-sent the interests of smaller nonprofit lenders. Members of Congress have far greater allegiance to the smaller lenders because they are distributed widely throughout states and congressional districts across the nation, whereas Sallie Mae had branches and employees in only a few localities. The failure to include them, some staffers commented, was in keeping with the organization's self-interested style; even policy actors allied with the lender remarked on its "tone-deaf" attributes (confidential interviews, 2010). In addition, the alternative did not satisfy congressional Repub-licans because it did not originate with private capital but with gov-ernment. From their perspective, it amounted to a "bloated direct loan program," with the added expense of fees paid to lenders (confidential interviews, 2010).

Within days, Miller repudiated the lenders' alternative, saying, "It's un-fortunate that a small number of lenders are using legislative gimmicks to mask the fact that their proposal would divert $15 billion into their own pockets at the expense of students" (Herszenhorn 2009). Instead, on July 21, he introduced legislation modeled on Obama's plans, calling for an end to the bank-based lending program and using the savings to direct funds to Pell Grants, community colleges, and other programs geared to help students. The committee approved the legislation that same day in a vote of 30 to 17, with all members voting along party lines except for two Republicans who also voted in favor, Tom Petri of Wisconsin and Todd R. Platts of Pennsylvania (Burd 2009; Peterson 2009). Interestingly, no member of either party introduced a substitute amendment representing the lenders' alternative proposal.

Surprisingly, Republicans—after years of working actively in tandem with the lenders—took a passive approach toward policy developments. Certainly, they spoke out frequently to lament the "government takeover" being launched by the majority. As articulated by the ranking member of the committee, John Kline of Minnesota: "The speed with which the Democrats are orchestrating a full government takeover of our classrooms and communities is astonishing. First, we saw a drive toward complete government takeover of our nation's health care system. Now we see government seizing control of student lending, forcing the private sector out and welcoming a mountain of public debt. I'm almost afraid to ask: What part of our lives will be handed over to government next?" (Lederman 2009a)

Yet, aside from such rhetoric, Republicans refrained from putting forward a serious alternative that might have gleaned support from moderate Democrats, a plan that could have done more for small lenders than the option advanced by Sallie Mae. The only substitute amendment, offered by Republican Brett Guthrie of Kentucky, essentially asked Congress to proceed more slowly, retaining the existing student loan system while conducting a study intended to find "a new model for maintaining a strong public-private partnership for student lending" (U.S. Congress 2009b).[6] It was rejected by the same group of twenty-eight Democrats and two Republicans that approved the legislation (U.S. Congress 2009c). The lack of more energetic opposition to the termination of the bank-based system reflects, in part, the Republicans' current political strategy of unwillingness to compromise with the Democrats. As one staffer put it, "If we had been willing to modify some components of the legislation, it would have appeared as if we endorsed others put forward by the majority, when in fact there are wide philosophical differences between us." In addition, the minority party's passivity on student lending reveals the practical impossibility amid current economic circumstances of successfully devising a feasible alternative to direct lending that both originates with private capital and offers government cost savings (confidential interviews, 2010).

With the opposition effectively silenced, the full House proceeded quickly to approve Obama's plans. Just a few days later, in votes mostly along party lines, the chamber passed the spending bill for the labor, education, and health and human services components of the federal budget. In keeping with the terms of the stimulus bill, it included $17.8 billion for Pell Grants, setting the maximum grant at $5,500. It surpassed the president's plan by including $146 million more for historically black and tribal colleges and institutions enrolling large numbers of minority students (Lederman 2009c; Field 2009b). Lenders had developed close allegiances over the years with financial aid officers at minority-serving institutions and with members of the Congressional Black Caucus; those groups, in turn, had supported them in the struggle to preserve FFEL, and so such funds were deemed necessary to shift their support to the president's approach (Basken 2010d).

In mid-September, the full House approved the Student Aid and Fiscal Responsibility Act (HR 3221, which became known as SAFRA) by a vote of 253 to 171. Six Republicans joined Democrats in support and four Democrats allied with Republicans in opposition (U.S. Congress 2009e).[7] The legislation mandated the end of FFEL, requiring all colleges to shift to direct federal lending by July 1, 2010; it permitted lenders to compete to service loans, but no longer to originate them. The legislation used $40 billion of the projected savings from FFEL to boost Pell Grants, not by making the grants a formal entitlement, but by ensuring annual increases of CPI plus 1 percent. As such, the maximum award was set to grow from $5,350 to $5,550 in 2010, with additional increases that would bring it to $6,900 in 2019. Obama's plans for community colleges were also included: $10 billion for the AGI, aimed to elevate the number of graduates by 5 million by 2020; plus an expansion of the existing College Access Challenge Grant program, which awards grants to individual colleges and states that put forward innovative approaches to elevating enrollment and graduation rates (Lewin 2009a; Field 2009c; Lederman 2009d; U.S. Congress 2009d).

Republicans once again put forward a substitute amendment calling for a commission to develop a new private-sector model for student lending, preserving FFEL in the meanwhile; the vote was 165 votes in favor and 265 opposed. Other Republican amendments proposed elimination of specific parts of the bill and using the funds instead for deficit reduction. Representative Virginia Foxx (R-NC), for example, a former president of a community college, objected to the community college funds on the ground that the graduation initiatives would interfere with students' privacy. Her amendment, like the others, failed (U.S. Congress 2009e).

In effect, the House granted the president everything he wanted with the exception of making Pell Grants an entitlement. Democratic leaders confidently predicted that the Senate would also pass the legislation within a few short weeks. Such optimism soon proved to be misguided.

MOBILIZATION AND COUNTERMOBILIZATION DURING THE LONG WAIT

As the autumn proceeded, the Senate stalled in its efforts to act on the president's top priority, health care reform. Leaders decided to forestall the chamber's action on higher education policy in hopes of leaving the door open to combining the two issues in a reconciliation package, only one of which is permitted per session, if necessary. This strategy was not without risks because the chairman of the budget committee, Senator Conrad, whose support would be necessary for the approach to work, had expressed reservations about attempts to enact major policy changes through budget reconciliation (Delisle 2010). Moreover, Conrad had never been a strong supporter of direct lending, likely because student lending by the Bank of North Dakota provided a significant number of jobs and revenues to his home state (Delisle 2010). Nonetheless, under the circumstances, the gamble seemed the best the Democrats could manage.

Lenders used the delay to mobilize at the grassroots and elite levels, attempting to fight the proposed changes to student lending and to retain a more significant role for themselves in its future. Sallie Mae mobilized workers and residents in the towns where it employed the greatest numbers: Fishers and Muncie, Indiana; Lynn Haven, Florida; and Wilkes-Barre, Pennsylvania. In Fishers, more than 81,000 individuals signed a petition urging Congress to preserve a role for lenders. At a rally of company employees, hundreds of whom donned matching t-shirts that read "Protect Indiana Jobs," Sallie Mae CEO Albert Lord attempted to stir populist anger, declaring, "There's Washington, and then there's the rest of the country. This is the rest of the country" (Nelson 2009; Lichtblau 2010).

Meanwhile, on Capitol Hill, lenders set the goal of gaining support from at least five moderate Democratic senators to retain the FFEL program. They devoted millions of dollars to lobbying; Sallie Mae alone spent more than $4 million on it in 2009, the second-largest amount it had ever spent in one year (slightly less than in 2007). To lobby on its behalf, the company hired former Clinton administration official Jamie Gorelick and Democratic fundraiser Tony Podesta, whose brother John had led the Obama transition (Alarkon 2009; Herszenhorn 2009; Knight 2009; Dreas 2009).

By November, the lenders appeared to be gaining ground: analysts predicted that Obama's proposal lacked the support of enough senators to pass (Dreas 2009). Democrat Bob Casey from Pennsylvania, together with eleven moderate Democrats, announced their support for a revised version of the lenders' alternative approach (Boles 2009). Yet, according to staffers on the Hill, they never offered "a serious compromise proposal." Just as the lenders' alternative had not been introduced in the House Education and Labor Committee, neither did either Casey or his colleagues put forward a bill containing its provisions in the Senate. In fact, some of the senators admitted privately that they felt they had to speak out about their concerns about job losses in their states, but that they would ultimately vote in support of legislation similar to SAFRA (confidential interviews, 2010).

As lenders struggled to oppose loan reform, the two broad-based membership organizations that address student aid issues, the United States Student Association (USSA) and U.S. Public Interest and Research Group (PIRG), worked energetically to promote it. As the financial crisis brought state budget cuts for public universities and colleges, these organizations found their memberships rolls on the rise. The leadership of both organizations had spent years working to replace FFEL with direct lending; the achievement of that goal combined with improved student aid in the 2009 and 2010 legislation made it a focal point for mobilizing their grass roots. And as one organizational leader put it, "Students have been waiting for a while to get behind something they felt would impact them directly." During one week in September, PIRG and its member groups around the nation collected petitions from students indicating the amount of debt they would have once they graduated, and attached each to a brick; displayed in combination, the bricks constituted a "Wall of Debt" that powerfully depicted the issues students faced. In October, USSA, PIRG, and other associations united forces for a "Raising Pell" Week of Activism, in which they used social networking sites to reach students and mobilized them in two days of a national youth call-in and fax-in calling on the Senate to pass SAFRA. They recruited numerous organizations to be fellow signatories on an ad to the leaders of the Senate HELP committee that was published in *Politico*, highlighting the need for student aid reform (confidential interviews, 2010, 2011).

The student organizations generated heightened activity in states across the country in which senators were considered swing votes, often because the student loan industry employed residents. The groups helped stimulate the publication of newspaper editorials in numerous locations, and organized a financial aid hearing with Casey in Pennsylvania. In some instances, they not only activated students but also coordinated their efforts with labor organizations, including the AFL-CIO and the Service Employees International Union (SEIU), and with civil rights organizations such as the NAACP and La Raza. In some local areas where lenders argued that the demise of FFEL would mean lost jobs, labor organizations probed deeper; in at least one case they revealed that the new servicing activities would actually require Sallie Mae and others to move jobs back to the United States, thus increasing employment (confidential interviews, 2010, 2011).

Meanwhile, the battle over the future of student loans encompassed a broader scope of conflict by involving the administrative state. Under the leadership of Obama appointees, the Department of Education reversed its posture of the past several years and actively encouraged colleges to switch to direct lending (Lewin 2009b). In July 2009, department officials sent a letter to college presidents announcing plans to facilitate a "smooth process for the transition of schools into the Direct Loan Program." They promised to expand the capacity of an automated system to aid in loan disbursement, and to award private firms contracts for servicing them (Taggart 2009). Officials pointed out that ECASLA, the law through which government had shored up the lenders during the credit crisis, was set to expire on July 1, 2010; furthermore, SAFRA, as passed by the House in September 2010, dictated that all schools convert to direct lending by that date. If schools did not take advance action, they would not be prepared to make the change once the Senate approved the legislation (Lewin 2009b; confidential interviews, 2010). Such efforts appeared effective: by later in 2009 the market share of direct lending relative to FFEL loans had increased to 42 percent, up from 29 percent one year earlier (*Chronicle of Higher Education* 2009).

Congressional Republicans strenuously objected to the Department's advocacy for direct lending, arguing that it was pushing change that lawmakers had not yet approved. In November, several of them who were members of the House Education and Labor Committee wrote to Secretary Duncan, criticizing the agency for attempting to mobilize college leaders in support of the administration's agenda rather than serving as an "impartial agent" (Kline 2009). The following month, Republican leaders from both the House and Senate drafted an open letter to college and university leaders: "Contrary to recent statements made by the Department of Education, the elimination of the FFEL program is not imminent. There remains widespread, bipartisan support in Congress to continue the FFEL program during these difficult times" (Enzi 2009).

Although these efforts to mobilize support and opposition to the student aid legislation persisted, in the Senate chamber itself the issue remained on hold. Democratic leaders, so confident in early fall that a bill would gain approval quickly through normal voting procedures, grew less certain as the months dragged on. Finally, on December 24, the Senate approved a health care bill by the requisite sixty votes, and Congress recessed for the holidays. As 2010 began, Obama met with Democratic leaders to meld the health care bills passed by each chamber in preparation for final votes on the issue, and it seemed that higher education policy would soon have its own moment.

Then in the special Massachusetts Senate election on January 19, Republican Scott Brown surprised the nation and won the seat the late Ted Kennedy had held for forty-seven years. On a symbolic level, Kennedy's death had already devastated the higher education community: he had been widely regarded as the last surviving member of a cadre of congressional leaders who had governed on their issues successfully throughout past decades; with the others retired from Congress, his knowledge of the intricacies of reauthorization and such matters had been unsurpassed (confidential interviews, 2007). Now, the Brown victory terminated the Democrats' filibuster-proof majority in the Senate and upended legislative plans for health care reform and also, therefore, for the student aid bill. Although leaders had long envisioned the possibility of combining the two issues in the reconciliation process, the way forward was anything but clear.

THE GRAND FINALE

Seemingly undaunted by the Brown victory, a few days afterward Obama reinforced his commitment to his higher education goals in his State of the Union address, urging the Senate to pass the House bill: "To make college more affordable, this bill will finally end the unwarranted taxpayer subsidies that go to banks for student loans. Instead, let's take that money and give families a $10,000 tax credit for four years of college and increase Pell Grants" (2010).

The president's new budget underscored this administration's continuing commitment to student aid. Although it cut discretionary spending sharply in most areas across the board, nonetheless the president asked for additional increases in Pell Grants, for total spending on the program of $34.834 billion—double the amount spent annually before he took office (Lederman 2010c). Once again, he called for Congress to give Pell Grants entitlement status.

Yet, trouble was brewing. First, a few members of Congress favored health care legislation, but opposed the student aid legislation. In the House, for example, Paul Kanjorski (D-PA)—in whose district Sallie Mae employed many—was one such member. In attempting to assemble support for the final votes on the president's central initiative, Democratic leaders knew they could not afford to lose the support of such individuals.

Second, the CBO announced a new 2010 budget score for the student aid component that was drastically lower than the 2009 assessment: $61 billion instead of $87 billion. Ironically, the administration had become a victim of its early successes in two respects. First, that the Department of Education had successfully pushed many schools to adopt direct lending, even in advance of the legislation, meant that much of the costs savings of the shift away from FFEL had already been realized. In addition, the reduced CBO score was a result of the recession having led to soaring college enrollments and more students than ever qualifying for Pell Grants, thus elevating demand and program costs (confidential interviews, 2010; Lederman 2010a; de Vise 2010). To put these changes in perspective, Pell Grants cost the U.S. government $18.3 billion in 2008 and 2009, when they were delivered to 6.2 million students; for 2010 and 2011, they are expected to reach $32 billion, for 8.4 million students (Basken 2010c). The CBO's lower assessment of savings, if used, would mean substantially less money available for new spending.

At this stage, furthermore, Kent Conrad, as chair of the Senate Budget Committee, controlled the fate of the student aid legislation with his authority to deem whether its provisions met the criteria to be included in the reconciliation package. Such bills may not include new programs but only funding for existing ones, and the overall package must achieve budgetary savings. In the second week of March, in a stormy meeting in Speaker Nancy Pelosi's office, Conrad told fellow Democrats that higher education should be removed from the bill, delayed for some months and perhaps even until the reconciliation process in the next Congress (confidential interviews, 2010). "I think it threatens the health care bill," he said. "It would . . . sink them both" (Montgomery and Murray 2010). Advocates for the higher education provisions were stunned. They believed the legislation would die if delayed beyond the midterm elections.

The day after the divisive meeting, Senator Tom Harkin, chair of the Senate HELP Committee, and George Miller, of the House Education and Labor Committee, met with the Democratic Caucus. Majority Leader Harry Reid permitted each one five minutes to make the case for including the higher education provisions with health care reform. To the leaders' consternation, Conrad himself did not attend this meeting, citing previous engagements. Six moderate Democratic senators, moreover, sent a letter expressing concerns about job losses in their states if FFEL were terminated (Raju and Thrush 2010).[8]

Conrad finally conceded and agreed to include the higher education provisions, but on one condition: he insisted on using the new, lower 2010 CBO score for cost savings, meaning tens of billions less for student aid. This decision infuriated other Democrats, who knew that Conrad possessed the discretion to allow either score to be used, and that he had deemed the 2009 scores to suffice for determining the health care components of the bill (confidential interviews, 2010). Nonetheless, they were

forced to scale back the proposed increases for student aid. Of the $61 bil-
lion in estimated savings from loan reform, the leadership requested $19
billion to help finance health care reform and deficit reduction, with $9
billion and $10 billion directed toward each, respectively. The health care
bill, on its own, did not provide enough savings to be considered revenue
neutral; combining it with the higher education provisions thus enabled
its enactment (Basken 2010a). These changes left $43 billion—less than
half of what policymakers had expected as recently as one month earlier—
for the programs that aimed to expand access to college and to elevate
completion rates.

Over the next several days, staffers and group representatives wran-
gled in arriving at the final terms of the much leaner bill. Dominant voices
in the trade associations urged policymakers to prioritize Pell Grant funding; this choice left the community college portion of the bill to be gutted
severely. Whereas Obama had hoped to make Pell Grants an entitlement
and the House had proposed annual increases at the rate of inflation plus
one percent, the final bill mandated only that the grant levels must increase with inflation. In fact, with the growing demand for Pell Grants,
one-third of the monies allocated for it had to be used to pay for past funding shortfalls, not future increases. As a result, although the House had
planned for maximum Pell Grant awards to increase to $6,900 (up from
$5,350), the reconciliation bill puts them at $5,550 for the next two years
with gradual increases up to $5,975 in 2020 (Basken 2010c; confidential
interviews, 2010).

In news that devastated community college representatives, negotiators decided to axe Obama's signature American Graduation Initiative.
This was a blow, particularly after the House had approved $10 billion for
the program in SAFRA, and recent drafts of the final bill were rumored to
feature even greater funding and institutions' autonomy for innovation
and experimentation. Conrad apparently objected to AGI on the grounds
that it was a new program and therefore did not meet reconciliation requirements. Ultimately, Democratic leaders managed to find $2 billion to
grant awards somewhat consistent with AGI's rationale by providing
funds for a program already approved by Congress in the stimulus bill—
the Community College and Career Training Grant Program (confidential
interviews, 2010). Meanwhile, the College Access Challenge Grants, for
which the House had set aside $3 billion in SAFRA, were pared down to
$750 million. On balance, as one lobbyist for the community colleges put
it, "It was a huge disappointment, after what had been planned" (confidential interview, 2010).

A few other provisions filled out the education portion of the bill. As in
the House version, funds were provided to minority-serving institutions

($2.55 billion in the final bill). In addition, $1.5 billion was added to increase income-based repayment benefits for student loan borrowers. This program, which began with the College Cost Reduction and Access Act of 2007, enables those who work in low-paying jobs to have their payments reduced and stretched out over a longer period than the normal ten-year window; also, those employed in public service may have their debt forgiven after ten years of making payments (Becker 2009). Another $1.5 billion was set aside for loan servicing by the same companies that had long benefited from the profits FFEL had made possible (Carey 2010). One last-minute change to the bill came when Conrad asked to eliminate a provision he had negotiated earlier to exempt the Bank of North Dakota from loan reform. In a controversy that was reminiscent of the Cornhusker Kickback in health care reform, Republicans had begun to pillory Conrad's deal as the Bismarck Bank Job (Basken 2010b).

Remarkably, FFEL's termination—the most momentous aspect of the higher education provisions—attracted little attention at this final stage. One event in the reconciliation bill's final markup in the House Budget Committee indicated how much political capital the lenders had lost. When Representative Allen Boyd (D-FL), in whose district Sallie Mae employed many individuals, introduced an amendment to retain FFEL by adopting the lenders' alternative, only four committee members voted in favor, but thirty-two opposed it. This outcome would have seemed unimaginable as recently as four years earlier, when lenders still enjoyed a privileged relationship with and strong support from both Republicans and moderate Democrats on Capitol Hill. Still, when the full Senate voted on reconciliation, three Democratic senators—Nelson of Nebraska and Pryor and Lincoln of Arkansas, all vocal defenders of the bank-based student loan system and each of whom had voted in favor of health care reform in December—opposed it, as did all Republicans, for a vote of 56 to 43. This indicated that the higher education legislation likely could not have mustered enough support apart from the reconciliation procedures.

When the House approved the reconciliation bill in a vote of 220 to 211 near midnight on March 21, and the Senate followed a few days later, the occasion was clearly historic because of health care reform, yet it was also noteworthy because of the student aid provisions. It marked the culmination of the two-decade battle to terminate FFEL, a system that had long privileged lenders and inadvertently empowered them more than students. Part of the savings, though less than reformers had envisioned just a few weeks earlier, was directed to programs that would help less advantaged Americans attend college and complete degrees. As one staffer put it, "We have taken money from a vested interest and given it to some of the most low-income people in our country. We don't do that very often" (confidential interview, 2010). On March 30, at Northern Virginia Community College, President Obama signed the new bill into law.

THE RECONSTITUTED LANDSCAPE OF STUDENT AID POLITICS

Next to health care reform, the student aid legislation stands as one of the most significant accomplishments of Obama's presidency to date. Granted, the sea-change in the politics of higher education policy did not begin with his election. Its origins can be traced to the 2006 midterm elections and the high turnout among young people, followed by the revelation of inappropriate relationships between lenders, colleges, and the Department of Education. Remarkably, although the credit crisis of 2008 and the recession that ensued thwarted progress in some policy areas, those same circumstances actually provided a moment of political opportunity in which to reconstitute the political economy of student aid. Most obviously, the unavailability of credit rendered the bank-based system of student loans infeasible and made it clear that it could survive only with government's support. Furthermore, amid high unemployment rates, public officials viewed increased educational aid as a means toward building a more highly trained and resilient workforce. Even before Obama took office, Democratic leaders had begun to take advantage of the political openings created by these events, redirecting higher education policy away from the course it had followed for many years. Meanwhile, the beginnings of direct lending that had been signed into law by Bill Clinton, though holding only a fragile foothold up until the credit crisis, now appeared to be the entering wedge on which reformers could build.

Although circumstances were therefore ripe for an overhaul of student aid policy, Obama's leadership has been critical in bringing major change to fruition, first by underscoring the importance of education policy. As Obama articulated in his State of the Union address in 2010, "In the 21st century, the best anti-poverty program around is a world-class education." He considers educational policy to be essential to economic development as well, and the means by which to promote equal opportunity. Each of his budgets has underscored his administration's commitment to these principles, with the 2010 version devoting large funds to student aid even while scaling back other forms of discretionary spending. Obama's election ushered Democratic majorities into Congress that were just large enough to legislate effectively in this area—at least, as long as reconciliation procedures could be invoked. He also brought to Washington Bob Shireman, the reigning policy expert in the area, who stayed just long enough to oversee the transition to direct lending (Lederman 2010b). And though health care legislation consumed the headlines, the Obama administration kept the student aid bill in its sights. As a result, remarkably, when health care reform's chances hung in the balance after the Brown victory, the higher education policy provided the key to its enactment by offering the necessary cost savings when the two were combined and passed together through the reconciliation process. Of course, that strategy also robbed the student aid bill of some of its reformist edge.

Although the journey toward enactment of the student aid bill contained its share of drama, the most momentous achievements were carried out more easily than would have been the case in earlier years. Viewed against the struggle for direct lending during the Clinton administration and the entrenched power of the lenders since that time, in 2010 lawmakers finally toppled the bank-based system with remarkable ease. The formerly formidable system had been weakened severely by scandals and the credit crisis, and its defenders in the Republican Party had ceased to rally on its behalf. Obama also managed to expand tuition tax credits without much effort, as these fit the mold of the kind of social policy that has mustered broad support especially over the past two decades. But other policy goals proved insurmountable. Obama's plan to make Pell Grants an entitlement was halted immediately by Democratic congressional leaders. Finally, his bold plans for community colleges became the victim of budget politics as Democrats struggled to move both health care reform and higher education policy together through the gauntlet of the reconciliation process.

Viewing these policy outcomes in combination, how can we assess the administration's accomplishments, and what do they portend for the future? One could review this scorecard and conclude that policymakers prioritized the policies that benefit predominantly middle-income students, both student loans and tax breaks, but neglected to adequately improve the policies that stand to benefit especially low-income students, both Pell Grants and community college funds (Carey 2010). Such an assessment makes sense at first blush, but it overlooks the broader significance of what was accomplished in 2009 and 2010, and ignores some of the concurrent developments that have reshaped higher education policy.

First, the termination of the FFEL program effectively changes the political landscape of higher education policy. It signifies the end of the system that had evolved to privilege lenders and replaces it with a system that makes students' needs primary. In the process, it dismantles a political economy that had increasingly fostered iron-triangle-type relationships, strong interdependences between lenders, financial aid officers on campuses, federal agency staff, and members of Congress, particularly those in key committee positions. As long as those relationships existed, student aid politics revolved primarily around fights over the amounts of subsidies and terms for lenders, to the exclusion of attention to policy alternatives that might have broadened access or achieved other goals aiding students. The destruction of the existing system does not in and of itself create new channels for expanded access to college or means of elevating college completion rates, but it does clear the political space in which policies that might foster such ends could be considered.

Second, the administration's failure to gain entitlement status for Pell Grants should not overshadow the remarkable increase in Pell Grant recipients in the past couple of years, which itself simultaneously involves an uncelebrated achievement. The number of Pell recipients in fiscal year 2011 is projected to be 8.7 million, a 57 percent increase from fiscal year 2008, when Obama ran for office (U.S. Department of Education 2010). That increase implies broadened access to college, a marked improvement in the numbers of low- to moderate-income individuals enrolled.

Policy change brings not only new potential, of course, but also new risks. It is worth considering the particular vulnerabilities inherent in the new student aid policy arrangements, and the unintended consequences that might emerge and imperil their success. In the case of student loans, although the federal government has already had a decade and a half to develop expertise with direct lending, nonetheless the shift to 100 percent direct lending undeniably involves responsibilities of an unprecedented scale for the Department of Education. Some opponents of the 2010 legislation predicted that "the chickens will come home to roost," suggesting that the new policy will yield its own challenges over time (confidential interviews, 2010). If direct lending becomes victim to financial crises or management scandals, government itself will become implicated. The policy could also be jeopardized when foes of the policy next win the White House and staff the agencies. Despite these risks, it is worth noting that when Republicans won back control of the House of Representatives in November 2010, they quickly made plans to try to repeal health care reform, but made no efforts to restore bank-based student lending. Representative Virginia Foxx, the conservative North Carolina Republican who became the new leader of the Subcommittee on Higher Education in the House, expressed interest in oversight of direct lending, but not in trying to revive the defeated system (Lederman 2011).

In the case of Pell Grants, soaring costs may threaten the program's long-term sustainability. Already in December 2010, during the lame-duck Congress, funding for the program hung in the balance, facing a shortfall of $5.7 billion that would have forced a 15 percent cut in the maximum award. After student groups mobilized and a story in the *New York Times* garnered attention to the issue, Congress included the necessary funding in a larger budget measure (confidential interviews, 2011). The future is still likely to involve repeated arduous struggles to fund Pell Grants at the levels legislators have promised, subject to such shortfalls and the strain of ever-rising tuition. College completion rates may not improve unless policymakers can find the funding for benefits that are generous enough to allow students to afford to remain in school through graduation. Institutions that enroll large numbers of Pell Grant beneficiaries typically need to provide additional funding to permit them to remain enrolled; such colleges and universities may increasingly make the case that they are deserving of additional institutional support, as some leaders have begun to suggest.

The changes in higher education policy that have occurred thus far during the Obama administration are unlikely by themselves to restore the United States to its role of world leader in educational attainment or to deal with other pressing issues related to costs. The demise of FFEL does not alone open the doors to college to those who are low to moderate income. Given their design and structure, neither will the new tuition tax credits, extended for two additional years in the tax compromise the Obama administration pushed Congress to adopt in December 2010, do much to expand access to college. Matters still to be addressed include the practices of for-profit colleges, which enroll sharply growing numbers of students but often leave them heavily indebted and without marketable skills. The Department of Education has sought to curtail such practices through efforts to create a "gainful employment rule," terminating federal aid to such schools if they have a poor track record. Republicans in recent years have protected the interests of the for-profits, and will likely attempt to come to their aid now that they have regained the majority in the House. The issue that is the elephant in the room is soaring tuition rates; it attracts bipartisan attention but is an issue that the trade associations would clearly like to avoid. Community colleges received more attention than in the past in the 2010 legislation, but in the end the organizational representatives of more affluent institutions prevailed in setting the agenda; these institutions that educate so many Americans with so few resources will need to develop a more powerful political voice if they are to benefit from greater federal largesse.

Nonetheless, the numbers of low- to moderate-income students in college have increased dramatically during Obama's short tenure in office, and such students receive higher Pell Grant benefits than had existed to date. Although the administration's novel approaches to fostering enrollment and degree completion were decimated in the 2010 legislation, the restructuring of student aid politics may allow policymakers to revisit such proposals in the future. As Obama said on the evening of March 21 after the House passed the reconciliation bill, "This is what change looks like." In the case of higher education policy, it does not encompass all aspects of what reformers might have hoped for, but viewed against the backdrop of the past thirty years, it marks a significant transformation.

Julianna Koch provided superb research assistance for this project. I am also grateful to the numerous individuals involved in the policymaking process in Washington, D.C., who allowed me to interview them in 2007, 2010, and 2011: they generously took time out of their busy schedules and spoke thoughtfully and with candor. The Spencer Foundation helped fund this research.

NOTES

1. These interviews lasted one hour on average, ranging from a half hour to two hours. All interviews were conducted in person and on the condition of anonymity; I will use neither names nor identifying information.

2. This pattern of development resembles that identified by Jacob Hacker as "drift" (see Hacker 2004).

3. In what now appears as an irony of political development, in 1965 banks opposed the creation of the guaranteed student loans, not wanting what they viewed as government control over rates and terms, whereas in 2009 Republicans called the proposed shift to direct lending "just another government takeover" because it would replace the system of government-subsidized lending on which they have become dependent (Mettler and Rose 2009; U.S. Congress 2009e).

4. Adding further complexity to this development, despite its initial stance on direct lending the Clinton administration took other actions that undermined efforts to expand access to higher education. First, Clinton promoted the privatization of Sallie Mae in 1996 and did so without stipulating that the company make substantial contributions back to the federal government. Second, Clinton himself promoted a goal that had been strongly resisted by Democrats beginning with Johnson: the adoption of tuition tax credits. He singlehandedly pushed the HOPE and Lifelong Learning Tax Credits, signing them into law in 1997 as part of the Taxpayer Relief Act. Immediately the tax credits, which offer institutions a perverse incentive to raise tuition and which fail to expand access, cost more in lost federal revenues than Pell Grants (see Mettler 2009).

5. Higher education benefited from several other smaller provisions of the stimulus bill, including research monies channeled through the National Science Foundation and National Institutes of Health, $200 million for the work-study program, and $53.6 billion for the state fiscal-stabilization fund for modernizing college facilities and mitigating cuts to colleges.

6. Most of the other amendments were uncontroversial and passed by voice vote.
7. The Republican supporters were Vern Buchanan, Joseph Cao, Timothy Johnson, Thomas Petri, Todd Platts, and Ileana Ros-Lehtinen. The Democratic opponents were Paul Kanjorski, Stephanie Herseth Sandlin, Michael McMahon, and Allen Boyd.
8. The letter was signed by six senators: Thomas Carper (D-DE), Blanche Lincoln (D-AR), Ben Nelson (D-NE), Bill Nelson (D-FL), Mark Warner (D-VA), and Jim Webb (D-VA) (Herszenhorn 2010).

REFERENCES

Alarkon, Walter. 2009. "Beneficiaries of Sallie Mae, Nelnet Fight Obama's Student-Aid Proposal." *The Hill.com*, March 9, 2009. Available at: http://thehill.com/homenews/news/18654-beneficiaries-of-sallie-mae-nelnet-fight-obamas-student-aid-proposal (accessed January 28, 2011).

Basken, Paul. 2007. "Student-Loan Industry Losing Friends in Education Department." *Chronicle of Higher Education*, July 27, 2007. Available at: http://chronicle.com/article/Student-Loan-Industry-Losing/33945 (accessed January 28, 2011).

———. 2010a. "Student-Loan Bill Begins Showdown Week." *Chronicle of Higher Education*, March 15, 2010.

———. 2010b. "Final Student-Loan Bill Offers Aid to Colleges and Students." *Chronicle of Higher Education*, March 19, 2010.

———. 2010c. "Historic Victory for Student Aid Is Tinged by Lost Possibilities." *Chronicle of Higher Education*, March 25, 2010.

———. 2010d. "Minority-Serving Colleges Benefit from a Student-Loan Change They Fought." *Chronicle of Higher Education*, April 4, 2010.

Baum, Sandy, and Marie O'Malley. 2003. "College on Credit: How Borrowers Perceive Their Education Debt." Results of the 2002 National Student Loan Survey. Wilkes-Barre, Pa.: Nellie Mae Corporation. Available at: http://www.nelliemae.com/library/research_10.html (accessed January 28, 2011).

Becker, Amanda. 2009. "Graduates Can Find Help Scaling Mountains of Debt." *Washington Post*, July 5, 2009.

Boles, Corey. 2009. "Alternate Senate Student Loan Plan Would Retain Role for Banks." *Dow Jones News Wire*, December 2. Available at: http://www.advfn.com/news_Alternate-Senate-Student-Loan-Plan-Would-Retain-Role-For-Banks_40615283.html (accessed January 30, 2011).

Burd, Stephen. 2009. "Sallie Mae's Influence Peddling." *Higher Ed Watch*, August 6, 2009. Available at: http://www.newamerica.net/blog/higher-ed-watch/2009/sallie-maes-influence-peddling-13759 (accessed September 21, 2009).

Carey, Kevin. 2010. "Taking an Incomplete: The Disastrous Education Compromise That Marred Obama's Best Week in Office." *The New Republic*, April 13,

2010. Available at: http://www.tnr.com/article/politics/taking-incomplete (accessed January 28, 2011).

CBS News Poll/*New York Times*. 2010. "The Tea Party Movement: What They Think." April 5–12, 2010. Available at: http://www.cbsnews.com/htdocs/pdf/poll_tea_party_041410.pdf?tag=contentMain;contentBody (accessed January 30, 2011).

Center for Responsive Politics. 2010. Website. Available at: http://www.open secrets.org/ (accessed January 20, 2011).

Chronicle of Higher Education. 2009. "Direct-Loan Program Gains Bigger Share of Federal Student Lending." *The Ticker*, October 20, 2009. Available at: http://chronicle.com/blogPost/Direct-Loan-Program-Gains/8539 (accessed March 1, 2010).

College Board. 2004. "Trends in Student Aid 2004." Trends in Higher Education Series. New York: The College Board. Available at: http://www.collegeboard.com/prod_downloads/press/cost04/TrendsinStudentAid2004.pdf (accessed January 28, 2011).

Consumer Bankers Association. 2009. "Fed Proposes Major TILA Changes for Mortgages and Home Equity Lines." *CBA Bankalert*, July 23, 2009. Available at: http://www.cbanet.org/files/ FileDownloads/Mortgage-HELOC.pdf (accessed January 30, 2011).

CQ Weekly. 2009. "Details of the Stimulus Plan." January 19, 2009, p. 127.

De Vise, Daniel. 2010. "House Approves Huge Changes to Student Loan Program." *Washington Post*, March 22, 2010.

Delisle, Jason. 2009. "Student Loan Purchase Programs under the Ensuring Continued Access to Student Loans Act of 2008." Washington, D.C.: New America Foundation. Available at: http://www.newamerica.net/publications/policy/student_loan_purchase_programs_under_ensuring_continued_access_student_loans_act_2008_0 (accessed May 19, 2010).

———. 2010. "Senator Conrad's Choice on Student Loan Bill." *Higher Ed Watch*, January 19, 2010. Available at: http://higheredwatch.newamerica.net/blog posts/2010/senator_conrads_choice_on_student_loan_bill-26445 (accessed May 19, 2010).

Dreas, Maryann. 2009. "Private Lenders Focus on Jobs in Student Loan Fight." *The Hill*, November 30, 2009. Available at: http://thehill.com/business-a-lobbying/69873-private-lenders-focus-on-jobs-in-student-loan-fight (accessed January 30, 2011).

Dynarski, Susan. 2000. "Hope for Whom? Financial Aid for the Middle Class and Its Impact on College Attendance." *National Tax Journal* 53(3)(2): 629–62.

Enzi, Michael B., United States Senate. 2009. An Open Letter to College and University Leaders. December 15. Available at: http://republicans.edlabor.house.gov/Media/file/PDFs/121509FFELLetter.pdf (accessed on March 1, 2010).

Field, Kelly. 2009a. "For Community Colleges, Federal Aid Would Come with

Strings Attached." *Chronicle of Higher Education*, July 29, 2009. Available at: http://chronicle.com/article/article-content/47493 (accessed January 28, 2011).

———. 2009b. "On Higher-Education Spending, the White House and Congress Agree, to a Point." *Chronicle of Higher Education*, August 17, 2009. Available at: http://page1.com/article/On-Education-Spending-the/48007 (accessed January 28, 2011).

———. 2009c. "Houses Passes Bill to End Bank-Based Lending." *Chronicle of Higher Education*, September 17, 2009. Available at: http://chronicle.com/article/House-Passes-Bill-to-End/48499 (accessed January 28, 2011).

———. 2009d. "Congress Is Poised to Ease Passage of Obama's Plan to End Bank-Based Lending." *Chronicle of Higher Education*, April 27, 2009. Available at: http://chronicle.com/article/Congress-Is-Poised-to-Ease/47214 (accessed January 28, 2011).

———. 2009e. "Lenders and Guarantors Offer Alternatives to President's Loan-Overhaul Plan." *Chronicle of Higher Education*, July 1, 2009. Available at: http://chronicle.com/article/LendersGuarantors-Offer/47349 (accessed January 28, 2011).

Gerstein, Josh. 2009. "Dems Take Aim at W.H. on Student Loans." *Politico*, March 25, 2009.

Gladieux, Lawrence E., and Arthur M. Hauptman. 1995. *The College Aid Quandary: Access, Quality and the Federal Role.* Washington, D.C.: Brookings Institution.

Gladieux, Lawrence E., and Thomas R. Wolanin. 1976. *Congress and the Colleges: The National Politics of Higher Education.* Lexington, Mass.: Lexington Books.

Hacker, Jacob S. 2004. "Privatizing Risk without Privatizing the Welfare State: The Hidden Politics of Social Policy Retrenchment in the United States." *American Political Science Review* 98(2): 243–60.

Herszenhorn, David M. 2009. "Obama Student Loan Plan Wins Support in House." *New York Times*, September 10, 2009, p. A9. Available at: http://www.nytimes.com/2009/07/11/education/11educ.html (accessed January 28, 2011).

———. 2010. "Obama's Student Loan Overhaul Endangered." *New York Times*, March 10, 2010. Available at: http://www.nytimes.com/2010/03/11/us/politics/11loans.html (accessed January 28, 2011).

Howard, Ed. 2009. "Nelson Cited as 'Emblematic' of Administration's Problems." *Nebraska State Paper*, April 1, 2009. Available at: http://nebraska.statepaper.com/vnews/display.v/ART/2009/04/01/49d355604df9c (accessed January 28, 2011).

Jaschik, Scott. 2009. "The Obama Plan." *Inside Higher Ed*, July 15, 2009. Available at: http://www.insidehighered.com/news/2009/07/15/obama (accessed September 20, 2009).

Kane, Thomas J. 2004. "College-Going and Inequality." In *Social Inequality*, edited by Kathryn M. Neckerman. New York: Russell Sage Foundation.

Keller, Josh. 2009. "Education Dept. Gets a Nominee Who Champions the Under-served." *Chronicle of Higher Education*, April 17, 2009. Available at: http://chronicle.com/article/Education-Dept-Gets-a-Nomi/13630 (accessed January 28, 2011).

King, Jacqueline E. 2000. "2000 Status Report on the Pell Grant Program." Washington, D.C.: American Council on Education, Center for Policy Analysis.

Kingdon, John W. 1995. *Agendas, Alternatives, and Public Policies*, 2nd ed. New York: HarperCollins.

Kline, John, U.S. House of Representatives, Committee on Education and Labor. 2009. Letter to Honorable Arne Duncan, U.S. Department of Education. November 3, 2009. Available at: http://republicans.edlabor.house.gov/media/file/PDFs/110309LettertoDuncan.pdf (accessed March 1, 2010).

Knight, Danielle. 2009. "Lobbying Showdown over the Future of Student Loans." *Huffington Post*, July 29, 2009. Available at: http://www.huffingtonpost.com/2009/07/29/lobbying-showdown-over-th_n_247506.html (accessed September 21, 2009).

Lederman, Doug. 2009a. "Aid Bill Moves, amid Misgivings." *Inside Higher Ed*, July 22, 2009. Available at: http://www.insidehighered.com/news/2009/07/22/house (accessed January 28, 2011).

———. 2009b. "Big Savings from Loan Proposal." *Inside Higher Ed*, March 23, 2009. Available at: http://www.insidehighered.com/news/2009/03/23/budget (accessed January 28, 2011).

———. 2009c. "Help from the House." *Inside Higher Ed*, July 27, 2009. Available at: http://www.insidehighered.com/news/2009/07/27/approps (accessed January 28, 2011).

———. 2009d. "House Passes Student Aid Bill." *Inside Higher Ed*, September 18, 2009. Available at: http://www.insidehighered.com/news/2009/09/18/aid (accessed January 28, 2011).

———. 2010a. "What Now for Student Aid Bill?" *Inside Higher Ed*, March 8, 2010. Available at: http://www.insidehighered.com/news/2010/03/08/safra (accessed January 28, 2011).

———. 2010b. "Mission Accomplished." *Inside Higher Ed*, May 18, 2010. Available at: http://www.insidehighered.com/news/2010/05/18/shireman (accessed January 28, 2011).

———. 2010c. "Renewed Push on Pell." *Inside Higher Ed*, February 1, 2010. Available at: http://www.insidehighered.com/news/2010/02/01/budget (accessed January 28, 2011).

———. 2011. "The House's New Higher Ed Leader." *Inside Higher Ed*, January 14, 2011. Available at: http://www.insidehighered.com/news/2011/01/14/interview_with_virginia_foxx_new_head_of_house_higher_education_subcommittee (accessed January 28, 2011).

Lewin, Tamar. 2009a. "House Passes Bill to Expand College Aid." *New York Times*,

September 18, 2009, p. A15. Available at: http://www.nytimes.com/2009/09/18/education/18educ.html (accessed January 28, 2011).

———. 2009b. "Colleges Are Pushed to Convert Loan System." *New York Times*, October 27, 2009, p. A15. Available at: http://www.nytimes.com/2009/10/27/education/27college.html (accessed January 28, 2011).

Lichtblau, Eric. 2010. "Lobbying Imperils Overhaul of Student Loans." *New York Times*, February 5, 2010, p. A1. Available at: http://www.nytimes.com/2010/02/05/us/politics/05loans.html?_r=1 (accessed March 6, 2011).

Long, Bridget Terry. 2003. "The Impact of Federal Tax Credits for Higher Education Expenses." NBER working paper no. 9553. Cambridge, Mass.: National Bureau of Economic Research.

McLean, Bethany. 2005. "Sallie Mae: A Hot Stock, a Tough Lender." *CNN Money*, December 14, 2005. Available at: http://money.cnn.com/2005/12/14/news/fortune500/sallie_fortune_122605/index.htm (accessed March 6, 2011).

Mettler, Suzanne. 2008. "From Passing Out Roses to Passing Out Thorns: Transformations in Congress and the Politics of Higher Education Policy, 1973–2007." Paper prepared for the annual meetings of the Midwestern Political Science Association Conference. Chicago (April 3–6, 2008).

———. 2009. "Promoting Inequality: The Politics of Higher Education Policy in an Era of Conservative Governance." In *The Unsustainable American State*, edited by Lawrence Jacobs and Desmond King. New York: Oxford University Press.

Mettler, Suzanne, and Deondra Rose. 2009. "Unsustainability of Equal Opportunity: The Development of the Higher Education Act of 1965." Paper prepared for delivery at the Annual Meeting of the American Political Science Association, Toronto, Ontario. (September 3–6, 2009).

Montgomery, Lori, and Shailagh Murray. 2010. "Key Senators Balk at Adding Student Loan Overhaul to Health Care Legislation." *Washington Post*, March 11, 2010. Available at: http://www.washingtonpost.com/wp-dyn/content/article/2010/03/10/AR2010031003934.html (accessed January 28, 2011).

Mortenson, Tom. 2007. "Bachelor's Degree Attainment by Age 24 by Family Income Quartiles, 1970 to 2007." Oskaloosa, Iowa: Postsecondary Education Opportunity. Available at: http://www.postsecondary.org (accessed January 28, 2011).

Nelson, Libby. 2009. "Sallie Mae Fights for Student-Loan Role in a Campaign That's All about Jobs." *Chronicle of Higher Education*, November 22, 2009. Available at: http://chronicle.com/article/Sallie-Mae-Fights-for-Stude/49224 (accessed March 1, 2010).

Obama, Barack. 2006. *The Audacity of Hope: Thoughts on Reclaiming the American Dream*. New York: Three Rivers Press.

———. 2007. "Remarks of Senator Barack Obama: Reclaiming the American Dream." Bettendorf, Iowa, November 7, 2007. Available at: http://www.barack

obama.com/2007/11/07/remarks_of_senator_barack_obam_31.php (accessed September 18, 2009).

———. 2009a. "Remarks of President Barack Obama—Address to Joint Session of Congress." February 24, 2009. Washington: The White House, Office of the Press Secretary. Available at: http://www.whitehouse.gov/the_press_office/Remarks-of-President-Barack-Obama-Address-to-Joint-Session-of-Congress (accessed September 19, 2009).

———. 2009b. "Remarks by the President on Higher Education." April 24, 2009. Washington: The White House, Office of the Press Secretary. Available at: http://www.whitehouse.gov/the_press_office/Remarks-by-the-President -on-Higher-Education (accessed September 21, 2009).

———. 2010. "Remarks by the President in State of the Union Address." January 27, 2010. Washington: The White House, Office of the Press Secretary. Available at: http://www.whitehouse.gov/the-press-office/remarks-president-state-union -address (accessed January 30, 2011).

OECD. 2007. "Education at a Glance: OECD Briefing Note for the United States." Paris: Organization for Economic Cooperation and Development. Available at: http://www.oecd.org/dataoecd/22/51/39317423.pdf (accessed January 30, 2011).

Office of Management and Budget. 2009. "President Obama's Fiscal 2010 Budget: Opening the Doors of College and Opportunity." Washington: The White House. Available at: http://www.whitehouse.gov/omb/fy2010_key_college (accessed September 19, 2009).

Onink, Troy. 2009. "The New Improved College Tax Credit." *Forbes*, March 10, 2009.

Peterson, Molly. 2009. "Obama's Student-Loan Overhaul Passes House Committee." *Bloomberg.com*, July 21, 2009. Available at: http://www.bloomberg.com/apps/news?pid=20601213&sid=ai0WwIo6jyAg (accessed September 20, 2009).

Price, Derek V. 2004. *Borrowing Inequality: Race, Class, and Student Loans*. Boulder, Colo.: Lynne Rienner.

Raju, Manu, and Glenn Thrush. 2010. "Conrad, Dems Split in Loan Spat." *Politico*, March 19, 2010. Available at: http://www.politico.com/news/stories/0310/34664.html (accessed January 30, 2011).

Shapira, Ian. 2007. "Bush Signs Sweeping Student Loan Bill into Law, Adding an Asterisk." *Washington Post*, September 28, 2007. Available at: http://www .washingtonpost.com/wp-dyn/content/article/2007/09/27/AR200709270 0958.html (accessed January 30, 2011).

Skowronek, Stephen. 1982. *Building a New American State: The Expansion of National Administrative Capacities, 1877–1920*. New York: Cambridge University Press.

Taggart, William J. United States Department of Education, Chief Operating Officer. 2009. Letter to College Presidents. Available at: http://ifap.ed.gov/

eannouncements/attachments/070809AttachTaggartLetterJuly8.pdf (accessed February 28, 2011).

U.S. Congress. House of Representatives. 2009a. "American Recovery and Reinvestment Act of 2009." HR 1. 111th Cong., 1st sess. Available at: http://frwebgate.access.gpo.gov/cgi-bin/getdoc.cgi?dbname=111_cong_bills&docid=f:h1enr.pdf (accessed January 30, 2011).

———. 2009b. "Amendment to the Amendment in the Nature of a Substitute to HR 3221. Offered by Mr. Guthrie of Kentucky." House Education and Labor Committee markup. 111th Cong., 1st sess.

———. 2009c. "Roll Call 1 HR 3221." House Education and Labor Committee markup. 111th Cong., 1st sess.

———. 2009d. "Student Aid and Fiscal Responsibility Act of 2009." *Congressional Record* 155(131)(September 16): H9594–637.

———. 2009e. "Student Aid and Fiscal Responsibility Act of 2009: Roll Call Votes 710–719." *Congressional Record* 155(132)(September 17): H9675–702.

U.S. Department of Education. 2009. "The American Recovery and Reinvestment Act of 2009: Education Jobs and Reform." February 18, 2009. Washington: Government Printing Office. Available at: http://www.ed.gov/policy/gen/leg/recovery/factsheet/overview.html (accessed September 19, 2009).

———. 2010. "Federal Pell Grants: Fiscal Year 2011 Budget Request." Washington: Government Printing Office. Available at: http://www2.ed.gov/about/overview/budget/budget11/justifications/p-pell.pdf (accessed August 11, 2010).

Washington Post. 2006. "Top 100 Executives by Total Compensation." Available at: http://projects.washingtonpost.com/post200/2006/executives-by-compensation (accessed January 30, 2011).

Chapter 4 | The Contest of Lobbies and Disciplines: Financial Politics and Regulatory Reform

Daniel Carpenter

ON JULY 21, 2010, President Obama signed into law the Dodd-Frank Wall Street Reform and Consumer Protection Act. The Dodd-Frank Act—so named after its two congressional cosponsors, Connecticut Senator Christopher Dodd and Massachusetts Representative Barney Frank—represents the most sweeping overhaul of financial regulations in the United States since the New Deal. More so than the American Recovery and Reinvestment Act of 2009, the so-called stimulus package, the Dodd-Frank Act represents the Obama administration's main structural attack on the financial crisis of 2008 and the Great Recession that followed it. And, compared with Obama's health care reform package, the Dodd-Frank financial reform bill stood to wither less if congressional Republicans were to gain House or Senate majorities in the November 2010 midterm elections. The Obama administration's financial reform proposals engendered substantial controversy and hundreds of millions of dollars in lobbying on various sides of the debate. These high stakes of financial politics reflect the massive transformations set in motion by the act.

The Dodd-Frank Act takes large investment banks and, in some ways, fundamentally dismantles them. One provision cleaves trading operations in derivatives and swaps from deposit-taking functions. Another provision allows only so much of a bank's capital to be deployed in proprietary trading. A critical set of provisions—largely unnoticed in the late-stage debate on the Dodd-Frank bill and the aftermath of its summer 2010 passage—establishes stringent governance of credit rating agencies, such as Moody's or Standard and Poor's, and weakens their power in the global

139

economy and government policymaking. The act boosts the requirements for how much basic capital banks must keep on hand as they engage in lending and investing. And the Dodd-Frank Act establishes, for the first time in American history, a federal agency explicitly dedicated to the regulation of consumer financial products such as mortgages, credit cards, and commodity loans. It puts into law the idea of financial safety for consumers and the economy as a whole. For banks large and small, for mortgage lenders and credit card companies, and for federal and private agencies that rate and regulate risk, there will be new business models in the years to come.

To be certain, both the process and the outcome of financial reform generated broad criticism and controversy. These laments came from conservatives who saw the new regulations as far too intrusive in American and global capital markets, and from progressives who wished for a return to New Deal institutions of financial governance.[1] Stronger versions of an independent consumer agency and of splitting derivatives operations from depository institutions were set aside, often in quieter moments of politics. Yet the momentous nature of the changes should not be understated. The politically successful proposals are notable for their breadth. As a result of the 2010 law, there will be substantial limitations on leverage, proprietary trading, and swaps operations at major financial institutions, and relatedly there will be stronger rules for minimum capital requirements, especially for so-called Tier 1 capital. A new consumer protection bureau has been added to the Federal Reserve, and the vigor with which its appointments politics was fought out suggests, if nothing else, that it carries the possibility of expansive regulatory capacity and action.

From a global and historical perspective, one less noticeable but deeply political transformation took place: the limited democratization of finance policymaking. Over the course of the late twentieth century, the policy networks of American finance became increasingly restricted. Whether in Democratic or Republican presidential administrations, appointments to top financial positions came increasingly from large Wall Street banks and from regulatory skeptics in economics and business faculties. Often enough, Democratic appointments to top financial posts were partners and colleagues of the very men Republicans had appointed to those positions, and vice versa. Most issues were decided not in legislative forums or in public, but in rule-making. And the academic and advisory circles that hosted discussions of financial reform were characterized more commonly by scholars with finance and economics doctorates than by scholars from law or the behavioral social sciences.

Yet, as the debates of 2009 and 2010 unfolded, this gilded network began to crack open. Issues that would have been covered entirely in rule-making among small cliques of regulators and financiers just five years earlier were suddenly thrown open for wider debate. Labor unions, consumer advocates, and scholarly voices from outside the academic-banking complex of modern finance policy became pivotal contributors to the policy agenda. Legislators heard voices from academic psychology, sociology, and housing studies. Within Congress, new members proposed and backed transformative new amendments that passed. Bureaucratic agencies that had enjoyed stable claims to policy turf and expertise quickly saw their credibility and their jurisdictions under attack. Whether this aperture of the finance policy network persists is not clear, but for a moment in political time, the making of finance policy was partially democratized.

CRISIS AND REFORM: SOME FINANCIAL FACTS AND CONCEPTS

Unlike the health care debate, the essential context for financial reform was not a decades-long fight by the Democratic Party to bring American policy to a par with other advanced democracies. Instead, financial reform's place on the agenda was set and secured by a global crisis of capital, risk, and economic security, a crisis whose reach has not been equaled since the Great Depression of the 1930s. Put differently, unlike health care reform, financial reform was not a decades-long wish of embedded movements within the Democratic Party and the liberal or progressive movements. The crisis of 2008 and the Great Recession that followed it damaged the fortunes of the wealthy and ripped away the jobs and health insurance of the working poor, the working class, and the middle class. More than 8 million jobs vanished, many of them never to return. The national housing crisis was historic in its own right—homeowners lost their shelter and their equity at record levels as lenders repossessed 2.3 million homes from December 2007 to September 2010—and the housing tumult engendered a crisis in banking, with bank failures and plummeting asset values for major investments (including institutional pension accounts, retirement funds, and foundation and university endowments). A structural implosion in housing generated an implosion in major financial institutions and their assets, which in turn decimated employment and incomes, worsening the housing crisis. The local world destabilized the global one, and the global returned the insult.

The two-year crisis damaged individual consumer fortunes and the accumulated wealth of the most powerful financial organizations on the planet. It hit both the consumer financial realm and the systemic financial realm,[2] and hard. Past stock market crashes were not as deeply embedded in the consumer finance market—witness the crash of 1987, the problems of Long-Term Capital Management and its international investments in 1998, and the popping of the tech and NASDAQ bubbles in 2000. In contrast to the 2008 crisis, in none of these events was the American housing market deeply implicated, and only in one was a set of overvalued household-level investments (many of them institutional, in the IT bubble of the 1990s) partially involved. At the same time, the crisis in homeownership and consumer finance is certainly lucid now, but its roots have been spreading for the better part of two decades. For a number of reasons, median income per capita stagnated over the last decade even as the costs of health care, education, and housing continued to rise (Warren and Tyagi 2003; Immergluck 2009; Krugman 2000; for a political economy interpretation of this widening trend of inequality, see Bartels 2009). And even as the costs of these goods have risen, Americans are becoming more enamored with them, sacrificing long-term savings and other expenditures to gain access to education, health care, and owned housing.

By most accounts, the financial crisis unfolded from contexts that reveal deeply political, social, and economic dimensions. The last twenty years have witnessed explicit and implicit financial deregulation, most markedly in the 1999 repeal of the Glass-Steagall Act that had formerly split commercial and depository from investment institutions in banking. This 1999 law culminated twenty years of lobbying efforts by the U.S. and global financial services industry. Income inequality has been growing in the United States and is now, by some measures, perched at levels not witnessed since the late nineteenth century. This has led to what some analysts call surplus capital among the wealthy, who have abundant assets with which to invest and who may compete on ever-higher returns. It has also led to the genesis of new financial and loan instruments that claim to permit financially constrained consumers to purchase homes they could not otherwise afford. So, too, different analyses have revealed the degree to which the new financial instruments were aimed at ethnic and racial minorities, disadvantaged peoples whose ability to seek shelter under consumer bankruptcy laws has been deeply curtailed since the Bankruptcy Abuse Prevention and Consumer Protection Act (BAPCPA) of 2005 (on the possible linkage of Glass-Steagall's repeal to the recent explosion of bank failures, see Moss 2009; Klein 2010).

Changes in Financial Products

In combination with these structural developments, companies have begun to offer new and much more complicated financial products to consumers. Each of these financial products can be reduced to a contract that contains its fundamental components—a promise of the lender to provide money now in return for a series of payments by the citizen later. The explosion of credit cards over the last two decades—by 2008, the average adult American carried ten or more of these on their person—is perhaps the most familiar evidence that financial products have revolutionized our lives. Yet it is not just credit cards but their contractual terms that have been transformed. The diversity and complexity of credit card contracts is bewildering. Most cards require no monthly fee for card use but some still do, and many more did just a decade or more ago. Cards differ in the fees that kick in—and the transparency with which they kick in—when payments for accumulated balances come in late or not at all. Citizens can use credit cards to accumulate money for airline flights, to make purchases at favored merchandisers, and even to make implicit contributions to their alma mater or a charity.

The array of other consumer financial products has also exploded in diversity and complexity. For much of the twentieth century the dominant form of home loan was a thirty-year fixed-rate mortgage with a certain percentage of the housing value down (20 to 30 percent, usually). In recent years, however, homeowners were able to purchase homes using an array of mortgages that allow purchasers to put very little money down and, in addition, provide little or no documentation (the euphemism for these products being "no-doc" or "low-doc" home loans). In combination with credit cards, these products were marketed with increasing psychological and sociological sophistication to the working class, the working poor, recent immigrants, and those in particular religious and social communities where homeownership was prized both culturally and even spiritually (on the intimate connections between the prosperity gospel movement and the subprime mortgage crisis, see Rosin 2009).

In tandem with these new consumer products arose a wide range of systemic financial products—collateralized debt obligations, securitized asset bundles such as residential mortgage-backed securities (RMBS), derivatives sold institutionally as well as in individual transactions. Of these products, most of the policy attention has focused upon two sorts. First is the class of financial products known as over-the-counter derivatives.[3] Derivatives are simply financial products derived from other financial products, and these can be traded on an exchange like that in South Korea or the Eurex institution of Europe, or over the counter between a party and a counterparty. The lack of a major exchange for derivatives trading in the United States is a peculiar feature of the American market, and one that renders the American derivatives market largely unregulated, both institutionally through the exchanges and governmentally.[4] The second set of products that have come in for criticism are bundles of consumer products or bundles of those bundles—residential mortgage-backed securities and credit default swaps (CDSs). The RMBS is a bundle of mortgages, each of varying quality, where quality levels correspond to slices or *tranches*, and in which the aggregation of individual mortgages is theoretically supposed to reduce the risk. The CDS is a hedge that a party makes on another party's default on a bond or loan; it could be (and often was), for instance, a hedge that a bank makes on the probability that another bank's RMBS-backed purchase of a bond will default. Again, these hedges can be used to reduce risk, and it was not uncommon for banks (or their associates) to take out credit default swaps on some of the very loan products they were providing to other borrowers. Again, the construction and sale of these products has been largely unregulated in the United States over the last two decades.

Political and Institutional Characteristics of the Finance Realm

The political and institutional characteristics of the finance realm also figured prominently in the production of new policy. The American financial sector has in the last decade served as one of the top contributors to congressional and presidential campaigns and has spent far more money lobbying, through payments to lobbying organizations and firms, than in direct campaign contributions. According to the Center for Responsive Politics, from 1998 to 2010 the industrial sector represented by "real estate, finance and insurance" spent more than $4 billion lobbying Washington officials, placing it at the top of all aggregated sectors in lobbying, including health and energy (see figure 4.1). In 2009 and the first quarter of 2010, when the financial reform package was making its way through Congress, this same aggregated sector spent an estimated $592.5 million (Americans for Financial Reform 2010).[5] And unlike the contributions of many sectors, this lobbying and contributions behavior was strategically and skillfully bipartisan, with major banks like Goldman Sachs contributing heavily to Democratic as well as Republican campaigns. Tellingly, the financial services and banking industry contributed more to the Obama campaign than to the McCain campaign in the 2008 general election cycle.

Another critical feature of the financial industry is its broad employment of workers across the United States, especially its wealthier employees in critical constituencies in the Northeast. In a Democratic presidency, where North Atlantic and New England legislators took pivotal positions in drafting financial reform legislation, the concentration of financial institutions and employment in the northeastern states became a major advantage for this sector. A large number of major investment banks are headquartered in New York, but many of their top officials and employees live

Figure 4.1   Total Lobbying Expenditures by Sector, 1988 to 2010

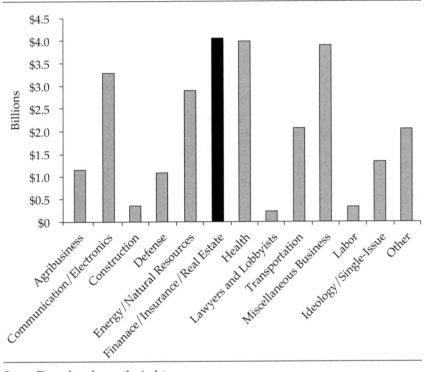

Source: Figure based on author's data.

not in the city, but in neighboring Connecticut or New Jersey. In addition, Boston, Philadelphia, and North Carolina harbor major banks and major employment centers, and credit card companies and financial services firms employ tens of thousands of workers in low-tax, rural states such as Iowa, Nebraska, and South Dakota. Smaller players in the financial industry such as community banks and lenders have branches and employees that are widely distributed across the nation's congressional districts. In congressional politics more than the executive-branch politics of financial reform, the political power of small banks would be felt as strongly as that of large Wall Street players.

Consider next that the the U.S. executive branch and the American states each possess hundreds of various agencies that regulate features of systemic and consumer finance. These range from the Federal Reserve to state insurance regulators. At some level, these various agencies aggregate to more administrative capacity than in other realms of state activity, but the multiplicity of regulatory organizations in American finance also engenders the politics of boundaries. The boundaries are in part suggestive of turf wars that congressional committee scholars and bureaucratic politics scholars have examined with increasing frequency in the last two decades (King 1994; Carpenter 2001). In other respects, the dividing lines of regulatory politics are as much about nonagency boundaries—the battles between and among professions, federalism (state versus federal authority), and even ideas and methods (free-market economics and efficient markets theories versus behavioral finance versus more populist approaches to regulation that are grounded outside of the economics profession and its embedment in American government).

Beyond the various executive agencies—and in some sense above them—lie the various counsels of policymaking associated with the White House and the president himself. Some of these are more bureaucratized and enduring, such as the Office of Management and Budget or the Office of Science and Technology Policy. Others are less formalized in their structure but nonetheless critical to policy development by virtue of their proximity to the president. This includes the National Economic Council, where the formidable Lawrence Summers (former president of Harvard and, before that, secretary of the treasury himself) was observed to have President Obama's ear for much of the first eighteen months of the administration.

Second, the industrial organization of finance policy is less decentralized in Congress as compared with, say, health care. Although their jurisdictions are far from watertight, the House Financial Services Committee and the Senate Finance Committee each control finance policy more than any single House or Senate committee controls health policy, environmental policy, or energy policy in their respective chambers. The two chairs of the congressional finance committees—Barney Frank of Massachusetts and Christopher Dodd of Connecticut—had commonalities and differences that played out in important ways during the finance regulation debate. Both were northeastern liberals from socially progressive states and both had abundant constituents who worked for or depended on the health of their state's financial sector. Both men had served over two decades in Congress and both were well versed in financial politics—this experience gave each ties to important financial constituencies and players who could lobby them. Yet the experience also gave each committee chair, and the committee's more experienced staff, some degree of independence from these constituencies, insofar as the expertise accumulated in each committee was substantial.

As with the late George W. Bush administration, where Treasury Secretary Henry Paulson occupied a central position in the development of the Troubled Asset Relief Program (TARP) and the Bush administration's response to the global financial crisis, so too in the Obama administration did the Treasury Department occupy a critical agenda-setting role in the American financial reform initiative. Officials in the Obama Treasury Department—not only Secretary Timothy Geithner but particularly deputy and assistant secretaries, including Michael Barr and Eric Stein—spent much of the transition period and the winter and spring of 2009 writing up the administration's reform initiative. A number of academic lawyers and economists also advised Treasury, including Jeremy Stein and Sendhil Mullainathan of Harvard's Economics Department.

Cross-Branch and Cross-Chamber Linkages: The Dodd-Treasury Alliance and the Filibuster

In a separated powers system, it is critical to pay attention to the linkages and (informational and incentive) dependencies across the executive and legislative branches. Two of these are worth discussion here. First, numerous observers and participants have documented very close ties between Senator Chris Dodd and the Treasury Department. It was Dodd who, according to interviewees, helped to vocalize some of the Treasury Department's opposition to particular forms of capital requirements on major banks, and it was the Treasury Department that later prevailed on Dodd to give up a minor battle on those same leverage restrictions. Ties between Dodd and Treasury also figured prominently in the development of an independent consumer protection agency, in the eventual placement of that agency in the Federal Reserve, and in the pitched battle over whether Elizabeth Warren would be nominated as its first director. Of course ties between committee chairs and executive agencies have existed for well over a century—witness the long-standing portrait (sometime inaccurate but nonetheless telling) of "iron triangles" in 1950s and 1960s political science. What is interesting in this light is that no ties as strong as those between Dodd and Treasury were observed between top Treasury officials and the House Financial Services Committee or its chairman, Barney Frank. Frank and his staff maintained regular liaison with the Treasury Department and with other executive branch financial agencies, yet Frank seemed less willing to form a solid alliance with Treasury officials, both against the Republicans but also against the progressive-liberal wing of Democratic politicians.

A second linkage across the legislative players was induced by the Senate filibuster. Those interviewed repeatedly suggested that House Democrats felt it critical, in a number of policy realms, to produce unanimous or near-unanimous agreement among Democratic representatives so as to minimize opportunities for Senate Democrats to defect from a Democratic coalition and thus endanger legislative prospects. This signal-of-unity logic was a strategy mentioned repeatedly in interviews, and it is difficult to tell whether it was pursued for all or many of the various planks in the legislation. Nonetheless, it was deemed important for the House majority (acting first) to present as unified a front as possible to the Senate majority. This cross-chamber dependency is somewhat different from that usually examined by political scientists, insofar as the supermajority institutions of the Senate not only induce the abandonment and revision of bills in the House and even before the legislative process (Krehbiel 1998), but also affect the crafting of coalitions within the lower chamber and its committees.

THE OBAMA AGENDA AND THE GILDED NETWORK

When President Obama took office in 2009, it appeared that a good portion of the gilded network was still intact. Mere days after his election, on November 10, 2010, Obama announced his selection of Rahm Emanuel as his White House chief of staff. Emanuel was a veteran of the Chicago politics scene and a principal recipient—in the House of Representatives, the top recipient by a fair margin—of political contributions from hedge funds and top Wall Street banks such as JP Morgan.[6] In economic policy appointments, too, Obama's principal choices came from networks rooted in New York investment banks, cliques whose members had long known one another and were skeptical of financial regulation. Former Clinton-era Treasury Secretary Robert E. Rubin was a member of the Obama transition team and, at the time of Obama's election, chairman of Citigroup (on Geithner's ties in the New York financial community, see Becker and Morgenson 2009; on Rubin as a central figure in this network, see Kuttner 2008; see also *New York Times* 2009; on Rubin's leadership of Citigroup in the financial crisis, see Dash and Creswell 2008).[7] Chief economic advisor Lawrence Summers had also served as treasury secretary and advocated for financial deregulation in the 1990s. Obama's choice for treasury secretary, Timothy Geithner, was head of the Federal Reserve Bank of New York and was widely described as a protégé of Rubin. In his role at the Fed, Geithner had assisted Bush administration Treasury Secretary Henry Paulson in the bailout of American International Group.[8]

From an historical perspective, too, Obama's ties to Wall Street were tighter than for previous Democratic presidents. It is worth noting that, where President Franklin Delano Roosevelt had excoriated Wall Street in his presidential addresses, Obama did not lash out. He instead kept up a modest tone of criticism and was much more likely to criticize Republican financial policies than the financial industry.

Although many forces internal to the Obama administration displayed this conservative tendency toward financial reform, there were no less powerful macro-level forces impelling the president and Congress toward significant regulatory change. The juxtaposition of the financial crisis with the TARP—or financial bailout—meant that, in a symbolic sense, investment banks were seen as both the cause of the Great Recession and the primary beneficiaries of the earliest policies to combat it. In the media coverage given to this stream of emotion, journalists described this "bailout furor" as a form of "populist rage." And the rage and furor set in early. In February 2009, the second month of the Obama presidency, a poll conducted by CNN and the Opinion Research Corporation (ORC) reported that 62 percent of Americans thought that the second half of the TARP money should be not be released to financial institutions. Amplifying this broader pressure was strong participation from labor unions and consumer groups whose voices and votes had been critical to the Obama campaign. The Service Employees International Union (SEIU) and Consumer Federation of America both participated actively and consistently in the campaign for reform. Both joined the umbrella group Americans for Financial Reform, and SEIU leader Andy Stern organized some critical anti–Wall Street protests that brought media attention to the financial reform cause (Bowman and Rugg 2010; on an exemplary SEIU protest, see Americans for Financial Reform 2009).[9]

To be sure, Republicans and economic conservatives did not fade to irrelevance in this debate. Yet their contribution was one more of obstruction than of shaping the policy agenda. This partial failure came not for lack of trying. The conservative and libertarian talking points that emerged in 2008 and 2009 linked the financial crisis with the government's support of the housing market for minorities and poorer citizens. Some of the support, they alleged, came from direct government intervention in the housing market through the mortgage giants Fannie Mae and Freddie Mac. Some of it came through the Community Reinvestment Act and its support for homeowning among poorer and minority families. The problem with this attack was twofold. First, Republicans were in a poor position from the start to make these arguments, being in the minority and in a position of deep unpopularity coming out of the Bush years. Second, their argument linking toxic mortgages lacked accuracy. As the housing scholar Dan Immergluck has shown, only a small portion of the run-up in adjustable-rate mortgages with teasers and other tricks was due to federal provision (2009, 41–43, 86).[10]

POLICY PROPOSALS OF SPRING 2009

In the year following Obama's inauguration, a debate raged about how to respond to the global financial crisis, at both the systemic and the consumer levels. Various reform proposals emerged from think tanks, university scholars, advocacy groups, and members of Congress. The Bush administration Treasury Department contributed in ways that have been largely overlooked, especially Secretary Henry Paulson, when he released a blueprint for financial reform in June 2007. Paulson's plan had little to say about derivatives regulation and consumer finance, but it called for cross-agency financial coordination, and bowed toward international capital standards by promising to complete rule-making in wake of the Basel II accords.[11]

The Treasury Department occupied a critical agenda-setting role when it released a draft proposal in June 2009. For this reason, important symbolic and structural patterns differentiated health care, where the Obama administration let Congress take the lead in drafting proposals, and financial reform, where the executive branch took the lead and Congress largely followed. The outline of reforms the Treasury Department proposed was published in a heavily read and much-anticipated document, *Financial Regulatory Reform: A New Foundation*, in June 2009. The U.S. House of Representatives passed many of these measures in December 2009. Like the Treasury proposal, this bill, which was reported by the House Financial Services Committee, chaired by Massachusetts Democrat Barney Frank, was interpreted as a bold, progressive strike against Wall Street interests on a number of fronts. The Treasury proposal and the House bill each contain a dizzying array of elements, but five common themes are of interest here.

1. Leverage restrictions and minimal capital requirements for systemic risk (skin-in-the-game reforms)

2. Regulation of over-the-counter (OTC) derivatives or the requirement that they be traded on institutional exchanges

3. Restrictions on the practices and business models of large banks—the most notable of these coming after the House bill, called the Volcker rule, which was a more recent proposal by the president in January 2010

4. New regulations for credit rating agencies (CRAs)

5. A consumer financial protection agency

In the months before and after this proposal, various personalities and lobbies tossed in their suggestions for reform. Harvard Law School professor Elizabeth Warren, appointed to chair the congressional oversight panel for the TARP program, became an especially forceful advocate of an independent agency to regulate consumer financial products. Her public profile, her perch at a congressional position, and her incredible skill at addressing professional and public audiences made Warren a political entrepreneur with unrivaled influence on financial reform. Labor unions and progressive groups continued to pour resources into lobbying for the bill, though their energies were also diverted in part by the debate over health care reform.

Against these forces the various lobbies representing American and global finance entered the debate. These included the American Bankers' Association and the U.S. Chamber of Commerce. Conservative think tanks such as the American Enterprise Institute sponsored scholars and pundits—among them Charles Calomiris, Robert Hahn, Peter Wallison, and Todd Zywicki—who also expressed their doubts about financial reform and its effect on "financial innovation." When the Obama health care reform passed Congress and was signed into law, bankers' lobbies knew that financial reform was next on the national agenda, and they sprung into new and more visible forms of action (Dennis and Mufson 2010).

On July 21, 2010, a number of these reforms were struck into law in the Dodd-Frank Wall Street Reform and Consumer Protection Act. In the aftermath of President Obama's signature to that act in July 2010, some concomitant issues assumed the status of a litmus test for progressives, such as the appointment of Elizabeth Warren to the leadership of the newly established Bureau of Consumer Protection. If a theme emerges from the legislation, its politics, and the aftermath, it is that much of the real work of reform has just begun, with rule-making and enforcement patterns comprising the truly significant realms of American government activity.

In the following sections, I take up these themes one by one, and examine the change in legislation that took place from the initial Obama proposal to the final enactment of legislation. These changes are outlined in table 4.1, which offers a brief summary of the proposal and legislation as it wound its way through the House and Senate.

Capital Requirements and Leverage Restrictions

Financial reform witnessed major battles over the shape and content of capital requirements, namely the thorny question of how much hard capital banks should be required to keep versus how much of their capital they expose to risk-heavy trading and speculation activities. In the main, these battles did not receive the kind of media coverage and popular attention commanded by other features of financial reform, such as Senator Blanche

Table 4.1 Simplified Timeline of Major Provisions in Financial Reform, 2009 to 2010

Component of Financial Reform	Obama Administration Proposal (June 2009)	House Bill (December 2009)	Senate Bill (May 2010)	Final Act (July 2010)
Prudential regulation coordination	Financial Stability Oversight Council (FSOC)—oversees large, interconnected financial firms and banks		FSOC	FSOC—makes recommendations to Fed; with two-thirds vote, can force lenders into higher capitalization, or divest holdings for grave threat cases.
Leverage restrictions and capital requirements	Proposal for stronger capital and prudential standards for all firms; higher for "large, interconnected firms."	Moss proposal; 15 to 1 ratio of total capital to Tier 1 capital for all, higher requirements (lower ratio) for systemically central firms.	Susan Collins proposal of 25 to 1 capital ratio for banks with more than $250 billion in assets; different definition of regulatory and Tier 1 capital. (Treasury opposes.)	Delegates capital requirement setting to "appropriate Federal banking agencies" (Sec. 171). Systemic risk outlined; Tier 1 concept included but weakly defined. Keeps Collins amendment that prohibits bank holding companies from maintaining less capital than their small bank subsidiaries. Banks forced to drop trust-preferred securities (TruPS), with transition phase.

Restrictions on proprietary trading (Volcker rule)	Not in original June 2009 proposal; introduced in January 2010 by Obama.	No restrictions on proprietary trading or hedge funds.	Volcker rule adopted; regulators ban proprietary trading by insured depository institutions (Sec. 619).	Weakened Volcker rule (Maximum of 3 percent of Tier 1 capital for large firms. Bank capital can compose maximum 3 percent of any hedge fund invested in). Less discretion given to regulators.
Derivatives regulation	Call for comprehensive regulation.	Mandates trading on exchange for most derivatives (Peterson-Frank Amendment). Spin-off provision (Stupak) defeated.	Mandates trading on exchange for most derivatives. Lincoln proposal requiring CDS spin-off adopted for almost all derivatives and swaps.	Mandates trading on exchange for most derivatives. Lincoln spin-off proposal weakened, but spin-off required for commodity (agriculture and metal), energy and noninvestment grade CDS derivatives into nonbank entity (Sec. 721). Limitation on funding/bailing of swaps (Federal Reserve Act, Sec. 23A; Sec. 716). New swap product listing requirement at CFTC/SEC (Secs. 717–18).

(Table continues on p. 154.)

Table 4.1 *(Continued)*

Credit rating agencies (CRAs)	Calls on SEC to further regulate CRAs. Calls on regulators to rely less or no longer on CRAs in their institutional evaluations. Bans conflicted advising: CRAs can't market their consulting services to firms whose credit or debt they are rating.	Mandates annual SEC review and SEC rule-making for disclosure. Drops requirement that mutual funds limit their investments to top-rated assets. Adds legal expert liability for CRAs. Keeps conflicted advising ban.	SEC regulations from House bill, with Office of Credit Rating established in SEC. Franken amendment adopted to have unified government rating of credit agencies. LeMieux proposal adopted to divorce FDIC from reliance on CRA ratings.	SEC regulations from House bill preserved. Office of Credit Rating established in SEC. Franken amendment dropped. Statutes and federal agencies divorced from reliance on CRA credit ratings (Sec. 931).
Systemic risk—shut down	Calls for creation of financial institution shut-down plans.	Permits FDIC to liquidate risky firms through "orderly receivership." $150 billion liquidation fund established through fees on firms.	Liquidation through common agreement of Treasury, Fed, and FDIC. Defeated Sessions amendment to substitute bankruptcy for liquidation. Liquidation fund limited to $50 billion.	Liquidation provisions: Liquidation through common agreement of Treasury, Fed, and FDIC. No orderly liquidation fund from bank fees; monies instead from TARP residual (Title II, Sec. 201).
Consumer protection regulator	Independent agency, appointment by president.	Independent agency, appointment by president.	Partially independent bureau in Fed. Appointment by president. Budget from Fed transaction fees. Rule-making overseen by regulator council, not OIRA-OMB.[a]	Partially independent bureau in Fed. Appointment by president. Budget from Fed transaction fees. Rulemaking overseen by regulator council, not OIRA-OMB.[a]
Scope of consumer regulator	Retail financial products, insurance excluded and left to states.	Same as proposal.	Same as proposal.	Same scope as original, but auto dealers exempted from oversight.

Source: Author's compilation.

[a] OIRA-OMB: Office of Information and Regulatory Affairs in the Office of Management and Budget.

Lincoln's proposal for splitting commerical banks from their derivatives-trading operations and Elizabeth Warren's proposal for a new consumer protection agency in finance. Yet among and within the branches of American government, these were some of the most heavily pressured and watched battles.

It was commonly understood that a critical part of the financial regulatory reform would be to require certain kinds of banks to take on less risk. A basic idea was to separate commercial banks from using their privileged position of capital access, the Fed, and institutional backstopping, Federal Deposit Insurance Corporation (FDIC) guarantees for depository institutions, to take undue risks with capital.[12] The critical question throughout this debate was how much capital to require in various categories of risk, and how those categories of risk would be defined. The most commonly referenced concept was that of Tier 1 capital, which is essentially a bank's core investments in equity: direct company and asset investments, as differentiated from hedge funds, derivatives, or other secondary or tertiary asset markets. Well before the financial crisis, Tier 1 capital, as a percentage of assets or total capitalization, was interpreted as a measure of a bank's fiscal soundness.[13]

The Treasury Department's proposal was specific on a number of issues, but it was vague on capital requirements and on the importance of Tier 1 capital in particular. Instead the Treasury's blueprint of June 2009 suggested that stronger "prudential standards" should govern all firms and that "large, interconnected firms" should face stronger capital requirements. This more ambiguous stance reflected the Treasury Department's desire that prudential standards be delegated to regulators, namely to the Fed and the Treasury itself, as represented in the umbrella oversight body established by the legislation, the Financial Services Oversight Council (FSOC). Yet the Treasury Department's ambiguity created something of a legislative vacuum, and that space was quickly filled (in terms of a proposal) by the House Financial Services Committee. Working with the business historian David Moss of the Harvard Business School, Barney Frank's committee endorsed a proposal of a maximum 15 to 1 ratio of total capital to Tier 1 capital for all regulated firms, and a lower ratio, not fully specified but left to the FSOC, for systemically important and larger firms. This proposal, slightly modified, passed the House in December of 2009.

The 15 to 1 ratio provides an insightful example of the democratization of the reform process. In a world dominated by experts, regulators, and established committee chairmen, it was California Democrat Jackie Speier who assumed the critical legislative role in this saga. Speier worked with Moss more closely than any other member of Congress on this proposal, and her amendment was passed in committee and then adopted in the

House. Speier's amendment stemmed from an understanding of the failure of the Securities and Exchange Commission (SEC) in regulating capital requirements at major banking institutions. In 2004 the SEC offered an exemption on leverage and capital requirements to five major banks: Bear Stearns, Goldman Sachs, Lehman Brothers, Merrill Lynch, and Morgan Stanley. For three decades before the SEC exemption, broker dealers' capital ratio was set at a maximum of 12 to 1, but in the wake of the SEC's exemption, the five banks leveraged up well in excess of 20 to 1 and even above 30 to 1. It was a mark of how much had been opened in public debate about prudential regulation that a woman, a second-term legislator, and a relative outsider to finance politics could advance such an important amendment, and see that amendment pass through a powerful committee and the House. And the amendment came not from consultation with an economics doctorate, but from collaboration with a professional historian (Grim 2009).

The Senate took up the House proposal and, partly at the behest of the Treasury Department, proposed to reduce its specificity. Yet, in a critical but unexpected turn of events, a juncture that happened after Dodd introduced his bill, Senator Susan Collins (R-ME) in May 2009 offered her own proposal for leverage requirements.[14] Collins's proposal is more complicated than can be summarized fully here, but it had two critical planks: a mandated 25 to 1 ratio of total capital to Tier 1 capital, lower for systemically critical firms, and a tightened definition of Tier 1 capital, such that hybrid investment vehicles known as trust-preferred securities (TruPS) would no longer qualify as Tier 1 capital. In many respects, the Collins leverage proposal worried major banks even more than the House legislation did, and House legislators weakened it in the conference committee stage of legislation (Dixon and Younglai 2010). The Treasury Department again expressed its opposition to this proposal—now not only the ratios but the very concepts by which capital would be defined would be taken partially out of the department's orbit.[15] But with Collins centrally involved in the capital requirements game, Dodd could no longer function as an effective proposal stopper. With the victory of Scott Brown in the January 2010 Massachusetts Senate race, Collins became the kind of moderate Republican that Senate Democrats like Dodd sorely needed to get the bill through. Hence Collins could not be ignored. Whereas Dodd initially tried to stop the Collins proposal on behalf of Treasury, it was later on that the Treasury Department, realizing that Collins's proposal was likely to survive and that Democrats could not afford to alienate her, asked Dodd to relent and allow the Collins proposal through the Senate. Collins's proposal also had the backing of FDIC chairwoman Sheila Bair, a

Republican appointee and an experienced official widely respected among the conservative-leaning circles of American finance policy.

The final legislation embeds parts of the Collins proposal's more rigid definition of Tier 1 capital, though it delegates the question for study.[16] The exact capital requirements will, however, be delegated to "appropriate federal banking regulatory agencies"; even the recipient of delegated power is not precisely established under the statute. The final act keeps the Collins amendment that requires bank holding companies to hold at least as much Tier 1 capital as smaller banks, a requirement calibrated by reference to the smaller bank subsidiaries of these holding companies. Banks are also forced to drop TruPS from their Tier 1 capital requirements, with a long transition phase for doing so.

The capital requirements battle was only part of the larger financial reform package, but it expressed some of the more visible patterns of financial politics during the early years of the Obama administration and the 111th Congress—the relative independence of the House Financial Services Committee from the Treasury Department, compared with the Senate Finance Committee, and the unique power of unexpected proposals from structurally and symbolically pivotal legislators. The relevant planks of the legislation will depend heavily on regulators for enforcement.

Proprietary Trading Restrictions

Another important battleground in the reform debate was tied to observers' understanding of the financial crisis and past battles over financial innovation. The problem of moral hazard, as it was widely termed, was not simply a matter of government-backed banks abusing their protection by overleveraging themselves. It was also that government-backed banks had the status of depository institutions. The very risk-pursuant institutions were those that held the savings of the middle and working classes, and yet the banks that would get in the most trouble by this system of incentives were those that would place enormous aggregate liabilities on the federal government in the case of hedges gone bad. In this way, institutional moral hazard threatened not only consumers but also the federal government's balance sheet.

Neither the Treasury proposal nor the House bill entertained serious limitations on proprietary activities of commercial banks—the activities often associated with investment banks, such as foreign exchange trading, hedge fund management, or arbitrage-related operations. Yet in the midst of the financial reform debate of the fall of 2010, many commentators noticed that a critical act of the 1990s—the 1999 repeal of the Glass-Steagall

Act of 1933—had not been discussed as a possible contributor to the financial crisis.

Into the vacuum stepped former Federal Reserve chairman Paul Volcker. Volcker had the bipartisan credibility of someone who once served Republican causes—as Fed chairman he had consciously and controversially kept a lid on inflation during the early 1980s during the depth of that recession—and who had decades-long experience in global financial policy. Volcker advanced a proposal, one favored by President Obama in January 2009 when it was announced, which required that insured depository institutions be prohibited from proprietary trading activities. Again the Treasury Department did not endorse this proposal, and numerous commentators have suggested that its leadership—Secretary Geithner and Assistant Secretary Barr—opposed rigorous partitioning of commercial banking from proprietary trading. Again, however, the Treasury Department's hands were somewhat tied; in February 2010, five former Treasury secretaries came out in public support of the Volcker rule, stating in a letter to the *Wall Street Journal* that "banks benefiting from public support by means of access to the Federal Reserve and FDIC insurance should not engage in essentially speculative activity unrelated to essential bank services" (Carney 2010; Johnson 2010; Blumenthal et al. 2010).

The Volcker rule in its strict form was written into the Senate legislation by Oregon Democrat Jeff Merkley and Michigan Democrat Carl Levin. The clause passed the Senate, and soon after the passage of the Senate bill, the Obama Treasury Department hinted that it would support the proposal in negotiations over reconciling the House and Senate version (Lowrey 2010). In part because of the pivotal influence of Massachusetts Republican Scott Brown, however, the Volcker rule was diluted into what is known as the 3-percent Volcker rule. Only a maximum of 3 percent of Tier 1 capital can be invested by large firms in proprietary activities, including hedge funds and private equity funds, and no federally insured bank's investments can make up more than 3 percent of any single hedge fund. The discretion given to regulators under the final bill is reduced compared to that of the Senate proposal, and some observers see the Treasury Department as reluctant to write detailed (read, binding and specific) new rules for the Volcker rule's enforcement.[17]

Derivatives

A third area in which large investment banks and financial institutions would be potentially constrained in financial reform appears in the regu-

lation of derivatives markets, especially those sold over the counter between two or more counterparties and not cleared upon an exchange. It is
a more complicated story than can be told adequately here, but derivatives got their start in agricultural commodities, where bundles of futures
contracts, and bundles of those bundles, were the subject of massive speculation from the late nineteenth century onward in grain, meat, and other
agricultural markets. It is for this reason that a regulatory agency that initially had primary authority over agricultural commodities—the Commodity Futures Trading Commission (CFTC)—began to investigate the
regulation of derivatives in the 1990s. In a now legendary showdown, the
chair of that commission (Brooksley Born) advanced a proposal for derivatives regulation that earned the strident opposition of major financial
players in the Clinton administration, mainly Fed chairman Alan Greenspan, Treasury Secretary Robert Rubin, and (later) Treasury Secretary
Lawrence Summers.

The Treasury's June 2009 proposal again gave derivatives regulation a
rather ambiguous treatment, and the major proposal for regulation of derivatives—namely, moving them from over-the-counter trading to institutionally regulated trading on an exchange—came in the Peterson-Frank
amendment, which was incorporated into the House legislation. Many
amendments were offered to the House legislation, but two by Michigan
representative Bart Stupak demonstrated the relatively moderate nature
of the House bill's restrictions. Stupak proposed first that any derivative
must be traded on a federally registered exchange; this proposal failed by
a vote of 98 to 330. He then proposed that the Commodity Futures Trading
Commission or the Securities and Exchange Commission be empowered
to ban "abusive swaps." This amendment also failed. The large margins
against Stupak's two amendments suggest that the appetitite for derivatives regulation in the House was moderate.

Another amendment by New York representative Scott Murphy
was intended to weaken the application of derivatives regulation to the
major banks by constraining the definition of *major swap participant* in the
Peterson-Frank clause to "those firms that either do a substantial amount
of speculative trading or that have derivative positions that are large
enough to pose a threat to the financial system." The terms in the clause
would obviously be defined by future regulators, but there was a substantial chance that, if struck into law, the Murphy amendment would
limit derivatives regulation on Wall Street rather substantially, which according to observers was precisely Murphy's intent. Murphy was, however, especially interested in protecting smaller trading houses and capital firms, as opposed to major investment banks. In a surprise to House

Democratic leaders and a setback for Frank and the House Financial Services Committee, this regulation-weakening amendment passed on the House floor with the votes of many Republicans as well as those of many Democrats.

Murphy's intervention into the derivatives section of the reform initiative did not come merely from his own wishes. In a sequence of events whose coincidence has drawn the attention of federal investigators, Murphy and other conservative House Democrats met with Wall Street bankers in a private fundraiser just before critical votes in October 2009 and December 2009 (Roth 2010; Vekshin and Kopecki 2010). The itinerary for the event suggests that issues critical to systemically important investment banks were likely discussed immediately before House members took a vote on them (see figure 4.2).[18]

Some additional insight into the appeal of the Murphy amendment, as well as into the cross-cutting pressures applied to the House Democratic caucus, can be gleaned from examining the legislators who voted for the final measure but also for the Murphy amendment (see table 4A.1). This list suggests that a great number of legislators voting for the Murphy amendment may have been influenced by farm-state interests, as many agribusinesses and moderate-sized farmers used derivatives as a way of hedging against swings in factor (input) prices as well as against produced commodity prices. This hypothesis needs additional examination, yet a logistic regression (table 4A.2) shows that the usual economic ideology measure used in congressional studies (D-NOMINATE First Dimension), although predictive of whether a Democrat switched to support the Murphy amendment on the floor, did not exhaust the predictive power of other variables. The second dimension measure, often indicative of social liberalism-conservatism, was also strongly predictive of the Murphy switch. So, too, members whose voting records are simply harder to classify according to the usual criteria, measured by members associated with a higher prediction error in the construction of the D-NOMINATE indices, were also more likely to switch to the Murphy amendment. What this suggests is that the Murphy switchers were not easily identifiable by the standard party and ideology metrics used in legislative studies (see figure 4.3).

The Senate bill followed the House bill in that it mandated trading on exchanges for all but a small set of derivatives. Yet just when derivatives-trading operations felt that, with the Murphy amendment and the moderate nature of the Dodd bill, they had dodged a bullet, an unforeseen critical event happened again. Senator Blanche Lincoln of Arkansas, under a serious primary challenge from Attorney General Bill Halter of Arkansas, seized on derivatives regulation as a way to demonstrate her bona fides to

Figure 4.2   Itinerary for a Murphy-Crowley Meeting of October 2009

MONDAY, OCTOBER 12	
12:00 – 1:30:	Possible lunch arranged by Scott Murphy and Joe Crowley
1:30 – 2:30:	Open for meeting
3:00 – 4:30:	NewDems to meet with Goldman Sachs executives (Confirmed: Crowley, Scott Murphy, Giffords; Possible: Moore, Schiff, McCarthy)
6:00 – 7:30:	NewDem Reception at home of Larry Coben, (Confirmed: Crowley, Murphy, Giffords, Schiff; Possible: Moore, McCarthy)
TUESDAY, OCTOBER 13	
9:00 – 10:00:	Open for meeting
10:30 – 12:00:	NewDems to meet with 35-50 CEOs of Marsh & McLennan Companies, 1166 6th Avenue, NY,NY (Confirmed: Murphy, Himes; Possible: Adler, Moore)
2:15 – 3:00:	NewDems to meet with JP Morgan Executives (Confirmed: Bean, Murphy, Himes, Crowley, Adler)
3:00 – 3:30:	Return to DC for Tuesday evening votes

Source: Author's adaptation of a Talking Points Memo document (TPM 2010).

Arkansas Democratic primary voters. She introduced an amendment that would require all commercial banks to partition their derivatives-trading units into legally and organizationally separate entities. This spin-off proposal surprised and alarmed major banks and their lobbyists, who were neither expecting it nor pleased with its implications. Swaps units had become important profit centers for major commercial banks in the previous decade.

The Lincoln proposal, like the Collins proposal on capital requirements and Senator Scott Brown's weakening of the bill in conference in June 2010, demonstrated the enormous shadow of the Senate filibuster. Either to weaken or to strengthen the proposal, well-positioned senators (conservative Democrats or moderate Republicans) could hold up an entire legis-

Figure 4.3   Role Played by Variables Other Than Economic Ideology
in the Switch of December 2009

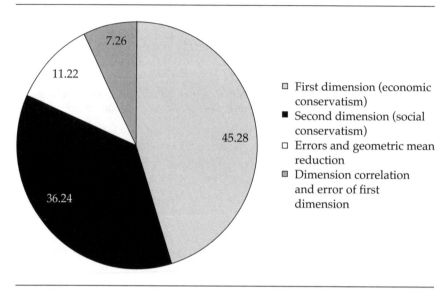

First dimension (economic conservatism)

Second dimension (social conservatism)

Errors and geometric mean reduction

Dimension correlation and error of first dimension

Source: Figure based on author's data.

Note: Pie entries are percentage of explained variance contributed by variable. Total explained variance is pseudo-R-squared of .2657, or just above a quarter of variance explained. Total variance explained by first-dimension ideology score (economic conservatism) is .1203 or 12 percent.

lative package because of the necessity of having sixty votes to proceed in the Senate. Strategically, the filibuster requirement was compounded by Senator Harry Reid's refusal to call Republicans' bluff and to compel them to filibuster popular legislation.

The Lincoln spin-off provision survived the Senate intact, and various interests (including the Treasury Department itself, allied with Dodd) immediately set about trying to weaken or kill it. In some measure, as the final structure of the legislation suggests, they succeeded. In other respects, Lincoln understood that the success of the proposal would be critical to her chances for a Senate primary victory as well as the (slim) prospect of her reelection in Arkansas in an off-year midterm season.

And perhaps most surprisingly, the fight over the derivatives provision in the conference committee—with various senators arguing for the strict Lincoln spin-off and others for weakening it, and House conferees largely favoring a more relaxed version—deflected attention and lobbying power from other issues and planks of the legislation. As in much political bargaining, especially at such a late stage of the game, players had to focus their attention on just a few issues. It was widely expected that conferees would attempt to weaken the consumer financial protection agency or perhaps the capital requirements; yet the immense push against the stringent form of the Lincoln amendment deflected attention away from those issues. In the absence of Lincoln's primary-induced proposal, not only derivatives regulation but also other planks of the Dodd-Frank Act would have looked quite different from their enacted form.

The final act preserved much of Lincoln's derivatives rule, mandating a spin-off for commodity-based derivatives (agriculture and metals), energy derivatives (such as those perfected and traded by Enron before its infamous demise), and non-investment-grade credit default swap derivatives. Any commercial bank must henceforth partition these operations in a nonbank entity, one without the protections and advantages of a federal bank chapter, FDIC insurance, or the Fed's credit window. In a little-noticed but fundamental revision to Section 23A of the Federal Reserve Act, financial institutions with derivatives operations can no longer use other funds and assets to bail out their derivatives operations, and in an odd resurrection of Congressman Bart Stupak's December 2009 amendment, the act mandates the vehicle listing of all "new derivative products" by the CFTC and the SEC (Sections 717 and 718 of the Dodd-Frank Act).

Reform and Regulation of Credit Rating Agencies

The role of credit rating agencies in the financial crisis of 2008 has been widely discussed. Much like the centrality of accounting firm Arthur Andersen to the corruption and demise of Enron, it is said, credit rating agencies facilitated the corruption and demise of major Wall Street firms by overrating the soundness of financial institutions and the risky mortgage-backed investments in which they were piling their capital. The Obama Treasury proposal gave particular specificity to CRA regulation, calling for the Securities and Exchange Commission to more strictly regulate them. In a move to give the government's financial regulators more independence and expertise, the Obama Treasury proposal also called on other government regulators to avoid using CRA ratings in their evaluations of the safety and soundness of financial institutions and asset classes. Finally, the Obama proposal banned conflicted advising, or the marketing by CRAs of their services or evaluations to firms whose debt or creditworthiness they were rating.

The case of CRA reform stands as one where, for all intents and purposes, the outline the Obama administration suggested was strengthened and rendered more specific by action in Congress. It is worth considering as something of a departure case whose development runs counter to the general tendencies of the various reform planks, most of which were watered down or heavily amended with generalities or exceptions in the House and Senate, and often yet again in conference. Led by Massachusetts Democrat Barney Frank, the House took the Obama proposal and specified a positive mandate for annual SEC review and reports on CRAs, including a disclosure of their potential conflicts of interest and their ratings decisions. The House also undermined a key girder of the CRAs' power, dropping the requirement that mutual funds limit their investments to top-rated investment classes—this too was Barney Frank's aspiration—and the House further added expert legal liability for CRAs, exposing them for the first time to tortiable claims at the federal level. The Obama administration's conflicted advising ban was kept.

The Senate did little to change the House bill on this front and further established an Office of Credit Rating in the SEC. Senator Al Franken introduced a controversial amendment to have a unified and systematic government rating of the various CRAs; this amendment would not survive the conference committee. The conference committee and the final bill did, however, retain the major planks the Treasury had promulgated a year earlier. It also severely limited the CRAs' power and legitimacy by divorcing regulatory agency judgments and mutual fund investments from the ratings.

A New Regulatory Agency

The most controversial proposal of the Obama financial agenda came in the form of the resurrection of an older idea about consumer financial protection, one implemented by the Canadian government in 2002. In 2007, Harvard law scholar Elizabeth Warren published a highly influential essay in the journal *Democracy* titled "Unsafe at Any Rate." The idea for an agency was built on work she had done with a new academic network, the Tobin Project, founded by Harvard Business School professor David Moss. Warren's idea was to create a separate agency for financial safety, one that echoed institutions the Canadian government had established almost a decade earlier. Even in the midst of the financial crisis of the fall of 2008, little legislative or media attention was given to this idea. The idea became legislatively tangible in March 2009, when it was formally introduced to Congress as a proposal for a Financial Products Safety Commission by Representatives William Delahunt of Massachusetts and Brad Miller of North Carolina. Key players in the Obama administration had been attracted to the idea—some, Assistant Treasury Secretary Michael Barr and the president, more than others, including Treasury Secretary Timothy Geithner and National Economic Council head Larry Summers—and the Treasury included the independent agency idea in its blueprint for financial reform in June 2009.

In the year after the Treasury plan was introduced, the independent agency idea attracted considerable attention, if not most of it, and conspicuous vitriol. Warren's brainchild was supported and attacked, surpassed only by health care and perhaps Afghanistan as front-page news and a front-burner priority for politicians. Yet other changes that are further off the radar screen have come in for strong opposition from banks, lending companies, and existing federal agencies with turf and fee-based revenues to protect.

A Threat, and the Fed's Response   The idea for a new independent consumer agency did not become tangible or threatening to existing regulators with turf to protect until March 2009, when a bill creating the Financial Product Safety Commission (FPSC) was introduced in the House of Representatives. The announcement for this bill came on March 5, 2009.[19] The formal bill was introduced to the Senate on March 10.[20] A number of Web-based news sources also began to discuss the legislative proposal for a new commission around this time (*Huffington Post* 2009). President Obama also mentioned the idea in an appearance that month on *The Tonight Show with Jay Leno*.[21]

In the bills introduced to Congress, and in the Obama administration's proposal as released in June 2009, the Consumer Financial Protection Agency (CFPA) posed clear threats to the turf of what may be called the status-quo regulators of U.S. consumer finance. What was undoubtedly concerning to officials at the Fed, the FDIC, the Federal Trade Commission (FTC), and other agencies was that significant parts of their governing authority, which one might call their policy turf, and in some cases their budgets and personnel would stand to be transferred to the new consumer agency. The FTC was one of the agencies to circle wagons most forcefully. Commissioner William Kovacic read the administration's bill as transferring "*all* consumer financial protection functions of the Federal Trade Commission" to the new agency. He also saw the legislation as defining "consumer financial protection functions so broadly as to include 'research, rulemaking, issuance of orders or guidance.' This expansive definition would include the Bureau of Economics' research as well as the FTC's enormously valuable public workshops and consumer education programs" (2009, 23). Kovacic saw in the bill an affront not merely to the agency as a whole, but to its Bureau of Economics and its Bureau of Competition in particular. Indeed, Kovacic's defense of the commission was so strong that he saw the financial crisis as a rationale for expanding the powers and responsibilities of the FTC: "Rather than divest the FTC of all of its consumer financial protection functions and give it hollow 'backstop authority,' a more promising approach could be to remove jurisdictional limits that currently constrain the FTC's regulatory and enforcement authority in the financial services sector" (25).

Yet given the size and expanse of the Federal Reserve—and its privileged funding structure among government agencies—it is not surprising that the Federal Reserve's mobilization against a fully independent consumer agency was larger and more forceful. Some observers saw in the CFPA proposal the largest threat to the Fed in four decades (Appelbaum 2009).[22] The bill passed by the House and initially considered in the Senate would have created and authorized the transfer of authorities, funds, and personnel from a number of national agencies, most notably the Federal Reserve.[23] Beyond this, the proposals had some of the CFPA's funding coming directly from the Fed. This proposed change was significant, given that the Federal Reserve's funding model differs from that of most federal agencies in that it is fee-based and less visible to the taxpayer. Of course, American consumers pay for the Federal Reserve's operations nonetheless, because banks undoubtedly pass along the direct costs of the fees, and the indirect administrative or compliance costs of paying them, to their customers. Banks and other lender organizations lobby against increases in these fees, and hence the size of aggregate fee revenue can only be so large before it is constrained by political resistance from banks and other fee-payors. Given such a constraint, each agency funded by fees has an incentive to capture the largest portion of the transaction and institution fee base that it can, hence the transfer of Fed funds to the CFPA would profoundly affect the Fed even though it did not alter the balance of spending and taxation.[24]

The Fed responded in speechmaking and in activity, both defending its statutory and historical prerogatives in consumer protection, and pumping up its enforcement activities. Fed official Daniel Tarullo offered the first comprehensive public statement on consumer protection regulation by top Fed officials in the entire aftermath of the financial crisis on March 19, 2009 (2009a).[25] Chairman Ben Bernanke did not mention regulation of consumer products in any speech following the crisis until April 2, right after (and well after) legislative energy for the proposal for consumer protection had begun. His major address on the issue came in mid-April 2009, when he addressed the issue of consumer protection for the first time in his response to the financial crisis. The first hint of opposition to the independent agency came in Bernanke's insistence that it would be his agency that would offer the appropriate response to government failures in financial consumer protection in testimony on July 21, 2009. This was followed by Governor Tarullo's warnings in testimony to the Senate on July 23, 2009. Then, two days after Bernanke defended his institution before Congress on July 21, and the very day that Tarullo warned Congress about the costs of transferring these important responsibilities to another agency, or any agency not under the Fed's penumbra, the Fed announced the first in a set of critical proposed rules changes, to Regulation Z for mortgage disclosures. Two months later, as the House began to take up the independent agency proposal in committee, the Fed proposed that credit cards should be subject to similar regulatory reforms, and Bernanke followed on the first of October with a proposal that Congress create a council of risk regulators. This proposal, which would have the effect of retaining the status-quo regulators for systemic and possibly consumer finance, echoed a plan for a council of consumer protection regulators that was then under consideration in the House, proposed by Idaho Democrat Walt Minnick. The House later defeated the Minnick plan and passed a financial regulatory reform bill that established the CFPA (see Bernanke 2009; Tarullo 2009b; Board of Governors 2009a, 2009b).

In July 2009, when Fed officials proposed a second set of revisions to Regulation Z, observers of financial markets and financial regulation noted two things. First, they were significant, with the *Wall Street Journal* calling them "sweeping new consumer protections for mortgages and home-equity loans." The new rules compelled simplified disclosures for mortgage costs and amortization terms, effectively banned yield spread premiums, directed lenders to create one-page documents demonstrating the risks of loans to consumers, and forced lenders to show consumers how their rate compares with rates of borrowers with better credit (see Holzer 2009). Second, observers noted the clear correspondence of these rules to the turf threat posed by a CFPA. As contributors for the financial website Fxstreet.com stated in an interpretation of the July 2009 proposed rules, "Bottom line: The proposed changes are in line with suggested reforms within the legislative process regarding the Consumer Financial Protection Agency (CFPA). The Federal Reserve may no longer regulate consumer financial products under certain iterations of the legislation backing the CFPA. Today's announcement is part of the feedback loop regarding this pending legislation and implications for the Federal Reserve's structure" (BBVA Bancomer Team 2009).

So, too, there was an odd and little noticed bump in Federal Reserve Bank enforcement patterns, especially starting in March of 2009. Using data listed on the Fed's website, announced enforcement actions against banks and lenders came at a snail's pace—just over three per month—

Figure 4.4   Fed Announced Enforcement Actions, Monthly Average

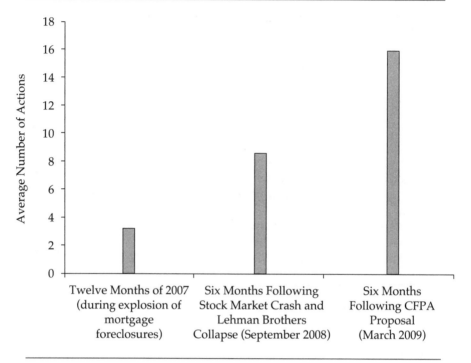

Source: Figure based on author's data.

during the very time that active foreclosures were hitting 1 million in statistical reports. Only when the crisis passed "from Main Street to Wall
Street," in September 2008, did Fed enforcement activity (again, its own
announcements) surge to about eight and a half per month. But the Fed's
announcements on its enforcement activity reached new and unprecedented heights when Congress took up the idea of an independent regulator in March 2009. From a postcrisis average of eight announced enforcement actions per month, the Fed nearly doubled its announcements to
sixteen actions per month. Every other day, or three out of four business
days per week, the Fed was publicly announcing a new enforcement action (see figure 4.4).

Full Circle, the Fed Gets a Consumer Bureau   Financial politics is rich
with ironies, and one of the richer ones is that the Dodd-Frank Act places

a consumer protection agency within the boundaries of the Federal Reserve. In a proposal released on March 15, 2010, Dodd proposed placing a consumer bureau inside the Fed, and, in a sign that Dodd and other legislators had done their political homework, independent agency advocate Elizabeth Warren endorsed the proposal. Although it is difficult to prove, the Federal Reserve's consumer protection push from March 2009 forward probably made the agency a more hospitable location for a consumer protection bureau. I have argued elsewhere that the Fed may be a poor place for a consumer protection bureau, given the agency's undistinguished consumer protection record, and its habit of shifting attention from consumer protection to monetary policy first, then prudential regulation second, when the chance permits. The issue has less to do with organizational capacity—there are skilled cadres of bank regulators and inspectors in the regional banks and offices of the Federal Reserve System—as with the lack of status that consumer protection activity has at the Fed. In light of the financial crisis, the reputational threats to the Fed, and the creation of the new consumer bureau, this status hierarchy may change considerably in the years to come (Carpenter 2010b; Chan 2010).

In theory, Dodd's proposal left the consumer agency within the Federal Reserve but autonomous (see the various subheadings in Title X where this aspect of the agency seems to be highlighted). But on this point, it is questionable whether the Fed can really commit to keeping its hands off of the consumer bureau. Consider again the reputational incentives. If the Fed's leadership would rather claim credit for consumer protection, or if it fears that an aggressive consumer rule will get in the way of its prudential regulation or the profitability of financial institutions, it may well try to tamp down on the agency by pressuring its oversight council, throwing procedural roadblocks in the way of consumer protection rules, or some other obstructionist measure. Rather uniquely among regulatory agencies, the consumer bureau will have its rules reviewed by other financial regulators.[26]

Nonetheless, progressive proponents of financial reform have genuine reasons to think that the new Consumer Financial Protection Bureau (CFPB) will have strong powers. Even though its rules will be reviewed by an oversight council, they will not be reviewed by the Office of Information and Regulatory Affairs (OIRA) in the Office of Management and Budget (OMB), where cost-benefit analysis has become entrenched in the last three decades. The independent funding stream from the Federal Reserve will insulate the bureau from appropriations politics. And the legislation even included the possibility of an interim director appointed through the Treasury Department, temporarily bypassing the Senate confirmation process.[27]

A late-stage legislative defeat for proponents of a consumer bureau came in the carve-out exemption won by independent auto dealers. California Republican John Campbell introduced the amendment, which passed on the House floor and again in the Senate after being introduced by Sam Brownback. Independent auto dealers are in every congressional district and, as one congressional staffer observed, "sponsor Little Leagues and soccer games." Their ubiquitous presence was enough to overcome opposition to the amendment from the House Financial Services Committee and the Obama administration. It was an example of the power of some of the smallest financial institutions in the odd and complicated politics of the 111th Congress.

In the two months following the passage of the Dodd-Frank Act, perhaps the most acrimonious fight came over the possible appointment of Elizabeth Warren as first director of the bureau. The issue did not arise until a July 15, 2010, report in the *Huffington Post* suggested that Treasury Secretary Timothy Geithner opposed Warren's appointment to the post, preferring instead his deputy Michael Barr. Progressive activists immediately and furiously set into motion, circulating a petition to the president for Warren's appointment that garnered a quarter-million signatures within a month (Nasiripour 2010).[28]

Liberal Democrats (including Barney Frank), skeptical economists (such as Simon Johnson and Paul Krugman), and progressive activists (SEIU and AFL-CIO on the labor side, as well as Web-based progressive groups such as Progressive Change Campaign Committee) openly lobbied Obama to nominate none other than Elizabeth Warren, brain-mother of the independent consumer regulator, to head the new agency. Republicans like Alabama Senator Richard Shelby announced their opposition to Warren, but others, such as Charles Grassley of Iowa, were viewed as possibly supportive. The Warren nomination assumed a symbolic status to the progressive wing of the Democratic Party that rivaled, if it did not surpass, the pressure that surrounded the public option concept in the national health care debate.

Senator Dodd complicated matters, perhaps intentionally given his ties to the Treasury Department, when he repeatedly expressed concern about whether Warren would be confirmable in the Senate. On September 17, 2010, Obama stood in the Rose Garden with Warren at his side and announced his appointment of her as a special assistant to the president, and to Secretary Geithner, for the purpose of managing the launch of the consumer bureau. Although some confusion set in about the precise nature of Warren's authorities and powers under the post, liberal groups and union leaders hailed the appointment.

Warren immediately set about creating the structural and human foundations of the bureau. She did so by recruiting top legal and financial talent to the agency, and by embedding an important principle in the very DNA of the agency's official structure. She focused regulatory attention on two central consumer financial products—mortgages and credit cards—and placed these at the top of her organizational chart for offices where rules would be written (figure 4.5). That chart also reflected an important principle, namely that rule writing would be deeply affected by research organized within the bureau. So, too, Warren's first appointments—Rajeev Date of the Cambridge Winter Center for Financial Institutions Policy as a senior advisor; Steven Antonakes, former commissioner of banks for Massachusetts, to lead depository supervision; Richard Cordry, former Ohio attorney general, to head enforcement; and David Silberman of Kessler Financial Services to head the establishment of the credit cards unit—reflected an emphasis on coalition-building, on legitimacy, and on quick and early action on mortgages and credit cards.

As important as structural work was political work. In at least three deft moves, Warren began to lay the foundation for a supportive coalition undergirding her agency. First, she began her appointment by striking a conciliatory stance toward the politically organized banking industry, appearing at a meeting of the Financial Services Roundtable in September 2010. Rather publicly, Warren pledged to work cooperatively with bankers' organizations and remarked, "It is now, right here at the beginning, that we have a remarkable chance to put aside misconceptions and preconceptions—whether they are yours or mine." Although some measure of distrust continued between the bankers' lobby and Warren, observers report that her public addresses eased the tension. Second, Warren began to invite state attorneys general to participate in establishing the agency and even consult making rules. This move headed off federalism-based objections and helped to cement the legitimacy judgments and the loyalty of the attorneys general. Finally, Warren continued to court community banks with assurances that the bureau's policies would help them compete on a more even playing field vis-à-vis larger banks and lending companies.[29]

FINANCIAL REFORM, ITS SIGNIFICANCE, AND ITS LEGACIES

In the aftermath of the signing of the Dodd-Frank Act, it is clear that major regulatory change has been accomplished in legislation. In light of the indeterminacy of financial reform, it is incontestable that considerable institutional change is being anticipated by major American and global banks, which have already begun to consult lawyers and boards to map out strat-

Figure 4.5 Planned Organization Chart of the Consumer Financial Protection Bureau, April 25, 2011

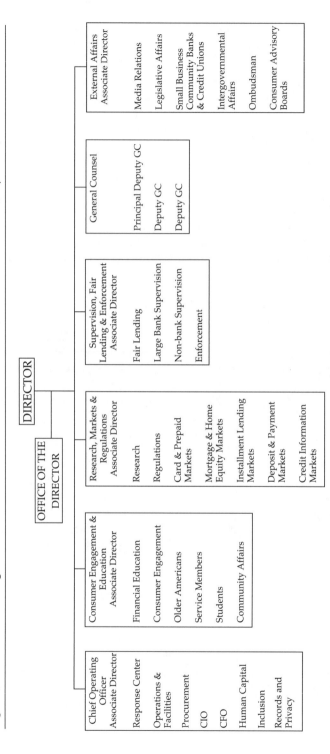

Source: From the Treasury Department's Consumer Finance Protection Bureau implementation team (http://www.consumerfinance.gov/the-bureau).

egies for separating parts of their operations from their core banking services (Yang 2010).

Another force shaping the evolution of financial reform will be the opposition and constraint emerging from the House of Representatives, where Republicans won a commanding majority in the midterm elections of November 2010. Republicans voted near-uniformly against the Dodd-Frank bill in the House and all but three (Scott Brown, Olympia Snowe, and Susan Collins) voted against the bill in the Senate. Although criticism of the act from incoming House Financial Services Committee chair Spencer Bachus has been considerable, it remains that the Republicans are less likely to act forcefully to water down the Dodd-Frank bill than they are to constrain its implementation through congressional oversight. It is, to begin with, quite telling that, unlike the case of the Affordable Care Act, which congressional Republicans have vowed to repeal, no such broad vows have been made by Republican leadership for repealing the Dodd-Frank Act. This difference stems not least from the broader popularity of the financial reform package and from the still-dubious public reputation of Wall Street and the American banking sector.

The newly elected Republican House majority aims to conduct strict oversight of the Consumer Financial Protection Bureau, but its hands are tied. Although congressional Republicans can use appropriations as an oversight tool to control many federal agencies, the CFPB receives its funding from the Federal Reserve budget, which is financed by transaction fees, not legislative appropriations. Although some congressional Republicans have voiced their intention to return the bureau to appropriations-based funding, this move would require a positive change in law and is unlikely to pass the Senate or the veto pen of President Obama. More likely, the early actions of congressional Republicans will focus on hearings and using publicity to shape the choices and agenda of the bureau.

One reason congressional Republicans may focus heavily on administrative implementation is that most of the critical action has been delegated to federal regulators. To some extent this pattern confirms a long-studied array of delegation decisions in political science, whereby politicians embrace the risk of losing control over policy by taking advantage of the superior expertise and capacity of administrative organizations (for literature on delegation in political science, see Epstein and O'Halloran 1999; Huber and Shipan 2002).[30] Yet the dynamics of financial reform in the Obama agenda gesture to a much more complicated (in some respects, more strategic but less predictable, ex ante or ex post) dynamic than political science models of delegation usually recognize. The financial realm in American politics is, as I suggested at the outset of this chapter, rather well populated by agencies with considerable capacity, especially when the United States is compared with other advanced industrial democracies. Delegation, in this context, was not merely the choice of a legislature as to whether to hand over policymaking authority versus the trade-off in expertise foregone by entrusting policymaking to congressional committees. Rather, existing financial agencies with stable funding models and thousands upon thousands of highly educated, centrally positioned, and legitimated employees lobbied aggressively for their agencies or their professional disciplines (quantitative finance, administative and contracts law, behavioral finance, and others). The result of the Dodd-Frank Act was as much due to the machinations of existing federal agencies, especially the Treasury and the Federal Reserve, as to the conscious decisions of legislators about where to place delegated authority. This is all the more so in the case of the Obama financial regulation initiative because the main blueprint for the entire effort was sketched out in the Treasury Department.

As evidence that administrative and bureaucratic politics lies at the center of past and present financial reform, the most pitched battles in the wake of President Obama's signing of the Dodd-Frank Act have come in appointments and rule-making. Combined with expressions of doubt by Senators Merkley and Levin, on the one hand, and the economist Simon Johnson, on the other, about the Treasury Department's seriousness in writing strong rules to enforce the Volcker provision, the fight over the Warren nomination suggests that the biggest battles of American financial reform have yet to be waged. And when they are waged, they will be fought in venues much less visible than those that hosted legislative debate over the last two years; progressive groups and consumer groups, sensing this reality, were pressing the Warren nomination for precisely this reason.

Yet the existence of this robust public debate, among other transformations, suggests that something changed, albeit temporarily, in the last two years. The financial crisis and the national debate over financial regulation opened a social aperture in finance policymaking. Progressive and liberal groups were fighting over appointments and rules precisely because they knew that the doors would soon close on public voice in the process, but also because they could credibly participate in a process where they had previously been invisible. Jackie Speier and David Moss—a second-term female legislator and a business historian—would probably have been unable, in previous decades, to introduce powerful new capital restrictions on systemically vital institutions. The gilded network cracked open because its experts in academia, on Wall Street, and in Washington have surrendered great legitimacy in the wake of the crisis. If previous justifications for a restricted circle of policy influence were premised on the expertise needed to contribute to financial policy debates, that rationale was powerfully undermined when so many observers saw in the financial crisis a multidimensional catastrophe of banking practices, the theory and methods of the economics profession, and the culture and rigor of the nation's regulatory agencies. The fall of the credit rating agencies—their excision from federal statute, their tight regulation, and the near-disappearance of their global and political status—remains one of the clearest markers of this transformation.

Still, the paths not taken in this saga remain informative. At least four major ideas were cast aside: an independent consumer protection agency, requirements for "plain vanilla" baselines for consumer financial products, the Volcker rule in its pure form, and a tax on larger banks to pay for the possible costs of future bailouts. The more stringent regulation of derivatives in the original House bill is also a casualty of the process, though the Lincoln amendment to the Senate legislation helped to resurrect these restrictions.

As I have intimated elsewhere (Carpenter 2010c), the strangulation metaphor may be apt here because these various proposals died a relatively quiet death. There was the pivotal politics of the Senate filibuster and the usual expression of multiple veto points, but those points were as much the result of culturally and institutionally privileged elites as they were of the calculus of supermajorities. Given that moments of major institutional reform in finance come only once a generation or two, and that general interest reforms are often quietly weakened in the years after their enactment (Patashnik 2008), obstruction by strangulation may leave a distinct policy legacy.

The coming appointments, draft rules, and early enforcement actions will tell us much about the longer arc of twenty-first-century financial reform. These actions, too, are Obama administration prerogatives, and their success or failure will mark an important Obama administration legacy. The salience of appointments for rule-making with new statutes is well known among administrative lawyers yet deeply understudied in the social science literatures. This salience underscores the symbolic and structural importance of Obama's impending consumer protection bureau appointment, and will in other ways shed considerable light on the appointments of regulators—ranging from Secretary Geithner to Barr and to Warren herself—who have been principally known for their advocacy and involvement in the legislative process.

Yet, for an enduring moment, the financial ball game changed because the gilded network was pried open by democracy. The structural changes being undertaken by some of the most powerful organizations on the planet are evidence that the financial reform initiative will have broad, transformative effects (for a similar inference strategy regarding American and global pharmaceutical companies and the power of the Food and Drug Administration, see Carpenter 2010a, chap. 10). Even under the most reluctant expression of rule-making and enforcement, there will now be strong restrictions on leverage at the largest financial institutions, a severe weakening and diminution of the power and discretion of credit rating agencies, a spin-off of dozens upon dozens of trading offices and derivatives and swaps operations at the nation's largest banks, and a consumer protection regulator writing and enforcing rules that do not need to pass through the OMB for review or to rely on congressional appropriations for funding.

APPENDIX

Table 4A.1   List of Switchers for the Murphy Amendment on Derivatives Regulation, December 2009

Name	State	District	Party	Name	State	District	Party
7. DAVIS	AL	7	100	118. LEWIS	GA	5	100
16. GIFFORDS	AZ	8	100	121. MARSHALL	GA	8	100
18. SNYDER	AR	2	100	125. BARROW	GA	12	100
21. THOMPSON	CA	1	100	126. SCOTT	GA	13	100
25. MATSUI	CA	5	100	129. MINNICK	ID	1	100
32. MCNERNEY	CA	11	100	131. RUSH	IL	1	100
39. CARDOZA	CA	18	100	133. LIPINSKI	IL	3	100
41. COSTA	CA	20	100	137. DAVIS	IL	7	100
58. HARMAN	CA	36	100	138. BEAN	IL	8	100
65. BACA	CA	43	100	144. FOSTER	IL	14	100
75. DAVIS	CA	53	100	151. DONNELLY	IN	2	100
77. POLIS	CO	2	100	161. BOSWELL	IA	3	100
78. SALAZAR	CO	3	100	166. MOORE	KS	3	100
79. MARKEY	CO	4	100	170. YARMUTH	KY	3	100
82. PERLMUTTER	CO	7	100	176. MELANCON	LA	3	100
86. HIMES	CT	4	100	182. MICHAUD	ME	2	100
87. MURPHY	CT	5	100	183. KRATOVIL	MD	1	100
90. BOYD	FL	2	100	184. RUPPERSBE	MD	2	100
91. BROWN	FL	3	100	187. HOYER	MD	5	100
105. MEEK	FL	17	100	189. CUMMINGS	MD	7	100
108. WASSERMA	FL	20	100	192. NEAL	MA	2	100
110. KLEIN	FL	22	100	207. SCHAUER	MI	7	100
112. KOSMAS	FL	24	100	209. PETERS	MI	9	100
115. BISHOP	GA	2	100	212. LEVIN	MI	12	100

Name	State	District	Party	Name	State	District	Party
216. WALZ	MN	1	100	312. WILSON	OH	6	100
220. ELLISON	MN	5	100	322. BOCCIERI	OH	16	100
224. CHILDERS	MS	1	100	332. BLUMENAU	OR	3	100
225. THOMPSON	MS	2	100	333. DEFAZIO	OR	4	100
230. CARNAHAN	MO	3	100	338. ALTMIRE	PA	4	100
241. BERKLEY	NV	1	100	342. MURPHY	PA	8	100
244. SHEA-PORTER	NH	1	100	344. CARNEY	PA	10	100
245. HODES	NH	2	100	347. SCHWARTZ	PA	13	100
248. ADLER	NJ	3	100	351. HOLDEN	PA	17	100
259. HEINRICH	NM	1	100	360. SPRATT	RI	5	100
261. LUJAN	NM	3	100	362. HERSETH SAN	SD	1	100
265. MCCARTHY	13	4	100	367. COOPER	TN	5	100
267. MEEKS	NY	6	100	368. GORDON	TN	6	100
268. CROWLEY	NY	7	100	370. TANNER	TN	8	100
271. TOWNS	NY	10	100	391. GONZALEZ	TX	20	100
274. MCMAHON	NY	13	100	394. RODRIGUEZ	TX	23	100
275. MALONEY	NY	14	100	400. GREEN	TX	29	100
278. ENGEL	NY	17	100	405. MATHESON	UT	2	100
280. HALL	NY	19	100	409. NYE	VA	2	100
282. MURPHY	NY	20	100	418. CONNOLLY	VA	11	100
286. OWENS	NY	23	100	419. INSLEE	WA	1	100
287. ARCURI	NY	24	100	420. LARSEN	WA	2	100
288. MAFFEI	NY	25	100	421. BAIRD	WA	3	100
290. HIGGINS	NY	27	100	424. DICKS	WA	6	100
293. BUTTERFI	NC	1	100	427. SMITH	WA	9	100
294. ETHERIDG	NC	2	100	428. MOLLOHAN	WV	1	100
300. KISSELL	NC	8	100	430. RAHALL	WV	3	100
303. SHULER	NC	11	100	433. KIND	WI	3	100
306. POMEROY	ND	1	100	438. KAGEN	WI	8	100
307. DRIEHAUS	OH	1	100				

Source: Author's compilation.

Table 4A.2   Results from Logistic Regression of Murphy Switch, December 2009

Logistic regression				Number of obs	=	418	
				LR chi2(5)	=	118.17	
				Prob > chi2	=	0.0000	
Log likelihood = –178.67693				Pseudo R2	=	0.2485	

murphy_swi~h	Coef.	Std. Err.	z	P>|z|	[95% C.I.]	
dwnom1	–3.349613	.5622545	–5.96	0.000	–4.451611	–2.247614
dwnom2	2.201922	.4298067	5.12	0.000	1.359517	3.044328
errors	–.0459016	.0150088	–3.06	0.002	–.0753183	–.0164848
nchoices	.0023234	.0023616	0.98	0.325	–.0023053	.0069522
gmp	–18.98761	5.476191	–3.47	0.001	–29.72074	–8.254469
_cons	14.94996	5.131283	2.91	0.004	4.892825	25.00709

Marginal effects after logit
$y = \text{Pr(murphy\_switch) (predict)}$
$= .16455799$

variable	dy/dx	Std. Err.	z	P>|z|	[95% C.I.]		X
dwnom1	–.4605002	.06073	–7.58	0.000	–.579529	–.341472	–.008639
dwnom2	.3027173	.05937	5.10	0.000	.186362	.419072	.009356
errors	–.0063105	.00214	–2.95	0.003	–.010501	–.00212	40.3995
nchoices	.0003194	.00033	0.98	0.327	–.000319	.000958	624.012
gmp	–2.610391	.78063	–3.34	0.001	–4.14039	–1.08039	.854222

Source: Author's compilation.

NOTES

1. To be sure, many progressive voices called for the reenactment of firm dividing lines between commercial banks and investment banks—as in the now-repealed Glass-Steagall Act of 1933. Yet that proposal was never on the legislative table in a realistic way, and in the meantime, the 3 percent Volcker rule appreciably constrains the major depository institutions from parlaying their government-backed access to capital into proprietary trading advantages and the outsized risk-taking that comes with them. In the weeks following the signing of the Dodd-Frank bill, major financial institutions have already begun to map out their divestment plans, and early accounts suggest that substantial organizational changes are under way (Yang 2010).

2. The world of finance and its regulation is a vast one, but for purposes of

analysis a simple binary—that between *systemic* and *consumer* risk—helps to simplify discussions. *Consumer risk* comprises the set of investments and assets in which individuals and households invest—retirement plans and pensions, life insurance, homeownership and mortgages, consumer and auto loans, equities and annuities, small bonds and the like. These are financial products historically provided by smaller and more localized credit institutions (credit unions, unions and employers, savings and loans, community banks, even the postal savings banks of the early twentieth century). *Systemic risk* comprises the institutional transactions and financial products—bank-to-bank transactions, collateralized debt obligations, hedge funds, securitized assets and mortgages, derivatives of various kinds, asset bundles with various tranches of quality—that constitute the world of Wall Street, large insurance companies and mass mortgage lenders. Bluntly and simply but somewhat inaccurately put, consumer risk is citizen-to-citizen; systemic is bank-to-bank (see Tufano 2009; Campbell 2006; for an excellent overview of the American housing finance system, see Immergluck 2009).

3. The gross market value of these derivatives in 2009 was estimated at approximately $20 trillion (see Bank of International Settlements 2009).

4. The well-known attempt by Commodity Futures Trading Commission head Brooksley Born was to regulate these derivatives, an endeavor apparently shot down by Fed chairman Alan Greenspan, Robert Rubin, and Larry Summers during the Clinton administration (Goodman 2008; Kirck 2009).

5. It is of course true that political science scholars have not found clear evidence linking legislative contributions and lobbying to voting patterns. However, numerous other forms of influence have been described. For one, skilled analyses of legislative participation make it clear that in many cases lobbyists are buying not votes but time, or, quite likely, the ability of legislators to work on setting the policy agenda (Hall and Wayman 1990).

6. The connections of Emanuel to financial interests were detailed in a *Washington Examiner* column by Timothy P. Carney, who wrote of Emanuel's brief career in the House of Representatives that "the $96,900 Emanuel pulled in from hedge funds places him above any Senator besides presidential candidates. In fact, Emanuel garnered from hedge funds more than the top eleven Republican lawmakers, combined." Carney also notes that "Goldman Sachs and JP Morgan are also in Emanuel's top-five career sources of campaign cash," and that "Emanuel received more money from the securities and investment industry—$600,500 as of September 30—than did any other member of the U.S. House, and more than two presidential candidates (including Joe Biden) and the chairman of the Senate Finance Committee. Commercial banks lined Emanuel's pockets, too, with $121,100, placing him fourth among House members" (2008).

7. Jo Becker and Gretchen Morgenson maintain that Geithner's "actions, as a

regulator and later a bailout king, often aligned with the industry's interests and desires, according to interviews with financiers, regulators and analysts and a review of Federal Reserve records" (2009, A1).

8. The question here is that of a counterfactual: whom else might Obama have appointed to these positions, and what did he do in other realms of policy? In economic policymaking positions, many progressives pushed for Paul Krugman and Joseph Stiglitz. In terms of policy areas, the proper comparisons are perhaps in environmental, health, and labor appointments, where Obama's choices are widely regarded as much more liberal. These include Hilda Solis as secretary of labor, Kathleen Sebelius as Department of Health and Human Services secretary (and later, Donald Berwick as head of Centers for Medicaid and Medicare Services), David Michaels as head of the Occupational Safety and Health Administration, Margaret Hamburg and Joshua Sharfstein as commissioner and principal deputy commissioner of the Food and Drug Administration, and Lisa Jackson at the Environmental Protection Agency.

9. After passage of the Act, SEIU officials attempted to mobilize bank employees to help enforce the act (Elk 2010).

10. As evidence that the Republican talking points have stuck, Congressman Barney Frank has at several junctures expressed his wish for structural reform of, and diminution of the role of, the federal housing agencies.

11. A summary of the Paulson proposal appears in a March 2008 Treasury Department press release, "Treasury Releases Blueprint for Stronger Regulatory Structure."

12. It is critical from the standpoint of legal and economic analysis, as well as from political and institutional analysis, to separate the question of capital requirements from three related policy questions: whether to bar or deter banks from certain activities altogether, whether to require banks to legally and organizationally split some activities (depository banking) from others (swaps and derivatives trading), and "skin-in-the-game" reforms that require banks to fully own associated hedge funds and trading operations. These various reforms have a common referent—namely the twin desires to limit undue risk-taking, and, relatedly, to regulate how much money banks keep in obscure investment harbors, and to prevent moral hazard from the government's backing of deposits. Yet they are separable from a policy standpoint and, more to the point, they mobilized different proposals and coalitions for and against.

13. Rather misleadingly, the Treasury Department would go on to define the most systemically important and interconnected financial firms as Tier 1 financial holding companies (FHCs). Tier 1 henceforth had the dual reference of implying the most robust kind of capital as well as the most pivotal firms in the larger financial system (firms whose possible failure would define systemic risk).

14. I use the terms *capital requirements* and *leverage limitations* somewhat inter-changeably here, but it is important to note that, for accounting purposes, capital requirements are usually risk-weighted valuations, whereas simple leverage is not risk-weighted in accounting practices used by regulators and institutional evaluators. These accounting distinctions turn out to be predic-tive of bank failures in Europe during the crisis (see Poghosyan and Čihák 2009).

15. The ability of government agencies—especially regulatory agencies—to set the terms of market transactions, investments, and even scientific inquiry is a form of power that I call "conceptual power" in regulation (for an application to global pharmaceutical regulation, see Carpenter 2010a).

16. This is still significant as it privileges the Collins definition as a focal point and starting point for future discussions, and requires the Treasury Depart-ment and the comptroller of the currency to revisit the issue in the future.

17. Perhaps in anticipation of this reluctance, Senators Merkley and Levin wrote on August 3, 2010, what Simon Johnson calls a "strongly worded letter" to the Treasury Department calling for strong rules that implement the Volcker rule (see Merkley 2010).

18. The itinerary appears online in the TPM Document Collection (Talkingpoints memo.com 2010). A December 2009 fundraiser by Crowley, as well as other fundraising events, are now under federal investigation for possible bribery charges, though at this writing no criminal charges have been filed against any member.

19. The timing of this bill introduction is one that I interpret as providing an im-portant threat, although agencies such as the Fed and the FTC may have learned earlier that the bill introduction was coming (see Americans for Fair-ness in Lending 2009).

20. "'The Financial Product Safety Commission Bill #S.566'—status—03/10/ 2009: Read twice and referred to the Committee on Banking, Housing, and Urban Affairs. (text of measure as introduced: CR S2975-2978); 03/10/2009: Sponsor introductory remarks on measure (CR S2974-2975); Committee/ Subcommittee Activity: Banking, Housing, and Urban Affairs: Referral, In Committee" (U.S. Senate 2009b).

21. The White House supports "getting back to some common sense regulations" for consumer financial products, President Obama said during his March ap-pearance on *The Tonight Show with Jay Leno* (Obama 2009).

22. On the magnitude of the threat, Vanessa Cross wrote that "according to finan-cial analysts, . . . the proposed 1,136-page Senate bill poses the biggest chal-lenge to the Fed's independence since it was codified into law in the 1970s" (2009).

23. See Restoring American Financial Stability Act of 2009, Title X (Consumer Financial Protection Agency), Subtitle F. Section 1061. (b) "(1) Board of Gov-

ernors.— (A) Transfer of Functions.—All consumer financial protection functions of the Board of Governors are transferred to the CFPA. (B) Board of
Governors Authority.— The CFPA shall have all powers and duties that were
vested in the Board of Governors, relating to consumer financial protection
functions, on the day before the designated transfer date" (U.S. Senate 2009a,
1000).

24. See Restoring American Financial Stability Act of 2009, Section 1018, (a)(1)(E)
(i) "IN GENERAL.—Each year (or quarter of such year), beginning on the
designated transfer date, and each quarter thereafter, the Board of Governors
shall transfer to the CFPA from the combined earnings of the Federal Reserve
System the amount estimated by the CFPA needed to carry out the authorities
granted in this title, under the enumerated consumer laws, and transferred
under subtitles F and H, taking into account such other sums available to the
CFPA for the following year (or quarter of such year), as requested by the
CFPA" (U.S. Senate 2009a, 881).

25. This statement again focuses only on publicly archived speeches and testimony at the Federal Reserve Board's website. The closest any Fed official
came to a pronouncement about consumer protection was in remarks by Sandra Braunstein (2009). Her remarks were not those of a governor, however,
and came after it was well known that a CFPA was a real legislative threat to
the Fed.

26. Since President Reagan's Executive Order 12291, regulatory agencies have
had their proposed rules examined continually by the Office of Management
and Budget, which is technically an extension of the president himself. But
having the rules reviewed by other congressionally created entities is quite
another matter.

27. In early January 2010, President Obama announced a general review of regulations. Early interpretations of this move suggest that it was undertaken as a
gesture to business executives and the business community. However, in a
sign that Obama intends to shield Dodd-Frank implementation from new
cost-benefit analyses, independent agencies that are critical in the administration of financial reform (such as the Fed and the CFPB, the FTC, and the SEC)
are exempted from this review (Montgomery 2011).

28. As of early October 2010, this single story generated over 8,000 comments on
the *Huffington Post* website, indicating the weight that progressive forces attached to the Warren nomination. It is not known whether Geithner actually
opposed Warren, and indeed Geithner denied opposing Warren for the position. Nevertheless, the *Huffington Post* story forcefully shaped the agenda for
the early establishment of the CFPB.

29. I should report that these interpretations of Warren's aims are exactly that—
interpretations. Although I have occasionally discussed financial regulation

and consumer protection issues with Professor Warren, I was not in contact with her from October 2010 through January 2011, and I have no direct evidence from her or her staff that she had these intentions and strategies. My evidence comes rather from financial reports and observers outside the bureau who have followed her activities (for the text of the speech, see Warren 2010).

30. Note, however, that the 848-page Dodd-Frank Act ("2,300 pages" in the jumbo congressional type referenced by bill opponents) is an example of how legislative action does not, in contrast to the assumptions of John Huber and Charles Shipan (2002), demonstrate that longer bills are those that more tightly constrain administrative discretion. Along with other enactments, the Dodd-Frank Act suggests that major legislation will often take up hundreds or thousands of pages preparing space, capacity, and funding models for agencies built from transfers of resources and parts from previously existing institutions. Legislative length is, at least in this case, a poor measure of statutory specificity; the latter concept often requires a more nuanced reading of legislation than quantitative political scientists have been willing to give it.

REFERENCES

Americans for Fairness in Lending. 2009. "Elizabeth Warren's Financial Product Safety Commission." March 5, 2009. Available at: http://americansforfairness inlending.wordpress.com/2009/03/05/elizabeth-warrens-financial-product -safety-commission (accessed May 2, 2010).

Americans for Financial Reform. 2009. "In These Times: SEIU Leads Protest Against Goldman's So-Called 'God's Work.'" *OurFinancialSecurity.org*, November 18, 2009. Available at: http://ourfinancialsecurity.org/2009/11/in-these -times-seiu-leads-protest-against-goldman%E2%80%99s-so-called-god%E2 %80%99s-work (accessed October 2, 2010).

———. 2010. "Post Passage Lobbying Statistics." *OurFinancialSecurity.org*, August 2, 2010. Available at: http://ourfinancialsecurity.org/2010/08/post-passage -lobbying-statistics (accessed October 1, 2010).

Appelbaum, Binyamin. 2009. "Business Digest: Deal Near on Senate Financial Reform Bill." *Washington Post*, December 24, 2009. Available at: http://www .washingtonpost.com/wp-dyn/content/article/2009/12/23/AR20091223 02948.html (accessed January 30, 2011).

Bank of International Settlements. 2009. "Semiannual OTC Derivatives Statistics at end-June 2009." Available at: http://www.bis.org/statistics/derstats.htm (accessed March 6, 2010).

Bartels, Lawrence M. 2009. *Unequal Democracy: The Political Economy of the Gilded Age*. Princeton, N.J.: Princeton University Press.

BBVA Bancomer Team. 2009. "US: Fed Revises Regulation Z." July 24, 2009. *FXStreet.com*. Available at: http://www.fxstreet.com/fundamental/economic -indicators/us-fed-revises-regulation-z/2009-07-24.html (accessed February 21, 2010).

Becker, Jo, and Gretchen Morgenson. 2009. "Geithner, Member and Overseer of Finance Club." *New York Times*, April 26, 2009, p. A1. Available at: http://www .nytimes.com/2009/04/27/business/27geithner.html (accessed January 30, 2011).

Bernanke, Ben. 2009. "Semiannual Monetary Policy Report to the Congress." Testimony before the House Committee on Financial Services, and Senate Committee on Banking, Housing, and Urban Affairs, U.S. Congress. July 21, 2009. Washington, D.C.: Federal Reserve Board. Available at: http://www.federal reserve.gov/newsevents/testimony/bernanke20090721a.htm (accessed July 3, 2010).

Blumenthal, Michael, Nicholas Brady, Paul O'Neill, George Shultz, and John Snow. 2010. "Congress Should Implement the Volcker Rule for Banks." *Wall Street Journal*, February 22, 2010. Available at: http://online.wsj.com/article/SB1000 1424052748703983004575074123680183534.html (accessed January 30, 2011).

Board of Governors. 2009a. "Banking and Consumer Regulatory Policy: Press Release." July 23, 2009. Washington, D.C.: Federal Reserve Board. Available at: http://www.federalreserve.gov/newsevents/press/bcreg/20090723a.htm (accessed January 30, 2010).

————. 2009b. "Banking and Consumer Regulatory Policy: Press Release." September 29, 2009. Washington, D.C.: Federal Reserve Board. Available at: http:// www.federalreserve.gov/newsevents/press/bcreg/20090929a.htm (accessed January 10, 2010).

Bowman, Karlyn, and Andrew Rugg. 2010. "TARP, the Auto Bailout and the Stimulus: Attitudes about the Economic Crisis." AEI Studies in Public Opinion working paper 100105. Washington, D.C.: American Enterprise Institute. Available at: http://www.aei.org/paper/100105 (accessed January 30, 2011).

Braunstein, Sandra. 2009. "Mortgage Lending Reform." Testimony before the Subcommittee on Financial Institutions and Consumer Credit, U.S. House of Representatives. March 10, 2009. Washington, D.C.: Federal Reserve Board. Available at: http://www.federalreserve.gov/newsevents/testimony/braunstein20 090311a.htm (accessed July 3, 2010).

Campbell, John. 2006. "Household Finance." *Journal of Finance* 61(4): 1553–1604.

Carney, John. 2010. "Treasury Department Is Already Saying That Volcker Rule Won't Change Goldman Sachs." *Business Insider*, February 2, 2010. Available at: http://www.businessinsider.com/treasury-department-is-already-saying -volcker-rule-wont-change-goldman-sachs-2010-2 (accessed August 15, 2010).

Carney, Timothy P. 2008. "Emanuel Will Be Wall Street's Man in the Obama White House." *Washington Examiner*, November 7, 2008. Available at: http://www

.washingtonexaminer.com/opinion/columns/TimothyCarney/Emanuel _Will_be_Wall_Streets_Man_in_the_Obama_White_House.html (accessed October 1, 2010).

Carpenter, Daniel P. 2001. *The Forging of Bureaucratic Autonomy: Reputations, Networks and Policy Innovation in Executive Agencies, 1862–1928.* Princeton, N.J.: Princeton University Press.

———. 2010a. *Reputation and Power: Organizational Image and Pharmaceutical Regulation at the FDA.* Princeton, N.J.: Princeton University Press.

———. 2010b. "Why Consumers Can't Trust the Fed." *New York Times,* March 16, 2010. Available at: http://www.nytimes.com/2010/03/17/opinion/17 Carpenter.html (accessed January 30, 2011).

———. 2010c. "Institutional Strangulation: Bureaucratic Politics and Financial Reform in the Obama Administration." *Perspectives on Politics* 8(3): 825–47.

Chan, Sewell. 2010. "Federal Reserve Nominees Are Clue to Its Future." *New York Times,* May 1, 2010. Available at: http://www.nytimes.com/2010/05/02/business/02fed.html (accessed January 30, 2011).

Cross, Vanessa. 2009. "Bipartisan Financial Reform Bill in U.S. Senate: Federal Reserve Board Chairman Bernanke Lobbies Against Reformation." *Suite101.com,* December 31, 2009. Available at: http://business-market-analysis.suite101.com/article.cfm/bipartisan_financial_reform_bill_in_us_senate (accessed February 21, 2010).

Dash, Eric, and Julie Creswell. 2008. "The Reckoning: Citigroup Saw No Red Flags Even as It Made Bolder Bets." *New York Times,* November 22, 2008. Available at: http://www.nytimes.com/2008/11/23/business/23citi.html (accessed October 1, 2010).

Dennis, Brady, and Steven Mufson. 2010. "Bankers Take Up Lobbying with Gusto." *Washington Post,* March 19, 2010, p. A18.

Dixon, Kim, and Rachelle Younglai. 2010. "House Panel Seeks to Weaken Bank Capital Rules." *Reuters,* June 17, 2010. Available at: http://www.reuters.com/article/idUSTRE65G6H820100617 (accessed January 30, 2011).

Elk, Mike. 2010. "SEIU Helps Bank Workers Become Whistleblowers." *Working in These Times,* September 13, 2010. Available at: http://inthesetimes.com/working/entry/6451/seiu_uses_new_financial_reform_laws_to_organize _bank_workers (accessed January 30, 2011).

Epstein, David, and Sharyn O'Halloran. 1999. *Delegating Powers: A Transaction Cost Politics Approach to Policy Making under Separate Powers.* New York: Cambridge University Press.

Goodman, Peter S. 2008. "The Reckoning—Taking Hard New Look at a Greenspan Legacy." *New York Times,* October 9, 2008. Available at: http://www.nytimes.com/2008/10/09/business/economy/09greenspan.html (accessed January 30, 2011).

Grim, Ryan. 2009. "Rep. Jackie Speier's Tough Bank Amendment Passes with

Room Nearly Empty." *Huffington Post,* November 20, 2009. Available at: http://www.huffingtonpost.com/2009/11/20/tough-bank-amendment-pass_n_365994.html (accessed January 30, 2011).

Hall, Richard, and Frank Wayman. 1990. "Buying Time: Moneyed Interests and the Mobilization of Bias in Congressional Committees." *American Political Science Review* 84(3): 797–820.

Holzer, Jessica. 2009. "Fed Unveils Rules to Protect Borrowers." *Wall Street Journal,* July 24, 2009. Available at: http://online.wsj.com/article/SB124837547483376651.html (accessed February 10, 2010).

Huber, John, and Charles Shipan. 2002. *Deliberate Discretion.* Cambridge: Cambridge University Press.

Huffington Post. 2009. "Financial Product Safety Commission: Dems Want Mortgages Regulated Like Toys, Drugs." March 10, 2009. Available at: http://www.huffingtonpost.com/2009/03/10/financial-product-safety_n_173691.html (accessed January 30, 2011).

Immergluck, Dan. 2009. *Foreclosed: High-Risk Lending, Deregulation, and the Undermining of America's Mortgage Market.* Ithaca, N.Y.: Cornell University Press.

Johnson, Simon. 2010. "The Treasury Position on the Volcker Rule." *Baseline Scenario,* August 5, 2010. Available at: http://baselinescenario.com/2010/08/05/the-treasury-position-on-the-volcker-rule (accessed January 30, 2011).

King, David. 1997. *Turf Wars: How Congressional Committees Claim Jurisdiction.* Chicago: University of Chicago Press.

Kirck, Michael. 2009. "The Warning." *Frontline,* October 20, 2009. Available at: http://video.pbs.org/video/1302794657 (accessed January 30, 2011).

Klein, Ezra. 2010. "Does Income Inequality Cause Financial Crises?" *Washington Post,* June 28, 2010. Available at: http://voices.washingtonpost.com/ezra-klein/2010/06/does_income_inequality_cause_f.html (accessed January 30, 2011).

Kovacic, William E. 2009. "The Consumer Financial Protection Agency and the Hazards of Regulatory Restructuring." *Lombard Street* 1(12)(September): 19–28. Available at: http://www.ftc.gov/speeches/kovacic/090914hazzrdsrestructuring.pdf (accessed February 21, 2010).

Krehbiel, Keith. 1998. *Pivotal Politics: A Theory of U.S. Lawmaking.* Chicago: University of Chicago Press.

Krugman, Paul. 2000. *The Return of Depression Economics.* New York: W. W. Norton.

Kuttner, Robert. 2008. "Team of Rubins." *Huffington Post,* November 24, 2008. Available at: http://www.huffingtonpost.com/robert-kuttner/team-of-rubins_b_145879.html (accessed October 1, 2010).

Lowrey, Annie. 2010. "Treasury's Wolin: Five Things Worth Fighting for in Fin-Reg." *Washington Independent,* May 27, 2010. Available at: http://washingtonindependent.com/85864/treasurys-wolin-five-things-worth-fighting-for-in-finreg (accessed August 15, 2010).

Merkley, Jeffrey. 2010. "Merkley, Levin Urge Strong Implementation of New Rules, End to 'Business-as-Usual' on Wall Street." Press release. Washington: Office of Oregon Senator Jeff Merkley. Available at: http://merkley.senate.gov/newsroom/press/release/?id=CB49AE3C-B8C4-4F8F-9081-5CD93833EFE8 (accessed January 26, 2011).

Montgomery, Lori. 2011. "Obama Orders All Fed Agencies to Review Regulations." *Washington Post*, January 18, 2011. Available at: http://www.washingtonpost.com/wp-dyn/content/article/2011/01/18/AR2011011801416.html (accessed January 20, 2011).

Moss, David. 2009. "An Ounce of Prevention: The Power of Public Risk Management in Stabilizing the Financial System." Working paper 09-087. Cambridge, Mass.: Harvard Business School. Available at: http://www.hbs.edu/research/pdf/09-087.pdf (accessed January 30, 2011).

Nasiripour, Shahien. 2010. "Geithner Opposes Nominating Elizabeth Warren to Head of New Consumer Agency." *Huffington Post*, July 15, 2010. Available at: http://www.huffingtonpost.com/2010/07/15/tim-geithner-opposes-nomi_n_647691.html (accessed January 30, 2011).

New York Times. 2009. "Mr. Geithner's World." Cartoon. April 27, 2009. Available at: http://www.nytimes.com/imagepages/2009/04/27/business/27geithner.graf01.ready.html (accessed January 30, 2011).

Obama, Barack. 2009. "Transcript: President Barack Obama on 'The Tonight Show with Jay Leno.'" *New York Times*, March 19, 2009. Available at: http://www.nytimes.com/2009/03/20/us/politics/20obama.text.html (accessed January 29, 2011); http://www.marketwatch.com/story/new-agency-would-protect-consumers (accessed February 21, 2010).

Patashnik, Eric S. 2008. *Reforms at Risk: What Happens after Major Policy Reforms Are Enacted*. Princeton, N.J.: Princeton University Press.

Poghosyan, Tigran, and Martin Čihák. 2009. "Distress in European Banks: An Analysis Based on a New Data Set." IMF working paper WP 9/09. Washington, D.C.: International Monetary Fund.

Rosin, Hannah. 2009. "Did Christianity Cause the Crash?" *The Atlantic*, December 2009. Available at: http://www.theatlantic.com/magazine/archive/2009/12/didchristianity-cause-the-crash/7764 (accessed July 3, 2010).

Roth, Zachary. 2010. "New Dems Met with Wall St. Execs While Pushing to Weaken Financial Reform." *Talking Points Memo*, January 5, 2010. Available at: http://tpmmuckraker.talkingpointsmemo.com/2010/01/conservadems_met_with_wall_st_execs_while_pushing.php (accessed March 16, 2010).

Talkingpointsmemo.com. 2010. "New Democrats' NYC Events Schedule." *TPM Document Collection*. Available at: http://www.talkingpointsmemo.com/documents/2010/01/new-democrats-nyc-event-schedule-1.php (accessed January 27, 2011).

Tarullo, Daniel K. 2009a. "Modernizing Bank Supervision and Regulation." Testimony before the Committee on Banking, Housing, and Urban Affairs, U.S. Senate. March 19, 2009. Washington, D.C.: Federal Reserve Board. Available at: http://www.federalreserve.gov/newsevents/testimony/tarullo20090319a .htm (accessed January 30, 2009).

————. 2009b. "Regulatory Restructuring." Testimony before the Committee on Banking, Housing, and Urban Affairs, U.S. Senate. July 23, 2009. Washington, D.C.: Federal Reserve Board. Available at: http://www.federalreserve.gov/ newsevents/testimony/tarullo20090723a.htm (accessed February 21, 2010).

Tufano, Peter. 2009. "Consumer Finance." *Annual Review of Financial Economics* 1(December): 227–47.

U.S. Senate. Committee on Banking, Housing, and Urban Affairs. 2009a. "Executive Session: To Consider Opening Statements on an Original Bill Entitled: 'Restoring American Financial Stability Act of 2009.'" Available at: http:// banking.senate.gov/public/_files/AYO09D44_xml.pdf (accessed January 29, 2011).

————. 2009b. "S. 566: Financial Product Safety Commission Act of 2009." Available at: http://www.govtrack.us/congress/bill.xpd?bill=s111-566 (accessed January 2011).

Vekshin, Alison, and Dawn Kopecki. 2010. "Dems, Wall Street Water Down Financial Reform: Moderate Group of Legislators Slowing Process, Trimming Key Changes." *Business Week*, January 4, 2010. Available at: http://www.msnbc .msn.com/id/34644156/ns/business-businessweekcom (accessed January 27, 2011).

Warren, Elizabeth. 2010. "A New Approach to the Regulation of Consumer Credit." Remarks as prepared for delivery at the Financial Services Roundtable Leadership Dinner. Washington, D.C. (September 29, 2010). Available at: http:// pubcit.typepad.com/files/38439729-elizabeth-warren-s-speech-to-the- financial-services-roundtable.pdf (accessed January 20, 2011).

Warren, Elizabeth, and Amelia Warren Tyagi. 2003. *The Two-Income Trap: Why Middle-Class Mothers and Fathers Are Going Broke.* New York: Basic Books.

Yang, Jia Lynn. 2010. "Banks Gird for Financial Overhaul's Ban on Speculating with Their Own Money." *Washington Post*, August 14, 2010. Available at: http:// www.washingtonpost.com/wp-dyn/content/article/2010/08/13/AR2010 081303688.html (accessed January 27, 2011).

Part II | Change through Regulation and Administrative Action

Chapter 5 | The Unsurprising Failure of Labor Law Reform and the Turn to Administrative Action

Dorian T. Warren

IN LATE APRIL 2010 the giant banner adorning the corner of the AFL-CIO headquarters that faces the White House was abruptly taken down.[1] The banner supporting organized labor's most important legislative priority— labor law reform known as the Employee Free Choice Act (EFCA)—had been up since the January 2009 inauguration of Barack Obama as president, a little over a year.[2] Of course, the labor movement's long-time organizational nemesis, the U.S. Chamber of Commerce, cheerily noted the banner's removal (U.S. Chamber of Commerce 2010a).[3] This unfurling of the EFCA banner symbolized the failure, yet again, of the American labor movement to achieve labor law reform under a Democratic president and Congress. It was not supposed to be this way.

Seizing the best political opportunity in half a century to achieve labor law reform with a pro-labor president and Congress, the hopes and expectations of organized labor were for victory by the 2010 midterm elections. On the night of his election in November 2008, Anna Burger, then president of Change to Win, the smaller of the two national labor federations, was exuberant. "At its foundation, this is a victory for working people by working people," said Burger. Obama's election signified a "historic and transformational moment for all Americans" and the "beginning of a new era for working Americans" (McKinney 2008). Several labor leaders planned to push for passage of EFCA within the first 100 days of the Obama presidency (confidential interviews, April to May 2010). In an interview with the *Los Angeles Times* a month before his inauguration, the president-elect reconfirmed his support for strengthening unions through

191

labor law reform: "When it comes to unions, I have consistently said that I want to strengthen the union movement in this country and put an end to the kinds of barriers and roadblocks that are in the way of workers legitimately coming together in order to form a union and bargain collectively" (*Los Angeles Times* 2008). These sentiments about the meaning of an Obama administration and the optimistic prospects for labor law reform were reiterated two years into Obama's term by the soon-to-be pro-labor chairwoman of the National Labor Relations Board (NRLB), Wilma Liebman: "The hopes of some (and fears of others) for the revitalization of labor law [were] enormous" (Liebman 2010).

There was, in fact, a very short window of opportunity in mid-2009 when organized labor and the Democratic Party came close to achieving labor law reform. With the switch in parties by Senator Arlen Specter (PA) and the swearing in of Al Franken (D-MN) in July 2009, there were fifty-eight Democrats in the Senate and two Independents who usually vote Democratic, creating a real possibility of reaching the magic number of sixty senators necessary to invoke cloture. This was the first time either political party controlled a filibuster-proof majority in the Senate since 1978 (Kane, Cillizza, and Murray 2009), the year that labor law reform failed to overcome a filibuster by only two votes (Dark 1999).[4] Expressing labor's optimism and even confidence, an AFL-CIO lawyer proclaimed seven months into the Obama administration, "We *will* have labor law reform" (Dube 2009). After all, candidate Obama made several labor policy reform promises to organized labor on the campaign trail in 2007 and 2008. These proposed reforms covered several areas of workers' rights with the most important being reforming labor law to stop the decline in union membership rates and enable unions to overcome employer opposition in organizing campaigns (Obama 2008).

Yet despite coming close to securing the sixty votes needed in the Senate and the overall high stakes for organized labor, the Democratic Party, and American workers weathering increasing inequality, labor law reform had little chance of success in the first two years of the Obama administration. Examined in the long view of American politics, the story of EFCA—and its failure—is unsurprising. In almost a half dozen attempts over the last sixty years, labor law reform has at best received lukewarm support from Democratic presidents and most often met its death in the Senate, where a supermajority has been the requirement for pro-labor policy reforms. But EFCA was just one of several top policy priorities in the Obama administration for labor, albeit the most important for its organizational survival. The labor movement did spend the first two years of the administration organizing around the economic crisis, both the Recovery Act and the financial reregulation, and health reform, two issues of vital importance to its members (chapter 1, this volume). Although not as exciting as policy areas like health care or financial reform, understanding the political dynamics over labor policy contests is key for analyzing the dynamics of inequality, political change, and governance in American democracy.

In this chapter, I analyze the most recent attempt at labor law reform during the first two years of the Obama administration. To account for its failure, I argue that several long-term institutional and political obstacles present throughout twentieth-century American politics, including the geographical concentration of labor and the conservative coalition in Congress, combined with antimajoritarian features of the American state, continued to be insurmountable for the labor movement. More short-term factors such as the Obama administration's policy sequencing, the role of interest groups, especially the Chamber of Commerce's intense opposition, organized labor's strategic choices, and declining public opinion of unions also help explain labor law reform failure in 2009 and 2010, but the more durable and structural longer-term factors are most important. However, in lieu of the unsurprising failure of labor law reform, President Obama has advanced some labor policy reforms through administrative politics—appointments and rule-making—with the potential to strengthen unions politically. Short of EFCA, whether these minor reforms and redirection of labor policy will be enough to change organized labor's trajectory has short- and long-term political implications for labor, the Democratic Party, and American politics.

A MOVEMENT IN CRISIS

Since its heyday in the 1950s, the American labor movement has lost millions of union members and been in decline as levels of economic and political inequality in the United States have increased dramatically over the last several decades. In the postwar era, unions' share of the workforce dropped from over 30 percent in the 1940s and 1950s to 12.3 percent of all workers and 7.2 percent of workers in the private sector in 2009, historic lows not seen since the Gilded Age (Bureau of Labor Statistics 2010).[5] In addition to declining union density, the demographics of union members have changed dramatically as well. Union membership in the private sector fell by 834,000 workers in 2009, making the public sector, at 52 percent, the majority of union workers for the first time in American labor history (Bureau of Labor Statistics 2010). This decline and changing composition of union members is consequential. Insofar as inequality continues to exist in American politics, whether through participation, government responsiveness, public policy outcomes, or public opinion, the U.S. labor movement is one of the few countervailing forces against increasing economic inequality (Rosenstone and Hansen 1993; Levi 2003; Jacobs and Skocpol 2005; Bartels 2008; Schlozman and Burch 2009; Winters and Page 2009). In the organizational combat that is American politics, big business and the affluent have regained power vis-à-vis little labor and the economically disadvantaged in contemporary politics (Hacker and Pierson 2010; Rosenfeld 2010).

With the steep decline of union membership rates and subsequent decline in bargaining power, the labor movement saw the 2008 election as critical for its survival in the twenty-first century. Organized labor is still the most powerful core constituency of the national Democratic Party by several measures, including campaign contributions, grassroots mobilization efforts of the party's key voters, lobbying, and setting the party's legislative agenda (Greenstone 1969; Dark 1999; Gottschalk 2000; Francia 2006). One cannot understand the politics of the Democratic Party today without understanding the central role of organized labor.[6] The labor movement spent more money than ever to get a Democrat elected to the White House in 2008 (Mayer 2009).[7] As a result, organized labor has had unprecedented access to the White House not seen since the Clinton administration (confidential interviews, April–May 2010).[8]

With a labor-friendly White House and Congress, organized labor began strategizing about how and when to push for their priority, the Employee Free Choice Act.[9] Reform of labor law was seen as important for three reasons. First, the future survival of the labor movement was at stake. Without a modernization of labor law that adapts to the new economic and political context, private-sector unionization and the overall power of labor will continue to decline. Second, in addition to revitalizing unions, labor law reform that encourages union organization would be a significant, if indirect, policy solution to the problem of growing economic inequality and the catastrophe of the Great Recession. Insofar as unions rectify the inequality in bargaining power between workers and employers, one of the original aims of the 1935 Wagner Act,[10] higher union density decreases wage inequality in the American labor market and increases consumer purchasing power (Freeman 2007; Western and Rosenfeld 2010). Yet, relative to other advanced industrialized democracies, organized labor is weakest in the United States; it is less encompassing, less centralized, and less powerful absent the institutional conditions for strong unions and an effective labor party (Levi 2003; Thelen 2001; Wallerstein and Western 2000). This matters for issues of economic inequality; in postindustrial economies, labor unions are often the necessary and decisive political actors in efforts to reduce inequality through redistribution (Bradley et al. 2003; Esping-Anderson 1990; Korpi 1983; Wallerstein 1989).

Stronger, more encompassing labor movements also reduce inequality through centralized wage bargaining negotiations with peak employer associations and government officials (Western 1997; Wallerstein 1999).

Last, but most important politically, labor law reform has broader political consequences, particularly for the ambitions of the Obama presidency and the future of the Democratic Party. Organized labor is a key player in the most central and important issues on the Obama administration's and the Democratic Congress's policy agenda: jobs and the economy, health care reform, financial regulatory reform, tax policy, immigration, energy and the environment, and the first major issue tackled by the administration, the stimulus package (American Recovery and Reinvestment Act, Public Law 111-5) aimed at immediate economic recovery. Across these issues, labor's importance for the Obama agenda is the strongest organizational force in the Democratic Party. As Larry Jacobs and Des King argue, analysts must take into account the central fact of imbalances in organized forces that pressure Congress and the White House on a range of issues (Jacobs 2010; Jacobs and King 2010). Absent a strong countervailing political constituency like organized labor, well-organized and more powerful stakeholders like business and industry groups are able to exert undue influence in American democracy (Lindblom 1977; Winters and Page 2009; Hacker and Pierson 2010). Measured by both members and money, the labor movement is the most powerful and resourceful political constituency on the political left in American politics. This is especially the case relative to the decline in mass membership organizations over the last half century (Skocpol 2003). The electoral implications are clear: if the labor movement does not stop the continued decline in union membership and spark a widespread renewal, it loses its ability to deliver votes and resources for the Democratic Party in future elections.

THE POLITICS OF LABOR POLICY AND THE WEAKENING OF UNIONS

The fate of the American labor movement is political, not economic, and labor policy is decisive in shaping its trajectory. Labor policy is a broad and expansive area comprising regulation of the American workplace as well as the promotion of international labor standards. Labor and employment policies are monitored and enforced by a patchwork of agencies such as the National Labor Relations Board, the Equal Employment Opportunity Commission, and the Department of Labor (which includes the Occupational Safety and Health Administration). These agencies are sometimes mutually reinforcing, yet often come into conflict (Frymer 2008). Workplace regulation encompasses more than 150 laws focused on setting workplace standards and protections for individual workers such as minimum wage, antidiscrimination, and health and safety standards. Labor and employment policy also includes enabling laws that govern labor relations for collectives of workers via union organization and representation. Aspects of trade policy also fall under labor policy, and have implications for labor standards around the world.

What determines the extent of organized labor's influence is its economic and political strength, which is in turn strongly shaped by the state and its role in structuring labor market institutions and the rules of the game for labor-business interactions (Hattam 1993; Olson 1965; Robertson 2000). Political conflicts around labor policy within American political economy are often characterized by business interests, on the one hand, attempting to shape markets to their benefit by mobilizing for favorable rules and subsidies, and labor, on the other, responding by pushing for social protections for workers and the disadvantaged, whether through social welfare legislation, favorable rules for organizing and collective bargaining, or other mechanisms (Polanyi 1944; Lindblom 1977; Block 2003; Silver 2003; Hacker and Pierson 2002, 2010). Yet these political contests do not occur in a vacuum; the political construction of racial and economic orders directly shapes social groups' rights and the political opportunities they have to organize and mobilize (King and Smith 2005; Warren 2010). As the sociologist Fred Block writes, "Labor markets, in short, are politically structured institutions in which the relative power of the participants is shaped by legal institutions that grant or deny certain baskets of rights to employers and employees. And this, in turn, generates an ongoing process of political contestation to shape and reshape these ground rules to improve the relative position of the different actors" (2003, 6). This central insight describes the always contentious politics of labor law in the United States, from slave codes in the eighteenth century, anticonspiracy efforts in the nineteenth, the Wagner Act and Taft-Hartley in the twentieth, to EFCA in the twenty-first (Forbath 1991; Orren 1991; Hattam 1993; Dubofsky 1994; Godard 2009). Labor law strongly shapes the development of labor movements as economic and political actors, but in racially specific ways in the case of the United States (Hill 1985; Frymer 2008). In response, labor movements also always attempt to shape this legal framework to their advantage; whether political elites offer inducements or constraints to labor is also a function of the power of organized labor at any given historical moment and under specific political conditions (Collier and Collier 1979; Farhang and Katznelson 2005).

From the moment the union-enabling 1935 National Labor Relations Act (NLRA) was ruled constitutional two years after its passage,[11] the right to organize, the right to collective bargaining, and the right to strike have each been under attack and severely curtailed by employers and their political allies. After recovering their temporarily displaced structural and instrumental power after the Great Depression (Hacker and Pierson 2002), employers fought for and won several significant victories from the 1940s and throughout the latter half of the twentieth century, from legislative reforms encoding their backlash to New Deal labor reforms that constrained the power of workers (1947 Taft-Hartley and 1959 Landrum-Griffin bills), to successful attempts to block progressive labor law reforms in the 1960s, 1970s, and 1990s (Dark 1999; Farhang and Katznelson 2005).

At age seventy-five, the Wagner Act is a relic of the industrial economic and political New Deal orders under which it was enacted (Plotke 1996). Scholars have described its "ossification" and inability to address the major challenges facing workers under a new economic regime with new norms and practices (Estlund 2002). Job instability and insecurity caused by increased global competition for goods and services, contingent and part-time work, short-term contracts and employment attachments, and volatile and frequent shifts in consumer demand requiring flexible management practices characterize the dominant features of the contemporary postindustrial, service-based, digital workplace (Stone 2004). But though these economic factors might account for many of the challenges facing the organized labor movement and describe its decline (Clawson and Clawson 1999), political explanations far better explain its plight (Hattam 1993; Hacker and Pierson 2010).

Taking advantage of such ossification of the Wagner Act over the last decades of the twentieth century, employers have become much more aggressive at violating workers' rights to organize under a much less protective labor law regime that, contrary to the intent of the NLRA, now provides perverse incentives for employers to break the law (Weiler 1990; Bronfenbrenner 2009). Although American employers have always been "exceptionally" hostile to workers and broader issues of workplace democracy (Jacoby 1997), since the 1970s firms have increased their "union avoidance" practices, particularly illegal ones, with drastic consequences for labor. The economists Richard Freeman and James Medoff first described this shift and its effects in their seminal 1984 book *What Do Unions Do?*[12] In 1984, they estimated 25 percent to 50 percent of the decline in union density was due to increased management opposition, as opposed to deindustrialization for workers' preferences. By 1994, the Clinton-appointed Dunlop Commission confirmed the increase in employer opposition and illegal conduct during union organizing drives (Dunlop 1994). The commission found that, "in the early 1950s, approximately 600 workers were reinstated each year because of a discriminatory discharge during a certification campaign. By the late 1980s, this number was near 2,000 a year" (70). From the mid-1950s to 1990, the commission concluded, "the probability that a worker will be discharged or otherwise unfairly discriminated against for exercising legal rights under the NLRA has increased over time" (79). A more recent study with data through 2003 finds that when workers attempt to unionize through NLRB elections, 57 percent of employers threaten to close the worksite, 47 percent threaten to cut wages and benefits, and most egregious, employers illegally fire pro-union workers in 34 percent of union election campaigns (Bronfenbrenner 2009). Even when workers are able to overcome intense employer hostility and vote successfully for union representation, a year after the election, more than half (52 percent) are still without a collective bargaining agreement due to employer resistance to bargaining in good faith (Bronfenbrenner 2009).

What explains this increased and effective employer hostility to unions in the contemporary postindustrial economic era? The identification of the plausible factors to answer this question determines the range of labor policy responses and illuminates the core assumptions behind key provisions of the Employee Free Choice Act. Scholars have advanced four explanations, each unsatisfactory alone: exceptionality of American employers, breaking of the postwar social contract, weak administrative state capacity, and regulatory capture by big business. The first explanation for the increased and effective hostility of employers is that management in the United States is exceptionally hostile toward workers who exercise collective action by unionizing. But this is not new. Historically, American employers have always been exceptionally antagonistic toward organized workers, often with the state on their side (Hattam 1993; Jacoby 1997). What the framing of employer hostility to unions in most accounts today implies (as do the data) is that there was an immediate postwar détente between labor and management, where employers implicitly agreed to a labor-management accord. It is the breaking of this postwar social contract that scholars offer as the second explanation for employer behavior today (Fraser and Gerstle 1989; Fantasia and Voss 2004; Clawson and Clawson 1999; Piven and Cloward 1997). Yet, as Nelson Lichtenstein argues, maybe there was never such an accord (2002). Instead, after their short-lived victory winning the 1935 Wagner Act and the rights to exist and engage in collective bargaining, unions were simply beaten back by employers, as symbolized by the passage of Taft-Hartley at the height of union power (Farhang and Katznelson 2005).

Although they advance this argument to explain the financial collapse and economic crisis of 2008 leading to the Great Recession, the third and fourth explanations for increased employer opposition to unions both reflect "a political crisis of the American state," to borrow from Jacobs and King (2010, 3). It is true that the federal government did itself become more hostile to organized labor, as infamously symbolized by former Screen Actors Guild president Ronald Reagan's firing of the Port Authority Transit Corporation (PATCO) workers in 1981. But the larger and longer-standing issue of the American state is its comparatively weak administrative capacity (Jacobs and King 2010). From its inception, the National Labor Relations Board lacked the adequate enforcement power to monitor and enforce labor law effectively (Gross 1985).[13] This might not have been as problematic in the early years when employers were still on the defensive and in some ways did adhere to certain norms, as the social contract proponents might argue (for a recent iteration of the norms–social contract argument, see also Western and Rosenfeld 2010). But beginning in the immediate postwar period and accelerating in the 1970s and 1980s, NLRB remedies for employer violations of the law have been ineffectual at best, and provide perverse incentives for employers to break the law at worst (Weiler 1990). Indeed, as early as the 1950s, unions were noting the rise of employer violations of labor law. Several labor officials testified about willful employer violations and the lack of strong enough penalties to discourage such behavior at a House subcommittee on the NLRB, known as the Pucinski Committee, in 1961 (Gross 1995, 153–56).

Weak administrative capacity is related to the fourth explanation: regulatory capture. Even if the NLRB had the capacity to monitor and enforce labor law effectively, it would still be prone to regulatory capture by business interests, as we have seen during periods of conservative governance (Gross 1995). Initiated by the sharp change in enforcement, the NLRB has been a fundamentally partisan agency, swinging back and forth between pro- and antilabor rulings depending on the party controlling the presidency (Gross 1995).

Taken together, all four of these explanations for effective management opposition under the ossified late twentieth-century labor law regime capture partial empirical truths. Each factor alone, but especially their interaction with each other, creates enormous historical, institutional, and policy constraints on the ability of the labor movement to halt the decline in unionization and rebuild itself as a real countervailing power to business and corporate interests. It is in this context of increasing hostility to workers' rights and unionization efforts that labor organizations have advocated for labor law reform to fix what they consider a broken system. Convinced of the need for reform by organized labor as a survival measure for both unions and the party, both candidate and President Obama, as well as the Democratic Party, committed to advance and pass labor law reform legislation. The hope for such reform was that it would reverse labor's organizational fortunes by changing the rules to make it easier to over-come management opposition in organizing drives to recruit new workers and increase the penalties on employers for violating the law.

UNSURPRISING FAILURE: LABOR LAW REFORM IN PERSPECTIVE

For more than sixty years, organized labor has attempted to reform labor laws that circumscribe and limit its strategies, tactics, and power. Labor advocates have attempted major labor policy reforms throughout American political history, with successes coming at rare and exceptional moments (Skocpol and Finegold 1982; Goldfield 1989; Hacker and Pierson 2002). Employer hostility to organized labor, with the national legal regime on its side, has been the more normal and routine state of affairs (Orren 1991; Hattam 1993; Jacoby 1997). Yet the story of labor law reform failure has deep historical roots and familiar political dynamics.

The business countermovement to retract the Wagner Act, labor's Magna Carta, began in 1939 when the powerful anti-New Dealer, anti-communist, and antilabor Representative Howard Smith (D-VA), a leader of the conservative coalition of southern Democrats and Republicans, led a congressional investigation of the National Labor Relations Board (Gross 1981, 1985).[14] Several of the resulting recommendations from the Smith Committee in 1940 found their way into Representative Fred Hartley's House bill in 1947, which became law after a Republican-led Congress overrode President Truman's veto of Taft-Hartley (Gross 1985). The final Taft-Hartley bill, enacted by the political alignment of southern Democrats with a majority of Republicans, many of whom had voted previously for the Wagner Act (Farhang and Katznelson 2005), included several provisions weakening the rules of the game for organized labor. Even the National Labor Relations Board, the administrative agency responsible for enforcing labor law, took an unusually active role in opposing its passage (Gross 1995, 15–25).

In 1947, a decade after the Supreme Court ruled the Wagner Act constitutional, business interests were finally able to accomplish their decade-long campaign to roll back the rights of workers and the national government's explicit encouragement of collective bargaining. Discontent with an inflationary economy and a strike wave in 1945 and 1946 propelled Republicans to gain control of Congress for the first time since 1928 in the midterm elections. Both chambers quickly went to work on legislation aimed at reversing much of the Wagner Act passed in 1935, the top domestic policy issue of the 80th Congress. Arguably the most important element of Taft-Hartley was Section 14(b), giving states the right to pass "right-to-work" laws that forbade "closed" and "union" shops.[15] Closed shops, workplaces where one is required to become a union member before becoming employed, and union shops, where one is required to pay union dues whether or not one supports the union, are two institutional mechanisms on which unions rely to overcome the "free-rider" problem (Olson 1965). This provision, along with the other aspects of the law, including anticommunist affidavits for union leaders and a ban on secondary boycotts, would have far-reaching implications for the development of the American labor movement. The new legal framework under Taft-Hartley would ensure that organized labor would remain geographically, economically, and politically contained in a minority of states in the North and far West for the rest of the twentieth century.

Thus was born the first effort to reform labor law. President Truman ran and was reelected on a platform of repealing Taft-Hartley in 1948. Organized labor was as confident then as it would be sixty years later; William Green, president of the American Federation of Labor, proclaimed a few weeks after election day that Taft-Hartley would be "past history" by March 1, 1949 (Stark 1948a, 1948b). In the Truman administration in 1949 and 1950, labor failed to muster the necessary votes in both the House and Senate. In every attempt at labor law reform since—in the Johnson, Carter, Clinton, and Obama administrations—the political alignment of the conservative coalition (southern and moderate Democrats with a majority of Republicans) and the supermajoritarian Senate has been the primary stumbling block for labor, despite unions garnering majority support for reform efforts in both chambers. Ironically, it was the Senate that previously served as the stumbling block for employers to reform labor law to their liking from 1935 until Taft-Hartley in 1947.

In the Johnson administration, labor had more access to the White House than it had had since the FDR administration and played a coordinating role on many of Johnson's most ambitious social policy successes, including civil rights and broad social welfare policies like Medicare and War on Poverty programs (Greenstone 1969; Draper 1994; Dark 1999). But after acquiescing to Johnson's demand to get his Great Society programs passed before labor law reform, he finally gave the green light in mid-1965. Labor law reform—to repeal Taft-Hartley—did pass the House in the summer by a vote of 221 to 203 over the opposition of the conservative coalition; southern Democrats, in contrast to their northern and western counterparts, voted overwhelmingly along with a majority of Republicans against the reform bill (Dark 1999). In late 1965, when labor law reform arrived in the Senate, a first cloture vote failed to reach a supermajority of two-thirds needed to invoke cloture. Again in 1966, the bill would suffer the fate of a successful filibuster even though labor did reach a majority for cloture. More than ten years ago, the political scientist Taylor Dark foreshadowed the first two years of the Obama administration and labor in describing unions and the Johnson administration: "Ultimately, the grand sweep of liberal accomplishment during the Johnson presidency would bypass a long-standing goal of the labor movement [to win labor law reform via repeal of Taft-Hartley]" (1999, 59).

With the election of Jimmy Carter in 1976 and strong Democratic majorities in the House and Senate in the immediate post-Watergate era, organized labor again saw a short political opportunity to achieve labor law reform. After first losing a more narrow "common situs" labor law reform bill in the House aimed at reversing a 1951 Supreme Court ruling limiting the ability and effectiveness of picketing and strikes, unions regrouped and proposed a broader reform bill. The Labor Law Reform Bill of 1978 dropped labor's previous goal of repealing Taft-Hartley, which it had pursued since the Truman administration, in favor of a bill that included several provisions aimed at addressing several of the causes of union decline as the labor movement then perceived it. The bill included faster elections (to be held within thirty days of requesting one with the requisite number of membership cards from workers in a bargaining unit), stronger remedy power for the Board, including increased penalties for employer violations of the law, expansion of the NLRB from five to seven members to expedite case handling to deal with delays, denial of federal contracts to employers who violated labor laws, back pay for workers in cases where the company refused to negotiate a first contract with a union after a successful certification election, and equal access to company property for unions during election campaigns (Gross 1995, 236–41; Dark 1999). Although this measure passed the House in late 1977 by a wide margin, it stalled in the Senate in 1978, despite majority support, after Senator Orrin Hatch (R-UT) successfully led a nineteen-day filibuster, defeating six attempted cloture votes that brought passage to within two votes (Gross 1995, 239). Again, the regionally based conservative coalition of southern Democrats and a majority of Republicans was able to use the supermajority rules in the Senate to block labor law reform over a majority in favor as well as lobbying by President Carter.

The next opportunity for labor law reform came with the 1992 election of Bill Clinton, the first Democrat to occupy the White House since Carter. With control of Congress, labor pushed a reform bill focused on ending the practice of the permanent replacement of strikers, as opposed to the second broader reform bill that was defeated under Carter. This proposed reform would help restore the greatly weakened strike tool for labor by banning the use of permanent replacement workers during economic strikes. Although the striker replacement bill won majority support in the

Table 5.1: Labor Law Reform, 1950 to 2010

Year: Administration	Reform	House	Senate	Reason
1949–1950: Truman	Repeal Taft-Hartley	Fail	Fail	Conservative coalition deny repeal
1965–1966: Johnson	Repeal Taft-Hartley	Pass	Fail	Senate filibuster
1977–1978: Carter	Labor Law Reform Act	Pass	Fail	Senate filibuster
1993–1994: Clinton	Striker replacement bill	Pass	Fail	Senate filibuster
2009–2010: Obama	Employee Free Choice Act	—	Fail	Senate filibuster

Source: Author's compilation.

House during the summer of 1993, it stalled and was ultimately defeated by filibuster over in the Senate. In the meantime, President Clinton appointed what became known as the Dunlop Commission to study the problems with labor law and make recommendations for legislative remedies. Unfortunately, although the commission described in detail the ineffectiveness of the national labor regime in protecting workers' rights and encouraging collective bargaining (as reported earlier), because of the unforeseen Republican takeover of Congress in the fall of 1994, "the work of the Commission was dead on arrival," in the words of Wilma Liebman, the current chair of the NLRB (Liebman 2010). See table 5.1 for a summary of labor law reform efforts over the years.

CLOSE, BUT NO CIGAR: THE FAILURE OF EFCA

The 2008 election of Barack Obama, paired with Democratic congressional majorities, opened the door for labor law reform for the first time since 1992. First introduced in 2003 and reintroduced in the 111th Congress in early March 2009 by Senator Tom Harkin (D-IA) and Congressman George Miller (D-CA), the Employee Free Choice Act, the labor movement's legislative priority, is the most significant labor law reform legislation in decades. EFCA is seen by many as the twenty-first-century version of the Wagner Act, which could alter the rules of the game for organizing workers into unions.[16] Based on the core assumptions of the problems leading to increased and effective management opposition to unionization described earlier, the Employee Free Choice Act would amend the National Labor Relations Act in three ways. First, it would allow union certification by the NLRB on the basis of a majority of signed authorization cards by employees in a bargaining unit. Often called card-check or majority sign-up, this mechanism for union recognition would be in addition to the traditional NLRB-sponsored secret-ballot elections, which most unions view as favoring employers. Second, the act would mandate first-contract mediation and arbitration through the Federal Mediation and Conciliation Service (FMCS) if a union and employer are unable to reach agreement on a contract within ninety days. This provision is meant to address the failure of almost half of newly unionized firms to reach a first contract a year after certification (Bronfenbrenner 1994, 2009; Ferguson 2009). Third, the act would increase penalties for employer violations of workers' rights under the NLRA. These would include treble back pay for workers illegally fired during an organizing or first-contract campaign, and, for the first time, civil penalties against employers of up to $20,000 per violation of the law.[17]

EFCA seemed to have momentum toward passage at various moments during the first two years of the Obama administration. At the start in January 2009, there was no foreseeable path to sixty votes in the Senate. Senator Tom Harkin (D-IA) proclaimed, "We're waiting for Mr. Franken to arrive. There's no doubt that has a bearing on it" (Cain 2009a). But once Pennsylvania's Arlen Specter switched parties and Al Franken (D-MN) was finally seated after sustained business opposition delayed his arrival for months, efforts around the bill began to heat up. A path to the sixty votes needed to overcome southern and conservative Democratic opposition and a threatened Republican filibuster in the Senate seemed possible. At one point during the summer of 2009, Harkin, chair of the Senate Labor Committee and the chief sponsor in that chamber, claimed he would force a vote on the bill before the August recess, only to later backtrack. "I was wrong," he said in one interview. "I think we're 80 [percent] to 90 percent there" (Bureau of National Affairs 2009a). But, in September, hopes were again revived that labor law reform had enough votes to pass when Specter (D-PA) announced to delegates at the AFL-CIO convention that a compromise deal had been reached on EFCA that he thought would "bring 60 votes for cloture," allowing passage "before the year is up" (Amber 2009). The compromise would drop the card-check provision from the bill, replacing it with measures for quick or "snap" NLRB elections, meant to speed up the process to rectify the issue of often illegal employer opposition during lengthy election campaigns. Although many union leaders privately agreed with Specter's assessment of the possibility of a compromise garnering the requisite supermajority in the Senate, very few said so publicly (confidential interviews, April–May 2010). In fact, there was no compromise according to top labor leaders; the AFL-CIO is "still on card check," proclaimed the newly elected head of the labor federation, Richard Trumka, in response (Amber 2009; confidential interview, April–May 2010).

Labor's strategy to advance EFCA was two-fold. First was to work with the Obama administration's policy priorities of the economic stimulus and health and financial reform to secure quick victories and wait for the "right time" for the president to push labor law reform (for more on labor's role, see Jacobs and Skocpol 2010). The second element was to reach the magic and necessary number of sixty pro-reform senators by continuing to apply grassroots pressure for EFCA on targeted Democratic moderates in sixteen states through letters, telephone calls, and civil demonstrations (confidential interviews, April–May 2010; Cain 2009a). For example, in July 2009, the AFL-CIO coordinated a rally of about 1,500 union activists and their allies at Senator Blanche Lincoln's Arkansas office to pressure her into supporting EFCA (confidential interview, May 3, 2010).[18]

But the short window of opportunity to pass labor law reform in late 2009 would come to an abrupt and surprising end at around the one-year mark of the Obama administration. With an already very narrow path to sixty votes in the supermajoritarian Senate, a nail in the coffin for EFCA was the surprise election in January 2010 of Republican candidate Scott Brown to Edward Kennedy's old Senate seat in Massachusetts, ending Democrats' short-lived sixty-vote majority in the chamber. When asked about the prospects for labor law reform in response, Senator Harkin replied, "Well, it's, it's, it's there. But it doesn't look too good. I'm not going to give up on it. I'll never give up on it" (Cummings 2010). Even Karen Ackerman, the AFL-CIO's political director, admitted that "there has not yet been laid out a clear strategy of how to win on the Employee Free Choice Act" (Cummings 2010). Proclaiming EFCA "dead" as a result a month later, a prominent liberal journalist declared that "for American labor, year one of Barack Obama's presidency has been close to an unmitigated disaster" (Meyerson 2010).

By early spring, the Obama administration sought to reassure unions that labor issues were still vital. Meeting with the AFL-CIO Executive Council in March 2010, Vice President Biden assuaged angry labor leaders, telling them that the administration had not given up on labor's priorities (Amber 2010a; confidential interviews, April–May 2010). Just a few weeks later, after a year-long battle with strong union support, President Obama signed health care reform into law, renewing labor's hopes that such a huge victory would change the tenor of American politics and shift focus to EFCA, a second stimulus, and financial reform legislation. Said one labor leader, "We expected the administration and Congress to pursue these other issues that had been on hold during the fight over health care. At that point, jobs and the economy, and a second stimulus to deal with unemployment and economic misery was a priority. And of course EFCA" (confidential interview, April 12, 2010). By late spring, as the president was still publicly supporting EFCA by proclaiming his administration was doing all it could "to make sure that people just get the fair chance to organize," the AFL-CIO was still trying to mobilize around labor law reform by "continuing to move the campaign on the field," according to one labor official (Cain 2009b). Yet organized labor was at a loss strategically as to how to score a victory. Fred Azcarate, an AFL-CIO official, hinted at defeat when he said that the labor federation was "investigating other ways to get it done. We are exploring lots of options [for passage] . . . this Congress or next" (Cain 2009b).

By early summer of 2010, Senator Harkin admitted what many knew but were reluctant to admit publicly: EFCA was dead. Admitting that he didn't have the votes to get to the supermajority sixty needed to invoke cloture, Harkin told a group of management attorneys that he was "within one vote, but something happened in Massachusetts" (Cain 2010a). By July, even AFL-CIO president Trumka acknowledged the death of EFCA in this Congress, yet still held out hope, telling a reporter, "We're looking for methods to pass it" (Rose 2010b). Harkin, trying to keep the labor law reform flame alive, claimed that EFCA might still be passed during the lame-duck session after the November midterm elections. "To those who think it's dead, I say think again. . . . A lot can happen before Election Day, or maybe in lame duck too" (Cain 2010b). In August, Obama again sought to reassure organized labor when speaking to the AFL-CIO Executive Council for his first time as president (on his forty-ninth birthday). Recommitting to fighting for and signing labor law reform, the president acknowledged that getting EFCA "through a Senate is going to be tough. It's always been tough, it will continue to be tough, but we'll keep on pushing" (Obama 2010).

Despite its death in the Senate, EFCA went further than expected according to some in the labor movement.[19] "The theory we had in 2005 that building our capacity in individual unions, rallying to elect a president in 2008, and then passing" labor law reform was a "totally thoughtful strategic plan that we got really far down the line," according to Andy Stern, the former president of the politically powerful Service Employees International Union (SEIU) and the most frequent visitor to the Obama White House during the first year of the administration (Amber 2009). At least publicly, Stern didn't doubt the strategy that labor took: "We did a good job of setting up EFCA that would have allowed that energy to be channeled in a new context that had a lot of possibility. I think we made the right decision, allocated the resources, chose the strategy, and tried to change the environment" (Amber 2009). External factors such as the pro-tracted struggle over health care reform—another one of labor's top legis-lative priorities—and the loss of sixty votes in the Senate with the election of Scott Brown (R-MA) in January 2010 were his attributed sources of fail-ure (Amber 2009).

But, privately, others in the labor movement were more critical of la-bor's strategy. One official at a national union explained that "the labor movement never really had a realistic nor coordinated strategy for getting to sixty independent of the president. It's not clear we ever really had Lin-coln (D-AR) or Nelson (D-NE). And none of us could foresee, even though we should have, the backlash to the president's agenda, especially health care reform" (confidential interview, May 3, 2010). Another top official at another union described how acquiescing to the administration's policy priorities and sequencing was possibly a mistake: "We should have gone along when it made sense, like on health care, but really pushed hard early on to force EFCA on the agenda . . . especially during those first 100 days" (confidential interview, April 12, 2010).

LABOR'S FOE: THE FILIBUSTER

Several institutional and political obstacles, including the supermajoritar-ian rules of the Senate, the role of interest groups, especially the Chamber of Commerce's intense opposition and organized labor's strategic choices, and the Obama administration's policy sequencing, explain labor law reform failure in 2009 and 2010. One factor is uniquely important over time, the filibuster. Every serious reform effort since 1950 has gone down to filibuster in the Senate, which requires a supermajority of sixty senators to invoke cloture.[20] And few issues arouse such persistent obstruction throughout the last sixty years of American politics as labor law reform. Why? Obviously, as discussed earlier, the stakes are high for shaping the rules of the game for labor-business interaction. But over the last decade, the number of filibusters has increased dramatically, with the 111th Con-gress setting the all-time record for cloture motions with 136 (U.S. Con-gress 2010). This is even more remarkable considering the change in Senate rule 22 in 1975, lowering the threshold for the number of senators required to overcome a filibuster. A quick summary of successful filibusters over labor law reform illuminates its importance:

- In fall of 1965 and again in 1966, Senate Minority Leader Everett Dirk-sen (R-IL) led successful filibusters against labor law reform (Dark 1999, 47–75).

- After fighting for two decades for filibuster reform, the labor move-ment rejoiced with the change in 1975 in Senate rule 22, which reduced the necessary number of votes for invoking cloture from two-thirds (sixty-seven) to three-fifths (sixty).

- Yet in 1978, organized labor was stymied again by a Senate filibuster, despite the lowered supermajority requirement for cloture, when senators came within two votes of defeating and winning on a labor law reform package substantively very similar to the current EFCA.

- In 1993, feeling hopeful from the Democratic presidential and congressional victories, organized labor pushed labor law reform in the form of a striker replacement bill. After passing the House, it was defeated by a Republican filibuster in 1994, led again by Senator Orrin Hatch (R-UT), who was joined by Bob Dole (R-KS) and Don Nickles (R-OK) (Logan 2007).

In 2007, the Employee Free Choice Act passed the House but stalled in the Senate. Its fate in 2009, when hopes were high, was similar: no action in the Senate due to a threatened filibuster and not enough votes to invoke cloture, the House deciding this time around to wait until the Senate voted successfully to pass the bill before taking action.

Tom Harkin explained in plain language why EFCA failed as a result of the inability to reach a supermajority in the Senate: "What happened? We had an election in Massachusetts. We lost our 60th vote," he said to a union audience in May of 2010 (Bureau of National Affairs 2010). As it had before in response to its failure to overcome filibusters of labor law reform in the 1950s and 1960s, the AFL-CIO again recently advocated for yet another change in Senate rule 22 to "end legislative gridlock" (AFL-CIO 2010b). One national union, the Communications Workers of America (CWA), went further than the vague AFL-CIO language by passing a resolution at their convention demanding that the "filibuster must be eliminated and the use of holds to deny the appointment of qualified individuals must come to an end" (Amber 2010d). By the beginning of the new 112th Congress in January 2011, these efforts by the AFL-CIO and CWA, along with the Sierra Club and fifty other liberal national organizations, had coalesced into an official coalition advocating for filibuster reform called Fix the Senate Now.[21]

PARTISAN DIVISION, UNITY, AND ORGANIZATIONAL COMBAT

Even though by July 2009 there were in theory sixty senators who might be convinced to vote for cloture, that magic number was always an uphill battle to attain. At various times, moderate Democratic senators like

Blanche Lincoln (D-AR), Mark Pryor (D-AR), or then-Republican Arlen Specter (D-PA) announced that they would not support the bill (MacGillis 2009b, 2009c).[22] Lincoln explained, in withdrawing her support for the card-check provision of the bill, which she had supported in the previous congressional session: "This is not the time or the place" (MacGillis 2009c).

Frustrated by the newly cohesive Republican obstruction and lack of Democratic party unity on the issue of labor law reform,[23] organized labor targeted Senator Blanche Lincoln's June 2010 primary race, pouring more than $10 million into an unsuccessful challenge by pro-labor challenger Lieutenant Governor Bill Halter.[24] Gerald McEntee, president of the American Federation of State, County, and Municipal Employees (AFSCME) and head of the AFL-CIO's political committee, explained labor's support for Lincoln's challenger by saying that she had "stood in the way" of labor law reform and that it was "time to draw a line in the sand" by "sending a message to others in the Senate" (Amber 2010a). By the summer of 2010, AFL-CIO president Richard Trumka was threatening to withhold support from antiunion Democrats: "We intend to run on issues less than on people, and we will support those who support those issues. We will be unpredictable partners—we will partner with Democrats when they operate in the interest of working people, and we will not when they do not" (Rose 2010a).

The direct conflict between the competing interests of employers and workers is one of the deepest and most enduring divides in modern societies (Dahrendorf 1959). Yet despite sustained opposition from the U.S. Chamber of Commerce, the National Association of Manufacturers (NAM), and other business groups, business can't be considered a monolith politically. In summer of 2009, several large employers, including Whole Foods, Starbucks, and Costco, supported a compromise on labor law reform at a moment when it appeared that EFCA had a chance to reach the supermajoritarian threshold in the Senate: a bill that would drop two of the three provisions of the bill, the card-check–majority sign-up and mandatory arbitration, but proffering a plan for quicker elections to minimize employer opposition (MacGillis 2009c). Comments from Howard Schultz, the CEO of Starbucks, hinted that at least some employers viewed labor law reform as inevitable and thus wanted to shape its final form: "The way the wind is blowing, we're heading toward a bill that is not the right approach. My responsibility is to not be a bystander but to offer a voice of reason, offer a more positive alternative that levels the playing field" (MacGillis 2009a). However, the dominant players among business groups, including the Chamber of Commerce and a 500-member employer coalition called the Coalition for a Democratic Workplace (CDW), strongly rejected any proposed alternatives (Bureau of National Affairs 2009b). The Chamber of Commerce was quite confident there would be no deal, as indicated by the response of one of its lobbyists, Glenn Spencer. In response to Senator Specter announcing a compromise bill to the AFL-CIO, Spencer claimed that the senator's announcement was "misplaced or wishful thinking" (Amber 2009). Recognizing the divide within the Democratic Party on EFCA, he continued, "There is no indication that other moderates will agree to take up the bill or pass it" (Amber 2009).

Yet fearing that Democratic moderates just might vote for a compromise bill, organized business, such as the NAM and the Chamber of Commerce, would continue to oppose any attempt at compromise. By the following summer, the National Association of Manufacturers reiterated its full opposition to labor law reform "in any form, including individual provisions such as forced arbitration and snap elections" (Bureau of National Affairs 2010). The business lobby also took aim at President Obama's prolabor administrative politics by encouraging its peers to "resist National Labor Relations Board rulemaking that overturns the long-established balance in management-labor relations" (Bureau of National Affairs 2009b).

A mobilized business community had been gearing up for such a fight around labor law reform since EFCA passed the House in the previous Congress in 2007. In addition to the efforts of the large employer coalition, Coalition for a Democratic Workplace,[25] the Chamber of Commerce alone allocated $20 million solely to defeat EFCA in 2009 and 2010 (Hamburger 2009). John Wilhelm, the president of the hotel, gaming, and food service workers union UNITE-HERE, summed up the outcome of the business effort around EFCA, saying, "The legislation is severely challenged. The unified business community has been so strident about the issue, they have effectively achieved solidarity among Republican senators" (Hamburger 2009). Another anonymous union official was more concise, saying, "We were outspent, outhustled and outorganized" (Hamburger 2009).

OBAMA ADMINISTRATION TIMING AND SEQUENCE

Another yet not nearly as significant reason for the failure of labor law reform under the Obama presidency is the administration's strategy for prioritizing and sequencing policies on its agenda. The president and his aides decided that the stimulus bill was most important to pursue during a moment of economic distress surpassed only by the Great Depression, followed quickly by the focus on health care reform (Alter 2010; chapter 1, this volume). This meant that the Employee Free Choice Act certainly would not be high on the agenda in 2009 or 2010, and organized labor acquiesced to the administration's and the Democratic Congress's priority. Of course, health care reform has been high on the list of labor's legislative priorities for some time (Gottschalk 2000), and unions regularly contribute resources to its successful passage. The same could be said of both the Recovery Act and financial reregulation, both strong union priorities in this legislative cycle. But one of the underlying assumptions of this strategy that proved wrong, shared by both the administration and the labor movement, was that a victory on health care reform would provide momentum for other legislative proposals such as labor law reform (Amber 2010c).

By the fall of 2009, the focus in Congress was on health care reform, banking and financial regulatory reform, and an energy bill, to which John Sweeney, then president of the AFL-CIO, said he agreed, as did other labor leaders (Amber 2010c; confidential interviews, April–May 2010). Indeed, at a Labor Day speech in September, while reiterating his support for EFCA, President Obama asked labor for its help in getting health care reform passed (Raupe 2009a). Yet this strategic choice sealed the fate for labor law reform. "The focus on other issues distracted from the fight for EFCA," said one labor leader (confidential interview, May 3, 2010). Furthermore, the timing and sequencing strategy of the administration, including health care reform "taking way too long," according to Andy Stern, guaranteed EFCA's failure (Amber 2010c).

This was not the first time the labor movement went along with a Democratic president's timing and sequencing of reform bills. Under Johnson in the mid-1960s, labor went along with the administration's focus on other policy priorities, both domestic (civil rights, antipoverty and health legislation) and foreign (escalating war in Vietnam), to the detriment of labor law reform. After much internal debate within organized labor on timing, with several unions pushing for the administration to take up labor law reform very early in the congressional session, labor leaders waited until early summer of 1965 to begin their campaign, only after Johnson gave them the green light (Dark 1999, 59). By the time the bill reached the Senate floor that fall, it was filibustered by Minority Leader Dirksen with the support of a significantly mobilized coalition of employers and undermobilized union members (Dark 1999; Gross 1995).

PUBLIC OPINION, UNION DENSITY, AND DIVIDED LABOR MOVEMENT?

Low union density, public opinion, and a divided labor movement are three popular explanations offered repeatedly for organized labor's inability to achieve labor law reform since the 1950s. Although these are important determinants of the fate of reform in their own right, these factors are often advanced in lieu of the more durable and longer-term obstacles such as the geographical concentration of labor, the conservative coalition in Congress, and the antimajoritarian features of the American state. The decline in union membership numbers, the argument goes, has resulted in a decline in labor political power. Where unions are strongest in numbers, particularly in the Northeast and Midwest, the bluer the state. There is an obvious correlation between levels of union density and whether a state tends to vote Democratic or Republican. Thus, many labor activists and scholars argue that as unions have lost members and overall density since their peak in 1955, so too have they lost political power and the ability to win labor law reform. As one labor leader told me, "Until we have higher union density, we won't have the political power we need to win EFCA" (confidential interview, April 5, 2010).

This explanation makes sense, and is even a seductive mantra for those hoping to build a stronger labor movement. But on closer inspection, it is not as convincing as other factors for explaining the failure of labor law reform. For instance, the logic of higher union density as the necessary condition for reform does not explain the failures of reform efforts under Presidents Truman, Johnson, and Carter against the successes under Clinton and Obama. Under Johnson, union density was double what it is currently, with strong Democratic majorities in Congress. This argument also can't explain how labor reforms unfavorable to labor were successful over labor opposition at the moments of highest union density in American history: most notably Taft-Hartley in 1947 at 31.9 percent, and Landrum-Griffin in 1959 at 28.9 percent (Troy 1965). Indeed, union density was low at the moment of the passage of the Wagner Act itself seventy-five years ago at only 13.3 percent, statistically insignificant from the 12.7 percent of 2009.

A second popular explanation offered for labor's failing fortunes is public opinion. Unions have fallen out of favor with the public and therefore can't muster enough public support to convince Congress to pass labor law reform. Recognizing the role of public opinion in labor's influence, one union leader explained, "We have to make a better argument to the American people why they should care about reforming our labor laws. . . . We're losing the framing battle to the Chamber [of Commerce]" (confidential interview, May 3, 2010). It is true that on many issues, politicians tends to follow public opinion over time (Page and Shapiro 1992), and attempts by business to tar unions in the public's mind have long been an explicit strategy in their efforts to win employer-friendly labor reforms (Gross 1995). And recent evidence suggests that business is winning; Americans' current attitudes about unions, in particular, do not bode well for significant support for labor policy reform. In the first year of the Obama administration, for the first time since Gallup first took a poll asking Americans their opinions about organized labor in 1936, the year after the NLRA was passed, a majority did not approve of unions. In 2009, only 48 percent of Americans approved, down from 59 percent in 2008, the high of 75 percent in 1953 and 1957, and 72 percent when the poll was first conducted in 1936 (Jones 2010).[26] And public approval of unions has declined overall since the first poll in 1936, supporting the thesis of a relationship between public opinion and labor law reform. In addition, public-sector unions have declined in the public's eyes, many Americans even becoming resentful at the perceived luxurious health and pension benefits many government employees are much more likely to have relative to their private-sector counterparts. Add the fiscal crises of most state and local governments to this mix, brought on by the economic downturn and partly by pension obligations, and public-sector union members—now the majority of all unionized workers—begin to look like the much reviled labor insiders in western European countries.[27] Indeed, in the wake of the November 2010 elections, newly elected governors and state legislators have proclaimed their goals of demanding wage and benefit cuts from state and local government employees to address budget deficits. This targeting of public-sector union contracts is a bipartisan affair, as both Republican and Democratic governors have taken nearly identical—and popular—policy stances (Braun and Rosenkrantz 2011).

Yet, it is important to note that public opinion of the labor movement has little to do with determining labor's political fate; approval of unions was much higher during periods of labor law reforms that unions opposed: 64 percent approved of unions in 1947 when Taft-Hartley passed, whereas 68 percent and 73 percent approved in January and August of 1959, respectively, the year Landrum-Griffin passed. What is important in the relationship between public opinion and efforts at labor law reform is the timing of the public's souring on unions. For instance, during the Johnson-era effort, a two-week strike of transportation workers in New York City in January 1966 provoked a backlash in public approval of unions and especially public-sector workers (Dark 1999, 60). Similarly during the Carter-era effort, a 110-day strike by United Mine Workers members from late 1977 through 1978 also irritated the public about the pending reform, providing political material for the National Association of Manufacturers and the Business Roundtable to lobby moderate congressional leaders to vote against the bill (Dark 1999, 110).

A third and final often-advanced explanation for the failure of reform is internal divisions within the labor movement. These internal divisions, it is argued, prevent a unified and coordinated strategy to garner all the resources of the labor movement to advance a unified approach to winning reform. A divided labor movement has in fact proved ruinous in previous reform efforts. During the effort under Truman, the American Federation of Labor explicitly refused to coordinate with the Congress of Industrial Organizations the legislative campaign to repeal Taft-Hartley (Gross 1995, 42–57). The AFL-CIO Executive Council was divided on its approach to reform during the Johnson administration, and there was broad "institutional disarray" in the House of Labor during the Carter administration (Dark 1999, 113). The most recent division, under Clinton, was between what John Logan calls traditionalists, who advocated for a limited reform in the guise of the striker replacement bill, and modernizers who wanted a much broader package of reform, similar in content to EFCA (Logan 2007).

Some labor movement officials attributed the failure of labor law reform in 2009 and 2010 to the divisions in the contemporary labor movement between the two rival federations, the AFL-CIO and Change to Win (confidential interviews, April–May 2010; Hamburger 2009). In particular, several national officials pointed to the highly contentious internal fight within SEIU over the national union's controversial trusteeship of its West Coast local of health care workers, the internal fight and divorce within UNITE-HERE, and the interunion squabble between SEIU and UNITE-HERE. Although it is true that many resources used to wage these internal battles might have been allocated toward a political strategy for advancing EFCA in Congress (via grassroots lobbying in targeted states and districts, or public opinion, and so on), it is unlikely that a unified labor movement could have overcome the deeper and longer-term structural obstacles, including the use of the filibuster and the Chamber of Commerce's lobbying effort to defeat reform.

THE TURN TO ADMINISTRATIVE POLITICS

Despite the most recent failure of labor law reform in Congress, the Obama administration has used administrative politics to enact significant labor policy reforms during its first two years. These include, most significantly, executive orders, appointments, and regulatory rule changes. The president himself described these efforts publicly to a labor audience: "There are a lot of things that we've been doing administratively to try to make sure that people just get the fair chance to organize." He continued, "So that when a union tries to organize, it doesn't take five years before you can even get a ruling, and then it turns out that the ruling somehow conveniently always is against the union" (Cain 2009b). Yet as public as President Obama has been about the use of administrative politics to achieve labor policy reforms considered both above and below the radar, what the

Chamber of Commerce calls "subregulatory initiatives," these actual and proposed changes have not gone unnoticed by pro-business groups like the Chamber, which are keeping close track of these changes with just as much—if not more—vigor as the AFL-CIO (U.S. Chamber of Commerce 2010b; Haas et al. 2010; AFL-CIO 2010a). For example, the appendix of a report on the Obama administration's labor policy by the Chamber of Commerce titled "Bearing Down on Employers: The New Labor and Immigration Landscape," which displays an ominous picture of a train engine approaching on its cover, consists of several sections with illuminating titles, including "Regulatory Initiatives: *The New Battleground*," and "Sub-Regulatory Initiatives: *Substantive Changes without Accountability*" (U.S. Chamber of Commerce 2010b, emphasis added). Although not new— labor policy battles are always fought on the terrain of administrative politics—increased attention is being paid by both labor and business to these efforts, which include recess appointments and rule changes at the NLRB, executive orders, appointments at the other labor agencies, including the Equal Employment Opportunity Commission (EEOC) and the Department of Labor (DOL), and rule changes at the National Mediation Board (NMB).

Executive Orders

On the campaign trail in 2008, candidate Obama promised to reverse several antilabor Bush administration executive orders. Issuing several prolabor executive orders in his first two months in office, President Obama got an early start to fulfilling those campaign promises, much to the chagrin of the Chamber of Commerce and other business lobbies. According to several sources (AFL-CIO 2010a; U.S. Chamber of Commerce 2010b; White House 2010), the administration has issued five executive orders (EOs) favorable to workers: prohibiting the use of government funds by federal contractors for antiunion expenditures (EOs 13494 and 13517); requiring the nondisplacement of qualified workers when federal contracts change service providers (EO 13495); requiring federal contractors to post notices in conspicuous places informing workers of their rights to organize and bargain collectively (EO 13496); encouraging federal contractors to use project labor agreements for construction projects (EO 13502); and reestablishing a labor-management council within the federal government (EO 13522).

Appointments

Overall, the Obama administration has appointed pro-labor and pro-worker officials to several agencies responsible for labor policy. These include the NLRB, the NMB, the EEOC, and the DOL—along with several important subdivisions, including the Occupational Health and Safety Administration (OSHA), the Mine Safety and Health Administration (MSHA), the Office of Federal Contract Compliance Programs (OFCCP), and the Wage and Hour Division. In addition, the administration has significantly increased funding to agencies that monitor and enforce workplace standards and protections. One result of increased funding has been the hiring of 710 new "enforcement personnel" in the various worker-related agencies as part of an overall effort to rebuild the capacity of worker-related federal agencies to advance workers' rights and workplace protections (White House 2010).

National Labor Relations Board

The National Labor Relations Board is a "'political animal' and had been 'since its inception,'" according to former Eisenhower-appointed board chair Guy Farmer (Gross 1995, 97). As such, the stakes are high when it comes to appointments, rule-making, and enforcement because "this is not pinochle we're playing here. It's not penny-ante. This battle is over control of one of the most powerful agencies that ever existed in Washington—the NLRB. This is no tea party" (Gross 1995, 97–98). Might then the NLRB achieve some of labor's goals through rule-making and enforcement that the labor movement wanted in EFCA? Nancy Schiffer of the AFL-CIO publicly responded in the negative, arguing that "it really requires legislation" (McGowan 2009). But business groups thought otherwise.

From the moment the president nominated them in July 2009, the Chamber of Commerce and National Association of Manufacturers strongly opposed the appointments of two pro-labor members to the NLRB. As a result, the NLRB was inescapably dysfunctional and ineffective during the first year of the Obama administration. In a March 2010 meeting with angry labor leaders, Vice President Biden admitted that the administration had not gotten "it done in terms of the NLRB . . . but we are going to get it done" (Amber 2010a). After more than a year of delay and obstruction by Senate Republicans, including their successful defeat of a cloture motion to end a filibuster on the nomination of Craig Becker, a long-time lawyer for the AFL-CIO and SEIU, the president finally used his recess appointment power in April 2010 to install Becker and Mark Pearce, the other pro-labor nominee, over the intense opposition of business groups. In his birthday address to the AFL-CIO, President Obama reminded his audience of his actions regarding the NLRB and one of his executive orders (EO 13494): "We are going to make sure that the National Labor Relations Board is restored to have some balance so that if workers want to form a union, they can at least get a fair vote in a reasonable amount of time. And we don't want, by the way, government dollars going in to pay for union busting. That's not something we believe in. That's not right. That tilts the playing field in an unfair way" (2010).

The board, now with a three-to-two pro-labor majority, had only two members, one Democrat and one Republican, for more than a year. During this period it ruled on hundreds of cases on which these two members agreed, postponing decisions on more than fifty of the most controversial cases. However, a federal appeals court ruled in 2010 that all of those decisions were not valid, because according to federal law the board must have a quorum of at least three. But two other federal appeals courts have ruled the opposite, and the Supreme Court will more than likely have to resolve these split decisions among the circuit courts. In the meantime, the NLRB now faces the possibility of having to add those hundreds of thrown-out cases to its already overloaded docket. Aside from the board's potential increased workload as a result of having to redecide hundreds of cases, the pro-labor majority has already issued significant rule changes favoring labor, and is considering several more. One of these potential rule changes in 2011—a proposal to implement ten-day "snap elections"— was the primary feature of the compromise to EFCA floated for a time in 2010 (confidential interview, 2010). These rule changes by the NLRB and NMB, described in the following section, have not gone without notice by employers. At a January 2011 session at the conservative Heritage Foundation, "Unionization through Regulation," several participants lamented the Obama administration's rule changes favoring unions. According to one panelist, Obama has shifted from legislative to administrative politics through a "quiet but very aggressive push the administration has been making to push unions on workers whether they want them or not" (Hobbs 2011).

Department of Labor

President Obama nominated Hilda Solis, a pro-labor member of Congress, to be his secretary of labor. Her appointment, along with other pro-labor personnel in key positions at the agency, meant that the administration would strongly monitor and enforce labor policy that affects individual workers, specifically, both wage and hour violations and health and safety violations. "The Department of Labor is back in the enforcement business," Solis said at the AFL-CIO convention in September (Raupe 2009b). Indeed, the administration allocated more resources to the department, resulting in the addition of 670 investigators, the most since 2001, and planned to hire an additional 250 in 2010 (Bologna 2009; Raupe 2009b).

OSHA and MSHA have stepped up their enforcement efforts with vastly increased funding and are also moving forward with changing rules around several hazards, including silica, coal dust, and construction cranes (AFL-CIO 2010a). The administration is proposing even more funding to enhance DOL's worker protection enforcement efforts, including a focus on minimum wage and overtime violations, and an effort to curtail "employee misclassification," which is a strategy employers increasingly use to label employees "independent contractors" to escape compliance with minimum wage and overtime laws, contributions to unemployment insurance, Social Security, workers' compensation, and a range of other worker protections.[28]

National Mediation Board

President Obama nominated Linda Puchala, former head of the flight attendants' union, to the vacant seat on the three-member National Mediation Board in March 2009. The NMB governs labor relations in the airline and railroad industries as created by the Railway Labor Act. Confirmed two months later, Puchala's appointment bore fruit a year after her confirmation when, in a two-to-one decision, she issued the decisive vote in May of 2010 to change a seventy-five-year-old rule overseeing union recognition in the transportation industry to labor's favor. Instead of requiring a majority of eligible voters in a bargaining unit to certify union representation, the new rule would make it easier for unions by requiring a simple majority of all those voting (Swisher 2010). This puts the Railway Labor Act in line with the National Labor Relations Act in terms of voting rules in union elections. In the near term, the implications are significant for labor absent legislative reform to make it easier to recruit new members. Transportation unions hope to organize about 3,000 workers at Piedmont, a U.S. Airways subsidiary, and 50,000 workers at Delta in 2010, after their merger with unionized Northwest Airlines, a not-insignificant number considering there were only 400,000 total newly unionized workers in 2009.

WILL ADMINISTRATIVE POLITICS BE ENOUGH?

Short of comprehensive labor law reform, might these reforms and redirection of labor policy at the agency level be enough to change organized labor's trajectory? The answer to this question has short- and long-term political implications for labor, the Democratic Party, and American politics. At the end of his final book in his trilogy on twentieth-century labor policy, historian James Gross describes the lukewarm relationship between the presidency and workers' rights in this way:

> In the White House, no matter who the occupant, courageous leadership has been lacking. No president has been willing to risk pursuing a clear statement of the rights of workers or delineating statutory solutions to serious labor relations problems. Instead, administrations have done the minimum necessary to respond, or at least appear to be responding, to political pressure, to gain political backing, or to reward business or organized labor for its support in election campaigns. They then go through the motions of seeking reform while manipulating the situation for maximum political gain. (1995, 276)

This historic pattern was on display yet again as President Obama addressed the AFL-CIO Executive Council, outlining his accomplishments but recommitting to labor's most important legislative priority. "We passed the Fair Pay Act to help put a stop to pay discrimination. We've reversed the executive orders of the last administration that were designed to undermine organized labor. I've appointed folks who actually are fulfilling their responsibilities to make sure our workplaces are safe, whether in a mine or in an office, a factory or anyplace else. And we are going to keep on fighting to pass the Employee Free Choice Act" (Obama 2010). These executive actions are vital, if small, victories for the labor movement. Indeed, in an attempt to educate its leaders and members in the lead-up to the midterm elections in November 2010, the AFL-CIO highlighted the important accomplishments of labor reforms through administrative politics, in addition to the significant legislative victories it supported such as health care reform, financial reregulation, and the stimulus package (AFL-CIO 2010a).

But even if EFCA had passed successfully, it is doubtful that it would be, although necessary, enough to spark a wholesale revitalization of the labor movement. Even the chair of the NLRB is not sanguine on this particular labor law reform, arguing that "EFCA does not represent comprehensive labor-law reform. What it represents, rather, is the prospect of an end to the ossification of our law" (Liebman 2010). Yet labor has always known that changing the law, by itself, is a necessary but not sufficient condition toward revitalizing the union movement. As one leader put it, "To change the plight of workers in this country, we can't just rely on the law. Unions themselves must change. Unions have to commit to organizing on a massive scale in spite of the law. We have to change the internal organizational cultures of unions to get them to support organizing. That way, we'll make gains while waiting for the law to come back on our side, but we'll also be ready to organize once it does" (confidential interview, May 3, 2010).

The author thanks Theda Skocpol, Larry Jacobs, Margaret Weir, Suzanne Mettler, Paul Frymer, Kate Bronfenbrenner, and the Market Cultures NYC group for comments on this chapter and is grateful to union officials and labor policymakers for agreeing to talk with me.

NOTES

1. The AFL-CIO is the larger of the two national—and rival—union federations. It has fifty-seven member unions, whereas Change to Win has only five.
2. The House version of this legislation was HR 1409, the Senate version S 560.
3. The title of the Chamber's blog post was "EFCA Comes Tumbling Down," and the post included photos of the unfurling.
4. The 2009 Employee Free Choice Act substantively mirrored the 1978 labor law reform bill.
5. Union density in 2009 was 12.3 percent, compared to 10.5 percent in 1929. Union density reached a postwar high in 1955 at 31.8 percent.
6. The critical 1932 election sparked a political realignment that permanently incorporated the labor movement as a core constituency of the twentieth-century Democratic Party, so much so that J. David Greenstone proclaimed organized labor as the "national electoral organization of the national Democratic Party" (Greenstone 1969, xiii).
7. According to Opensecrets.org, the labor sector spent more than $150 million during the 2008 election cycle, although business spending was more than double that amount (Mayer 2009). Another source puts the number at $250 million that labor spent (MacGillis 2008).
8. Andy Stern, until 2010 the president of SEIU, visited the White House twenty-two times during the first six months of 2009, more than any other visitor (Zeleny 2009).
9. The Recovery Act was also very high on labor's list of priorities, as was health care reform and financial reregulation (AFL-CIO 2009).
10. The National Labor Relations Act is also often referred to as the Wagner Act, after its champion and chief sponsor, Senator Robert Wagner (D-NY).
11. NLRB v. Jones and Laughlin Steel Corp, 301 U.S. 1 (1937).
12. Freeman strongly defends this argument twenty years later in a reassessment of the 1984 book (Freeman 2007).

13. Compare the remedies available to the NLRB versus its just as weak sister workplace agency, the EEOC. At least the EEOC has the ability to impose punitive damages on employers for violating employment law (Frymer 2008).

14. Smith, also a staunch segregationist, would later become chair of the House Rules Committee, where he often successfully stymied civil rights legislation in the 1950s and 1960s.

15. There were, of course, several other provisions of Taft-Hartley aimed at undercutting the power of unions.

16. Although many scholars see EFCA as not going nearly far enough.

17. Unlike most employment regulations, such as the 1964 Civil Rights Act, labor law has not allowed civil penalties for violators of the law, creating perverse incentives for employers to violate the law in union organizing or contract campaigns. According to recent research (Bronfenbrenner 2009), employers fire workers engaged in union activity in 34 percent of NLRB election campaigns.

18. A year later, the AFL-CIO funded a primary challenger to Senator Lincoln to the tune of $10 million, only to lose.

19. Having passed EFCA by a strong majority in the previous Congress, the House always had a majority of votes to pass the bill, but decided to wait for the supermajority Senate to pass it first this time around.

20. Before a change in rule 22 in 1975, the required number to invoke cloture was two-thirds, or sixty-seven.

21. The coalition's website is available at: http://fixthesenatenow.org (accessed January 3, 2011).

22. Specter would switch his party affiliation to Democratic a month later.

23. Unlike in earlier political eras, not one Republican supports labor law reform, making a cross-party coalition all but impossible. GOP senators are unified, but Democratic senators are not—anywhere from six to twelve expressing some opposition to reform.

24. What is notable in terms of party unity is how unified the contemporary Republican Party has been in opposition to labor law reform, a result of the increased party polarization over the last two decades.

25. See the Coalition's website, http://www.myprivateballot.com (accessed January 3, 2011).

26. Fifty-two percent of Americans approve of labor unions in the most recent Gallup poll in August 2010.

27. Teachers' unions are also driving this increasingly negative image of the labor movement, as both the Republican and Democratic Parties, including President Obama, have targeted education unions as the chief obstacles to public school reform.

28. The Chamber of Commerce report "Bearing Down on Employers" includes a detailed list of these protections (U.S. Chamber of Commerce 2010b).

REFERENCES

AFL-CIO. 2009. "AFL-CIO Legislative Guide 2009." On file with author.

———. 2010a. "Obama Administration Accomplishments." July. On file with author.

———. 2010b. "Senate Procedural Changes Needed to End Legislative Gridlock." Executive Council Statement, August 5, 2010. Washington, D.C.: AFL-CIO. Available at: http://www.aflcio.org/aboutus/thisistheaflcio/ecouncil/ec0805 2010d.cfm (accessed March 4, 2011).

Alter, Jonathan. 2010. *The Promise: President Obama, Year One.* New York: Simon and Schuster.

Amber, Michelle. 2009. "Specter Says Compromise Reached on EFCA, but AFL-CIO Says No Deal Yet." *Labor Relations Week* 23(September 17): 1478.

———. 2010a. "Biden Tells Labor Chiefs That Administration Is Not Abandoning Their Priorities Like EFCA." *Labor Relations Week* 24(March 4): 334.

———. 2010b. "Labor Backs Arkansas Lieutenant Governor in Challenge to Sen. Lincoln's Re-Election Bid." *Labor Relations Week* 24(March 4): 336.

———. 2010c. "As Retirement Nears, SEIU's Stern Says Shift in Work Processes Is Top Issue Facing Unions." *Labor Relations Week* (24)(April 22): 639.

———. 2010d. "AFL-CIO Joins One Nation, Calls on Senate to Change Rules to End Legislative Gridlock." *Daily Labor Report* 151(August 6): B-2.

Bartels, Larry M. 2008. *Unequal Democracy: The Political Economy of the New Gilded Age.* New York: Russell Sage Foundation; Princeton, N.J.: Princeton University Press.

Block, Fred. 2003. "Karl Polanyi and the Writing of the Great Transformation." *Theory and Society* 32(3): 275–306.

Bologna, Michael. 2009. "Solis Says Labor Department Focus Must Be on Strong, Safe, Sustainable Jobs." *Labor Relations Week* 23(September 10): 1432.

Bradley, David, Evelyne Huber, Stephanie Moller, Francois Nielsen, and John D. Stephens. 2003. "Distribution and Redistribution in Postindustrial Societies." *World Politics* 55(2): 193–228.

Braun, Martin Z., and Holly Rosenkrantz. 2011. "Public-Worker Unions Confront U.S. Governors over Benefits in Role Switch." *Bloomberg News,* January 20, 2011. Available at: http://www.bloomberg.com/news/2011–01–20/public-worker -unions-battle-governors-on-benefits-in-role-shift.html (accessed January 20, 2011).

Bronfenbrenner, Kate. 1994. "Employer Behavior in Certification Elections and First-Contract Campaigns: Implications for Labor Law Reform." In *Restoring the Promise of American Labor Law,* edited by Sheldon Friedman, Richard Hurd, Rudolph Oswald, and Ronald Seeber. Ithaca, N.Y.: Cornell University Press.

———. 2009. "No Holds Barred: The Intensification of Employer Opposition to

Union Organizing." EPI Briefing Paper 235. Washington, D.C.: Economic Policy Institute.

Bureau of Labor Statistics. 2010. "Union Members in 2009." Current Population Survey news release. Washington: U.S. Department of Labor. Available at: http://www.bls.gov/news.release/pdf/union2.pdf (accessed April 5, 2010).

Bureau of National Affairs. 2009a. "EFCA Vote Slips Until after August Recess, 'May Be Longer Than That,' Harkin Says." *Labor Relations Week* 23(July 30): 1212.

———. 2009b. "Business Groups Reject Alternatives to Proposed Employee Free Choice Act." *Labor Relations Week* 23(July 30): 1228.

———. 2010. "NAM Report Outlines Proposals on Growth, Opposes Labor Law Changes." *Labor Relations Week* 24(July 8): 1138.

Cain, Derrick. 2009a. "EFCA Introduced in Both House, Senate; Senate to Take up Bill after Easter Recess." *Labor Relations Week* 23(March 12): 385.

———. 2009b. "AFL-CIO Continues EFCA Pursuit Despite Lack of Votes in Senate." *Labor Relations Week* 24(May 6): 729.

———. 2010a. "Harkin Says He Does Not Have Enough Votes to Approve EFCA." *Labor Relations Week* 24(May 20): 820.

———. 2010b. "EFCA Could Be Taken up in Congress after November Elections, Harkin Says." *Labor Relations Week* 24(July 1): 1084.

Clawson, Daniel, and Mary Ann Clawson. 1999. "What Has Happened to the Labor Movement?" *Annual Review of Sociology* 25(January): 95–119.

Collier, Ruth Berins, and David Collier. 1979. "Inducements versus Constraints: Disaggregating 'Corporatism.'" *American Political Science Review* 73(4): 967–86.

Cummings, Jeanne. 2010. "Labor Helps Kill Its Own Top Priority." *Politico*, January 26, 2010. Available at: http://dyn.politico.com/printstory.cfm?uuid=6CD9 C06C-18FE-70B2-A8F39148A7BC8614 (accessed January 30, 2011).

Dahrendorf, Ralf. 1959. *Class and Class Conflict in Industrial Society*. Palo Alto, Calif.: Stanford University Press.

Dark, Taylor. 1999. *The Unions and the Democrats: An Enduring Alliance*. Ithaca, N.Y.: Cornell University Press.

Draper, Alan. 1994. *Conflict of Interests: Organized Labor and the Civil Rights Movement in the South, 1954–1968*. Ithaca, N.Y.: Cornell University Press.

Dube, Lawrence E. 2009. "ABA Speakers Continue EFCA Debate, Differing on Evidence of Need for Change." *Labor Relations Week* 23(August 6): 1259.

Dubofsky, Melvyn. 1994. *The State and Labor in Modern America*. Chapel Hill: University of North Carolina Press.

Dunlop, John Thomas. 1994. *Fact Finding Report: Commission on the Future of Worker-Management Relations*. Federal Publications, paper 276. Washington: U.S. Department of Commerce, U.S. Department of Labor. Available at: http://digital commons.ilr.cornell.edu/key_workplace/276 (accessed February 7, 2011).

Esping-Anderson, Gøsta. 1990. *The Three Worlds of Welfare Capitalism*. Princeton, N.J.: Princeton University Press.

Estlund, Cynthia L. 2002. "The Ossification of American Labor Law." *Columbia Law Review* 102(6): 1527–612.

Fantasia, Rick, and Kim Voss. 2004. *Hard Work: Remaking the American Labor Movement*. Berkeley: University of California Press.

Farhang, Sean, and Ira Katznelson. 2005. "The Southern Imposition: Congress and Labor in the New Deal and Fair Deal." *Studies in American Political Development* 19(Spring): 1–30.

Ferguson, John-Paul. 2009. "The Eyes of the Needles: A Sequential Model of Union Organizing Drives, 1999–2004." *Industrial and Labor Relations Review* 62(1): 3–21.

Forbath, William E. 1991. *Law and the Shaping of the American Labor Movement*. Cambridge, Mass.: Harvard University Press.

Francia, Peter L. 2006. *The Future of Organized Labor in American Politics*. New York: Columbia University Press.

Fraser, Steve, and Gary Gerstle. 1989. *The Rise and Fall of the New Deal Order, 1930–1980*. Princeton, N.J.: Princeton University Press.

Freeman, Richard B. 2007. *America Works: Critical Thoughts on the Exceptional U.S. Labor Market*. New York: Russell Sage Foundation.

Frymer, Paul. 2008. *Black and Blue: African Americans, the Labor Movement, and the Decline of the Democratic Party*. Princeton, N.J.: Princeton University Press.

Godard, John. 2009. "The Exceptional Decline of the American Labor Movement." *Industrial and Labor Review* 63(1): 82–108.

Goldfield, Michael. 1989. "Worker Insurgency, Radical Organization, and New Deal Labor Legislation." *American Political Science Review* 83(4): 1257–82.

Gottschalk, Marie. 2000. *The Shadow Welfare State: Labor, Business, and the Politics of Health Care*. Ithaca, N.Y.: Cornell University Press.

Greenstone, J. David. 1969. *Labor in American Politics*. New York: Alfred A. Knopf.

Gross, James A. 1981. *The Reshaping of the National Labor Relations Board: National Labor Policy in Transition, 1937–1947*. Albany: State University of New York Press.

———. 1985. "Conflicting Statutory Purposes: Another Look at Fifty Years of NLRB Law Making." *Industrial and Labor Relations Review* 39(1)(October): 7–18.

———. 1995. *Broken Promise: The Subversion of U.S. Labor Relations Policy, 1947–1994*. Philadelphia, Pa.: Temple University Press.

Haas, Mel, Steve Warren, Chuck Roberts, and Constangy, Brooks & Smith, LLP. 2010. "The 'Obama' National Labor Relations Board: The Potential Use of Rulemaking to Enhance Union Organizing." Washington, D.C.: U.S. Chamber of Commerce, Labor, Immigration, and Employee Benefits Division. Available at:

http://www.uschamber.com/sites/default/files/reports/1008_obamanlrb
.pdf (accessed January 30, 2011).

Hacker, Jacob S., and Paul Pierson. 2002. "Business Power and Social Policy: Employers and the Formation of the American Welfare State." *Politics and Society* 30(2): 277–326.

———. 2010. "Winner-Take-All Politics: Public Policy, Political Organization, and the Precipitous Rise of Top Incomes in the United States." *Politics and Society* 38(2): 152–204.

Hamburger, Tom. 2009. "Labor Unions Find Themselves Card-Checked." *Los Angeles Times*, May 19, 2009. Available at: http://articles.latimes.com/2009/may/19/nation/na-unions19 (accessed January 30, 2011).

Hattam, Victoria C. 1993. *Labor Visions and State Power: The Origins of Business Unionism in the United States*. Princeton, N.J.: Princeton University Press.

Hill, Herbert. 1985. *Black Labor and the American Legal System: Race, Work and the Law*. Madison: University of Wisconsin Press.

Hobbs, Susan R. 2011. "'Unionization through Regulation' Decried as End-Run in Favor of Union Organizing." *Labor Relations Week* 25(January 20): 103.

Jacobs, Lawrence R. 2010. "Democracy and Capitalism: Structure, Agency, and Organized Combat." *Politics & Society* 38(2): 243–54.

Jacobs, Lawrence R., and Desmond King. 2010. "Varieties of Obamaism: Structure, Agency and the Obama Presidency." *Perspectives on Politics* 8(3): 793–802.

Jacobs, Lawrence R., and Theda Skocpol. 2005. *Inequality and American Democracy: What We Know and What We Need to Learn*. New York: Russell Sage Foundation.

———. 2010. *Health Reform and American Politics: What Everyone Needs to Know*. New York: Oxford University Press.

Jacoby, Sanford M. 1997. *Modern Manners: Welfare Capitalism since the New Deal*. Princeton, N.J.: Princeton University Press.

Jones, Jeffrey M. 2010. "U.S. Approval of Labor Unions Remains Near Record Low." *Gallup*. Available at: http://www.gallup.com/poll/142007/americans-approval-labor-unions-remains-near-record-low.aspx (accessed March 4, 2011).

Kane, Paul, Chris Cillizza, and Shailagh Murray. 2009. "Specter Leaves GOP, Shifting Senate Balance." *Washington Post*, April 29, 2009. Available at: http://www.washingtonpost.com/wp-dyn/content/article/2009/04/28/AR200904280 1523.html (accessed January 30, 2011).

King, Desmond, and Rogers M. Smith. 2005. "Racial Orders in American Political Development." *American Political Science Review* 99(1): 75–92.

Korpi, Walter. 1983. *The Democratic Class Struggle*. London: Routledge and Kegan Paul.

Levi, Margaret. 2003. "Organizing Power: The Prospects for an American Labor Movement." *Perspectives on Politics* 1(1): 45–68.

Lichtenstein, Nelson. 2002. *State of the Union: A Century of American Labor*. Princeton, N.J.: Princeton University Press.

Liebman, Wilma B. 2010. "The Revival of American Labor Law." Comments prepared for Access to Justice Lecture Series, Washington University Law School. February 17, 2010. On file with author.

Lindblom, Charles. 1977. *Politics and Markets: The World's Political Economic Systems*. New York: Basic Books.

Logan, John. 2007. "The Clinton Administration and Labor Law: Was Comprehensive Reform Ever a Realistic Possibility?" *Journal of Labor Research* 28(4): 609–28.

Los Angeles Times. 2008. "Obama Focused on Economic Stimulus." December 10, 2008. Available at: http://articles.latimes.com/2008/dec/10/nation/na-obama-excerpts10 (accessed January 30, 2011).

MacGillis, Alec. 2008. "Labor Leaders Stress Unions' Importance for Obama." *Washington Post*, August 29, 2008. Available at: http://www.washingtonpost.com/wp-dyn/content/article/2008/08/28/AR2008082804003.html (accessed January 30, 2011).

———. 2009a. "Executives Detail Labor Bill Compromise." *Washington Post*, March 22, 2009. Available at: http://www.washingtonpost.com/wp-dyn/content/article/2009/03/21/AR2009032101449.html (accessed January 30, 2011).

———. 2009b. "Specter Will Vote to Block Union Bill." *Washington Post*, March 25, 2009. Available at: http://www.washingtonpost.com/wpdyn/content/article/2009/03/24/AR2009032401648.html (accessed January 30, 2011).

———. 2009c. "Union Bill's Declining Chances Give Rise to Alternatives." *Washington Post*, March 29, 2009. Available at: http://www.washingtonpost.com/wp-dyn/content/article/2009/03/28/AR2009032801753.html (accessed January 30, 2011).

Mayer, Lindsay Renick. 2009. "Labor and Business Spend Big on Looming Unionization Issue." Available at: http://www.opensecrets.org/news/2009/02/labor-and-business-spend-big-o.html (accessed January 30, 2011).

McGowan, Kevin P. 2009. "Congress May Turn to ENDA, Equal Pay Bill after Long Health Care Battle, Speakers Say." *Labor Relations Week* 24(April 1): 502.

McKinney, Amber. 2008. "Obama Win Start of New Era for Workers, Unions Say; Management Fears Policy Shifts." *Labor Relations Week* 22(November 13): 1603.

Meyerson, Harold. 2010. "Under Obama, Labor Should Have Made More Progress." *Washington Post*, February 10, 2010. Available at: http://www.washingtonpost.com/wp-dyn/content/article/2010/02/09/AR2010020902465.html (accessed January 30, 2011).

Obama, Barack. 2008. "Obama '08: Economy." *Organizing for America*. Available at: http://www.barackobama.com/issues/economy/index_campaign.php (accessed January 30, 2011).

———. 2010. "Remarks by the President to the AFL-CIO Executive Council." August 4, 2010. Washington: The White House, Office of the Press Secretary. Available at: http://www.whitehouse.gov/the-press-office/remarks-president-afl-cio-executive-council (accessed January 30, 2011).

Olson, Mancur. 1965. *The Logic of Collective Action: Public Goods and the Theory of Groups*. Cambridge, Mass.: Harvard University Press.

Orren, Karen. 1991. *Belated Feudalism: Labor, the Law, and Liberal Development in the United States*. Cambridge: Cambridge University Press.

Page, Benjamin I., and Robert Y. Shapiro. 1992. *The Rational Public: Fifty Years of Trends in Americans' Policy Preferences*. Chicago: University of Chicago Press.

Piven, Frances Fox, and Richard A. Cloward. 1997. *The Breaking of the American Social Compact*. New York: New Press.

Plotke, David. 1996. *Building a Democratic Political Order: Reshaping American Liberalism in the 1930s and 1940s*. New York: Cambridge University Press.

Polanyi, Karl. 1944. *The Great Transformation: The Political and Economic Origins of Our Time*. Reprint, Boston, Mass.: Beacon Press, 2001.

Raupe, Bebe. 2009a. "Obama Affirms Support of Public Option, EFCA Legislation at Ohio Labor Day Picnic." *Labor Relations Week* 23(September 10): 1431.

———. 2009b. "Solis Touts Changed DOL, Urges Passage of Health Care Overhaul Legislation, EFCA." *Labor Relations Week* 23(September 17): 1481.

Robertson, David Brian. 2000. *Capital, Labor and State: The Battle for American Labor Markets from the Civil War to the New Deal*. Lanham, Md.: Rowman and Littlefield.

Rose, Michael. 2010a. "Speakers Say Organizing, Economic Issues Key to Electing Worker-Friendly Candidates." *Labor Relations Week* 24(June 10): 955.

———. 2010b. "Trumka Says AFL-CIO's Focus on Economy Sets His Administration Apart from Others." *Labor Relations Week* 24(July 1): 1092.

Rosenfeld, Jake. 2010. "Little Labor: How Union Decline Is Changing the American Landscape." *Pathways: A Magazine on Poverty, Inequality, and Social Policy* (Summer): 3–6. Available at: http://www.stanford.edu/group/scspi/_media/pdf/pathways/summer_2010/summer_2010.pdf (accessed March 4, 2011).

Rosenstone, Steven J., and John Mark Hansen. 1993. *Mobilization, Participation and Democracy in America*. New York: Macmillan.

Schlozman, Kay Lehman, and Traci Burch. 2009. "Political Voice in an Age of Inequality." In *America at Risk: The Great Dangers*, edited by Robert Faulkner and Susan Shell. Ann Arbor: University of Michigan Press.

Silver, Beverly J. 2003. *Forces of Labor, Workers' Movements and Globalization since 1870*. New York: Cambridge University Press.

Skocpol, Theda. 2003. *Diminished Democracy*. Norman: University of Oklahoma Press.

Skocpol, Theda, and Kenneth Finegold. 1982. "State Capacity and Economic Intervention in the Early New Deal." *Political Science Quarterly* 97(2): 255–78.

Stark, Louis. 1948a. "Labor Chiefs Hail Vote as 'Mandate.'" *New York Times*, November 4, 1948.

———. 1948b. "Quick Return to Wagner Act Pressed on Congress by AFL." *New York Times*, November 15, 1948.

Stone, Katherine V. W. 2004. *From Widgets to Digits: Employment Regulation for a Changing Workplace*. Cambridge: Cambridge University Press.

Swisher, Larry. 2010. "NMB's Change in 75-Year-Old Policy Complies with RLA, APA, Court Finds." *Daily Labor Report* 124(June 30): A-9.

Thelen, Kathleen. 2001. "Varieties of Labor Politics in the Developed Democracies." In *Varieties of Capitalism: The Institutional Foundations of Comparative Advantage*, edited by Peter A. Hall and David Soskice. New York: Oxford University Press.

Troy, Leo. 1965. "Trade Union Membership, 1897–1962." *Review of Economics and Statistics* 47(1): 93–113.

U.S. Chamber of Commerce. 2010a. "EFCA Comes Tumbling Down." *Chamber Post*. Available at: http://www.chamberpost.com/2010/04/efca-comes-tumbling-down.html (accessed March 4, 2011).

———. 2010b. "Bearing Down on Employers: The New Labor and Immigration Landscape." Washington, D.C.: U.S. Chamber of Commerce, Labor, Immigration, and Employee Benefits Division. Available at: http://www.uschamber.com/reports/bearing-down-employers-new-labor-and-immigration-landscape (accessed March 4, 2011).

U.S. Congress. Senate. 2010. "Cloture Motions—111th Congress." Available at: www.senate.gov.pagelayout/reference/cloture_motions/111.htm (accessed January 3, 2011).

Wallerstein, Michael. 1989. "Union Organization in Advanced Industrial Democracies." *American Political Science Review* 83(2): 481–501.

———. 1999. "Wage-Setting Institutions and Pay Inequality in Advanced Industrial Societies." *American Journal of Political Science* 43(3): 649–80.

Wallerstein, Michael, and Bruce Western. 2000. "Unions in Decline? What Has Changed and Why." *Annual Review of Political Science* 3(June): 355–77.

Warren, Dorian T. 2010. "The American Labor Movement in the Age of Obama: The Challenges and Opportunities of a Racialized Political Economy." *Perspectives on Politics* 8(3): 847–60.

Weiler, Paul C. 1990. *Governing the Workplace: The Future of Labor and Employment Law*. Cambridge, Mass.: Harvard University Press.

Western, Bruce. 1997. *Between Class and Market*. Princeton, N.J.: Princeton University Press.

Western, Bruce, and Jake Rosenfeld. 2010. "Unions, Norms, and the Rise in American Wage Inequality." Unpublished manuscript.

White House. 2010. "Annual Report of the White House Task Force on the Middle Class." Washington: The White House. Available at: http://://www

.whitehouse.gov/sites/default/files/microsites/100226-annual-report-middle
    -class.pdf (accessed March 4, 2011).
Winters, Jeffrey A., and Benjamin I. Page. 2009. "Oligarchy in the United States?"
    Perspective on Politics 7(4): 731–51.
Zeleny, Jeff. 2009. "White House Visitors Log Includes Stars and CEOs." *New York
    Times*, October 31, 2009, p. A11. Available at: http://www.nytimes.com/2009/
    10/31/us/politics/31visitor.html (accessed March 4, 2011).

Chapter 6 | Surprising Momentum: Spurring Education Reform in States and Localities

Lorraine M. McDonnell

"The Recovery Act put a lot of money into schools, saved a lot of teacher jobs, made sure that schools didn't have to cut back even more drastically in every community across this country. But I think the single most important thing we've done is to launch an initiative called Race to the Top. We said to states, if you are committed to outstanding teaching, to successful schools, to higher standards, to better assessments—if you're committed to excellence for all children—you will be eligible for a grant to help you attain that goal. . . . So Race to the Top isn't simply the name of an initiative, it sums up what's happening in our schools. It's the single most ambitious, meaningful education reform effort we've attempted in this country in generations."

—Barack Obama, July 29, 2010

THE FEDERAL GOVERNMENT, as the junior partner with neither constitutional authority for elementary and secondary education nor a major role in its financing, has increasingly leveraged its limited resources by requiring that states and local school districts move in particular policy directions to obtain federal funds. The Obama administration has strengthened that leverage to an unprecedented level by including consistency with federal priorities as a basis for ranking states in the competition for education stimulus funds. With no assurance that they would receive any Race to the Top funding, seventeen states changed their laws to allow student test scores to be taken into account in evaluating teachers, thirteen removed caps on the number of charter schools that can be established in

230

their state, and forty-eight agreed to consider adopting common academic standards, thirty-four of which formally approved the new standards within a few months of their publication. After two rounds of competition among forty-seven applicants, eleven states and the District of Columbia were awarded $4 billion in Race to the Top funding. Yet the changes in state policies prompted by the competition extend beyond just the winners.

The administration has pushed states in a direction where many of them were already headed: policies aimed at narrowing persistent gaps in student achievement across race, ethnicity, social class, and geography; clearer lines of accountability for student learning; better prepared educators; and more rigorous academic standards. This policy course continues one begun by President Obama's two immediate predecessors. In its essential elements, then, the administration's agenda does not represent a critical juncture or radical departure from the trajectory of federal education policy over the last twenty years. What is unique, however, is the administration's use of stimulus policy to craft a substantive reform agenda, and the speed with which it altered long-standing political and institutional arrangements.

The Obama administration's K-12 policy agenda and the political response to it is a story about a president and a secretary of education acutely aware of the problems facing students in urban school districts, and influenced by a diverse group of policy entrepreneurs extending beyond the traditional education establishment. It is also a story echoing familiar themes from the education reforms of the last several decades recast to reflect the administration's concerns about students deprived of educational opportunity, and its willingness to try different approaches regardless of their ideological origins.

In designing parts of the American Recovery and Reinvestment Act as a down payment on his ambitious education reform goals, Obama accomplished what few other presidents have. The strategy gave his administration three distinct advantages: a large discretionary funding source with little congressional scrutiny, flexibility in pursuing education reform without crowding out other policies on the president's agenda, and the ability to shape the national reform discussion for more than a year on the administration's terms without being constrained by negotiations over a specific piece of legislation. Now the question is whether the Obama administration's political dexterity can be matched by skill in fashioning institutional arrangements that ensure the long-term sustainability of these reforms.

This chapter examines how the Obama administration was able to promote its K-12 agenda using the vehicle of economic stimulus policy, and how that agenda compares with earlier federal and state education policy. Of particular interest is why a Democratic administration would select policy strategies that have angered the teacher unions, one of the party's key constituent groups.

EDUCATION STIMULUS POLICY AS THE NEXT PHASE IN AN EVOLVING FEDERAL ROLE

Since its 1965 enactment, the Elementary and Secondary Education Act (ESEA)—with its focus on providing assistance to low-income, education-ally disadvantaged students—has been the main vehicle presidents and Congress have used to operationalize their education policy goals. It functions much like other categorical programs as an inducement through which the federal government seeks to change the behavior of state and local agencies by offering financial resources on the condition that they undertake certain activities. In its early years, Title I—the major program within ESEA—functioned separately from regular classroom instruction, providing supplemental pull-out services such as small-group instruction to eligible students and requiring state fiscal monitoring, but giving little attention to evidence of student progress. Over time, however, Title I has become more prescriptive in its regulations, and has moved the federal agenda closer to the core instructional program within schools.

Moving Federal and State Policy Closer to the Classroom

In the 1988 reauthorization of the Elementary and Secondary Education Act, states were required for the first time to define the levels of academic achievement that Title I eligible students should attain. The contours of a new federal role were further defined in the 1994 ESEA reauthorization that required states to establish content and performance standards in reading and mathematics and to design student assessments aligned with those standards. The policy idea that defined ESEA and other federal K-12 programs during the Clinton and George W. Bush administrations was standards-based reform. It is premised on the notion that setting high academic standards and then expecting schools to teach and students to learn to those standards can serve as a potent lever to improve overall educational quality. In formulating the concept, then dean of the Stanford School of Education and later deputy secretary of education in the Clinton administration, Marshall Smith, and his coauthor Jennifer O'Day viewed standards-based reform as addressing two persistent problems in U.S. education: unequal learning opportunities across race, social class, and school location; and the proliferation of fragmented policies unconnected in their design and implementation (Smith and O'Day 1991).

Although standards-based reform has taken a variety of forms at the federal, state, and local levels, four elements typically characterize it: a focus on student achievement; an emphasis on academic standards specifying the knowledge and skills students should acquire and the levels at which they should demonstrate mastery; a desire to extend the standards to all students, including those for whom expectations have been low traditionally; and a heavy reliance on achievement testing to spur the reforms and monitor their impact (Goertz 2007; National Research Council [NRC] 1997, 2008). When it was first articulated, the concept of standards-based reform emphasized the centrality of rigorous academic standards in guiding instruction for all students and in serving as the basis for linking instructional materials, teacher training, and student assessment policies. The assumption was that with coherent, aligned policies, local districts and schools could be held accountable for their students' progress, but they would also have greater flexibility in how they taught those students (Smith and O'Day 1991). However, in practice, as the assessment portions of standards-based reform have become more prominent and high-stakes, attention has focused less on either support for educators or local flexibility and more on using student assessment results to allocate rewards and sanctions.

As the current incarnation of the Elementary and Secondary Education Act, No Child Left Behind (NCLB) requires that states adopt academic content and performance standards; assess all students annually in reading and mathematics in grades 3 through 8 and once in high school; report test scores by school disaggregated by ethnicity, gender, low-income status, and educational need; and take specific actions to improve schools with chronically low student test scores. Despite complaints that NCLB represents unwarranted federal intrusion into state and local control of education, the legislation actually lagged behind what was already occurring in a number of states. In fact, the recent history of federal-state relations strongly suggests that NCLB was possible only because of profound changes in the state policy role over the previous twenty years, and that NCLB's development tells us as much about the depth of change in state policy as it does about any alteration in the federal role (McDonnell 2005).

In his analysis of the origins of No Child Left Behind, Paul Manna focuses on policy changes in the federal system, and develops the concept of *borrowing strength*. It "occurs when policy entrepreneurs at one level of government attempt to push their agendas by leveraging the justification and capabilities that other governments elsewhere in the federal system possess" (2006, 5). Manna argues that the passage of NCLB was possible because state governments had already enacted reforms organized around standards and assessments.[1] In most cases, the impetus for these reforms had come from governors such as Bill Clinton, Lamar Alexander, James Hunt, and later George W. Bush, who viewed improving the schools as a centerpiece of their state's economic development strategy. Policy entrepreneurs promoting NCLB were able to mobilize around the *license*, or arguments states had already made to justify the involvement of higher levels of government in classroom processes and outcomes, and the *capacity* and administrative structures state reforms had created. Even as its policies have become more directive over the last twenty years, the federal government remains the junior partner in elementary and secondary education. Although its proportion of the total cost of K-12 education has fluctuated over presidential administrations, the federal contribution has remained small, ranging on average from about 6 to 12 percent. Authority over teacher training and licensure, student attendance, course requirements, and curriculum remains a state prerogative.

Education Stimulus as a Down Payment on the Administration's K–12 Agenda

When President Obama took office in January 2009, ESEA-NCLB was already two years overdue for reauthorization. In several campaign speeches, Obama had indicated that he supported No Child Left Behind's goals, particularly its emphasis on narrowing achievement gaps between white and minority students. At the same time, he argued that because NCLB was underfunded, school districts were having difficulty in implementing it and parts of the law would need to be overhauled. In addition to advocating increased funding, Obama promised to work with the nation's governors and educators to create better assessments that would improve student learning by measuring critical thinking and problem-solving skills. Obama also promised significant funding increases for early childhood education, a major focus on improving the preparation and compensation of teachers, and a doubling of federal financial support for charter schools (Obama 2008, 75–82, 248–51). However, it was unclear during the campaign how he intended to translate these aspirations into a legislative agenda,

Obama's education agenda seemed even more tenuous in the face of his other policy priorities and the nation's serious economic problems. During the transition, the president-elect and his team recognized that the need for a stimulus package and his desire to make health care his top priority in the first year meant that other policy initiatives could not be advanced during the same period. Part of their calculus stemmed from a judgment that with too many proposals on the agenda at the same time, members of Congress, the media, and the public would become distracted, and attention would be diverted from the president's top priorities. The incoming administration was also concerned about how much the Democratic congressional leadership could handle at the same time, especially given that several proposals would have to pass through the same committees (for example, health care and education both fall within the jurisdiction of the same House and Senate committees).[2]

Just as he did in several other areas such as energy and health care, President Obama used parts of the stimulus bill as a down payment on advancing components of his education agenda even as the administration pursued countercyclical policy goals.[3] One early estimate of the recession's impact on K-12 public education projected that, absent increased taxes or federal stimulus funding, overall spending would fall 8.7 percent between fiscal years 2009 and 2011. As a result, approximately 574,000 jobs would be lost over the three years unless local school districts chose to reduce spending in other ways (Roza 2009). Not surprisingly, then, most of the funds designated for education in the Recovery Act were targeted for traditional stabilization purposes and allocated to states on a population-based formula: $48.6 billion in a state fiscal stabilization fund, including $39.5 billion available to local districts and higher education institutions for averting staff reductions and programmatic cutbacks and $8.8 billion for facilities modernization and repair. Other funding of approximately $30 billion augmented major federal categorical programs. In keeping with the focus on stimulating the economy, the first priority in the Department of Education's (ED) Recovery Act guidance to states was to spend quickly to save and create jobs.

Nevertheless, even the statutory language for this traditional countercyclical, formula-based portion took into account reform goals. It required that states provide "assurances" that they were taking actions in four substantive areas: achieving equity in the distribution of highly qualified teachers between high- and low-poverty schools and assuring that low-income and minority students were not taught at higher rates by inexperienced or unqualified teachers; establishing longitudinal state data systems for tracking individual student progress more reliably; enhancing the quality of state academic content and performance standards; and supporting low-performing schools through intervention strategies focused on school reorganization and improved approaches to instruction. These assurances, signaling the administration's substantive policy interests, would prove challenging to states: all are costly to implement, and the first and fourth require substantial political capital because of likely opposition from local education constituency groups. However, the need to allocate stimulus funds quickly meant that, at least for the first allocation to states, they were essentially aspirational goals with only limited federal enforcement.[4]

Consistent with the administration's interest in using the stimulus legislation as a down payment on future policy redesign, Congress also authorized and appropriated about $6.2 billion for initiatives intended to strengthen the K-12 infrastructure through expanded statewide data systems and improved educational technology, enhanced teacher quality, and stimulation of innovation. Included in this category are what have become the administration's most potent reform levers, the Race to the Top state competition and the Investing in Innovation (i3) Fund.

Although critics later questioned the administration's use of Race to the Top funds as a goad for major changes in state and local education policy, it was not a major concern during the debate over the stimulus bill. The debate centered on traditional stimulus issues: whether funds for education would immediately and significantly stimulate the economy and whether federally financed school construction would set a precedent for an expanded federal role in the future. In fact, the Democratic congressional majority kept the debate away from the substance of education reform. For example, when Republican senators argued that before increasing funding for ESEA programs through the Recovery Act, the program should be redesigned to ensure a greater impact on student achievement, Senator Tom Harkin (D-IA), chair of the Senate Appropriations Committee, argued that "the economic recovery bill should not be the vehicle for reauthorizing the No Child Left Behind Act. . . . It would be foolhardy, not to mention politically impossible, to try to enact major education reforms" in a few weeks' time (Klein 2009). What would subsequently become the Race to the Top and i3 competitive grant programs were only cursorily outlined in the Recovery Act legislation. The funds were reserved for the secretary of education to award as incentive grants to states that have made significant progress in meeting the four assurances (PL 111–5, Sec. 14006), and to eligible entities that "have made significant progress in closing the achievement gap," allowing them "to expand their work and serve as models for best practices" (Sec. 14007).[5]

Race to the Top as a Reform Lever

Secretary of Education Arne Duncan recognized the unique resources that the passage of the Recovery Act had given him: "What I love is opportunity, and this is a once-in-a-lifetime opportunity to do something special, to drive change, to make our schools better" (as quoted in Dillon 2009a). Not only was his department's budget more than doubled over the two-year duration of the Recovery Act, but he had been given unparalleled discretion in allocating the funds. As a *New York Times* article noted, "the $100 billion in emergency aid for public schools and colleges in the economic stimulus bill could transform Arne Duncan into an exceptional figure in the history of federal education policy: a secretary of education loaded with money and power to spend large chunks of it as he sees fit" (Dillon 2009a). In dozens of speeches over the ten months before the first Race to the Top applications were due, Duncan articulated the administration's education reform agenda and developed in greater detail themes introduced during the campaign.

The criteria for the Race to the Top grants competition allowed the administration to specify its reform goals precisely, but also gave it considerable leverage over the conditions imposed on states applying for the funds. When the Department of Education published draft guidelines for awarding the $4.35 billion in Race to the Top funds, the full import of what the administration hoped to accomplish with the education stimulus became clear. State applications were to be judged on nineteen criteria that included the extent to which they had been able to maintain K-12 funding at prerecession levels and the lifting of any caps on the expansion of charter schools. Another requirement was that applicant states could not have any laws barring the use of student achievement data in evaluating teachers and principals. To reinforce the administration's political investment in what would be major changes in the status quo, both the secretary of education and the president used publication of the draft guidelines to emphasize their commitment to these policy strategies. In a *Washington Post* op-ed article, Duncan called Race to the Top "the equivalent of education reform's moon shot," noting that the "fund marks a once-in-a-lifetime opportunity for the federal government to create incentives for far-reaching improvement in our nation's schools. Indeed, the $4.35 billion available in Race to the Top easily outstrips the combined sum of discretionary funds for reform that all of my predecessors as education secretary had" (Duncan 2009).

In what can only be described as a rare event in presidential history, President Obama came to the Department of Education in July 2009 to announce the draft guidelines. He mentioned the administration's efforts "to build a new foundation for growth and prosperity" through health insurance, energy, and financial reforms. "But even if we do all of these things, America will not succeed in the 21st century unless we do a far better job of educating our sons and daughters." In the remainder of his remarks, the president was quite specific about what the administration expected of states applying for Race to the Top funds. He discussed, for example, particular strategies for how states might turn around their lowest-performing schools, and the need to use a few key benchmarks to measure state progress on the quality of their standards and their effectiveness in closing the achievement gap. He promised that teachers would be brought into the process by which student performance would be linked to judgments about their performance, and that tests would be just one part of a broader evaluation. However, he warned, "Let me be clear: Success should be judged by results, and data is a powerful tool to determine results. We can't ignore facts. We can't ignore data" (Obama 2009c).[6]

In its guidance to states on the use of the formula-based stimulus funds and the criteria for the competitive grants, the Obama administration articulated an agenda firmly grounded in the standards-based reform philosophy that has defined state and federal education policy for more than two decades. At the same time, the administration extended the strategy in significant ways. Up to this point, the major policy instruments aimed at changing classroom instruction and student outcomes have been the state standards and, even more prominently, state assessments. Policymakers acknowledge the importance of what education researchers call the enabling conditions of standards-based reform: qualified teachers, instructional materials aligned with the standards, and schools organized to deliver instruction effectively. Yet federal and state policy has paid only minimal attention to these institutional and human capital factors (Cohen and Moffitt 2009). By making them an integral part of the conditions states had to take into account to be competitive for stimulus funding, the administration was reshaping the federal role.

POLICY IDEAS, INSTITUTIONAL REDESIGN, AND REALIGNED INTERESTS

As the Obama administration's K-12 policy agenda has emerged over the past two years, commentators have noted its surprising similarity to George Bush's approach, and the president's seeming willingness to challenge long-held positions of the education establishment. Although the political and educational consequences of Obama's policy choices are still unknown, how the president and Secretary Duncan have defined the shortcomings of the U.S. education system, coupled with their willingness to look to a diverse group of policy entrepreneurs for solutions, help explain an agenda that both continues and departs from past policy.

The Policy Ideas and Their Sources

Since the publication of *A Nation at Risk* almost thirty years ago, the primary rationale for the expanded role of the federal government and the states in education policy has been increasing U.S. competitiveness in the global economy. In *The Audacity of Hope* (2006) and in subsequent speeches,

Obama has used the same rationale. However, he typically ties it back to the students who are being shortchanged because of the quality of the schools they attend. "We've become accustomed to such stories, of poor black and Latino children languishing in schools that can't prepare them for the old industrial economy, much less the information age" (160). Statistical data on the achievement gap between affluent and low-income students and between students of color and white students give credence to these stories. For example, the proportion of elementary schools where the overwhelming majority of students are poor is much higher in urban areas (40 percent) than in suburbs (13 percent) or rural communities (10 percent).[7] More than 60 percent of the enrollment in these high-poverty schools are students of color. Teachers in high-poverty schools are more likely to be inexperienced (21 percent with fewer than three years of teaching experience) than those in low-poverty schools (16 percent). In addition, on average, one-fifth of the faculty in high-poverty schools turn over each year. Students in high-poverty schools consistently score lower on reading and mathematics tests than their peers in more affluent schools (National Center for Education Statistics 2010). Perhaps the most troubling indicator, and one that Obama has stressed, is the significant disparity in high school graduation rates. Of the students who began high school in 2001, nationwide 71 percent graduated four years later. However, the proportion was only 53 percent in the fifty largest school districts; the graduation rate for African American students was 55 percent and for Latino students 58 percent, as compared with 78 percent for white students (Swanson 2009).

In advancing solutions, Obama has argued that past reforms have been inadequate . . . because the more far-reaching ones have been stymied by ideological conflicts:

> Unfortunately, instead of innovation and bold reform of our schools . . . what we've seen from government for close to two decades has been tinkering around the edges and a tolerance for mediocrity. Partly this is a result of ideological battles that are as outdated as they are predictable. Many conservatives argue that money doesn't matter in raising educational achievement; that the problems in public schools are caused by hapless bureaucracies and intransigent teachers' unions; and that the only solution is to break up the government's education monopoly by handing out vouchers. Meanwhile, those on the left often find themselves defending an indefensible status quo, insisting that more spending alone will improve educational outcomes. Both assumptions are wrong. (Obama 2006, 160–61)

Although espousing a range of initiatives from early childhood education to longer school days, Obama has placed the greatest emphasis on the need for good teachers. To ensure an adequate supply, he has called for improved preparation programs and higher compensation. At the same time, "in exchange for more money, teachers need to become more accountable for their performance—and school districts need to have greater ability to get rid of ineffective teachers" (2006, 162). From the president's perspective, good teachers are the most critical resource in providing a high-quality education. Therefore, ensuring that all students have equal access to competent teachers should be the ultimate goal of any reform effort even if it means changing well-established rules for how this resource is managed and distributed.

The selection of Arne Duncan, chief executive officer of the Chicago Public Schools and a "basketball buddy" of Obama's, as secretary of education provides a clue to the source of many of the president's ideas. Duncan, along with former superintendents Joel Klein in New York City, Michelle Rhee in Washington, D.C., and Michael Bennett in Denver, was among a group of urban superintendents who espouse a different approach to school reform. They place management of human capital at the core of their strategies and have pressed for changes in the criteria used in assigning teachers to schools; for higher teacher compensation in exchange for basing it partly on performance, including how well a teacher's students score on standardized tests; and for reconstituting chronically low-performing schools using strategies that involve replacing the leadership and in some cases contracting with third-party providers. Some of these superintendents, often described as "hard-charging," work in cities where the mayor has assumed direct responsibility for the schools, thus giving them additional political clout through the chief executive to whom they report.[8]

Sources of Support

These urban reformers have been assisted by a tight cluster of foundations, nonprofit third-party providers, and interest groups. Included in this network is the Carnegie Corporation of New York, which has funded Teach for America, The New Teacher Project, and New Leaders for New Schools—nonprofits designed to recruit and train educators through alternatives to the traditional university-based schools of education.[9] Another prominent player in this network is the Bill and Melinda Gates Foundation, which has invested hundreds of millions of dollars in a variety of education reform initiatives, including efforts to redesign high schools and to change how teachers are evaluated. It was also one of the funders supporting the development of common state standards, and provided $250,000 each to states applying for Race to the Top grants if they agreed to abide by eight conditions, including the adoption of standards common across multiple states and the linking of student data to teachers.[10]

The major interest group is a political action committee, Democrats for Education Reform (DFER), based in New York City. It raised approximately $2 million in the 2008 campaign, and was vocal in its support of charter schools and differential pay for teachers. DFER's fundraising capacity does not match that of the major teacher union, the National Education Association (NEA), which along with its state and local affiliates raised at least $40 million for Democratic candidates. However, DFER was active at the 2008 Democratic national convention and during the transition in advancing a reform agenda often opposed by traditional Democratic constituencies (Klein 2008).[11] At a press conference before the DFER seminar held at the Democratic convention, Mayor Cory Booker of Newark argued that debate over issues such as performance-based compensation for teachers and the expansion of charter schools is a "battle at the heart of the Democratic party. . . . As Democrats, we have been wrong on education. It's time to get it right." At the same seminar, several panelists, including Michelle Rhee, argued that teacher unions were putting the interests of their members ahead of the educational needs of students (Hoff and McNeil 2008).

State officials have been less visible in the national media than urban reformers, and their willingness to change state laws to conform with federal priorities has stemmed largely from a desire to obtain additional funding under tight fiscal conditions. Nevertheless, in a number of states, officials saw Race to the Top as an opportunity to move their own reform agendas. For example, former Tennessee Governor Phil Bredesen requested that the state legislature pass a reform package that included the requirement that student achievement data be used in teacher evaluations as well as provisions strengthening the state's ability to intervene in chronically low-performing schools. In doing so, Bredesen was "borrowing strength" from the federal government, as it had done itself previously in using state reforms as a rationale for No Child Left Behind and similar changes in federal policy. Bredesen noted that the education stimulus offered a unique opportunity to gain political traction for significant policy changes. "The whole Race to the Top just provided a focal point for a whole range of things that might have been difficult to do in other times" (as quoted in Robelen 2010).

Similarly, legislators in Michigan indicated that a package of reforms they enacted allowing the state to take over the lowest-performing schools and even whole districts, establishing new routes to teacher and principal certification, linking student performance to teacher and principal evaluations, and allowing for an increase in the number of charter schools were changes that had been discussed for years. However, they probably would not have been passed were it not for the financial incentives Race to the Top offered (Robelen 2010). This assessment was echoed by officials in other states who characterized Race to the Top as allowing them to undertake needed reforms more quickly than would have been possible without the potential of a large infusion of federal funding. However, now that cash-strapped states, such as Michigan and California, have been unsuccessful in winning Race to the Top funds, they are likely to lack the resources to implement the reforms authorized in new legislation, thus making it easier for opposition groups to delay or block the changes.

Teacher Union Opposition

The two national teacher unions, the NEA and the American Federation of Teachers (AFT), have resisted several elements of the education reform agenda that has taken shape over the last decade and that the Obama administration is now pursuing. The unions oppose charter schools because, though they are public schools, their independence from local districts means that, with a few exceptions, the teachers are not unionized. The AFT and the NEA have also been highly critical of the growing emphasis on standardized testing, and the use of test scores in negatively labeling schools whose students fall short of expected gains. They note that the growing emphasis on standardized testing in only a few subjects has narrowed the curriculum and compromised teachers' professional judgment about how best to educate their students. Recent moves to base teacher compensation partly on their students' test scores have further intensified union opposition to the testing regime that defines No Child Left Behind and state policies.

In expressing opposition, the NEA and AFT are protecting the interests of their members. However, they also argue that these reforms fall considerably short of advocates' claims and in some cases are actually counterproductive in improving student learning and closing the achievement gap. Unfortunately, research evidence on the effectiveness of charter schools, incentive pay for teachers, and other popular reform strategies is either incomplete, inconsistent, or highly contested. For example, a recently completed, three-year study in which nearly 300 middle-school mathematics teachers in Nashville were randomly assigned to experimental and control groups to test whether awarding financial bonuses of up to $15,000 annually would lead to higher student scores found that students of teachers eligible for rewards did not outperform students whose teachers were assigned to the control group (Springer et al. 2010). Although the study casts doubt on the effectiveness of a central Obama administration reform strategy and seems to reinforce union arguments, it leaves unanswered other relevant questions. These include whether incentive pay would attract and retain a different group of people as teachers, and how adding other features such as differential responsibilities to an incentive pay system would affect the results. Although research on charter schools is more developed than that on teacher compensation systems, its inconsistent findings have been the subject of ongoing controversy (Henig 2008). At this point the most reasonable conclusion is that, like traditional public schools, the quality of charters varies significantly, depending on the state in which they operate, how they are organized, and what types of students they serve. In a variety of areas, the lack of solid evidence that the administration's reform proposals will lead to significant improvements over the status quo has provided ammunition for union opposition and added a distinctly political dimension to the debate over how best to educate students.

Obama understood that in espousing an institutional redesign agenda he was challenging core union tenets. Several commentators have argued that because both unions supported Hillary Clinton in the Democratic primaries, Obama owed them little (Alter 2010; Colvin 2009). Nevertheless, his approach has been to remain firm about his redesign strategies, but to suggest that these changes can be made with teacher and union involvement. At the press conference nominating Duncan, Obama argued, "If pay-for-performance works and we work with teachers so they don't feel like it's being imposed on them but instead they've got an option for different compensation mechanisms in order for us to encourage high performance, then that's something we should explore. If charter schools work, let's try that. You know, let's not be clouded by ideology when it comes to figuring out what helps our kids" (CQ Transcripts Wire 2008).

Before nominating him, the president-elect indicated to Duncan that his education agenda should rest on two principles: all policy should revolve around what is best for kids, not adult interest groups; and the administration should avoid putting a stick in anyone's eye. Obama's admonition to Duncan was "let's engage, not attack," likening his education reform effort to Nixon going to China (Alter 2010, 90–91). His choice of Duncan reflected a belief that substantial change could be pursued without alienating the teacher unions. While CEO in Chicago, Duncan had maintained a cordial relationship with the local AFT affiliate even as he introduced a pay-for-performance plan and contracted with third-party providers to operate seventy-five new schools.

The AFT and the NEA worked hard to elect Barack Obama, and they supported Duncan's nomination as secretary of education. Consequently, until announcing its opposition to the Race to the Top draft rules, the NEA was careful to avoid disparaging the administration's education reform agenda. However, both unions became vocal in their criticisms during the summer of 2009. In its comments, the NEA asserted that "we cannot support yet another layer of federal mandates that have little or no research base of success and that usurp state and local governments' responsibilities for public education" (Sawchuk 2009). The AFT made similar comments, arguing that Race to the Top "would simply layer another top-down accountability system on top of the current faulty one," and its president, Randi Weingarten, suggested that ED's intent seemed to be to have Race to the Top go much further than just replicating proven programs and promoting promising ideas, "effectively creating and implementing education policy outside of a legislative process" (McNeil 2009). Among the 1,135 comments ED received on the draft guidelines were ones from other groups and elected officials who raised concerns about aspects of the Race to the Top program. However, the ones from the national teacher unions were among the most critical, and they were reinforced by comments from their state and local affiliates, which also objected to the emphasis on charter schools and performance-based compensation.[12]

The unions' opposition to the Race to the Top application criteria had tangible consequences for states competing for grants. They needed to show that local districts and their teacher unions had agreed to participate in the state's proposed reform agenda, with a state's plans for its teacher quality system counting for up to 138 of the 500 points on which applications were judged. Several states that observers assumed would be competitive received lower scores in the first round because of limited local district and union buy-in. For example, in contrast to the two first-round winners, Delaware and Tennessee, which had near-universal support from their districts and teacher unions, only 8 percent of Florida's districts participating in its teacher evaluation plan had buy-in from their local unions (McNeil and Maxwell 2010). However, an analysis by *Education Week* of second-round Race to the Top applications suggests that local teacher union buy-in broadened, with the proportion of local unions signing on to state applications increasing by 22 percentage points on average among the twenty-nine states that applied in both rounds. The reasons vary by state, and some even lost union support. However, those that made significant gains, such as Florida, Michigan, and Wisconsin, involved the unions more in the application process, and where student data have become a required part of teacher evaluations, local implementation is typically subject to collective bargaining (McNeil 2010a).

The media highlighted the growing rift between the teacher unions and the administration, pointing especially to the absence of any Obama administration official at the AFT's and NEA's annual conventions in 2010. Commentators have also noted the NEA delegates' vote of no confidence in the Race to the Top guidelines and proposed use of competitive grants in the reauthorized Elementary and Secondary Education Act (Luce 2010; Dillon 2010a; Sawchuk 2010; Brill 2010).[13] In speeches at their respective conventions, AFT president Randi Weingarten and NEA president Dennis Van Roekel expressed their disapproval of the administration, both criticizing Obama's and Duncan's positive mentions of the firing of eighty-nine teachers at a Rhode Island high school, the emphasis on standardized test scores as the primary measure of student progress and teacher quality, and the tenor of public discussion with the problems of public education blamed almost entirely on teachers. Their views were captured in Weingarten's comment, "Never before have I seen so few attack so many, so harshly, for doing so much—often with so little" (2010).

Yet like Albert Shanker, one of her predecessors as AFT president, Weingarten seems to recognize that the education status quo is changing, and that the interests of unionized teachers are better protected if they participate in reform discussions and adapt to changed circumstances rather than oppose a movement they cannot stop.[14] She has used this reasoning in her support of a Colorado law and her active participation in collective bargaining negotiations in Washington, D.C., where the result in both cases has been policies linking teacher job security more directly to classroom performance. However, union leaders like Weingarten have to balance the recognition that longer-term social and political trends need to be accommodated with the short-term concerns of their members. As a result, in a few localities where unionized teachers and other public employee unions are strong and where they perceive reform candidates to have unfairly criticized teachers or been overly supportive of charter schools, the unions have retaliated by supporting their opponents, especially in low-turnout Democratic primaries. Examples include the defeat of Adrian Fenty in the Washington, D.C., mayoral election at least partly because of his support of schools chancellor Michelle Rhee, and the defeat by union-backed candidates of three New York state senate candidates who strongly support charter schools. Still, regardless of what happens in the near future, the longer-term effect of the Obama K-12 agenda may be to allow progressive union leaders to borrow strength in much the same way as some governors and mayors have done in persuading their constituents to accept major reforms.

Summary: Education Reform from an Urban Perspective

The Obama administration justified its down payment stimulus policies on much the same basis as its immediate predecessors did for traditional education policy: focusing on closing the achievement gap as a strategy for enhancing U.S. competitiveness in the global economy. However, Barack Obama's urban political roots have given him a different perspective on the problem and the policy ideas to address that problem. Over the last decade, a group of foundation leaders, urban education reformers, and elected officials have coalesced around the recognition that urban schools with their high dropout rates are the Achilles heel of U.S. education, and that incremental approaches will not remedy this growing crisis. Some of the solutions they propose are either untested or have produced weak or mixed effects. Yet the resources and political influence available to this group of reformers have propelled their ideas to the top of the national education policy agenda, and have made them a counterweight to groups representing the education establishment. President Obama's strategy is not without political costs in diminished support from a core constituency. However, the administration seems to have calculated that the costs are likely to be short term and concentrated in a few localities, and that they will be offset by the potential benefits of addressing an increasingly serious problem that threatens the country's economic and social well-being.

This combination of policy ideas anchored in human capital strategies and the redesign of institutional rules and structures—supported by an influential coalition of interests—allowed the Obama administration to use stabilization policy in an unprecedented way. However, its reform agenda will remain only a fleeting opportunity unless it is institutionalized in more permanent federal legislation. Once it enters that arena, the administration stands to lose much of the rhetorical and political advantage it enjoyed for some eighteen months.

FROM TEMPORARY STIMULUS TO ONGOING POLICY AND PRACTICE

What had been a preview of the Obama administration's education reform agenda culminated in March 2010 with the publication of *A Blueprint for Reform* (U.S. Department of Education 2010a). In it, the administration outlines its plan for the reauthorization of the Elementary and Secondary Education Act. It retains some of the core elements of No Child Left Behind, including the mandate that all students in grades 3 through 8 be tested in mathematics and reading each year, and that their scores be disaggregated and publicly reported by race-ethnicity, low income, and special populations such as students with disabilities. However, the administration also proposed significant changes reflecting directions it introduced as part of the education stimulus. These include linking Title I funding to state adoption of college- and career-ready standards, defining *effective teachers* based partly on student outcomes, and offering *turnaround* grants for implementing intervention models that require replacing the principal in the lowest-performing schools. At the same time, the administration has recommended greater flexibility in how student proficiency is measured, in how schools that miss proficiency targets for only a few student groups are treated, and in granting greater autonomy and rewards to schools that demonstrate progress in closing the achievement gap.

Like other presidential administrations since the inception of the Elementary and Secondary Education Act in 1965, Obama's education reform agenda has now moved into the traditional arena of presidential-congressional politics. Here the president has limited influence on the legislative schedule, on which issues become central in committee and floor deliberations, and how supporters and opponents frame those issues. Despite being long overdue for reauthorization, ESEA's legislative course is uncertain.

Reauthorization under Altered Political Dynamics

The shift to a Republican majority in the House after the 2010 midterm election complicates predictions about the ESEA reauthorization. John Kline (R-MN) replaced George Miller (D-CA), an Obama ally and defender of the administration's reform strategy, as chair of the House Education and Labor Committee. Given the Republican focus on deficit reduction, it is safe to assume that the administration will no longer have substantial discretionary funding to pursue its reform objectives, and House Republicans will exert greater oversight over how Secretary Duncan uses what funds are available to him. However, the timeline for the ESEA reauthorization and the shape of the ultimate legislation are less certain.

In response to the *Blueprint,* Miller and his senate counterpart Tom Harkin held a series of informational hearings in spring 2010 focused on topics such as secondary schools, standards and assessments, teachers and education leaders, and school turnaround models. The hearings were designed to inform committee members about research, exemplary practices, and potential problems related to the future legislation. Yet neither the House nor Senate committees drafted legislation. Part of the reason for the Democrats' decision not to move more decisively while they still held a majority in both houses was the memory of unsuccessful efforts to reauthorize ESEA in 2007. At that time, Miller encountered opposition from the teacher unions and some freshman Democratic members who opposed including in a draft bill a competitive grants program for local districts willing to experiment with rewarding teachers for student achievement gains, and from the Bush administration and some civil rights groups opposed to basing evaluations of school progress on multiple measures in addition to standardized test scores.[15]

Although few observers are willing to offer solid predictions about when ESEA will be reauthorized or how closely it will reflect the administration's *Blueprint*, two factors will certainly shape the process and the final legislation. First, ESEA's reauthorization is likely to be less divisive and partisan than other domestic policies such as health care, immigration, and taxation. The major reason is that federal education policy has traditionally been formulated in a bipartisan manner with Democratic and Republican staffs working closely together and the committee chairs and ranking members consulting regularly.

The norms of bipartisanship have been strengthened over the past two decades with the centrality of standards-based reform and school choice as the two big ideas guiding federal (and state) policy. However, the broad consensus around these two ideas and the lack of competing alternatives have by no means eliminated partisan disagreement over such issues as what the size of the federal financial contribution should be, whether the federal government should support vouchers or just charter schools, and how tightly federal directives should constrain state and local action. Nevertheless, even in the midst of serious disagreements over these and other issues, the legislative process has been reasonably collaborative and rarely as rancorous as in some policy areas. This pattern is likely to continue. Secretary Duncan and other administration officials have been working with Kline, and both Duncan and Kline report having a collegial relationship (Dillon 2010b).

The second factor influencing the ESEA reauthorization is a consensus that elements of No Child Left Behind are not working as intended, and that the legislation should be thoroughly overhauled. Although there is less agreement among the various affected interests about exactly how NCLB should be changed, the primary focus of everyone's concern is the accountability system and the criteria used to label schools as needing improvement. This broad-based press for changes to NCLB, coupled with less agreement about specific strategies, has been reflected in the mixed reaction to the administration's *Blueprint*.

Interest Group Mobilization

Education establishment groups have expressed support for parts of the *Blueprint* that address some of the more problematic aspects of NCLB. Organizations representing school boards and administrators are pleased that the *Blueprint* eliminates adequate yearly progress (AYP) as the measure of a school's effectiveness under NCLB. AYP, the basis on which schools are judged to be meeting student proficiency goals, compares a cohort of students in a given year with the cohort from the previous year. It is a technically flawed measure and most policymakers and educators agree that it should be changed. Building on pilot projects begun during the Bush administration and taking advantage of new state longitudinal data systems, the Obama administration recommends that states measure achievement gains using growth models that compare changes in individual students' test scores from one year to the next. Similarly, the *Blueprint* recommends eliminating the NCLB requirement that all students reach proficiency on state assessments by 2014. Instead, it proposes that states, districts, and schools aim to have all students graduate from high school prepared for college or a career by 2020, but does not establish the date as a firm deadline. In some areas, the *Blueprint* provides greater local flexibility than NCLB. For example, schools that fail to meet achievement targets would not be automatically required to offer their students the option of transferring to another public school or to provide tutoring from outside vendors funded by local Title I resources.[16]

Criticisms of the administration's recommendations have focused on elements of the Obama reform agenda already operative in Race to the Top. In addition to the teacher unions' opposition to incentives for performance-based compensation, the continued emphasis on large-scale annual student testing and the expansion of charter schools, three other issues have emerged as potentially divisive. The first is the recommendation that as a condition for states receiving Title I funding, they either upgrade their own standards in collaboration with their four-year university system or work with other states to develop standards that build toward college- and career-readiness. State officials, members of Congress, and education interest groups have strongly supported developing standards common across multiple states and having the federal government encourage such efforts through the education stimulus. However, the idea that more rigorous standards might become a condition for Title I funding has drawn criticism from groups such as the National Conference of State Legislatures and the National School Boards Association, which, though indicating support for bottom-up, state-led efforts, have called the administration's plan "unnecessary overreach by the federal government" (Klein 2010a). These groups can count on a positive response from Republican members of Congress intent on scaling back the federal role in education and allowing greater discretion for states and local school districts.

A second administration recommendation that has drawn criticism is its interest in having states and districts apply one of four specific turnaround models to the lowest-performing 5 percent of schools in each state (approximately 5,000 schools nationwide). The administration proposes giving schools that miss proficiency targets for one or two of their student subgroups greater flexibility in how they decide to remedy the problem than they have under No Child Left Behind. At the same time, it wants the reauthorized Elementary and Secondary Education Act to be more pre-scriptive about how states are to fix the lowest-performing schools. All four models involve replacing the principal: the first also requires that teachers reapply for their jobs with no more than half of them rehired; the second requires turning the school over to a charter school operator, a charter management organization, or an education management orga-nization; the third strengthens the school's staffing and implements a research-based instructional program and a new governance structure; and the fourth involves closing the school and enrolling the students in a higher-performing school in the same district.

The NEA and a coalition of civil rights groups, including the NAACP and the National Urban League, have opposed the prescriptiveness of the turnaround models. The civil rights coalition, the National Opportunity to Learn Campaign (OTL Campaign), argues that the *Blueprint* places too much emphasis on school closures and the reconstitution of school staff, and it "urges an end to the federal push to encourage states to adopt federally-prescribed methodologies that have little or no evidentiary sup-port" (2010). Miller has questioned the turnaround model in which a large proportion of teachers are dismissed, suggesting that educators at under-performing schools may have the potential to be effective but lack ade-quate support and assistance. Senator Michael Enzi of Wyoming, the ranking Republican on the Senate committee, has questioned whether these models apply to rural schools, and has suggested that they rely on research that is "at best sketchy" (Klein 2010c).[17] Like several other changes recommended by the administration, opposition to the turnaround mod-els cuts across traditional partisan and ideological divides.

The third issue in dispute—the proportion of Elementary and Second-ary Education Act funds that should be formula driven and the propor-tion distributed to states and local districts through competitive grants—reflects policy feedback originating in ESEA's initial enactment. To ensure its passage, the allocation formula was designed so that all congressional districts and the overwhelming majority of school districts receive funds. That formula created state and local constituents who view ESEA funds as an entitlement. In subsequent reauthorizations, those broad-based inter-ests have blocked attempts to target funds more efficiently either to dis-tricts and schools with the greatest need or to ones organized to deliver instruction more effectively. Specialized targeting of Title I funds has been largely restricted to new monies appropriated in excess of the formula funding.

The Obama administration has recommended that competitive grants become a more central part of the Elementary and Secondary Education Act, and that the Race to the Top and i3 programs be continued. At the same time, Secretary Duncan has maintained that even with proposed increases in competitive grants in the administration's 2011 budget and their being included in the *Blueprint*, 80 percent of federal K-12 programs would be formula based (Duncan 2010). Nevertheless, several groups, including the OTL Campaign coalition, have spoken out in opposition to continuing competitive grant programs like Race to the Top. The Campaign's argument is that because only a few states will receive competitive grants, "most children in most states will experience a real decrease in federal support when inflation and state and local budget cuts are taken into consideration." Instead of competitive grants to a few states, it calls for conditional incentive grants to all states "provided they adopt systemic, proven strategies for providing all students with an opportunity to learn" (National Opportunity to Learn Campaign 2010).

Administration Defense of Its Reform Agenda

It is unclear what the administration's response will be once it must negotiate over the details of specific legislative language. Until now, Secretary Duncan has been responsive to groups expressing criticism and recommending alternatives to the *Blueprint*.[18] At the same time, the administration—most notably President Obama—has identified elements of the education agenda on which it is unwilling to compromise. The clearest evidence of that came in the president's speech to the National Urban League three days after the group joined in issuing the OTL Campaign framework with its criticisms of Race to the Top and other parts of the administration's program.[19]

Calling his speech an "honest conversation," the president spent more than forty minutes defending all the major elements of his education reform agenda. He began by challenging the concern

that Race to the Top doesn't do enough for minority kids, because the argument is, well, if there's a competition, then somehow some states or some school districts will get more help than others. Let me tell you, what's not working for black kids and Hispanic kids and Native American kids across the country is the status quo. That's what's not working. What's not working is what we've been doing for decades now. So the charge that Race to the Top isn't targeted at those young people most in need is absolutely false because lifting up quality for all children—black, white, Hispanic—that is the central promise of Race to the Top. And you can't win one of those grants unless you've got a plan to deal with those schools that are failing and those young people who aren't doing well. (Obama 2010)

The president then reiterated that "the whole premise of Race to the Top is that teachers are the single most important factor in a child's education from the moment they step into the classroom." He repeated his support for higher teacher salaries, better training, and a supportive work environment. But, he added, "if we're not seeing results in a classroom then let's work with teachers to help them become more effective. If that doesn't work, let's find the right teacher for that classroom" (Obama 2010). In the rest of his speech, the president argued for states voluntarily adopting common standards that are higher than current ones. He defended better tests whose use can inform teaching and learning, and charter schools not as a "magic bullet" but as a chance for states and local districts to try new things.

Toward the end of his talk, Obama made a promise that had already shaped the "edujobs" stimulus legislation Congress passed in August 2010: "I'll . . . continue to fight for Race to the Top with everything I've got, including using a veto to prevent some folks from watering it down" (Obama 2010). During the deliberations over the $10 billion appropriation aimed at saving the jobs of 160,000 teachers, Representative David Obey (D-WI) vowed to fund it by taking $500 million from Race to the Top, $100 million from charter school grants, and $200 million from the Teacher Incentive Fund that supports the establishment of performance-pay plans. After Obama threatened to veto the bill if these cuts were included, the offsets were taken from other education programs and a large proportion from the food stamp program.

The Likely Shape of ESEA Legislation and Challenges Ahead

Even if President Obama and his administration hold fast to the reform agenda they have pursued through the education stimulus, all the elements will not be incorporated in the Elementary and Secondary Education Act. Based on past reauthorizations and current politics, it is likely that when ESEA is reauthorized, it will remedy the most serious problems with No Child Left Behind. Growth models will replace average yearly progress in calculating school progress; schools failing to meet some of their proficiency targets will have greater flexibility in improving their performance; and the 2014 deadline for 100 percent student proficiency will be replaced with a "softer" goal. However, standards and assessments will continue to constitute the core of ESEA. The high-stakes testing regimes established by some states more than twenty years ago and strengthened by NCLB will endure, albeit with more valid tests developed through federal stimulus funding.

What the Obama administration is unlikely to obtain in the ESEA reauthorization is a requirement that chronically low-performing schools can only use one of its four prescribed turnaround models. There will likely be a heightened emphasis on these schools, but states will be given greater flexibility in the strategies they select. The administration will likely succeed in getting several competitive grant programs included in ESEA. Several will be augmented versions of existing ESEA programs such as the Teacher Incentive Fund and grants to establish charter schools. The others most likely will build on the Recovery Act programs, but will be authorized at lower funding levels, and not supported at the expense of the formula grants.

Regardless of what is included in the reauthorized Elementary and Secondary Education Act, the long-term question will be whether it makes a difference for those students who "through a turn of fate . . . happened to be born in the wrong neighborhood" (Obama 2010). For more than forty years, federal officials have encountered significant challenges in moving their policies into classroom practice and in attempting to change the learning conditions for low-income students and those with special needs. In their thoughtful history of ESEA Title I, David Cohen and Susan Moffitt explain why the program has continued to fall short of its goals:

> The traditions and structure of U.S. education and government meant that instructional capability was not a matter that state and federal agencies either were inclined to attend to, or with which they could readily offer much help. State and federal agencies thus tended to over-invest in the instruments that were familiar and relatively easy for them to deploy, such as tests, and to under-invest in measures, such as curricula and professional education, that could help to build schools' capability to improve education. The result was a collision between policy pressure for more ambitious work at the state and federal level, and weak capability in practice, in local schools and school systems. (2009, 218–19)

To its credit, the Obama administration has paid greater attention than its predecessors to the design of the institutions and the capability of the people who implement top-down policy. However, the way the stimulus policies have been framed and the fiscal context in which they have been advanced may constrain their long-term effectiveness. As with many previous education reforms, the Obama administration has emphasized the central role of teachers—how they are recruited, trained, evaluated, and compensated. In doing so, it faces a classic dilemma: the group the administration has identified as a central part of the problem is the one on whom it must depend to solve that problem (Cohen and Moffitt 2009). Consequently, like earlier generations of education reformers, the Obama administration and its partner state governments must convince educators that this menu of reforms is in their interest and equally important, it must invest in enhancing educators' capability to move policy into classroom practice. Building such capability requires sustained support and continuing resources of time and expertise. At this point, it is too early to predict whether states can maintain that critical capacity. However, experience with federal seed grants and the opportunistic nature of state behavior with regard to the Race to the Top competition lead to concerns about their political will and their ability to institutionalize whatever they began with temporary stimulus funds.

COMPETITIVE GRANTS AS A FEDERAL LEVERAGE STRATEGY

Race to the Top's success in motivating governors and legislators to change state laws to be competitive for funding raises the question of whether such a strategy might be broadly applicable in gaining greater federal leverage over state and local programs. A variant on this model is the i3 Fund, the other competitive grants program included in the education stimulus. Although i3 has been less visible, its design may be more applicable across the federal government because it supports different levels of innovation and a broader range of organizations are eligible to compete.

The i3 Fund distributed $650 million to local school districts, nonprofit organizations, and institutions of higher education that competed for three levels of funding: up to $50 million per project to "scale up" programs with a strong track record of effectiveness; up to $30 million for "validation" grants to expand programs with emerging evidence of success; and up to $5 million per "development" grant to refine promising ideas.[20] More than 1,600 proposals were received, and in early August 2010 awards were made to forty-nine applicants.[21] The i3 Fund requires that awardees secure 20 percent of the amount requested in matching funds from private-sector sources.

In addition to Race to the Top and the i3 Fund, the Obama administration has also established a $50 million Social Innovation Fund (SIF) authorized under the Edward M. Kennedy Serve America Act and managed by the Corporation for National and Community Service in close collaboration with the White House Office of Social Innovation and Civic Participation (OSICP). SIF's public funding has been augmented by $74 million in private funds from sources such as the Broad and the Open Society Foundations. Its purpose is to provide capital to replicate effective programs focused on economic opportunity, health care, and youth development in communities facing similar social and economic challenges.

Although minuscule in comparison to the total federal domestic policy budget, these efforts represent a strategy that the administration hopes to implement in multiple federal agencies. It is part of a larger movement focused on social innovation, or social entrepreneurship, taking hold in the United States and Great Britain. A central premise of the movement is that solutions to society's most intractable problems require partnerships among government, private capital, social entrepreneurs, and the public. Advocates see social innovation as more than just private-sector contracting for the delivery of public services—a trend that has accelerated over the past two decades. Rather, social entrepreneurship is defined as bringing innovative ideas, often drawn from the private sector, to the solution of social problems (*The Economist* 2010).

In assessing the implications of the Race to the Top, i3, and Social Innovation Fund models for other policy areas, it is useful to consider the three different, but related, purposes they serve. The first is encouraging innovation in the organization and delivery of social, educational, and health care services. Although the federal government could do more in this area, it has a well-established track record supporting basic, applied, and clinical research through its existing funding programs located in multiple agencies. The White House OSICP is hoping that federal agencies can use cash prizes, in addition to research funding, to encourage social innovation, and the administration is promoting legislative changes that would allow agencies to offer incentive prizes (*The Economist* 2010). It is not clear that such prizes would make a significant difference to the rate or quality of social innovation. However, a modest infusion of additional resources and greater visibility would likely help the effort.

The second purpose of these models is leveraging others' resources. In the case of Race to the Top, it has been the statutory authority of state governments. Although the speed with which states changed their laws is unprecedented, two factors limit the inferences that can be drawn from this experience. The first is the unique nature of stimulus policy: the speed with which the Recovery Act was enacted and funds allocated, the states' desperate need for funding, and the limited debate and scrutiny of the program's design. Race to the Top's link to the Recovery Act, with its promise of substantial funding distributed quickly, provided a strong political rationale for the majority of states to compete. It offered even greater political leverage for states whose leaders were already predisposed to the reform strategies embodied in Race to the Top but who had been reluctant to move on them because of potential opposition from powerful interests. The second factor is that changing state law does not automatically result in revised local policy and practice. Removing the cap on charter schools does not necessarily mean new ones will open, and evaluating teachers on student test scores can take a variety of forms depending on subsequent compromises and local implementation. With Race to the Top or any other competitive grant program, the federal government can only encourage the implementation of preferred policy changes and help create the enabling infrastructure. However, it lacks the authority and administrative capacity to enforce all its regulations, or to ensure that other governmental levels and private-sector organizations have the political will and capacity to meet federal expectations.

In the case of i3 and the Social Innovation Fund, the leveraging has been for resources from private foundations, and the result has been remarkable though not without criticism. In April 2010, a dozen major foundations announced that they were creating the Foundation Registry i3. They were committing $506 million to leverage the federal government's i3 funds. The collaborative is not a pooled fund: each foundation retains control over its contribution and decides how it will award the funds. The expectation is that foundations will contact i3 awardees, who have uploaded their proposals onto the Registry website, with offers of matching grants and additional funding. By early August when the Department of Education announced the i3 winners, forty-three foundations had joined the Registry.

Although the Department of Education plays no role in allocating the Registry funds, it is pleased with the size of the match. It planned to hold a summit to spotlight other highly rated projects that the department was unable to fund, in the hopes that some foundations would support them (U.S. Department of Education 2010c). The foundations have been enthusiastic about the arrangement because it allows them to leverage their limited funds without losing autonomy and gives them greater visibility and focus. Criticisms of the arrangement have been muted, but some researchers have suggested that by linking a substantial portion of their resources to the federal program, foundations run two risks. They may either miss potentially significant innovations that do not yet have federal approval, or the Registry may crowd out private funds that would otherwise support ventures the federal government either cannot or would not fund (Robelen and McNeil 2010).

The third purpose, scale-up, is the most challenging and no governmental level has been particularly successful at accomplishing it. Programs shown to be effective at small scale often have difficulty maintaining that effectiveness when replicated more widely (Granger 2011). A necessary condition for scale-up of social policy interventions is solid evidence of their effectiveness, often through research based on random-controlled trials. During the review process for the i3 Fund, experts evaluated the research base supporting applications, and those requesting scale-up funds had to meet the most stringent evidence requirements. At the point of scale-up, the emphasis is less on innovation and more on effectiveness and what works.

A solid evidence base is a necessary but not sufficient condition for moving from small- to large-scale implementation. The sufficient condition relates to the ability to adapt an intervention developed and tested in a few locations to different local contexts—to the politics, existing organizational capacity, motivations of implementers, and nature of client groups. The i3 Fund scale-up and validation projects have a higher likelihood of succeeding than earlier attempts. Their funding levels are substantial enough to do more than just "plop" an off-the-shelf intervention into new locales. The $30 to $50 million project budgets allow for the time and expertise to adapt to local conditions, for considerable capacity-building, and the resources for impact evaluations. The funding base for the i3 projects contrasts with the first eleven projects funded under the Social Innovation Fund, with the largest funded at $10 million and eight of the eleven at $5 million or less.

The Obama administration has decided that competitive grants are a potentially productive strategy for pursuing its social innovation goals. However, the design of Race to the Top and i3, with considerably greater resources from the Recovery Act, seems more promising than the smaller, more symbolic Social Innovation Fund. Innovation can be encouraged with relatively small amounts of money, but if scale-up efforts are to surmount previous limitations, more resources and improved designs sensitive to local conditions are required. The unanswered question is whether such initiatives can be expanded outside the unique circumstances of a major economic crisis and, if so, can they be sustained once federal support is decreased or terminated. That question may not be answered anytime soon because, in the short term, the political prospects for competitive grants as a strategy to promote policy innovation are not good. Congressional Republicans have made clear that they do not support additional funding for Race to the Top or i3, and even some congressional Democrats are lukewarm about a program that creates winners and losers among their constituents.

LOOKING AHEAD

In an interview at the end of his first year in office, President Obama commented that "we've done as much on education reform as any administration in the last twenty years, and nobody knows it" (as quoted in Alter 2010, 338). To a large extent, that low visibility—outside traditional presidential-congressional relations and just beyond the view of a public focused on recession and health care reform—allowed the administration to launch its education agenda at warp speed. The substance of what has been accomplished is less noteworthy than the swiftness with which it occurred. The Obama administration can take credit for putting human capital strategies and institutional redesign at the core of its reform agenda in a more complete and focused way than previous administrations. However, these are not new ideas, and use of third-party providers, new forms of teacher compensation, and more rigorous and uniform academic standards were already spreading from a handful of states and urban districts to other locales when Obama assumed office.

The political skill the administration has demonstrated in handling K-12 policy is less about what was done than about how it was done. Secretary Duncan pursued a meaningful agenda without getting in the way of the administration's higher policy priorities, and without wasting time in negotiations with Congress and interest groups. With the president's assistance at key points, he was able to define the terms of the national reform discussion for eighteen months, and encountered only limited pushback from the education establishment.

The question for the administration going forward is whether it can maintain the same policy trajectory and momentum as it moves from stimulus policy into the traditional decision-making arena of the Elementary and Secondary Education Act reauthorization. Three scenarios are possible. The first is to keep moving at the current speed. This scenario is highly unlikely, as evidenced by the slow-moving ESEA reauthorization, the 2010 midterm election results, state and district coping strategies as stimulus funding ends, and by what more than thirty years of implementation research tells us about the long, complex process of moving top-down policy into classroom practice.

In a second scenario, a countermovement emerges that at least temporarily derails the current policy trajectory. Although this scenario seems quite unlikely at this time, the course of the common standards movement in individual states may alter that prediction. In the 1990s, state standards and assessments became a basis for mobilization by cultural conservatives and other groups, resulting in the "math and reading wars" (McDonnell 2004). Today there is broader agreement about how mathematics and reading should be taught, and the common standards are currently not particularly visible even in states that have approved them. Nevertheless, public school curriculum has long been a rallying point for cultural conservatives, and one could imagine this issue being joined to the Tea Party movement if taxes and health care began to lose their mobilizing force.

The third and most likely scenario is that the Obama K-12 agenda will keep moving in its current direction, but at a slower speed. Its critical elements are anchored in the standards-based reform philosophy that has dominated American education for more than two decades and there is no reason to assume that it will disappear in the near future. The challenge for the administration will be to keep its vision of reform focused on the students most in need of the promised benefits and to advance that agenda through the difficult slog of congressional politics, underresourced schools, and hard-pressed teachers who may be part of the problem but are also the solution.

I am grateful to Suzanne Mettler and James Morone for their thorough and instructive reviews of the chapter. Their comments, along with those of the editors and the other members of the working group, were especially helpful as I clarified the intricacies of state and federal education policy and analyzed them in light of Barack Obama's broader domestic policy agenda.

NOTES

1. At the time that No Child Left Behind was enacted, only six states used standards-based assessments to test students in all the subjects and grade levels required by NCLB, but twenty were testing students in English–language arts and mathematics in grades 3 through 8 and once in grades 10, 11, or 12. Forty-seven states had some type of program requiring standardized testing of K-12 students on their mastery of state-adopted academic content standards, and most of these programs had been in place for a decade or more (Rentner et al. 2003).

2. The basis for the president-elect and his transition team's decision to pursue some agenda items through the stimulus was confirmed in a confidential discussion with a senior advisor to the Obama campaign.

3. In his first weekly address after his inauguration, the president noted, "This is not just a short-term program to boost employment; it's one that will invest in our most important priorities, like energy and education, health care and a new infrastructure that are necessary to keep us strong and competitive in the 21st century" (Obama 2009a).

4. As part of the application process for the second round of stimulus funding, governors were required to report more specific data with regard to each of the four assurances; for example, as indicators of enhanced standards and assessments, data to be reported included the quality of assessments and the inclusion of students with disabilities and those with limited English proficiency, high school graduation rates, college enrollment, and college course completion (U.S. Department of Education 2009a). Department of Education officials described these reporting requirements as a part of a strategy to shine a spotlight on underperforming school systems with the expectation that making such information public would drive reform (Dillon 2009b).

5. Although Race to the Top was not a focus of public debate, Jonathan Alter (2010) reports that there were disagreements and negotiations behind the scenes between the administration and George Miller (D-CA), chair of the House Education and Labor Committee, on one side and David Obey (D-WI), chair of the House Appropriations Committee, and his Senate colleague Tom Harkin, on the other. Miller wanted to offer states what he called "applesauce"—additional funds "to resist entrenched interests and swallow some reform" (91). Obey wanted to allocate as much of the stimulus funds as possible through existing state aid formulas. Consequently, he resisted the idea of competitive grants, and was skeptical that major reforms could be accomplished through this strategy. Secretary of Education Arne Duncan had originally proposed $15 billion of the $100 billion education stimulus be reserved for what would become Race to the Top. After Obey and Harkin tried to kill this portion of the stimulus completely, they compromised with Miller on $5 billion.

6. The Race to the Top competition was conducted in two rounds. In the first, forty-one states applied with sixteen named as finalists based on the numerical scores they received from reviewers. Only two, Delaware and Tennessee, were selected as winners. In the second round, thirty-six states applied; eighteen and the District of Columbia were selected as finalists; nine states—Florida, Georgia, Hawaii, Maryland, Massachusetts, New York, North Carolina, Ohio, and Rhode Island—and the District of Columbia were selected as winners.

7. School poverty is measured by the proportion of students who qualify for free or reduced price lunch through the National School Lunch Program. High-poverty schools are those where 76 to 100 percent of the students are eligible; in low-poverty schools, up to 25 percent of students are eligible.

8. Although most of the policy ideas in the Obama education agenda can be traced back to policy entrepreneurs focused on urban reform, the impetus for the common standards movement came mainly from a group of former governors—James Hunt of North Carolina, Roy Romer of Colorado, and Robert Wise of West Virginia—who had been advocating common standards for several years. In a speech to twenty governors in June 2009, Secretary Duncan

announced that he would designate $350 million of the stimulus funds for grants to craft new assessments measuring student progress on mathematics and reading standards common across multiple states. He noted that standards had historically been a "third rail," and that what would be needed to move beyond the current system of standards unique to each state would be political courage on the part of governors. According to Duncan, developing standards would be relatively inexpensive, but developing assessments is "a very heavy lift financially" and federal funding would keep the initiative—and one of the administration's top education priorities—from stalling (Associated Press 2009a). The efforts of the former governors, whose activities were supported by several foundations and the National Governors Association, were significantly advanced by Duncan's pledge of funding and by a major speech on education that President Obama delivered to the Hispanic Chamber of Commerce in March challenging states "to adopt world-class standards that will bring our curriculums to the 21st century" (Obama 2009b).

9. The head of the New Leaders for New Schools is Jon Schnur, who was a policy advisor to the Obama campaign and for a period at the beginning of the administration was a counselor to Secretary Duncan. In that capacity, Schnur worked with Duncan to design the Race to the Top program, including coming up with the name and shaping the competition's overall direction (Brill 2010).

10. The Gates Foundation originally announced that it planned to give $250,000 to each of fifteen states of its choosing to fund the preparation of their Race to the Top applications. However, after officials in some of the nonselected states protested, and at the urging of the National Governors Association and the Council of Chief State School Officers, the foundation agreed to fund any state that met its conditions (Associated Press 2009b).

    Alter reports that Bill Gates called to urge Obama to nominate an education secretary who would be bold in the reforms he pursued, and that the two found they were in near-complete agreement on accountability issues (2010, 62). The closeness between the Obama administration and the Gates Foundation was further strengthened when Duncan selected two of its former staffers to join his senior staff. Margot Rogers, who had been special assistant to the Gates education program director, was Duncan's first chief of staff, and James Shelton, the former program director of the Gates education division, is Duncan's assistant deputy secretary for innovation and improvement.

11. One of the founding members of DFER, Kevin Chavous, a former school board and city council member in Washington, D.C., maintains that one of the reasons the organization can be effective is because many Democratic policymakers will embrace redesign strategies such as charter schools if given the kind of political cover that DFER affords (Klein 2008).

12. In the final rules for the Race to the Top program, the administration intro-

duced greater flexibility—for example, while still emphasizing charter schools, it invited states to describe innovative public schools other than charter schools operating in their districts. Nevertheless, the point system for evaluating applications continued to encourage the use of student test scores as one element in teacher evaluations, and the implementation of turnaround models that required dismissing the staff in failing schools (U.S. Department of Education 2009b).

13.   Although no roll call vote was taken, the standing vote indicated that the no-confidence motion passed by a thin majority. Those supporting the motion criticized Race to the Top's emphasis on standardized testing and its focus on teacher accountability without requiring that they be provided with the necessary resources. Those opposed noted that the NEA state affiliates in Delaware and Tennessee were participating in those states' successful Race to the Top bids, and that the motion did not represent the diversity of member opinion of the program. Other delegates were concerned about the political ramifications, especially that opposition might lessen NEA's influence on the ESEA reauthorization process (Sawchuk 2010).

14.   In the 1980s, after the publication of *A Nation at Risk*, Shanker recognized that education policy was moving in new directions, and that if the AFT resisted, it might win some temporary victories, but the long-term effect could very well be the undermining of public education through the widespread introduction of vouchers. As a result, the national AFT leadership began to discuss ideas such as a board of professional teaching and to single out union locals that were implementing new roles for teachers such as peer evaluation and assistance plans and school-site decision-making. To a large extent, Weingarten's philosophy seems to be moving toward Shanker's, as expressed more than twenty-five years ago:

> In a period of great turmoil and sweeping changes, those individuals and organizations that are mired in what seems to the public to be petty interests are going to be swept away in the larger movements. Those organizations and individuals who are willing and able to participate, to compromise, and to talk will not be swept away. On the contrary, they will shape the directions of all the reforms and changes that are about to be made. This is what we in the AFT intend to do. We intend to be on board shaping the direction of every change in education. (Shanker 1983)

15.   Miller's ability and that of his Senate counterpart, the late Senator Edward Kennedy, to craft a bill was further hindered by the politics of the upcoming presidential election and by the fact that members of Congress had already introduced more than 100 bills to amend NCLB (Klein 2007).

16.   This recommendation for greater flexibility reflects Secretary Duncan's strong

dislike of NCLB's supplemental services provision. As chief executive officer of the Chicago Public Schools (CPS), he fought regularly with the Bush administration to allow CPS, rather than private providers, to offer tutoring services even though CPS had failed to make AYP. He even refused to stop providing the services after ED told him to stop, but in 2006, he and several other urban district leaders were granted waivers to provide federally funded tutoring services (Klein 2010b)

17. The argument in the OTL Campaign document and Senator Enzi's remark about the research base reflect a common rhetorical strategy in education policy debates. Over the past decade, policymakers in both parties have emphasized that education policy and the interventions it supports should be grounded in scientifically based research, with the NCLB legislation including the term in more than a hundred places. The research base for some policy strategies such as the design and use of standardized testing and the teaching of early literacy skills is robust. However, as noted, in other areas, such as the effectiveness of charter schools and the relationship between teacher compensation and student achievement, the research base is incomplete, inconsistent, or in dispute. Consequently education policy debates often revolve around competing claims about the quality of the evidentiary base.

One example of criticism of the research base the Obama administration has offered in support of the *Blueprint* recommendations is a series of papers commissioned by the National Education Policy Center at the University of Colorado at Boulder. These papers were prepared by researchers from several universities, and all conclude that the six research summaries accompanying the *Blueprint* are of considerably lower quality than what is required for a national policy discussion. The reviewers' major criticisms focus on a lack of peer-reviewed research and the biased sources used to support the administration's recommendations (Mathis and Welner 2010).

18. For example, he promised the civil rights groups that he would work with them to tighten the provisions of ESEA mandating that funds be distributed equitably by requiring that districts be more transparent in reporting how resources such as experienced teachers are allocated across schools (U.S. Department of Education 2010b). At the same time, in a meeting with these groups, Duncan was adamant in arguing that "Race to the Top has done more to dismantle the barriers to education reform . . . than any federal law in history." He then went on to state that those who think the Education Department is not investing heavily in formula programs are either "intentionally misleading or profoundly misinformed" (as quoted in McNeil 2010b).

19. The president's speech was warmly received (and interrupted with applause fifty times) by those attending the Urban League conference, as was Secretary Duncan's on the previous day. The Urban League and the NAACP subse-

quently released a statement stressing "broad areas of agreement" with the administration and reaffirming their commitment to work with it on education reform (McNeil 2010b).

20. The i3 Fund is currently disbursing the Recovery Act funds on a one-time basis. However, the Obama administration requested $500 million in its FY 2011 budget request to continue the program, and i3 is also included in the *Blueprint* as a recommended component of the reauthorized ESEA.

21. Four organizations received scale-up grants in the $50 million range: the KIPP Foundation, which runs charter schools, will use its i3 funds to train 1,000 school leaders so it can double the number of students it serves to 55,000 over five years; Ohio State University, which will work with fifteen other universities to train an additional 3,750 teachers in Reading Recovery, a tutoring program for first graders experiencing serious difficulty in learning to read; Teach for America, which plans to expand its teaching corps from 7,300 to 15,000 members, allowing it to provide more than 20 percent of new hires in high-poverty schools in thirty-five states; and the Success for All Foundation will implement its school turnaround model in approximately 1,100 additional elementary schools in at least nineteen districts. Fifteen organizations were awarded validation grants, and thirty received development grants (U.S. Department of Education 2010c).

REFERENCES

Alter, Jonathan. 2010. *The Promise: President Obama, Year One.* New York: Simon and Schuster.

Associated Press. 2009a. "Education Chief Hopes Stimulus Will Push Standards." *Education Week,* June 15, 2009. Available at: http://www.edweek.org/ew/articles/2009/06/14/281654usededucationstandards_ap.html?qs=Education_Chief_Hopes_Stimulus_Will_Push_Standards (accessed June 29, 2009).

———. 2009b. "Gates Seeks to Leverage 'Race to the Top' Aid." *Education Week,* October 26, 2009. Available at: http://www.edweek.org/ew/articles/2009/10/26/309404usbillgateseducationinfluence_ap.html?qs=Gates_Seeks_to_Leverage (accessed August 12, 2010).

Brill, Steven. 2010. "The Teachers' Unions' Last Stand." *New York Times,* May 17, 2010. Available at: http:///www.nytimes.com/2010/05/23/magazine/23/race-t.html (accessed May 18, 2010).

Cohen, David K., and Susan L. Moffitt. 2009. *The Ordeal of Equality: Did Federal Regulation Fix the Schools?* Cambridge, Mass.: Harvard University Press.

Colvin, Richard. 2009. "Straddling the Democratic Divide." *Education Next* 9(2; spring): 11–17. Available at: http://www.educationnext.org/straddling-the-democratic-divide (accessed July 22, 2010).

CQ Transcripts Wire. 2008. "Obama Announces Arne Duncan as Education Secretary." December 16, 2008. Available at: http://www.washingtonpost.com/

wp-dyn/content/article/2008/12/16/AR2008121601325.html (accessed August 3, 2010).

Dillon, Sam. 2009a. "For Education Chief, Stimulus Means Power, Money and Risk." *New York Times*, February 17, 2009. Available at: http://www.nytimes.com/2009/02/17/education/17educ.html (accessed August 12, 2010).

———. 2009b. "Education Secretary Says Stimulus Aid Hinges on New Data." *New York Times*, April 2, 2009. Available at: http://www.nytimes.com/2009/04/02/education/02educ.html (accessed August 12, 2010).

———. 2010a. "Teacher Union Shuns Obama Aides at Convention." *New York Times*, July 4, 2010. Available at: http://www.nytimes.com/2010/07/05/education/05teachers.html (accessed July 19, 2010).

———. 2010b. "New Challenges for Obama's Education Agenda in the Face of a G.O.P.-Led House." *New York Times*, December 11, 2010. Available at: http://www.nytimes.com/2010/12/12/us/politics/12education.html (accessed December 13, 2010).

Duncan, Arne. 2009. "Education Reform's Moon Shot." *Washington Post,* July 24, 2009. Available at: http://washingtonpost.com./wp-dyn/content/article/2009/07/23 (accessed October 15, 2009).

———. 2010. "The Quiet Revolution." Remarks at the National Press Club, July 27, 2010. Available at: http:///www.ed.gov/news/speeches/quiet-revolution-secretary-arn-du (accessed August 1, 2010).

The Economist. 2010. "Let's Hear Those Ideas." August 12, 2010. Available at: http:///www.economist.com/node/16789766 (accessed August 12, 2010).

Goertz, Margaret E. 2007. "Standards-Based Reform: Lessons from the Past, Directions for the Future." Paper presented at "Clio at the Table: A Conference on the Uses of History to Inform and Improve Education Policy." Brown University (June 2007).

Granger, Robert C. 2011. "A Learning Agenda for the Scale-Up Movement." *Pathways* (winter).

Henig, Jeffrey R. 2008. *Spin Cycle: How Research Is Used in Policy Debates: The Case of Charter Schools*. New York: Russell Sage Foundation and The Century Foundation.

Hoff, David J., and Michele McNeil. 2008. "Top-Notch Education 'a Moral Obligation,' Obama Tells Throng." *Education Week*, September 3, 2008. Available at: http://www.edweek.org/ew/articles/2008/08/29/02dems.h28.html (accessed February 27, 2011).

Klein, Alyson. 2007. "Host of Lawmakers Offer Bills to Revise NCLB." *Education Week*, September 5, 2007. Available at: http://www.edweek.org/ew/articles/2007/09/05/02nclb.h27.html (accessed April 9, 2010).

———. 2008. "Democratic Education PAC Hopes for Its Moment under Obama." *Education Week*, December 3, 2008. Available at: http://www.edweek.org/ew/articles2008/12/03/14dfer.h28html (accessed May 13, 2010).

———. 2009. "Stimulus Debate Raises Issues Involving K-12 Funds." *Education*

Week, February 9, 2009. Available at: http://www.edweek.org/ew/articles/2009/02/09/21stimsenate-2.html (accessed April 9, 2010).

———. 2010a. "Critics Pan Obama Plan to Tie Title I to Standards." *Education Week*, February 26, 2010. Available at: http://www.edweek.org/media/2010/02/26/23esea_miller.jpg (accessed February 26, 2010).

———. 2010b. "Administration Unveils ESEA Renewal Blueprint." *Education Week*, March 13, 2010. Available at: http://www.edweek.org/articles/2010/03/13esea.h29html (accessed March 15, 2010).

———. 2010c. "Education Initiatives Hit Political Head Winds." *Education Week*, June 16, 2010. Available at: http://www.edweek.org/ew/articles/2010/06/16/35congress.h29.html (accessed July 19, 2010).

Luce, Edward. 2010. "US School Reform Report Awaits Grades." *Financial Times*, July 28, 2010. Available at: http://www.ft.com/cms/s/91015f8a-9a7b-11df-87fd-00144feab49a,d (accessed August 1, 2010).

Manna, Paul. 2006. *School's In: Federalism and the National Education Agenda*. Washington, D.C.: Georgetown University Press.

Mathis, William J., and Kevin G. Welner. 2010. "Introduction: Assessing the Research Base for *A Blueprint for Reform*." Boulder, Colo.: National Education Policy Center. Available at: http://nepc.colorado.edu/publication/blueprint-introduction (accessed October 31, 2010).

McDonnell, Lorraine M. 2004. *Persuasion, Politics, and Educational Testing*. Cambridge, Mass.: Harvard University Press.

———. 2005. "No Child Left Behind and the Federal Role in Education: Evolution or Revolution?" *Peabody Journal of Education* 80(2): 19–38.

McNeil, Michelle. 2009. "Proposed 'Race to the Top' Rules Seen as Prescriptive." *Education Week*, September 14, 2009. Available at: http://www.edweek.org/ew/articles/2009/09/02/03stim-rac.h29.html (accessed October 14, 2009).

———. 2010a. "Race to Top Buy-In Level Examined." *Education Week*, June 16, 2010. Available at: http://www.edweek.org/ew/articles/2010/06/16/35buyin_ep.h29.html (accessed July 19, 2010).

———. 2010b. "Duncan Deflects Civil Rights Groups' Criticism: You're 'Wrong.'" *Education Week*, July 28, 2010. Available at: http://blogs.edweek.org/edweek/campaign-k-12/2010/07/duncan_answ (accessed August 1, 2010).

McNeil, Michelle, and Leslie A. Maxwell. 2010. "$3.4 Billion Remains in Race to the Top Aid." *Education Week* 29(28)(April 7): 1, 30–31.

National Center for Education Statistics. 2010. *The Condition of Education 2010*. Washington: U.S. Department of Education. Available at: http://nces.edu.gov/pubs2010/2010282.pdf (accessed September 30, 2010).

National Opportunity to Learn Campaign. 2010. *Civil Rights Framework for Providing All Students an Opportunity to Learn through Reauthorization of the Elementary and Secondary Education Act*. Available at: http://www.otlcampaign.org/resources/civil-rights-framework-providing-all-students-opporta (accessed March 1, 2011).

National Research Council. 1997. *Educating One and All*. Committee on Goals 2000 and the Inclusion of Students with Disabilities. Lorriane M. McDonnell, Margaret J. McLaughlin, and Patricia Morison, eds.Washington, D.C.: National Academies Press.

———. 2008. *Common Standards for K-12 Education? Considering the Evidence: Summary of a Workshop Series*. Alexandra Beatty, rapporteur. Committee on Standards in Education. Washington, D.C.: National Academies Press.

Obama, Barack. 2006. *The Audacity of Hope: Thoughts on Reclaiming the American Dream*. New York: Three Rivers Press.

———. 2008. *Change We Can Believe In*. New York: Three Rivers Press.

———. 2009a. "The President's Weekly Address." January 24, 2009. Washington: The White House, Office of the Press Secretary. Available at: http://www.whitehouse.gov/video/YWAO12409 (accessed August 6, 2010).

———. 2009b. "Transcript of Remarks to the Hispanic Chamber of Commerce March 10 as Provided by the White House." *New York Times*, March 10, 2009. Available at: http://www.nytimes.com/2009/03/10/us/politics/10text-obama.html (accessed May 19, 2009).

———. 2009c. "Remarks by the President on Education." July 24, 2009. Washington: The White House, Office of the Press Secretary. Available at: http:///www.whitehouse.gov/the_press_office/remarks-by-the-president (accessed August 6, 2009).

———. 2010. "Remarks by the President on Education Reform to the National Urban League Centennial Conference." July 29, 2010. Washington: The White House, Office of the Press Secretary. Available at: http://www.whitehouse.gov/the-press-office/remarks-president-educat (accessed August 1, 2010).

Public Law 111–5 (HR 1). American Recovery and Reinvestment Act of 2009. February 17, 2009. 123 Stat. 115. (As amended by Public Law 111–8 [HR 1105]. Omnibus Appropriations Act of 2009, Division A, Section 523. March 11, 2009. 123 Stat. 524).

Rentner, Diane Stark, Naomi Chudowsky, Tom Fagan, Keith Gayler, Madlene Hamilton, and Nancy Kober. 2003. *From the Capital to the Classroom: State and Federal Efforts to Implement the No Child Left Behind Act*. Washington, D.C.: Center for Education Policy.

Robelen, Eric W. 2010. "States Change Policies with Eye to Winning Federal Grants." *Education Week*, January 6, 2010. Available at: http:///www.edweek.org/ew/articles/2010/01/06/16states-2.h29.html (accessed April 15, 2010).

Robelen, Eric W., and Michelle McNeil. 2010. "Push to Spur Innovation Raises Hopes—and Eyebrows." *Education Week*, May 7, 2010. Available at: http:www.edweek.org/ew/articles/2010/05/07/31stim-philan.h29.htm (accessed August 12, 2010).

Roza, Marguerite. 2009. *Projections of State Budget Shortfalls on K-12 Public Education Spending and Job Loss*. Bothell: University of Washington, Center on Reinventing

Public Education. Available at: http://www.crpe.org/cs/crpe/view/csr _pubs/266 (accessed April 7, 2010).

Sawchuk, Stephen. 2009. "NEA at Odds with Obama Team over 'Race to the Top' Criteria." *Education Week*, September 2, 2009. Available at: http:///www .edweek.org/ew/articles/2009/08/25/02nea.h29.html (accessed August 1, 2010).

———. 2010. "NEA's Delegates Vote 'No Confidence' in Race to the Top." *Education Week*, July 4, 2010. Available at: http://blogs.edweek.org/edweek/teacher beat/2010/07/neas_delegates_vote_no_confide_2.html (accessed August 1, 2010).

Shanker, Albert. 1983. "Albert Shanker's Address to the AFT Convention." Washington, D.C.: American Federation of Teachers. Available at: http://www.eric .ed.gov/PDFS/ED245801.pdf (accessed January 30, 2011).

Smith, Marshall, and Jennifer O'Day. 1991. "Systemic School Reform." In *The Politics of Curriculum and Testing*, edited by Susan Fuhrman and Betty Malen. San Francisco: Jossey-Bass.

Springer, Matthew G., Dale Ballou, Laura Hamilton, Vi-Nhuan Le, J. R. Lockwood, Daniel F. McCaffrey, Matthew Pepper, and Brian M. Stecher. 2010. *Teacher Pay for Performance: Experimental Evidence from the Project on Incentives in Teaching*. Nashville, Tenn.: National Center on Performance Incentives at Vanderbilt University.

Swanson, Christopher B. 2009. *Closing the Graduation Gap: Educational and Economic Conditions in America's Largest Cities*. Washington, D.C.: Editorial Projects in Education Research Center.

U.S. Department of Education. 2009a. "American Recovery and Reinvestment Act Strategic Planning." Powerpoint presentation, November 10. Washington: U.S. Department of Education, Office of the Deputy Secretary. Available at: http:// www2.ed.gov/policy/gen/leg/recovery/presentation/strategic-planning.ppt (accessed January 30, 2011).

———. 2009b. "Race to the Top Fund: Final Rule. 34 CFR Subtitle B, Chapter 2." *Federal Register* 74(221)(November 18): 59688–834.

———. 2010a. *A Blueprint for Reform: The Reauthorization of the Elementary and Secondary Education Act*. Washington: Government Printing Office. Available at: http://www2.ed.gov/policy/elsec/leg/blueprint/blueprint.pdf (accessed April 7, 2010).

———. 2010b. "Duncan Highlights Education Department's Civil Rights Agenda." July 28, 2010. Washington: Government Printing Office. Available at: http:/// www.ed.gov/news/press-releases/duncan-highlights-education (accessed August 1, 2010).

———. 2010c. "Nation's Boldest Education Reform Plans to Receive Federal Innovation Grants Once Private Match Is Secured." August 5, 2010. Washington: Government Printing Office. Available at: http://www.ed.gov/news/

press-releases/nations-boldest-education-reform-plans-receive-federal
-innovation-grants-once-pr (accessed August 12, 2010).

Weingarten, Randi. 2010. "Saving Public Education, Not as We Know It, But as We Know It Ought to Be." Remarks at the American Federation of Teachers Convention. Seattle, Wash. (July 8, 2010). Available at: http://www.aft.org/pdfs/press/sp_weingarten070810.pdf (accessed August 1, 2010).

PART III | Failed Bargains and Intensifying Conflict

Chapter 7 | Obama's Immigration Reform: A Tough Sell for a Grand Bargain

John D. Skrentny

THE UNITED STATES has always been a nation of immigrants, but in the twenty-first century, the policy debate is about becoming a nation of illegal immigrants. President Obama promised "comprehensive immigration reform," but he will be judged on how he handled illegal immigration. The challenge is a daunting one. Members of Congress thought they had successfully dealt with it a quarter of a century ago, but the demographic statistics—as well as the legislative record since then—tell a very different story.

The U.S. Department of Homeland Security estimates that about 10.8 million foreigners live in the United States without authorization (Hoefer, Rytina, and Baker 2010). That number is nearly equal to the population of Ohio. It is about one-third of the entire population of all foreign-born in the United States (Passel and Cohn 2011). An international comparison also highlights the scale of the problem: Russia is second only to the United States in numbers of immigrants, but Russia's total foreigner population, 12.3 million, is comparable to the number of illegal immigrants in the United States (United Nations 2009). The dominant questions in the often very emotional immigration debate are whether and how this massive population should be legalized and what should be done to prevent a new illegal population from developing.

Debate may be too generous a word to describe the discourse: legalization advocates and immigration restrictionists share little common ground. They are not even able to agree on terms. (I use here the more neutral *legalization* rather than *amnesty*, and use *illegal, unauthorized,* and *undocu-*

mented interchangeably.) Both legalization advocates and immigration restrictionists do agree, however, that the current border control effort fails to achieve its goals (Cornelius and Tsuda 2004). Both sides also agree that most migrants come here to work, and that there is at least some relationship between employers' demand for low-cost, low-skilled labor and the high number of illegal immigrants already here.

For several years, reformers' attempts to deal with the matter have been based on a common model, the grand-bargain approach. That legislative model has its origins, ironically, in one of the great policy failures of American history, the Immigration Reform and Control Act of 1986 (IRCA).

IRCA-style grand bargaining has two defining parts. First is a massive legalization package that would, with various procedures and requirements, move the vast majority of the millions of illegal aliens to permanent legal status. Second is a package of enforcement reforms that would seal the porous border. Although one grand bargain passed in 1986, since then enactment of a bill that satisfies all interests has been maddeningly elusive (Tichenor 2009). The basic dilemma is this: IRCA's failure to seal the border taught restrictionists not to make any more grand bargains. But the more reformers offer to entice the restrictionist side, the more they alienate and anger those fighting for legalization. The result is stalemate.

The long shadow cast by IRCA is not the whole story of the failure of immigration reform to advance during Obama's term, but it is a key factor. I argue here that IRCA led to negative perceptions and meanings of immigration reform—and in particular, mass legalization—that are widespread in Congress and in the electorate, but they work in concert with long-standing negative perceptions of undocumented immigrants. Equally important is the institutional structure of the American government that provides many veto points for highly motivated opponents to stop legislation.

The negative perceptions of legalization and the undocumented and the institutional leverage afforded by multiple veto points help us understand not only the inability of Obama's reform to gain traction, but George W. Bush's immigration reform failures as well. Immigration reform is distinctive from the other reform areas in this volume in that it is not just an Obama goal, or a Democratic goal. Obama's reform is similar to a reform George W. Bush propounded only a few years earlier. However, several factors are distinctive to the Obama presidency that, though not decisive, play a part in thwarting reform. These include the extreme partisanship displayed by Republicans in Congress, the dismal state of the economy, and a controversial law targeting illegal immigrants in Arizona. These all make reform more difficult—though, as previous failures during the Bush administration showed, they are not essential to blocking reform.

Last are three factors that social scientists usually link to policy change—

namely, public opinion, expert ideas, and interest groups—that all play a supporting actor role in the current failure of reform. That is, they work in concert with or are driven by the other factors but are not feature actors in this drama.

Potentially much is at stake with immigration reform. There are great concerns about the rule of law, Latino voters, and economic imports. Regarding economics, the complexity of the causal chains makes definitive statements surprisingly difficult. Despite some economic benefits to the status quo on undocumented immigration, costs—real and perceived— help drive the issue. The economist Gordon Hanson (2009) notes that about 50 percent of undocumented immigrants have payroll taxes deducted due to use of fake Social Security numbers. While these funds go to the federal government, costs are mostly borne by cities, counties, and states. Estimates of the precise fiscal impacts vary and depend in part on how they are measured. For example, the sociologists Frank Bean and Gillian Stevens (2003) put the short-term costs of immigration at $200 per household per year nationally and $1,200 in California. However, a Congressional Budget Office report on illegal immigration downplayed the costs to locals, arguing that though illegal aliens impose costs on education, health care, and law enforcement, those costs amount to less than 5 percent of total costs on average. Even in high-immigration areas, in states such as California where costs were in the tens of billions, those costs were still less than 10 percent of total expenditures (Congressional Budget Office 2007). Nevertheless, the perception of unjustified costs creates taxpayer resentment.

Looking at the wage effects, Hanson (2009) argues that illegal immigration redistributes income from low-skilled native workers to employers. It also leads to a net gain in overall income because employers can be more productive, though Hanson estimates that the "immigration surplus" is only .03 percent of GDP. Nevertheless, former Federal Reserve chair Alan Greenspan has testified to Congress regarding the employer benefits of immigration in relieving labor supply pressures (Greenspan 2000).

The economist George Borjas (2003) argues that legal and illegal immigration have helped reduce average wages in the United States by 3 percent between 1980 and 2000 and the wages of those without a high school degree by 9 percent. There is also evidence that some workplaces intentionally replaced American workers with immigrants and, in particular, easily exploitable undocumented immigrants (Waldinger and Lichter 2003; Skrentny 2007). This is true in a variety of low-wage jobs, especially meatpacking, where wages and work conditions have plummeted since the 1980s. Although the precise impacts on native black and white workers of displacement by immigrants are not clear, some social scientists argue that immigrant displacement of native black and white workers in some industries is correlated with higher native crime rates (Shihadeh and Barranco 2010a, 2010b).

What would be the distributive effects were Obama to succeed at legalizing the undocumented, sealing the borders, and providing legal guestworkers for employers who needed them? No one really knows and estimates are all over the map. A leading pro-legalization think tank, the Center for American Progress, argues that by boosting wages for both native workers and the newly legalized, reform would add $1.5 trillion to the GDP over ten years. On the other hand, deporting or otherwise losing the illegal worker population would reduce GDP by $2.6 trillion over ten years, and though the wages of low-skilled workers would rise, they would decline for higher-skilled workers and job loss would be widespread (Hinojosa-Ojeda 2010).

On the other hand, the Heritage Foundation sees current immigration policy as "importing poverty." Arguing that one-third of all immigrants live in families where the head of the household lacks a high school degree, the Heritage study finds that the 6 million legal immigrants without a high school degree will cost U.S. taxpayers half a trillion dollars over their lifetimes, and the 5 million illegal immigrants lacking high school diplomas, if legalized, will cost another half trillion dollars. Adding the cost of educating their children, this study finds the price tag for not encouraging these migrants to go home to be $2 trillion (Rector 2006).

The Cato Institute parries this thrust, and argues that legalization plus a visa tax would yield $180 billion to the GDP over ten years. Hanson is perhaps the most provocative when he notes that having *legal* workers will produce greater costs because these workers will be eligible for programs that the federal government now withholds. He suggests having these workers pay a fee to come or taxing employers who use them (2009).

As the battle of numbers rages inside the Beltway, the big story with Obama's comprehensive immigration reform remains that, unlike other areas of his agenda, such as health care and financial regulation, immigration reform has languished. Obama has pushed the issue, but no administration grand-bargain bill has materialized. Although Congress quickly passed an enforcement package in August 2010, and a narrow legalization provision aimed at illegal immigrants who are students or served in the military failed in September and the otherwise productive December lame-duck session, no committee in the Senate or the House has considered a major reform bill. Most focus has centered on a proposal initially propounded by Senators Charles Schumer (D-NY) and Lindsey Graham (R-SC).

In the section that follows, I show how we arrived at the current situation: why we have so much illegal immigration, how IRCA failed, and what happened when President Bush tried to reform immigration policy.

ILLEGAL IMMIGRATION AND THE HISTORY OF POLICY FAILURE

It is a truism that you cannot have undocumented immigrants without immigration control, yet the point is worth making. For much of American history, America's border with Mexico was mostly unmonitored. Mexican migrants tended to move freely back and forth across it, typically to work in agriculture. From World War II to 1964, they also came as part of the Bracero (from the Spanish word for *arm*) temporary work visa program (Gutiérrez 1997; Massey, Durand, and Malone 2002). Undocumented immigration was in a sense created by the 1965 Immigration and Nationality Act's immigration quotas and the end of Bracero (Jenkins and Perrow 1977; Martin 2003; see appendix table 7A.1). The law created a limit of 20,000 visas for each country in the Eastern Hemisphere, and an overall quota of 120,000 for the Western Hemisphere. Congress extended the 20,000-visa treatment to each country in the Western Hemisphere in 1976 (Massey, Durand, and Malone 2002; Reimers 1985).

Lacking access to Bracero guest-workers or other immigrant labor, agricultural interests as well as other businesses began to hire undocumented workers. Thus began the new era of illegal immigration: the number of unauthorized migrants swelled, more migrants stayed, and they spread across the United States (Massey, Durand, and Malone 2002; Navarro 2005).

IRCA and the Grand-Bargain Approach

By the mid-1970s, illegal immigrants were moving into jobs in construction, manufacturing, and low-skilled services, taking advantage of the growth of the unsteady, nonunion "secondary" labor market that grew in the wake of deindustrialization and globalization (Piore 1979; Bluestone and Harrison 1982). To deal with the growing problem, task forces under Presidents Ford, Carter, and Reagan, as well as a congressionally created commission, all advocated some version of the grand-bargain approach that has shaped immigration politics ever since: build a winning congressional coalition by combining border enforcement with legalization (Tichenor 2002; Graham 2003; Zolberg 2006).

Congress eventually responded in 1986 with the Immigration Reform and Control Act. The effort began with notable cooperation across party lines as well as between the House and Senate. Senator Alan Simpson (R-WY) and Representative Roman Mazzoli (D-KY) introduced identical bills in each chamber and held joint hearings.

But the bipartisan bill split both parties. Democrats close to labor unions opposed greater legal or illegal immigration because of the belief that a greater labor supply drives down wages. Democrats close to Latinos and other immigrants were concerned about discrimination issues and maintaining opportunities for family reunification, and supported more open borders. On the other side, Republicans sympathetic to employer interests in cheap labor sided with Democrats who wanted more open borders. But Republicans tied to social conservatives worried about a loss of law and order, taxpayer subsidies for lawbreaking foreigners, and changes to the national identity and culture. They did not want to reward lawbreakers with job opportunities, access to services, and eventual legal residence (Schuck 1992; Gimpel and Edwards 1999).

Expansionists won an amnesty for about 3 million undocumented persons then in the country and a prohibition of discrimination in employment on the basis of citizenship status. The latter provision was necessary to appease the expansionists because the restrictionists had won a novel control measure: penalties on employers who knowingly hired illegal workers. However, it was very important that an employer was in trouble only if he or she knowingly hired an illegal alien. An illegal immigrant job applicant only had to produce documentation indicating that he or she was legal. It did not have to be good documentation (Gimpel and Edwards 1999, 166; Massey, Durand, and Malone 2002; see table 7A.1).

IRCA was a stunning failure. The negative consequences were manifold. First, the legalization part of IRCA went without a significant hitch—but then personal ties to a legalized migrant itself became a significant predictor of who was likely to migrate illegally. Second, the control aspects not only miserably failed to control illegal immigration, but also had a series of deleterious consequences. Millions of migrants came to America, but, as the sociologist Douglas Massey and his colleagues show, after 1986, average wages of all low-skilled workers fell, including undocumented workers but especially legal migrants. Because of a crackdown in California, illegal immigrants began to spread across the country more quickly—bringing wage-reducing effects with them. Moreover, the California crackdown pushed the migrant transit points eastward into the deserts, and their fees to smugglers—as well as their death rates—skyrocketed (Sisco and Hicken 2009; Massey, Durand, and Malone 2002).

President Bush and the Failed Reform Attempts of 2006 and 2007

President George W. Bush, building on a Latino-friendly governorship, urged fellow Republicans to support reform in the IRCA mold. In his first term, the 9/11 terrorist attack sidetracked his reform plans by thrusting national security to the top of the immigration agenda, and led to a reorganization of the immigration bureaucracy. A new agency, Immigration and Customs Enforcement (ICE), was created within the new Department of Homeland Security (DHS) (Hing 2006; see appendix table 7A.2). In his second term, however, Bush worked hard for legalization and broader reform.

It was a tough sell. Restrictionist Republicans led passage in the House of the Border Protection, Antiterrorism and Illegal Immigration Control Act in December 2005. This enforcement-only bill would have made illegal migration a felony, criminalized assistance to illegals, provided more penalties on employers, and built more border fences (Wroe 2008, 194; O'Rourke 2006). The bill led to dramatic and massive protests, numbering at least in the hundreds of thousands, in Los Angeles, Chicago, and other cities. Rather than work to soften the bill, however, the Senate simply ignored it (Wroe 2008).

Instead, the Senate worked on a bipartisan bill more in line with what Bush wanted. Senators Edward Kennedy (D-MA) and John McCain (R-AZ) worked with Republicans Mel Martinez (R-FL), Chuck Hagel (R-NE), and Arlen Specter (R-PA) to produce a bill that would offer different legalization schemes for different groups of undocumented immigrants depending on when they arrived. Those in the United States the longest had the most favorable terms—but even they would have to pay fines and back taxes and wait five years before becoming legal. Others would have to leave the country before they could claim legal status. Those in the country the least amount of time (less than two years) would be ineligible for legalization. The bill also would have provided more work visas, including 325,000 guest-worker visas, and more border security; required employer use of an Electronic Employment Verification System, also known as E-Verify, to limit the use of fake documents; and imposed more penalties on employers.

On May 16, 2006, President Bush went on national television to promote immigration reform. He explained that he opposed an amnesty—by which he meant a legalization like that in IRCA, where undocumented migrants could be become legalized without paying a fine, without leaving the country, and without having to wait for a visa. He called an approach that attached these requirements a legalization or a path to citizenship rather than an amnesty. Bush, Vice President Cheney, and White House Senior Advisor Karl Rove lobbied Congress as well as conservative radio hosts to support the Senate bill.

Not all Democrats were on board: some had reservations about the bill's guest-worker program. Labor unions were divided on this point, with the Change to Win coalition supporting it and the AFL-CIO fearing that employers would use it to bring down wages, benefits, and work conditions (Waldinger 2008; Wroe 2008).

The bill passed the Senate with bipartisan support—and opposition. It passed on a 62 to 36 vote, with Republicans voting 23 to 32 and Democrats showing more support for Bush and voting 39 to 4. However, the bill died in the House, where the Republican leadership refused to let the bill come to a vote (Wroe 2008; see appendix table 7A.2).

A grand-bargain bill with legalization thus failed with Republicans controlling Congress and the White House. The Democrats took control of Congress in 2007, and conditions seemed ideal: a pro-grand-bargain, Republican White House with influence over fellow Republicans and a pro-grand-bargain Democratic Congress. Working with several leading Republicans and Democrats, the bargaining team once again sought to find the right balance between legalization and border enforcement, to find just the right combination that would bring about a successful vote. They tinkered with details such as what undocumented workers would have to do to earn legalization, when legalization would become available (known as the trigger—usually linked to the establishment of border security), how much and what kinds of new border security to provide, mandatory E-Verify, and the number and nature of guest-worker visas. In a bigger change that promised more business support, the 2007 effort would have shifted the balance of legal visas more toward skills rather than family reunification. Despite all of the tinkering, antilegalization forces remained opposed. Citizens flooded their senators' offices with phone calls and emails objecting to the legalization provisions. Negotiations collapsed, and the 2007 bill failed without even getting out of the Democratic Senate (Pear 2007; Wroe 2008, 213).

GHOST OF IRCA: EARLY ADMINISTRATIVE MOVES AND THE SENATE PROPOSAL

Continuing his reform-friendly stance as a senator, Obama's campaign promised grand-bargain, IRCA-style reform, as well as smaller, practical changes that would appeal to immigrants without angering either side (Obama and Biden 2008).[1] Although President Obama has offered various sweeteners for legal migrants, his overall legislative approach is similar to the failed bills from 2006 and 2007: those without documents would have to take various steps to be legal, and enforcement measures would be strengthened. But the Democrat Obama has done more for enforcement than his Republican predecessor.

Showing Off by Toughening Up

In office, Obama put priority on other issues, including the economic stimulus, health care, and financial regulation. But a delay on immigration appeared to be necessary anyway: one of the legacies of IRCA and the failures in the 2000s is that many in Congress demand an enforcement-first strategy (Tichenor 2009). To gain credibility for legalization, therefore, Obama used the powers of the presidency for a variety of new enforcement measures. Although not following any established program, Obama's efforts here resembled in essence the so-called third-way politics advocated by centrist groups such as the Democratic Leadership Council (Marshall and Schram 1993).[2] In other words, Obama sought to achieve some of the goals of restrictionists, but not by use of restrictionists' favored means.

For example, rather than indiscriminate deportations, Obama has demonstrated immigration control by ramping up deportation but focusing his effort on undocumented criminals. Deporting criminals saves taxpayers' incarceration dollars and is less likely to involve the high drama and psychological injury that sometimes accompany family break-ups. Obama's administration set a record in fiscal year 2009 by deporting more than 380,000 people—tens of thousands more than Bush's record high. Fully one-third of these individuals were criminals. In fall 2010, Obama was on pace to deport a record 604,133 people for that year (Kaye 2010; Newton-Small 2010; Preston 2010a).

To target criminals, and the most severe among them (and thus least deserving of legalization), Obama has modified the policies that regulate ICE's cooperation with local police. In 1996, a Republican Congress passed the Illegal Immigration Reform and Immigrant Responsibility Act. This law contained a section, known simply as 287(g), that authorized the DHS secretary to make agreements with state and local police to perform some immigration law duties. Homeland Security Secretary Janet Napolitano reformed this process to standardize the agreements and took measures to ensure that police did not detain individuals simply because they suspected they were undocumented (U.S. Department of Homeland Security 2009). Napolitano has also put energy into expanding a program begun in 2007, called Secure Communities, in which local authorities send to the federal government the fingerprints of criminal aliens so those in the United States illegally can be identified. ICE may then deport the illegal aliens who are criminals, prioritizing those who have committed the most serious crimes (U.S. Department of Homeland Security 2010).

Obama and Napolitano have also sought a third-way approach to workplace enforcement. Rather than (literally) chasing and handcuffing fleeing migrants in dramatic raids as in the past, Obama has ICE focus on prosecuting employers. This approach uses mostly civil law, focusing on fines and penalties, rather than criminal law. For example, ICE gave thirty days to clothing maker American Apparel to prove a suspicious third of its workforce had authorization to work in the United States. The company faces $150,000 in fines; no arrests have been made, though the company fired about 1,800 workers (Hsu 2009; Preston 2009a, 2009b). ICE has now audited employee files at nearly 3,000 companies and issued a record $3 million in civil fines. There was a single day in July 2009 when ICE audited more employers' hiring practices than it had in all of 2008 (Napolitano 2009; Preston 2010b).

Obama's enforcement-first strategy dictated his budget requests. He requested $4 billion to support 20,000 Border Patrol agents, $112 million for the E-Verify system (required for employers with federal contracts but otherwise voluntary), as well as money for streamlining visa application services (Office of Management and Budget 2009; for analysis, see Martinez 2009). His Southwest Border Initiative doubled the number of agents on Border Enforcement Task Forces, tripled the number of border intelligence analysts, brought new canine teams to the border, continued work on the fence, and created more partnerships with local police (Cummings 2010; Napolitano 2009).

Congress moved on immigration enforcement in time for the midterm elections. Though it was not the comprehensive reform Obama promised, the $600 million enforcement-only border security bill, which he signed on August 13, 2010, fit with the enforcement-first strategy that is the legacy of IRCA. It authorized and funds the hiring of more than 1,000 new border agents, new ICE officers, improved communication, and more use of surveillance drones. Obama stated, "These steps will make an important difference as my administration continues to work with Congress toward bipartisan comprehensive immigration reform to secure our borders, and restore responsibility and accountability to our broken immigration system" (2010a).

Inching toward Legislation as Republicans Run from Reform

Unlike the August enforcement bill, which sailed through Congress, comprehensive reform has hardly moved. The legislative effort began on June 25, 2009, when Obama met with a bipartisan group from Congress, including Senators John McCain and Lindsey Graham—two Republicans long sympathetic to legalization of undocumented migrants. Obama then announced that Napolitano would take the administration's lead in crafting legislation (Obama 2009). In a speech to the Center for American Progress on November 13, 2009, Napolitano laid out the administration's early line.

She argued that proper reform was like a three-legged stool. It would enforce the law on the border, improve "legal flows for families and workers," and provide a "firm but fair" plan to deal with the millions of un-documented already here. But her emphasis was on enforcement. Although Napolitano acknowledged the moral difficulties that many Americans had with illegal immigration (the problem of undocumented workers was "an affront to every law-abiding citizen and every employer who plays by the rules"), she admitted that the reason for the enforcement-first strategy was to show Congress that unlike other post-IRCA presidents, the Obama administration was serious about enforcing the law, and therefore a new grand bargain would not fail like IRCA.

However, she also argued that legalization was important to protect American workers from being undercut by exploitable illegal workers, and supported a labor-friendly guest-worker program as well as provisions for more high-skilled immigrants. Notably, she argued that the timing was right because of—rather than in spite of—the economic downturn. The time was right for reform because reform was, along with the stimulus, health care reform, and clean energy, part of the things that must be done "to fortify America for the long run" (Napolitano 2009).[3]

Not surprisingly, finding Republican allies in the Senate has proven to be more difficult for Obama than it had been for Bush. In a tough primary challenge from an immigration restrictionist, long-time reform supporter McCain abandoned the effort. But throughout 2009, according to insiders interviewed for this chapter, Lindsey Graham worked on a proposal, mostly behind closed doors, with Obama's major Democratic ally, Chuck Schumer of New York, who was another long-time supporter of reform (Schumer and Squadron 2007; Connally 2010). On March 19, 2010, they unveiled the outline of their plan in a *Washington Post* op-ed (Schumer and Graham 2010). Their approach was very similar to Napolitano's, though they emphasized an idea that in various forms had been kicked around since IRCA: a fraud-proof (now biometric) Social Security card that the government would require of all Americans.

About a month later, however, Graham walked away from his own plan. Officially, he stated that he would not support reform if, as Majority Leader Harry Reid (D-NV) was promising, the Democrats pushed it before another Graham priority—an energy and climate bill (Kornblut and Hsu 2010). Graham believed the Democrats were pushing immigration reform only to score political points with Latinos. As he explained in a letter to John Kerry (D-MA) and Joseph Lieberman (I-CT), leaders on the energy and climate bill, "Moving forward on immigration—in this hurried, panicked manner—is nothing more than a cynical political ploy. I know from my own personal experience the tremendous amounts of time, energy, and effort that must be devoted to this issue to make even limited progress. . . . Let's be clear, a phony, political effort on immigration today accomplishes nothing but making it exponentially more difficult to address in a serious, comprehensive manner in the future" (Eilperin 2010). Democrats countered that Graham's move was inspired by his desire to take attention off of John McCain's flip-flop on immigration (Stewart 2010). Indeed, on the day that Democrats unveiled their proposal, Graham switched his support to a border security bill instead, put forth by McCain and fellow Arizonan Jon Kyl (Klein 2010; O'Brien 2010). This left post-IRCA immigration reform in worse shape than it had ever been in: zero Republican supporters in the Senate.

Obama could not count on similar unity among Democrats. Senators from conservative states preferred that Obama focus on jobs and the economy rather than on immigration. Arkansas Democrats Mark Pryor and Blanche Lincoln, as well as Nebraska's Ben Nelson, all resisted the reform effort (Bolton 2010a).

Despite the GOP wall of opposition and the lack of consensus in their own party, Democrats supportive of reform went ahead and unveiled their plan on April 29. Their twenty-six-page proposal, based on the Graham-Schumer ideas but then called Real Enforcement with Practical Answers for Immigration Reform (REPAIR), offered legalization after eight years if applicants learned English, had no criminal record, and paid back taxes. The proposal also (of course) offered more funding for border security. It would also create a new biometric Social Security card (Bacon 2010). Obama went on the telephone to win Republican support, focusing on Dick Lugar (R-IN), Judd Gregg (R-NH), Lisa Murkowski (R-AK), Scott Brown (R-MA), and George LeMieux (R-FL). None joined the effort (Hunt 2010; Lee and Hunt 2010).

By June, immigration reform was off the agenda but not quite on the backburner. In the House, Luis Gutiérrez (D-IL) continued to fight hard for a bill, but the Obama administration showed little interest in that effort. In the Senate, Democrats appeared to move to a strategy of trying to win Latino votes by blaming Republicans for inaction or backward steps. Robert Menendez (D-NJ) told *Politico* that a chance for a bill before the midterm elections was small: "Here are the clear facts," he explained. "If we put a bill on the floor tomorrow, we need Republican votes" (Raju 2010). In a meeting with reform advocates behind closed doors, Democrats admitted that not only did they not have GOP votes, but they had also not secured all Democrats, either, and that some were considering giving up the grand bargain strategy and moving to a focus on undocumented children or agricultural workers (Raju 2010).

Some of Obama's most prominent moves on immigration in the summer of 2010 included a July 1 speech on reform that featured a call for legalization—in which, not surprisingly, he blamed Republicans for obstruction (Obama 2010b). On July 6, the Justice Department sued the state of Arizona for a controversial new law that required police officers to check the documents of persons they stop for another purpose when they have "reasonable suspicion" that the persons are here illegally; on July 28, a federal court agreed to block those provisions. On August 13, Obama quickly—though quietly, with no reporters present—signed the $600 million border enforcement bill that the Senate had passed the day before.

The biggest move for reform came during the lame-duck period, when the Obama administration made a big push to pass the Development, Relief, and Education for Alien Minors Act (DREAM Act), which would have offered legalization to a limited set of illegal immigrants who were brought to the United States by their families and fulfilled a set of educational or military requirements. The bill, which had a long, bipartisan history, passed the House but on December 18, 2010, forty-one senators voted against ending debate and only fifty-five in favor, five votes short of the sixty needed. The bill won three Republican votes, but five Democrats went against Obama's position and did not support it (Preston 2010c; see appendix table 7A.3 for a summary of actions under Obama).

WHY NO REFORM (YET)?

There is no one reason why, by the beginning of 2011, Obama had not yet been able to follow through on his promise of comprehensive immigration reform. The situation is obviously more complex than that, and requires identifying several factors—some specific to immigration, some specific to the Obama presidency, and others more general—that collectively have stymied reform.

Perceptions, Meanings, and Resistance to Reform

Understanding how policymakers perceive policies or their beneficiaries helps us to understand whether and how policies develop (Skrentny 2002; Steensland 2008). Put another way, perceived reality is what matters in politics. Critically, the failure of IRCA appears to have shaped the perception of immigration reform and especially legalization. Inside the Beltway and out, many people simply do not believe enforcement will work, and thus any legalization will be an IRCA-style giveaway. This explains why Obama sets records in deportations and workplace audits. It explains Obama's support for the $600 million border bill. It also explains the intense resistance to legalization among many in Congress, including some Democrats, that both Obama and George W. Bush have confronted.

The political scientist Daniel Tichenor notes that in 2007 the public was very skeptical of the Senate bill that ultimately failed: more than 80 percent polled said that it would not reduce illegal immigration (2009, 18). Though immigration control in general has been a bipartisan failure, more Democrats than Republicans supported IRCA and support legalization today. The public now trusts Republicans more than Democrats to handle illegal immigration, 46 to 36 percent (Polling Report 2010).

Inside the Senate in 2007, Tichenor shows, veterans of both parties revealed their skepticism. Byron Dorgan (D-ND) complained that in 1986 he believed the enforcement claims of IRCA supporters, but learned that "none of them were true, and three million people got amnesty. There was no border security to speak of, no employer sanctions to speak of, and there was no enforcement." Robert Byrd (D-WV) vowed not to make the same mistake again. Chuck Grassley (R-IA) said, "I was fooled once, and history has taught me a valuable lesson" (Tichenor 2009, 18).

The phrase *comprehensive immigration reform* is thus saddled with a very negative meaning, which makes passage more difficult now—despite the growth in the Latino electorate—than it was in 1986. But another problem of negative perceptions, which was around in 1986 but is stronger or at least better mobilized now than in 1986, is the negative perceptions of undocumented immigrants themselves as morally unworthy of help (Newton 2008).

Scholars in political science and sociology recognize the power of perceptions of moral worthiness in politics (Skrentny 2006). As Theda Skocpol has written, "Institutional and cultural oppositions between the morally 'deserving' and the less deserving run like fault lines through the entire history of American social provision" (1992, 149). Indeed, moral understandings can be a major driver of a wide variety of issues in American politics (Morone 2003).

In the view of many, undocumented immigrants are illegal, they are lawbreakers, and thus they are unworthy of any government aid. For many Americans, undocumented immigrants are quite like other controversial groups, such as gays and lesbians, in that their actions are an affront to American morality. Economic, cultural, or racial interests may also matter, but these are tied up with moral meanings that become the public frame for the issue. In this view, illegal aliens violate moral boundaries regarding rule of law, personal responsibility, and national sovereignty.

By themselves, of course, negative perceptions of particular groups such as undocumented immigrants cannot have any effect, and it is true the negative moral meanings have long been there, including when IRCA passed. However, in 1986, restrictionist groups and conservative media did not have the reach that they do today. For example, FAIR (Federation for American Immigration Reform) started in 1979, but its grassroots operation did not get under way until the 1990s (Tichenor 2002). Opinion leaders now have their influence enhanced by a media environment that segments Americans into distinct groups who are now more likely to perceive distinctly different realities (Shapiro and Jacobs 2011). With these forces now able to use powerful moral frames, transmitted through grassroots organizations and a combination of print, broadcast, and Internet media to mobilize restrictionist voters, legalization has become radioactive for many in Congress.

Moreover, immigrants have spread far beyond their traditional destinations of California, Texas, New York, Illinois, and Florida. New gateways of immigration have opened up across the country, attracting increasing numbers to states such as Georgia, North Carolina, and Nevada (Singer 2008), and leading to immigration controversies in increasing numbers of congressional districts and states. More specifically, anti-immigrant hostility is most likely found in new gateways, and it is found there when (as now) it is activated by national political discourse highlighting the new threats (Hopkins 2010). It is now easier, therefore, for restrictionists to find large numbers of voters to oppose grand-bargain reform in general and legalization in particular.

The morality politics of illegal immigration is best demonstrated if we compare it with that of legal immigration. Legal migrants are similar to illegal migrants in terms of race, though illegals are somewhat more Latino and somewhat less educated. However, since the 1940s, strong norms of human rights and nondiscrimination have shaped legal immigration politics, and pro-immigration interest groups police those boundaries with zeal (Skrentny 2002; Tichenor 2002; Wong 2006). Despite the recommendations of a bipartisan commission to limit at least some family visas (U.S. Commission on Immigration Reform 1995), Congress has had little success in limiting legal migration since the 1920s. On legal immigration, politicians offer sentimental paeans to the contributions of newcomers and the glorious tradition of America's "golden door." Lobbying by ethnic organizations, religious groups, business interests, and others takes place in a quiet, "client politics" mode (Wilson 1980; Freeman 1995). Legal-immigration restrictionists are easily on the defensive. They tread carefully or not at all (Graham 2003).[4]

It is a different story with Obama's priority: legalizing the illegal. Illegal immigration is the last stand for Republican immigration restrictionists, but it is an area where they can make a strong stand. Emphasizing law, as well as fairness to legal migrants, who commonly wait years for visas, it is not too difficult to make restriction arguments without appearing to be racist or mean-spirited.[5] Indeed, the closest the current congressional Republicans have come to advocating restrictions on legal migration—Lindsey Graham's short-lived interest in hearings on repeal of the Fourteenth

Amendment's guarantee of birthright citizenship (Barr 2010b; Cook 2010)—actually focused most attention on the morality of illegal parents who exploited American law to (in Graham's words) "come here to drop a child." Lawmakers on the national stage and in most GOP districts, therefore, can have a principled stand against legalization and for strong border enforcement without driving away many independent voters.[6]

The morality politics of illegal immigration has led reformers to invest considerable time and resources to find ways to talk about legalization while not offending the American public's moral sensibilities. The pro-immigration interest group America's Voice and the liberal think tank Center for American Progress did extensive polling with stalwart Democratic consultants Stan Greenberg, Celinda Lake, and Guy Molyneux to learn how to talk about reform. The results were sobering. Surveys in swing districts highlighted deep voter frustration. The pollsters ended up urging reformers to use the term *illegal immigrants* instead of *undocumented workers*. Drew Westen, a political consultant, advised, "When [voters] hear 'undocumented worker,' they hear a liberal euphemism, it sounds to them like liberal code." Even the language of *earned path to citizenship* sounded to voters like a gift to the unworthy. A winning message, the pollsters concluded, should emphasize toughness and practicality (Brown 2010a).

Political Institutions: Leverage for No

Although morality shapes the perceptions and motivations of restrictionists, it is the structure of American political institutions that gives them leverage. Scholars studying American political development have long observed that the fragmented nature of the American state creates multiple veto points to prevent reform (see, for example, Amenta 1998). The multistep legislative process means that antireform groups and the citizens they mobilize do not need to equal the strength of reformers. They have multiple opportunities to register their opposition, and restrictionist members of Congress can of course use these same veto points, as well as various procedural maneuvers, to prevent reform. For example, this was demonstrated clearly in 2006 when the Republican leaders in the House simply refused to consider a bipartisan Senate bill they feared had enough votes to pass.

It was apparent in my discussions with antireform forces that they knew that they did not have to do anything just yet. They knew that their job was easier. Should a legalization bill take shape and come to a vote, FAIR, NumbersUSA, and other antilegalization voices would mobilize their grass roots and fight it at each step.

Unique Challenges: Unprecedented Partisanship, the Great Recession, and a Rogue State

Though not necessary to stop reform in the past, another barrier for Obama is the growing partisanship in Congress. Obama confronts what may be the highest point of a decades-long partisanship trend (Layman, Carsey, and Horowitz 2006; Lee 2009). Parties are increasingly unified and responsive to party leadership rather than constituents. Immigration specifically has become an increasingly partisan issue since the 1980s (Gimpel and Edwards 1999). In an analysis of all votes on the 2006 and 2007 failed reform bills, Benjamin Marquez and John Witte (2009) found a strong party effect with Democrats on the pro-reform side and Republicans against.

To be sure, immigration reforms of the past few decades—1986, 1990, 1996, and the failed efforts in 2006 and 2007—had Republicans and Democrats on both sides of the issue. McCain and Graham attended a meeting with Obama in June 2009 and Graham helped draft the 2010 proposal. As of this writing, however, there is not a single Republican senator willing to support a grand-bargain reform that includes legalization. What changed?

Although this may be the most polarized Congress in modern history (Galston 2010), the pullback seems driven more by partisan strategy than by ideology. Republicans have supported a strategy of no because as the minority party—as one reform advocate reminded me—responsibility to govern falls mostly on the majority party. Obama himself said in his July 2010 address on immigration reform, "Now, under the pressures of partisanship and election-year politics, many of the eleven Republican senators who voted for reform in the past have now backed away from their previous support" (Obama 2010b). Opposing legalization is a potentially winning GOP strategy, at least in the short term, as I discuss in the final section of this chapter. The key point here is that as long as Republicans remain totally unified in opposition, no legalization reform can get through the Senate.

Second, perceptions of economic challenges are often associated with rises in immigration restrictionism (Citrin et al. 1997). Though the Great Recession was not necessary to stop reform for Bush, it certainly makes things more difficult for Obama. Reformers in general and Obama's spokespersons in particular have tried to make the best of a bad situation. They have indicated a strong desire for reform still exists, and they have skillfully turned the traditional argument on its head: reform is a good idea precisely because of the weak economy, because it will aid the economy and protect American workers. I heard the same position from the Democratic staffer with whom I spoke, who noted that, "fortunately for us," studies show that legalization will be good for the economy because it will lead to increased tax revenues. In addition, the influx of younger workers will help Social Security. Another reform advocate stated that Americans "can't build a strong economy on the basis of a broken immigration system."

Yet restrictionists know that the recession provides yet another arrow in their own quiver. One Republican staffer, who expressed great concern that the "economy is in the toilet," said that in the fight against amnesty, the poor economy is "the gift that keeps giving." Legalization, in this view, will simply open up even more Americans to unwanted competition for jobs once legalized workers can emerge from the shadow economy and work anywhere. Similarly, Rosemary Jenks, director of government relations for NumbersUSA, which opposes legalization, told me firmly, "The unemployment rate makes it impossible to justify amnesty." Taking these points seriously, one legalization advocate admitted to me that there is reason to worry that taking up immigration now will make Obama and allies in Congress vulnerable to the charge of ignoring the job concerns of ordinary Americans.

One could see the effects of the economy on immigration politics when Democratic governors pressed their concerns in a meeting with Obama in July 2010. Unhappy with the Justice Department's decision to sue Arizona, Tennessee's Phil Bredesen said, "Universally the governors are saying, 'We've got to talk about jobs.'. . . And all of a sudden we have immigration going on. . . . It is such a toxic subject, such an important time for Democrats" (Goodnough 2010).

Finally, the Arizona law itself also creates new challenges for immigration reform. The press made much of Arizona's new law allowing the police to demand identification from persons they suspect are undocumented. This attention fired up many pro-reform advocates, and in some ways provided arguments for reformers who framed the law as harsh or inhumane, as well as an unworkable and unconstitutional intrusion into a federal matter. However, this effect was balanced by another effect that takes some wind out of the reform sails: Democrats could then cast themselves as pro-Latino simply by playing defense rather than reforming law. They can loudly criticize the Arizona law, and others that may spring up in the next few years, take legal action, as the Justice Department did on July 6, 2010, and do their best to tag Republicans with the law's anti-Latino symbolism. A July 28 federal court ruling that blocked the key parts of the law did little to quiet the issue. As one Democratic House aide said, "There are always politicians who see this as a good political football vs. a policy problem to be solved. . . . They would rather have the fight over immigration to fire up Latino voters than jump into this with both feet"

(Wong 2010). Moreover, polls showing that small but consistent majorities support the Arizona law give more arguments for restrictionists (Polling Report 2010).

Supporting Actors: Public Opinion, Expert Ideas, Interest Groups, and Reform Stalemate

Democratic theory predicts that political leaders give the people what the people say they want. Evidence indicates that at least at some periods in the past, particularly the mid-twentieth century, policy tended to move with public opinion (Page and Shapiro 1983; Burstein 2003). Is reform failing because the public is against it?

The problem with this explanation is that many if not most polls—and particularly those in the immigration area—are difficult to interpret and highly sensitive to question wording. Poll data suggest both that the public tends toward immigration restriction and supports strong border enforcement (Simon 1985; Graham 2003; Schuck 2007; Polling Report 2010), and that it also supports comprehensive reform and in particular legalization programs.

For example, in a review of polling data on the key elements of reform since 2001, the political scientist Deborah Schildkraut found consistent results that were surprisingly liberal (2009). On the most controversial aspect of Obama's plan, she concluded that between 2001 and 2009, an average of only 33 percent of Americans opposed earned legalization for undocumented immigrants whereas an average of 61 percent supported it. Using the word *amnesty* in the question increased opposition, though not always producing majorities. Forty-three percent of Americans supported deporting undocumented immigrants, and 51 percent opposed it.[7]

These results do not sway opinion in Washington. One problem is they do not capture the intensity of restrictionist opinion, though they are misleading in other ways as well. For example, when I discussed the pro-legalization results with NumbersUSA's Rosemary Jenks, she quickly pointed out that the deportation position is a straw man and expressed frustration with any poll or discussion of undocumented immigration that offered as the only policy options legalization or deportation. Her organization supports "attrition through enforcement," where undocumented immigrants would voluntarily go home when they realize they cannot work in the United States any longer. Jenks argued that a 2006 Zogby poll, commissioned by the restrictionist Center for Immigration Studies, showed that when given the choice between the conditional legalization approach, as in the 2006 Senate bill, and the House's 2006 attrition-through-enforcement model, majorities chose the latter. Specifically, when given a three-way choice between the Senate's legalization, the House's attrition, and simple deportation, public support was 28 percent, 56 percent, and 12 percent, respectively (Camarota 2006).

It is therefore not surprising that a Democratic staffer close to the process told me flatly that poll results do not shape their approach to the bill because of their sensitivity to question wording. Instead, this staffer reported that the pro-legalization side used poll results to shape their arguments for positions they already held, especially when trying to frame legalization in a way that might persuade Republicans to support their cause. In other words, following the argument of Lawrence Jacobs and Robert Shapiro (2000), they use polls to try to change public opinion, rather than to follow the public's wishes.

Alternatively, some scholars have argued that consensus expert ideas, such as general causal models of how the world works—for example, whether deregulation leads to economic growth—can explain policy development (Derthick and Quirk 1985; Campbell 2002). In the case of comprehensive immigration reform, however, there is no consensus. Both sides use expert ideas in the same instrumental ways that they use polls: to win arguments and to persuade the undecided. Moreover, both sides rely on the ideas generated by their favored think tanks rather than the ostensibly more neutral academia. For example, one Democratic staffer told me that the pro-legalization side closely monitors expert ideas, and indeed looks at "everything that comes out"—and this staffer did list a wide range of sources of ideas, including the Brookings Institution, the Cato Institute (libertarian and thus a supporter of opening borders), and the Center for American Progress. Yet this staffer did not mention the ideas that were put forth to me as definitive and authoritative by a Republican staffer—the restrictionist Robert Rector at the Heritage Foundation—whose work emphasizes the costs of legalization.

Finally, is the failure to reform due simply to restrictionist groups being stronger (with more funds, better organization, and larger memberships) than legalization forces? The answer is no. Though restrictionist groups are stronger than in 1986, they still are outnumbered and outresourced (for a scorecard, see Marquez and Witte 2009). They are also excluded from the process of writing comprehensive reform bills.

The pro-reform side, according to a Democratic staffer, is in dialogue with several ethnic-oriented advocacy groups, including America's Voice, the National Immigration Forum, and the National Council of La Raza, as well as major labor organizations, such as the AFL-CIO and the Service Employees International Union (SEIU), and, to a lesser extent, the U.S. Chamber of Commerce, which is focused more on future flows of legal workers rather than legalization.[8] The two big labor unions, which in the past had differences on guest-worker programs, are now unified (Jost and

McCullough 2009). Religious leaders of both Catholic and Protestant denominations have also been proponents of legalization. When I asked a pro-reform interest group advocate who was involved in shaping the proposal, the answer was, "Everyone under the sun!"

However, when I asked if "everyone" meant that the restrictionist organizations, such as FAIR or NumbersUSA, weighed in on what they wanted, I was set straight: "No." Although opposition groups with electoral clout typically receive some deference (Mayhew 2004), NumbersUSA's Jenks confirmed to me that her group was not invited to participate in any way. Still, the antireform side can rely on highly motivated individuals to mobilize the antilegalization public and use institutional veto points to exert pressure on Congress. In short, a drastic growth in the power of the pro-reform coalition is needed for interest group strength to be decisive.[9]

PATHWAYS TO REFORM?

Obama and the Democrats failed to push through their desired immigration reform in Obama's first two years, and now face a Republican majority in the House of Representatives. Does this mean that reform is dead for the Obama presidency? The answer is not simple, but several observations may clarify possible moves forward.

Rebranding the Grand Bargain

First, for the reasons already described, a grand-bargain reform with a mass legalization package seems very unlikely to pass in the near future. What is needed would be a massive rebranding of the moral meanings of legalization and illegal immigrants, and to give political cover for members of Congress to support reform, that rebranding would have to come from the right or with the significant involvement of the Republican base.

This is not as far-fetched as it sounds. A potentially significant development has been new pro-reform activity by a reliably conservative and Republican interest group: evangelical Christians. Though some evangelical leaders admit that part of their motivation is to proselytize among the sometimes-only-nominally Catholic Latino migrant population (Gerstein and Smith 2010), their public message on legalization, along with that of mainline Protestant, Catholic, and Jewish organizations, is moral and based on Bible teachings to welcome strangers. The National Association of Evangelicals (NAE), representing 30 million believers, decided in 2009 to support legalization and has held reform vigils. On May 13, 2010, NAE paid for a full-page ad in support of legalization in *Roll Call* (Goodwin 2010). An evangelical leader introduced Obama for his July 2010 speech on immigration and others, including the NAE president, were in the front row (Goodstein 2010). Other religious leaders have banded together to form the Christians for Comprehensive Immigration Reform (Christians for Comprehensive Immigration Reform 2009).

NumbersUSA's Rosemary Jenks argued to me that the religious leadership is out of touch with the church members, and that the members will not go along with legalization. A Zogby International poll does show a significant split between leaders and flock on desired levels of immigration (Neefus 2009). Leaders themselves have acknowledged the challenge in changing opinion (McKinley 2010). Yet evangelicals have shown power to mobilize voters in the past (Rozell and Wilcox 1996; Wilcox and Sigelman 2001), and if they can mobilize those in the pews to support legalization, the shift in interest group power will be important, because the moral thrust of their argument could also shift the public perception of legalization. Religious groups could help rebrand illegal immigrants as something closer to friendly strangers who need generosity and support.

Another potentially important change in the interest group landscape is the creation of a high-status, deep-pocketed reform coalition. Michael Bloomberg, mayor of New York City, joined forces with News Corp CEO Rupert Murdoch to lead creation of this new group, the Partnership for a New American Economy. Other members include mayors of Los Angeles, San Antonio, Philadelphia, and Phoenix, as well as major corporations, including Hewlett-Packard, Walt Disney, Marriott International, Boeing, and Morgan Stanley. The group vowed to fight for the key elements of a grand bargain, including legalization, border enforcement, and other reforms to supply the labor market with migrant labor at both the high- and low-skilled levels (Ioffee 2010; Finnegan 2010). The new group is significant because it showed large business interests moving on legalization as an issue. They may operate only behind the scenes, but if they use their deep pockets on ads to reframe and rebrand the issue (Kinder 1998; Goldstein and Ridout 2004), a group such as the Partnership could help make a grand-bargain reform possible.

An immigration reform in Utah, which stunned many in the Obama administration, provides a blueprint for future reform through re-branding by the right. In that state, a conservative religious group—the Mormon Church—joined forces with a deep-pocketed business group—the Salt Lake City Chamber of Commerce—to promote a reform that would legalize many of the state's undocumented migrants. On March 15, 2011, Republican Governor Gary Herbert signed a bill that would allow most law-abiding illegal workers and their families to pay a fine of up to $2500 in order to receive documents authorizing work in the state. He also signed a restriction measure that required Utah police to check the immigration status of those arrested for felonies or serious misdemeanors. In essence,

Utah passed a conservative-led grand bargain. The measures were preceded by a document, created by business and civic groups and endorsed by the Mormon Church, called the "Utah Compact." It committed signees to support business-friendly and family-centered immigration policies. Utah reformers are trying to take their approach to other states and the federal government (Riccardi 2011).

Political Boundaries and Possible Action

Absent this rebranding of mass legalization, immigration politics is likely to be played within nebulous but very real boundaries. On the reformer side, there may be immigrant-friendly developments, including small-scale legalizations, but these will stop short of opportunities for mass legalization, including even those plans with penalties and Byzantine requirements. On the restrictionist side, border enforcement must steer clear of bills that reformers can credibly cast as anti-Latino, racist, or mean-spirited.

The reasons for the boundaries for reformers have already been described. Yet mirror-images of these factors also affect the restrictionists. For example, reformers can use the ample opportunities to torpedo enforcement bills that restrictionists have used to kill reform. Edward Alden, a senior fellow at the Council on Foreign Relations and the director of a bipartisan task force on immigration that recommended grand-bargain reform (Alden, Bush, and McLarty 2009), told me, "The central dynamic of the next couple of years, I think, will be Republicans in the House pushing for restrictionist legislation, and the pro-reform side mobilizing to block it. The essence of the current stalemate is that each side has enough power to stop the other, but not enough to move ahead forcefully with its agenda" (Alden, personal correspondence, November 22, 2010).

In addition, just as Obama was stymied by Republican opposition, restrictionists will need significant Democratic support in the Senate to get anything done. Both need bipartisanship. As Tamar Jacoby, leader of the pro-reform small business federation Immigration Works USA, observed in a conversation with me before the midterm election, "Only when both sides get serious about governing together will things get done."

The morality politics of legalization has a flipside for restrictionists as well: don't be too harsh. Exactly when enforcement and border security goes too far and becomes mean-spirited or racist is not clear, but it is certainly not the case that any restriction bill can pass. For example, the House bill in 2006 that criminalized aiding illegal immigrants failed. A bill to eliminate birthright citizenship is also likely outside the bounds; one House staffer on the Democratic side predicted that despite some tough GOP talk on a statute that would end birthright citizenship, no bill was likely to get out of committee. Legislatures in conservative states may try to act on their own, however (Preston 2010d). In general, tough treatment at the border has been acceptable in national politics, but the politics becomes more unpredictable and perilous for aggressive enforcement and exclusionary strategies deep inside the nation's borders or when directed at long-term, otherwise law-abiding illegal residents.

So where is the middle ground on immigration? Moderate moves can and likely will include more efforts at enforcement: more officers patrolling the border, more fences, more and better surveillance technologies. There always seems to be more to be done, and even if they cannot be shown to actually work, increased efforts to protect American borders—American sovereignty—make for good politics. Although supportive of the $600 million August 2010 bill, Republicans such as McCain immediately said it was not enough (Associated Press 2010).

As long as many politically active Americans and many in Congress perceive the border as porous, the negative meanings created by IRCA's failure suggest that increased enforcement will remain a popular policy option even for reformers. Either through administrative action or legislation, we are likely to see more restriction effort, especially to seal the border. Reformers have a strong interest in portraying the border as controlled so they can get to the promised land of a mass legalization. Restrictionists will support those efforts but, as McCain did in 2010, will call for yet more efforts to fortify the border. Restrictionists also know that one of the legacies of IRCA is that as long as the border is perceived as unsecure, there can be no mass legalizations.

There are also some workplace enforcement measures that are in the middle ground of immigration politics and ripe for action—especially as long as jobs are a top political issue. E-Verify has become the standard workplace enforcement measure in reform bills, and also will likely be expanded. Workplace enforcement has the political advantage of promising to reduce employment opportunities for illegal immigrants without the dramatic raids that sometimes divide families and can make for bad press. Given the Great Recession's devastating impact on jobs, any immigration restriction efforts that can be sold to voters as part of a job protection strategy will likely receive bipartisan support. However, the array of privacy and individual liberty groups that oppose reformers' most innovative idea, the biometric Social Security card, will likely keep that idea outside the playing field.

Other possible reforms focus on legal migration. For example, new policies to attract skilled migrants, and in particular, to make it easier for foreign graduates of America's universities to stay in the country, have some advocates. Other policies within the boundaries of immigration politics and thus likely to attract bipartisan support include a temporary work permit program to allow for a flexible, low-skilled labor supply, and efforts to reform family reunification visas, which currently suffer from backlogs that force migrants to wait for years (for these and other policy fixes, see Alden, Bush, and McLarty 2009).

Finally, also within the boundaries of the possible are limited and targeted legalizations (Marquez and Witte 2009). One popular strategy with significant grassroots mobilization remains the DREAM Act, which would offer legalization to undocumented immigrants who came to the United States before they were sixteen years old, lived in the United States for at least five years, and finished college or two years of military service. Senator Orrin Hatch (R-UT) originally introduced the DREAM Act in 2001 with bipartisan support, seven Republicans and twelve Democrats.[10] Although DREAM is usually included in grand-bargain bills, it lost a vote as a standalone bill in 2007. Senators Richard Durbin (D-IL) and Richard Lugar (R-IN) have nevertheless continued to reintroduce the measure. Durbin and Lugar asked DHS not to deport those who would be eligible for the act in the hopes that it may yet pass (Durbin 2010; Preston 2007; Curry 2007). Although no agreement has been formalized, DHS has complied: of the nearly 825,000 who would likely achieve legalization (Batalova and McHugh 2010), almost none have been deported. John Morton, head of ICE, told the *New York Times*, "In a world of limited resources, our time is better spent on someone who is here unlawfully and is committing crimes in the neighborhood. . . . As opposed to someone who came to this country as a juvenile and spent the vast majority of their life here" (Preston 2010a). DREAM supporters argue that the bill's provisions weaken the moral arguments against legalization because it benefits only those who did not choose to violate U.S. laws and whose legalization is in the U.S. interest (Bruno 2007, 2010).

Another targeted legalization approach that, like DREAM, Congress has considered as both a stand-alone bill and part of most grand bargains is the Agricultural Jobs, Benefits, and Security Act (AgJOBS). This bill would emphasize economic need more than morality. The AgJOBS approach would offer "blue card" and then eventual green card status to undocumented workers who met a series of requirements, including having performed agricultural work in the past, and would come with requirements of three to five years more agricultural work. It would offer the same legalization benefits to spouses and children (Bruno 2010). Although Lugar has been the only Republican sponsor in the Senate, potential for more support from farm state conservatives exists (Bolton 2010b).[11]

The DREAM Act failed twice under Obama in his first two years. In September 2010, Reid brought DREAM to a vote, though he did so in a way that made it difficult for it to pass: as an amendment to a Defense Department authorization bill that also included an end to the military's ban on soldiers who are openly gay, lesbian, or bisexual. Democrats refused to allow Republican amendments to the bill. Predictably, Republicans filibustered (Herszenhorn 2010a). A stand-alone version of DREAM also failed during December's lame-duck period, despite significant retooling to make the bill costless—for example, beneficiaries would not be eligible for any grants. Yet DREAM remains alive. Durbin told the *Washington Post* that some Republicans did not want to pass the bill during the lame-duck period, but might support it in the future. "Some of those who voted against it and spoke against it, and were the angriest over it being offered, have told me they want to sit down and talk, and I want to hold them to it," he explained (Murray 2011).

Even narrowly targeted legalizations will not come easily, however. These provoke strong restrictionist email, telephone, and fax activity that worries lawmakers. A targeted legalization would be most likely to pass if reformers included several GOP lawmakers in drafting the bills and paired legalization with restriction provisions to provide political cover for restrictionists and to mitigate the negative meanings of reform and legalization. In other words, it would look like a grand-bargain bill but would offer far more to restrictionists than to reformers.

Party Strategy and the Latino Vote: High Stakes and Big Gambles

I have so far described ways that immigration legislation is likely to go forward during Obama's presidency and after. But it is possible that one or both parties will use a very different strategy, or even avoid the legislative route entirely. Understanding the final possibilities requires us to first focus on the question that both parties will have to decide: how important is immigration reform to win the growing Latino vote? Each side approaches the question differently.

Currently, the Democratic leadership's answer to this question goes like this: we support reform, including legalization, because it sends a message to the rapidly growing numbers of Latinos that Democrats are on their side; Latinos will remember this, and reward us for decades just like African Americans have done. As one senior Democratic Party official told the *Washington Post*, "The fight over immigration is a proxy for tolerance. It's a proxy for diversity" (Shear 2010). In this view, the Republicans are doomed. A Democratic strategist explained confidently, "Look: The Republicans, if you do the math, cannot be successful as a national party if they continue to alienate Latinos" (Shear 2010). Answering Republican calls for more border security, then, actually increases pressure on Republicans to support legalization, because they would be losing excuses to resist, and forced to appear more nakedly anti-Latino or racist. Racist Republicans are good for Democrats. Democrats recognize that support for legalization could hurt them in the short term, especially in more conservative states and districts, but if Texas's rapidly growing Latino population flips that state from red to blue a few years down the road, the White House is theirs to lose.

But is Democratic support for border control the right way to use immigration to win Latino voters? Obama and the Democrats must decide whether they should give up on the enforcement-first strategy. Alden has argued that such a strategy is a losing game for reformers because there is no clear benchmark for border control—and no likely success. During the Cold War, he notes, the border between East and West Germany featured fifty guards per square mile with shoot-to-kill orders, landmines, electric fences, and barbed wire, yet about 1,000 people each year were able to cross (Alden 2010). Alden suggested to me a kind of reversal of the Democrats' current enforcement-first strategy: the only way to get a grand bargain may be "for the administration to start dragging its heels on enforcement in a much more systematic way and setting up a real confrontation with congressional Republicans." In this view, "the essential message would be that the price for continued tough enforcement is some progress on other elements of the reform agenda." Alden argued that the Obama policy in 2009 and 2010 was essentially the restrictionist strategy of "attrition through enforcement," and that "as long as the administration keeps giving the restrictionists almost everything they want for free, there will be no political incentive for the restrictionist side to negotiate." Senator Jon Kyl (R-AZ) has maintained that Obama has already flirted with this strategy. According to Kyl, Obama told him, "If we secure the border then [Republicans] won't have any reason to support comprehensive immigration reform," and therefore border security had to be paired with legalization in a grand bargain (Barr 2010a).

This would be a high-risk strategy, and it could alienate independents and many Democrats. Future Democratic party strategy will depend greatly on what the leadership believes is necessary to continue to attract the majority of Latino votes.

In 2009 and 2010, Republican logic on the question of the place of immigration in winning the Latino vote went like this: Latinos are not like African Americans. On many issues, Latinos are conservatives whose votes are up for grabs, and they will vote based on their conservatism, not on the issue of legalization. Therefore, restrictionism will pay short-term benefits with little long-term risk. This appears to remain the dominant view, though there is still a strong reform group in the GOP who are worried about the growing Latino vote, and believe that a pro-immigration stance is necessary to attract it.

My discussions with insiders in both parties regularly turned up acknowledgment of the Republican predicament, and there are many public statements from Republicans expressing concern. For example, GOP consultant Mike Murphy is among those who thinks the anti-immigrant—even the anti-undocumented immigrant—strategy is a political loser. Shortly after the 2008 presidential election, Murphy noted Indiana's switch to the Democrats and commented, "That's right, GOP, you've entered a brave new world ruled by Latino Hoosiers, and you're losing." He warned his colleagues starkly: "Illegal immigrants can't vote. Their children will" (Murphy 2009).

Lionel Sosa, who has advised George W. Bush and John McCain, similarly warned that opposing reform "comes off as insensitive, uncaring to the Latino community" (Shear 2010). Representative Jeff Flake (R-AZ) told *Politico*, "Republicans see a short-term benefit because of the popularity of the Arizona law. But then, a lot of Republicans realize, long term, this is not a winner for the party to take a position that is so distant from the largest-growing demographic" (Wong 2010). After the midterm elections, both the *Wall Street Journal* and the *Weekly Standard* featured calls from Republicans to other Republicans to support some attempt to legalize illegal immigrants in the United States (Jacquot and Rivkin 2010; Bergner 2010). Pro-reform Republicans can point to California, where GOP-supported restrictionism drove out many Latinos (Waters and Jiménez 2005, 114) but also solidified the remaining Latinos' allegiance to Democrats without a counterbalancing increase in GOP support by non-Latino whites (Bowler, Nicholson, and Segura 2006).

But the dominant view in the Republican leadership remains cool to immigration reform. GOP pollster Neil Newhouse counters, "I'd rather win [Latinos] over on economic issues and taxing-and-spending issues than on the issue of illegal immigration. . . . Democrats are rolling the dice that this is going to help them more in '12 than it's going to hurt them in '10. That calculation is very risky" (Shear 2010). Moreover, a *National Journal* poll of members of Congress found that only 24 percent of Democrats thought that their own party had the advantage on immigration, whereas 67 percent of Republicans thought that the GOP was best positioned (Cohen and Bell 2010).

The view that Republicans can oppose grand-bargain reform or any legalization bill and still win Latino votes was bolstered after the 2010 midterm election. Although voters returned some Democrats to the Senate in states with large and growing Latino populations, such as California and Nevada, there was much in the returns for restrictionist Republicans to crow about.

Consider the *Washington Post* op-ed penned by Lamar Smith (R-TX), a restrictionist and the new chair of the House Judiciary Committee, which oversees immigration. Smith observed that House Republicans won 38 percent of the Latino vote in 2010—about 8 percent more than in 2006 and 2008—and "many Hispanics" voted for pro-enforcement and antilegalization Republicans. In addition, some prominent antilegalization Latino Republicans won major offices: Susana Martinez (New Mexico governor), Brian Sandoval (Nevada governor), and Marco Rubio (Florida senator). Five Latino Republicans joined the U.S. House of Representatives. Smith argued, "On many of the most important issues of our day—jobs, education, support for small businesses and the economy—the Republican positions line up with Hispanic values" and that "the right way to attract Hispanic support is to emphasize our shared values" (Smith 2010).

There is evidence that Smith's view is becoming more entrenched in the Republican Party. At a new GOP event designed to build ties with Latinos, the Hispanic Leadership Network Conference, even pro-reform Republicans significantly dialed down their immigration message. Held in January 2011 in Florida, the event brought prominent Republicans, either live or on video, to deliver messages filled with appeals to Latino voters. Yet featured speakers, including presidential hopefuls such as Tim Pawlenty and Newt Gingrich, assiduously avoided talking about immigration. Even former Florida governor Jeb Bush, long a supporter of grand-bargain reform, avoided immigration talk. He told the conference that ignoring the Latino vote would be "incredibly stupid," but his four-point plan to reach Latino voters did not even mention immigration. The simple plan was to be mindful of tone, have a broad agenda, appoint Latinos to prominent government posts, including the judiciary, and develop Latino candidates to run for office (Brown 2011). Explaining the tone issue, Bush maintained that "if you send the signals of 'them v. us' you're not going to be able to get the desired result" and that "leaders have to lead and that means they have the responsibility of civility as well as having a tone that draws people toward our cause and not against it" (Reinhard 2011).

Divided government, we need to remember, does not necessarily lead to gridlock and may actually lead to considerable policy innovation as both parties seek to claim credit for legislation (Mayhew 2004). Can divided government be as productive in today's unprecedentedly polarized political and media environment as it has been in the past, and can it be productive on immigration policy? That is unclear. The only certainty is that all of Obama's political skills will be needed to move out of IRCA's shadow and make progress on this most difficult and emotional of issues.

APPENDIX
Table 7A.1   Summary of Immigration Reform Legislation (1965 to 1996)

	Amendment to Immigration Act (Hart-Cellar Act) October 3, 1965	Immigration Reform and Control Act (IRCA) November 6, 1986	Immigration Act November 29, 1990	Personal Responsibility and Work Opportunity Reconciliation Act August 22, 1996	Illegal Immigration Reform and Immigrant Responsibility Act September 30, 1996
Name of Act Date					
Status	Passed	Passed	Passed	Passed	Passed
Summary	• Eliminated national-origins quota system. • Created visa preferential categories according to immigrants' familial ties or special occupational skills. • Limited total immigration from Eastern Hemisphere (120,000) and Western Hemisphere (120,000). • Established requirement that entering immigrant workers will not affect the employment, wages, and working conditions of American workers.	• Authorized legalization of undocumented aliens living in the United States since January 1, 1982. • Established penalties for employers who knowingly employ unauthorized aliens. • Increased border enforcement. • Established new category for seasonal agricultural labor and provisions for legalization. • Extended registry date for adjustment to permanent resident status to January 1, 1972.	• Raised cap on total immigration to 700,000 from 1992 to 1994, and to an overall flexible cap of 675,000 from 1995 onwards. • Modified all reasons for exclusion and deportation, particularly those on political and ideological grounds. • Authorized attorney general to grant temporary protected status to undocumented aliens from countries with armed conflict and natural disasters.	• Restricted eligibility of legal immigrants for means-tested welfare programs. • Broadened restrictions on welfare for all aliens.	• Created measures of border control, work-site enforcement, and for the removal of deportable aliens. • Increased restrictions on welfare benefits for aliens. • Created requirements for educational institutions to collect information on foreign students' status and nationality for the INS.

Source: Author's summary of appendix in Waters and Ueda (2007).

Table 7A.2   Summary of Immigration Reform Legislation (2001 to 2008)

Name of Act	Patriot Act	Homeland Security Act	Real ID Act	Border Protection, Antiterrorism, and Illegal Immigration Control Act	Comprehensive Immigration Reform Act (Hagel-Martinez Bill)	Secure Fence Act
Date	October 26, 2001	November 25, 2002	May 11, 2005	December 16, 2005	May 25, 2006	October 26, 2006
Status	Passed	Passed	Passed	Passage of bill only in House	Passage of bill only in Senate	Passed
Summary	• Increased personnel and improved monitoring technology at immigrant checkpoints. • Required attorney general and FBI to provide state and INS with access to specified criminal histories. • Broadened scope of aliens inadmissible or deportable for terrorism.	• Transferred functions of INS of the Department of Justice to the Department of Homeland Security (DHS). At the DHS, the Directorate of Border and Transportation Security and the U.S. Citizenship and Immigration services took on immigrant enforcement and immigration service functions, respectively.	• Established federal restrictions on state-issued driver's licenses and ID cards, and denied them to undocumented aliens. • Enhanced procedural requirements in asylum-granting procedures. • Granted Homeland Security additional authority to construct additional barriers and roads at border.	• Criminalized unlawful presence and the assistance of undocumented immigrants. • Increased penalties on employers hiring unauthorized immigrants and imposed requirement for the verification of employees' Social Security numbers. • Required state and local authorities' enforcement of federal immigration law. • Funding for an extended border fence.	• Introduced temporary worker program • Established provisions for earned legalization by undocumented aliens according to their length of stay. • Increased employment-based visas, and established nonagricultural temporary worker visas.	• Authorized construction of 700-mile border fence.

Source: Author's compilation based on data from Wroe (2008), Waters and Ueda (2007), and Library of Congress (2005).

Table 7A.3   Summary of Immigration Reform Legislation and Executive Actions (2009 to 2010)

Name of Act	Comprehensive Immigration Reform for America's Security and Prosperity Act of 2009 (CIR ASAP).	Real Enforcement with Practical Answers for Immigration Reform Plan.	Justice Department Lawsuit against State of Arizona to enjoin implementation of SB 1070 in District Court of Arizona.
Date	December 15, 2009	April 29, 2010	July 6, 2010
Status	In committee.	—	—
Summary	• Establishes a Southern Border Security Task Force and border relief grants for local police agencies. • Requires minimal conditions for immigration law enforcement and detention. • Establishes non-immigrant status for undocumented immigrants with possibility of naturalization. • AgJobs Act.	• Establishes eligibility for legalization for undocumented immigrants in eight years if they learn English, do not commit a crime, and pay taxes. • Create biometric Social Security cards. • Increase federal funding for border security.	• Invalidates SB 1070 and prohibits its implementation because of its violation of Supremacy Clause of U.S. Constitution.

Source: Author's compilation based on data from Bacon (2010), U.S. Department of Justice (2010), Library of Congress (2009, 2010a, 2010b, 2010c, 2010d), Preston (2010e), and Herszenhorn (2010b).

Thanks to the Russell Sage Foundation, the Center for Comparative Immigration Studies, and the UCSD Committee on Research for support for this project. David Keyes, Micah Gell-Redman, Gary Lee, and John Whittemore provided invaluable research assistance. Edward Alden, Wayne Cornelius, Zoltan Hajnal, Minh Ho, Tom Medvetz, Stanley Skrentny, members of the Obama Agenda Project, and external reviewers provided helpful conversations and helpful comments. Finally, I would like to give special thanks

Making emergency supplemental appropriations for border security for the fiscal year ending September 30, 2010, and for other purposes.	National Defense Authorization Act for Fiscal Year 2011 [pledge by Senator Reid to attach Development, Relief, and Education for Alien Minors (DREAM) Act]	Comprehensive Immigration Reform Act of 2010	Removal Clarification Act of 2010 [includes Development, Relief, and Education for Alien Minors (DREAM) Act of 2010]
August 13, 2010	September 21, 2010	September 29, 2010	December 18, 2010
Passed	Cloture not invoked in Senate	In committee	Passage of bill only in House
• Places $600 million in supplemental funding for enhanced law enforcement and border security (additional staffing, infrastructure and technology) along the Southwest border.	• DREAM Act: Authorizes the adjustment of the status of undocumented minors with degree of higher education or military service (two years) to conditional non-immigrant status, with possibility of permanent residence.	• Enhances border and internal immigration law enforcement Includes • AgJobs Act [legalizes undocumented farmworkers and reforms farmworker visas]. • DREAM Act. • Uniting American Families Act [recognition of permanent partners].	• DREAM Act: Authorizes the adjustment and subsequent extension of the status of undocumented minors with degree of higher education or military service (two years) to conditional non-immigrant status, with possibility of permanent residence.

to all of the immigration reform insiders, on both sides of the issue, who were so generous with their time in answering my questions.

NOTES

1. In the Senate's 2007 bill, Obama cosponsored an amendment to maintain immigration visas based on family reunification, arguing that visas based on skills preferences would hurt Latinos (Washington Post Votes Database 2010).

2. The Democratic Leadership Council has given strong support to the policies of Obama's Department of Homeland Security secretary, Janet Napolitano, implemented when she was governor of Arizona (Democratic Leadership Council 2008).

3. At an event at the Center for American Progress on December 16, 2009, Labor Secretary Hilda Solis and Commerce Secretary Gary Locke also made the economic argument for immigration reform by saying that it will strengthen pay and benefits for all workers and allow collection of billions in taxes (2009).

4. In the 1990s, Senator Alan Simpson (R-WY) led a failed effort to reduce legal immigration by 135,000 to 540,000 a year. A 1996 effort to limit legal immigrants' access to various welfare programs succeeded, though much of it was restored in 1998 (Graham 2002; Gimpel and Edwards 1999; Wroe 2008).

5. One can see an analogous political dynamic in the politics of affirmative action. In a study that I conducted during the 1990s, I asked Republican congressional staffers why they did not follow through on their promises to end affirmative action. I was told that Republicans were divided, with the majority fearing that ending affirmative action would make them appear racist (Skrentny 2001).

6. The unworthiness of illegal migrants could also be seen when the issue intersected with Obama's health care reform effort. Though taxpayers have subsidized illegal immigrants for decades through Medicaid payments to hospitals, especially by reimbursing hospitals for their pregnancies (DuBard and Massing 2007), these payments were obscure and the process opaque. Yet the issue of taxpayer funding of illegal immigrants' health care exploded during Obama's health care speech to Congress when Representative Joe Wilson (R-SC) yelled, "You lie!" after Obama claimed that undocumented immigrants would be ineligible for benefits in the new health care plan (MacGillis 2009). In fact the plan excluded undocumented immigrants, but many Republicans believed that more stringent exclusions were needed. Democrats countered that increased controls were unnecessary, costly, and caused burdens to citizens. Conservative talk radio hosts rallied behind Wilson, and within just a few days, Obama gave in. He sought a tougher position, banning illegal aliens from even buying insurance on the exchanges the program would create.

7. More specifically, a poll conducted by ABC News/*Washington Post* in April 2009 found that a plurality of Americans favored a pathway to citizenship for undocumented migrants (beating out two other options—letting them stay as guest-workers and deporting them (44, 21, and 30 percent, respectively). CBS News/*New York Times* found in the same month that 61 percent of Americans favored a pathway to legal residence if undocumented migrants paid a fine. Majorities of Republicans also favor conditional legalization (see Polling Report 2010; also see Pew Research Center for the People and the Press 2007). In December 2009, a Benenson Strategy Group poll of independent voters

found that 67 percent supported passage of "comprehensive immigration reform" and 72 percent supported conditional legalization. When offered the choice of conditional legalization, temporary stay, or deportation, 61 percent supported conditional legalization, 10 percent supported temporary stay, and 27 percent chose "they must leave the country" (American Voice 2010).

8. Business groups had been active on immigration reform, but mostly focused on increasing legal opportunities for foreign workers to come to the United States. For example, the U.S. Chamber of Commerce helped sponsor a study showing the benefits of increased immigration of the highly skilled (2010). There are some business interests who support legalization, however, including ImmigrationWorks USA, a federation of small business owners led by prominent pro-reform advocate Tamar Jacoby.

9. One element in the Schumer bill, the biometric Social Security card for all Americans, may bring new groups to the bargaining table. The idea has been promoted before, especially after the terrorist attack of September 11, 2001, and by both pro-reform forces (including Senators Diane Feinstein [D-CA] as well as Schumer and Graham) and center-left experts (such as the Migration Policy Institute and former Immigration and Naturalization Service commissioners Doris Meissner, who served under Clinton, and James Ziglar, who served under George W. Bush), as well as by immigration restriction organizations such as FAIR. Feinstein's support came as early as 1997 (Bernstein 1997). The Migration Policy Institute created the bipartisan Independent Task Force on Immigration and America's Future, made up mainly of pro-reform forces, which recommended a national biometric Social Security card in 2006. FAIR has an elaborate proposal on their website that includes biometric identifiers for all Americans (see FAIR 2002). But national ID cards have long been controversial in the United States because of privacy and civil liberties concerns (Eaton 1986). The American Civil Liberties Union (ACLU) organized a very diverse coalition to sign on to an April 23, 2010, letter to the reform leaders opposing the biometric card requirement in the Schumer proposal, in which it states that "a National ID would not only violate privacy by helping to consolidate data and facilitate tracking of individuals, it would bring government into the very center of our lives by serving as a government permission slip needed by everyone in order to work" (ACLU 2010). Joining the ACLU are the Americans for Tax Reform, the Consumer Federation of America, and a variety of privacy organizations.

10. "Bill Summary & Status, 107th Congress (2001–2002), S.1291, All Information." Available at: http://rs9.loc.gov/cgi-bin/bdquery/z?d107:SN01291:@@@L&summ2=m& (accessed October 4, 2010).

11. Supporters of the grand bargain have been reluctant to support DREAM or AgJOBS alone or paired in a small reform bill in the past because they believed passage would make it less likely to pass other reforms, and particu-

larly a mass (if still conditional) legalization. In a meeting with education and technology leaders in San Diego, Bob Filner (D-CA) explained that reformers resist DREAM—as well as a visa program for foreign graduates of American universities—as stand-alone bills because they hope these sweeteners will lure votes for a grand-bargain reform bill. (These remarks were made in response to my question at the CONNECT Public Policy Forum, La Jolla, California, August 11, 2010.) One advocate noted to me that most undocumented immigrants are not children or do not have children, and explained, "The problem is it's really hard to dial back. People view [DREAM] as a compromise—they don't see how winning one thing, it leads to another. . . . If you start with the DREAM Act, there is such a pent-up demand for [comprehensive reform], now all of the different interests will say that if you are going to do *one* thing, why not *their* thing?" Obama's public statement on the DREAM Act (to Spanish-language newspaper *La Opinion*) suggests he continues to prefer grand-bargain reform: "I just don't want anybody to think that if we somehow just do the DREAM Act, that that solves the problem. . . . We've got a bigger problem that we have to solve. We still need comprehensive immigration reform. The DREAM Act can be an important part of that, and, as I said, I'm a big supporter of that. But I also want to make sure that we don't somehow give up on the bigger strategy" (Brown 2010b).

REFERENCES

ACLU. 2010. "Comprehensive Immigration Reform Must Respect Civil Liberties and Privacy, Says ACLU." April 13, 2010. Available at: http://www.aclu.org/immigrants-rights-technology-and-liberty/broad-coalition-urges-president-obama-and-congress-oppose-b (accessed June 26, 2010).

Alden, Edward. 2010. "The Meaningless Mantra of 'Border Security.'" *Wall Street Journal*, June 1, 2010. Available at: http://online.wsj.com/article/SB100014240 52748704269204575270810940585150.html (accessed November 22, 2010).

Alden, Edward, project director, and Jeb Bush and Thomas F. McLarty III, chairs. 2009. "U.S. Immigration Policy." Independent Task Force Report 63. New York: Council on Foreign Relations.

Amenta, Edwin. 1998. *Bold Relief: Institutional Politics and the Origins of Modern American Social Policy*. Princeton, N.J.: Princeton University Press.

America's Voice. 2010. "Independent Voters Back Comprehensive Immigration Reform." January 2010 update. Available at: http://amvoice.3cdn.net/a948e3 f8e4f6c724b2_9zm6bxqun.pdf (accessed March 28, 2010).

Associated Press. 2010. "Obama Signs $600 Million Border Security Bill into Law." *Washington Post*, August 13, 2010. Available at: http://www.washingtonpost .com/wp-dyn/content/article/2010/08/13/AR2010081302827.html?hpid =moreheadlines (accessed August 13, 2010).

Bacon, Perry, Jr. 2010. "Democrats Unveil Immigration-Reform Proposal." *Washington Post*, April 29, 2010. Available at: http://www.washingtonpost.com/wp-dyn/content/article/2010/04/29/AR2010042904512.html?hpid=topnews (accessed April 29, 2010).

Barr, Andy. 2010a. "White House Says Jon Kyl Story Not True." *Politico*, June 21, 2010. Available at: http://www.politico.com/news/stories/0610/38789.html (accessed June 21, 2010).

———. 2010b. "Graham Eyes 'Birthright Citizenship.'" *Politico*, July 29, 2010. Available at: http://www.politico.com/news/stories/0710/40395.html#ixzz0vC0Vc3CR (accessed October 2, 2010).

Batalova, Jeanne, and Margie McHugh. 2010. "DREAM vs. Reality: An Analysis of Potential DREAM Act Beneficiaries." *MPI Insight*, July 2010. Available at: http://www.migrationpolicy.org/pubs/DREAM-Insight-July2010.pdf (accessed October 4, 2010).

Bean, Frank, and Gillian Stevens. 2003. *America's Newcomers and the Dynamics of Diversity*. New York: Russell Sage Foundation.

Bergner, Jeff. 2010. "As Simple as One, Two, Three: A Legislative Strategy for the House Republicans." *Weekly Standard* 16(9)(November 15): 30–33. Available at: http://www.weeklystandard.com/articles/simple-one-two-three_515079.html (accessed January 23, 2011).

Bernstein, Nina. 1997. "Goals Clash in Shielding Privacy." *New York Times*, October 20, 1997. Available at: http://www.nytimes.com/1997/10/20/us/goals-clash-in-shielding-privacy.html (accessed June 26, 2010).

Bluestone, Barry, and Bennett Harrison. 1982. *The Second Industrial Divide*. New York: Basic Books.

Bolton, Alexander. 2010a. "Desire to Tackle Immigration Reform Splits Reid from Centrist Democrats." *The Hill*, April 14, 2010. Available at: http://thehill.com/homenews/senate/92079-immigration-splits-reid-from-centrist-colleagues?page=5 (accessed July 28, 2010).

———. 2010b. "Immigration Groups Eye Piecemeal Reform as Reid Focuses on Energy Bill." *The Hill*, June 5, 2010. Available at: http://thehill.com/homenews/senate/101561-immigration-groups-eye-piecemeal-reform-as-reid-focuses-on-energy-bill (accessed July 28, 2010).

Borjas, George J. 2003. "The Labor Demand Curve Is Downward Sloping: Reexamining the Impact of Immigration on the Labor Market." *Quarterly Journal of Economics* 118(November): 1335–74.

Bowler, Shaun, Stephen P. Nicholson, and Gary M. Segura. 2006. "Earthquakes and Aftershocks: Race, Direct Democracy, and Partisan Change." *American Journal of Political Science* 50(1): 146–59.

Brown, Carrie Budoff. 2010a. "Dems' Tough New Immigration Pitch." *Politico*, June 10, 2010. Available at: http://www.politico.com/news/stories/0610/38342.html (accessed January 15, 2011).

————. 2010b. "Democrats Pivot on Immigration." *Politico*, September 14, 2010. Available at: http://www.politico.com/news/stories/0910/42153.html (accessed September 15, 2010).

————. 2011. "Jeb Bush: GOP 'Incredibly Stupid' to Ignore Hispanics." *Politico*, January 14, 2011. Available at: http://www.politico.com/news/stories/0111/47622.html#ixzz1Bb77VLP2 (accessed January 15, 2011).

Bruno, Andorra. 2007. "Unauthorized Alien Students: Issues and 'DREAM Act' Legislation." CRS Report RL33863. Washington: Government Printing Office. Available at: http://trac.syr.edu/immigration/library/P1606.pdf (accessed July 2, 2010).

————. 2010. "CRS Report for Congress: Unauthorized Aliens in the United States." CRS Report R41207. Washington: Government Printing Office. Available at: http://assets.opencrs.com/rpts/R41207_20100427.pdf (accessed July 2, 2010).

Burstein, Paul. 2003. "The Impact of Public Opinion on Public Policy: A Review and an Agenda." *Political Research Quarterly* 56(1): 29–40.

Camarota, Steven A. 2006. "New Poll: Americans Prefer House Approach on Immigration." Washington, D.C.: Center for Immigration Studies. Available at: http://www.cis.org/articles/2006/2006poll.pdf (accessed May 17, 2010).

Campbell, John L. 2002. "Ideas, Politics and Public Policy." *Annual Review of Sociology* 28(August 2002): 21–38. doi: 10.1146/annurev.soc.28.110601.141111.

Christians for Comprehensive Immigration Reform. 2009. "Statement of Principles." Available at: http://faithandimmigration.org/content/statement-principles (accessed July 2, 2010).

Citrin, Jack, Donald P. Green, Christopher Muste, and Cara Wong. 1997. "Public Opinion toward Immigration Reform: The Role of Economic Motivations." *Journal of Politics* 59(3): 858–81.

Cohen, Richard E., and Peter Bell. 2010. "Congressional Insiders Poll." *National Journal*, July 17, 2010. Available at: http://www.nationaljournal.com/njmagazine/ip_20100717_3880.php (accessed July 27, 2010).

Congressional Budget Office. 2007. "A CBO Paper: The Impact of Unauthorized Immigrants on the Budgets of State and Local Governments." Washington: Government Printing Office (December). Available at: http://www.cbo.gov/ftpdocs/87xx/doc8711/12-6-Immigration.pdf (accessed July 27, 2010).

Connally, Katie. 2010. "Immigration Reform Is Back on the Agenda: What's the Political Strategy?" *Newsweek*, March 11, 2010. Available at: http://blog.newsweek.com/blogs/thegaggle/archive/2010/03/11/immigration-reform-is-back-on-the-agenda-what-s-the-political-strategy.aspx (accessed March 28, 2010).

Cook, Dave. 2010. "Sen. Mitch McConnell Defends Hearings on Birthright Citizenship." *Christian Science Monitor*, August 5, 2010. Available at: http://www.csmonitor.com/USA/Politics/monitor_breakfast/2010/0805/Sen.-Mitch

-McConnell-defends-hearings-on-birthright-citizenship (accessed October 2, 2010).

Cornelius, Wayne A., and Takeyuki Tsuda. 2004. "Controlling Immigration: The Limits of Government Intervention." In *Controlling Immigration: A Global Perspective*, edited by Wayne A. Cornelius, Takeyuki Tsuda, Philip L. Martin, and James F. Hollifield. Stanford, Calif.: Stanford University Press.

Cummings, Jeanne. 2010. "Hispanics Unhappy with Dem Shift." *Politico*, May 6, 2010. Available at: http://www.politico.com/news/stories/0510/36844.html (accessed May 6, 2010).

Curry, Tom. 2007. "Lessons of the Dream Act Defeat." *MSNBC*, October 24, 2007. Available at: http://www.msnbc.msn.com/id/21456667/ns/politics/ (accessed May 18, 2010).

Democratic Leadership Council. 2008. "Policy Brief: Immigration Reform." Available at: http://www.dlc.org/ndol_ci.cfm?contentid=254702&kaid=139&subid=271 (accessed October 1, 2010).

Derthick, Martha, and Paul J. Quirk. 1985. *The Politics of Deregulation*. Washington, D.C.: Brookings Institution.

DuBard, C. Annette, and Mark W. Massing. 2007. "Trends in Emergency Medicaid Expenditures for Recent and Undocumented Immigrants." *Journal of the American Medical Association* 297: 1085–92.

Durbin, Richard J. 2010. "Durbin, Lugar Ask Secretary Napolitano to Stop Deportations of Dream Act Students." Available at: http://durbin.senate.gov/show Release.cfm?releaseId=324015 (accessed July 2, 2010).

Eaton, Joseph W. 1986. *Card-Carrying Americans: Privacy, Security and the National ID Card Debate*. Lanham, Md.: Rowman and Littlefield.

Eilperin, Juliet. 2010. "Sen. Graham Walks Away from Climate and Energy Bill—Multiplatform Editor." *Washington Post*, April 24, 2010. Available at: http://views.washingtonpost.com/climate-change/post-carbon/2010/04/sen_graham_threatens_to_halt_work_on_climate_and_energy_bill.html?hpid=topnews (accessed April 24, 2010).

FAIR. 2002. "FAIR: Agenda for Identity Document Security." Available at: http://www.fairus.org/site/News2?page=NewsArticle&id=16906&security=1601&news_iv_ctrl=1011 (accessed June 26, 2010).

Finnegan, William. 2010. "Borderlines." *The New Yorker*, July 26, 2010. Available at: http://www.newyorker.com/talk/comment/2010/07/26/100726taco_talk_finnegan (accessed July 28, 2010).

Freeman, Gary P. 1995. "Modes of Immigration Politics in Liberal Democratic States." *International Migration Review* 24(4): 909–13.

Galston, William. 2010. "Can a Polarized American Party System Be 'Healthy'?" *Issues in Governance Studies* 34(April): 1–20.

Gerstein, Josh, and Ben Smith. 2010. "Churches Eye Immigration's Upside." *Polit-

ico, July 20, 2010. Available at: http://www.politico.com/news/stories/0710/39938.html (accessed July 20, 2010).

Gimpel, James G., and James R. Edwards Jr. 1999. *The Congressional Politics of Immigration Reform*. Boston, Mass.: Allyn and Bacon.

Goldstein, Kenneth, and Travis N. Ridout. 2004. "Measuring the Effects of Televised Political Advertising in the United States." *Annual Review of Political Science* 7: 205–26. doi: 10.1146/annurev.polisci.7.012003.

Goodnough, Abby. 2010. "Governors Voice Grave Concerns on Immigration." *New York Times*, July 11, 2010. Available at: http://www.nytimes.com/2010/07/12/us/politics/12governors.html?_r=1&pagewanted=all (accessed July 23, 2010).

Goodstein, Laurie. 2010. "Obama Wins Unlikely Allies in Immigration." *New York Times*, July 18, 2010. Available at: http://www.nytimes.com/2010/07/19/us/politics/19evangelicals.html?_r=3&hp=&pagewanted=all (accessed July 19, 2010).

Goodwin, Liz. 2010. "Evangelicals' Full-Page Ad in D.C. Will Call for Immigration Reform." *Yahoo! News*, May 11, 2010. Available at: Available at: http://news.yahoo.com/s/ynews/20100511/ts_ynews/ynews_ts1994 (accessed May 11, 2010).

Graham, Hugh Davis. 2002. *Collision Course: The Strange Convergence of Affirmative Action and Immigration in America*. New York: Oxford University Press.

Graham, Otis. 2003. "Failing the Test: Immigration Reform." In *The Reagan Presidency: Pragmatic Conservatism and Its Legacies*, edited by W. Elliot Brownlee and Hugh Davis Graham. Lawrence: University Press of Kansas.

Greenspan, Alan. 2000. Testimony at Renomination Hearing, Senate Committee on Banking, Housing, and Urban Affairs (January 26). C-SPAN Video Library. Available at: http://www.c-spanvideo.org/program/154958-1 (accessed February 21, 2011).

Gutiérrez, David Gregory. 1997. *Between Two Worlds: Mexican Immigrants in the United States*. Lanham, Md.: Rowman & Littlefield.

Hanson, Gordon. 2009. "The Economics and Policy of Illegal Immigration in the United States." Washington, D.C.: Migration Policy Institute. Available at: http://www.migrationpolicy.org/pubs/Hanson-Dec09.pdf (accessed July 14, 2010).

Herszenhorn, David M. 2010a. "Move to End 'Don't Ask, Don't Tell' Stalls in Senate." *New York Times*, September 21, 2010. Available at: http://www.nytimes.com/2010/09/22/us/politics/22cong.html?_r=1 (accessed October 4, 2010).

———. 2010b. "Passion and Politics on Immigration Act." *New York Times*, September 21, 2010, p. A18. Available at: http://www.nytimes.com/2010/09/22/us/politics/22immig.html (accessed January 2011).

Hing, Bill Ong. 2006. "Misusing Immigration Policies in the Name of Homeland Security." *CR: The New Centennial Review* 6(1)(Spring): 195–224.

Hinojosa-Ojeda, Raúl. 2010. *Raising the Floor for American Workers*. Washington,

D.C.: Center for American Progress, American Immigration Council. Available at: http://www.americanprogress.org/issues/2010/01/raising_the_floor.html (accessed August 4, 2010).

Hoefer, Michael, Nancy Rytina, and Bryan C. Baker. 2010. "Estimates of the Unauthorized Immigrant Population Residing in the United States: January 2009." *Population Estimates*. January. Washington: Department of Homeland Security, Office of Immigration Statistics. http://www.dhs.gov/xlibrary/assets/statistics/publications/ois_ill_pe_2009.pdf (accessed July 28, 2010).

Hopkins, Daniel J. 2010. "Politicized Places: Explaining Where and When Immigrants Provoke Local Opposition." *American Political Science Review* 104(1): 40–60.

Hsu, Spencer S. 2009. "Little New in Obama's Immigration Policy." *Washington Post*, May 20, 2009. Available at: http://www.washingtonpost.com/wp-dyn/content/article/2009/05/19/AR2009051903404.html (accessed September 10, 2009).

Hunt, Kasie. 2010. "Lindsey Graham Lashes Out on Immigration." *Politico*, May 5, 2010. Available at: http://www.politico.com/news/stories/0510/36815.html (accessed May 5, 2010).

Ioffe, Karina. 2010. "US Cities, Companies Team Up on Immigration Reform." *Reuters*, June 24, 2010. Available at: http://www.reuters.com/article/idUSN2419811120100625 (accessed July 2, 2010).

Jacobs, Lawrence R., and Robert Y. Shapiro. 2000. *Politicians Don't Pander: Political Manipulation and the Loss of Democratic Responsiveness*. Chicago: University of Chicago Press.

Jacquot, Joe, and David B. Rivkin Jr. 2010. "The GOP's Immigration Opportunity." *Wall Street Journal*, November 19, 2010. Available at: http://online.wsj.com/article/SB10001424052748704312504575618520808255794.html (accessed November 19, 2010).

Jenkins, J. Craig, and Charles Perrow. 1977. "Insurgency of the Powerless: Farm Worker Movements (1946–1972)." *American Sociological Review* 42(2)(April): 249–68.

Jost, Ali, and Mark McCullough. 2009. "Change to Win and AFL-CIO Unveil Unified Immigration Reform Framework." April 14, 2009. Available at: http://www.seiu.org/2009/04/change-to-win-and-afl-cio-unveil-unified-immigration-reform-framework.php (accessed July 28, 2010).

Kaye, Jeffrey. 2010. "America's Fickle Welcome Mat." *Los Angeles Times*, March 23, 2010. Available at: http://www.latimes.com/news/opinion/commentary/la-oe-kaye23-2010mar23,0,5809816.story (accessed May 15, 2010).

Kinder, Donald R. 1998. "Communication and Opinion." *Annual Review of Political Science* 1: 167–97.

Klein, Ezra. 2010. "Sen. Lindsey Graham: 'I care equally about immigration and climate change.'" *Washington Post*, April 29, 2010. Available at: http://voices

.washingtonpost.com/ezra-klein/2010/04/sen_lindsey_graham_i_care_equa .html (accessed April 29, 2010).

Kornblut, Anne E., and Spencer S. Hsu. 2010. "Arizona Governor Signs Immigration Bill, Reopening National Debate." *Washington Post*, April 24, 2010. Available at: http://www.washingtonpost.com/wp-dyn/content/article/2010/04/23/AR2010042301441.html?hpid=topnews (accessed April 24, 2010).

Layman, Geoffrey C., Thomas M. Carsey, and Juliana Menasce Horowitz. 2006. "Party Polarization in American Politics: Characteristics, Causes, and Consequences." *Annual Review of Political Science* 9(2006): 83–110.

Lee, Frances E. 2009. *Beyond Ideology: Politics, Principles, and Partisanship in the U.S. Senate*. Chicago: University of Chicago Press.

Lee, Carol E., and Kasie Hunt. 2010. "White House Woos Republican Party on Immigration." *Politico*, May 4, 2010. Available at: http://www.politico.com/news/stories/0510/36786.html (accessed May 5, 2010).

Library of Congress. Congressional Research Service. 2005. *H.R. 418, REAL ID Act of 2005*. THOMAS (Library of Congress). Available at: http://thomas.loc.gov/ (accessed January 2011).

———. 2009. *H.R. 4321, CIR ASAP Act of 2009*. THOMAS (Library of Congress). Available at: http://thomas.loc.gov/ (accessed January 2011).

———. 2010a. *S. 3721, A Bill Making Emergency Supplemental Appropriations for Border Security for the Fiscal Year Ending September 30, 2010, and for Other Purposes*. THOMAS (Library of Congress). Available at: http://thomas.loc.gov/ (accessed January 2011).

———. 2010b. *S. 3454, National Defense Authorization Act for Fiscal Year 2011*. THOMAS (Library of Congress). Available at: http://thomas.loc.gov/ (accessed January 2011).

———. 2010c. *S. 3932. CIR Act of 2010*. THOMAS (Library of Congress). Available at: http://thomas.loc.gov/ (accessed January 2011).

———. 2010d. *H.R. 5281, Removal Clarification Act of 2010*. THOMAS (Library of Congress). Available at: http://thomas.loc.gov/ (accessed January 2011).

MacGillis, Alec. 2009. "Shout Draws Focus to Illegal-Immigrant Issue." *Washington Post*, September 11, 2009. Available at: http://www.washingtonpost.com/wp-dyn/content/article/2009/09/10/AR2009091004276.html (accessed September 12, 2009).

Marquez, Benjamin, and John F. Witte. 2009. "Immigration Reform: Strategies for Legislative Action." *The Forum* 7(3): Article 2.

Marshall, William, and Martin Schram, eds. 1993. *Mandate for Change*. New York: Berkley Books.

Martin, Philip L. 2003. *Promise Unfulfilled: Unions, Immigration and the Farm Workers*. Ithaca, N.Y.: Cornell University Press.

Martinez, Gebe. 2009. "Has Obama Forgotten Immigration?" *Politico*, March 9, 2009. Available at: http://www.politico.com/news/stories/0309/19564.html (accessed September 21, 2009).

Massey, Douglas S., Jorge Durand, and Nolan J. Malone. 2002. *Beyond Smoke and Mirrors: Mexican Immigration in an Era of Economic Integration*. New York: Russell Sage Foundation.

Mayhew, David. 2004. *Congress: The Electoral Connection*. New Haven, Conn.: Yale University Press.

McKinley, James C., Jr. 2010. "Houston's Clergy Unites to Urge Support for Immigration Reform." *New York Times*, July 4, 2010. Available at: http://www.nytimes.com/2010/07/05/us/05churches.html?scp=1&sq=houston%20clergy&st=cse (accessed July 4, 2010).

Morone, James A. 2003. *Hellfire Nation: The Politics of Sin in American History*. New Haven, Conn.: Yale University Press.

Murphy, Mike. 2009. "For Republicans, the Ice Age Cometh." *Time*, June 22, 2009. Available at: http://www.time.com/time/magazine/article/0,9171,1904136,00.html (accessed May 17, 2010).

Murray, Shailagh. 2011. "After Losing House, Democrats Will Try New Strategy: Bipartisanship." *Washington Post*, January 5, 2011. Available at: http://www.washingtonpost.com/wp-dyn/content/article/2011/01/04/AR2011010405626.html?hpid=topnews (accessed January 5, 2011).

Napolitano, Janet. 2009. "Prepared Remarks by Secretary Napolitano on Immigration Reform at the Center for American Progress." November 15, 2009. Washington: Department of Homeland Security. Available at: http://www.dhs.gov/ynews/speeches/sp_1258123461050.shtm.

Navarro, Armando. 2005. *Mexicano Political Experience in Occupied Aztlán: Struggles and Change*. Walnut Creek, Calif.: Rowman Altamira.

Neefus, Christopher. 2009. "Poll: Most Christians and Jews at Odds with Their Leaders over Illegal Immigration." *CNSNews.com*, December 31, 2009. Available at: http://www.cnsnews.com/news/article/59164 (accessed July 26, 2010).

Newton, Lina. 2008. *Illegal, Alien, or Immigrant: The Politics of Immigration Reform*. New York: New York University Press.

Newton-Small, Jay. 2010. "Why GOP Senators Won't Play on Immigration Reform." *Time*, May 10, 2010. Available at: http://www.time.com/time/politics/article/0,8599,1988149,00.html (accessed June 19, 2010).

O'Brien, Michael. 2010. "McCain Says Border Security Must Be Top Priority in Immigration Reform Efforts." *The Hill*, April 19, 2010. Available at: http://thehill.com/blogs/blog-briefing-room/news/93017-mccain-says-border-security-must-be-top-priority-on-immigration (accessed April 19, 2010).

O'Rourke, Allen Thomas. 2006. "Good Samaritans, Beware: The Sensenbrenner-King Bill and Assistance to Undocumented Migrants." *Harvard Latino Law Review* 9(Spring): 195–208. Available at: http://www.law.harvard.edu/students/orgs/llr/vol9/allenorourke.pdf (accessed January 25, 2011).

Obama, Barack. 2009. "Remarks by the President after Meeting with Members of Congress to Discuss Immigration." June 25, 2009. Washington: The White House, Office of the Press Secretary. Available at: http://www.whitehouse

.gov/the_press_office/Remarks-by-the-President-after-meeting-with
-members-of-Congress-to-discuss-immigration (accessed September 23, 2009).

———. 2010a. "Statement by the President on the Passage of the Southwest Border Security Bill." August 12, 2010. Washington: The White House, Office of the Press Secretary. Available at: http://www.whitehouse.gov/the-press-office/2010/08/12/statement-president-passage-southwest-border-security-bill (accessed August 13, 2010).

———. 2010b. "Remarks by the President on Comprehensive Immigration Reform." July 1, 2010. Washington: The White House, Office of the Press Secretary. Available at: http://www.whitehouse.gov/the-press-office/remarks-president-comprehensive-immigration-reform (accessed July 11, 2010).

Obama, Barack, and Joseph Biden. 2008. "Barack Obama and Joe Biden: Fighting for Comprehensive Immigration Reform." *Organizing for America*, September 6, 2008. Available at: http://www.barackobama.com/pdf/issues/Immigration FactSheet.pdf (accessed August 31, 2009).

Office of Management and Budget. 2009. "U.S. Department of Homeland Security." Washington: The White House. Available at: http://www.whitehouse.gov/omb/fy2010_department_homeland/ (accessed September 21, 2009).

Page, Benjamin I., and Robert Y. Shapiro. 1983. "Effects of Public Opinion on Policy." *American Political Science Review* 77(1): 175–90.

Passel, Jeffrey S., and D'vera Cohn. 2011. "Unauthorized Immigrant Population: National and State Trends, 2010." Washington, D.C.: Pew Hispanic Center.

Pear, Robert. 2007. "Experts Say Failure of Senate Immigration Bill Can Be Lesson for U.S. Congress." *New York Times*, June 30, 2007. Available at: http://www.nytimes.com/2007/06/30/washington/30immig.html (accessed June 30, 2010).

Pew Research Center for the People and the Press. 2007. "Mixed Views on Immigration Bill." Washington, D.C.: Pew Center for the People and the Press. Available at: http://people-press.org/reports/pdf/335.pdf (accessed January 28, 2011).

Piore, Michael. 1979. *Birds of Passage*. Cambridge: Cambridge University Press.

Polling Report. 2010. "Polling Report: Immigration." *Polling Report*. Available at: http://pollingreport.com/immigration.htm (accessed June 30, 2010).

Preston, Julia. 2007. "Bill for Immigrant Students Fails Test Vote in Senate." *New York Times*, October 25, 2007. Available at: http://www.nytimes.com/2007/10/25/washington/25immig.html?_r=3 (accessed May 18, 2010).

———. 2009a. "U.S. Shifts Strategy on Illicit Work by Immigrants." *New York Times*, July 3, 2009. Available at: http://www.nytimes.com/2009/07/03/us/03immig.html?pagewanted=1&_r=2&h (accessed September 15, 2009).

———. 2009b. "Immigration Crackdown with Firing, Not Raids." *New York Times*, September 29, 2009. Available at: http://www.nytimes.com/2009/09/30/us/30factory.html?_r=1 (accessed January 18, 2011).

———. 2010a. "Students Spared Amid Increase in Deportations." *New York Times*, August 8, 2010. Available at: http://www.nytimes.com/2010/08/09/us/09students.html?pagewanted=1&_r=2&hp (accessed August 8, 2010).

———. 2010b. "Illegal Workers Swept from Jobs in 'Silent Raids.'" *New York Times*, July 9, 2010. Available at: http://www.nytimes.com/2010/07/10/us/10enforce.html?_r=1&hp=&pagewanted=all (accessed July 10, 2010).

———. 2010c. "Immigration Vote Leaves Obama's Policy in Disarray." *New York Times*, December 18, 2010. Available at: http://www.nytimes.com/2010/12/19/us/politics/19dream.html?_r=1 (accessed December 18, 2010).

———. 2010d. "Political Battle on Immigration Shifts to States." *New York Times*, December 31, 2010. Available at: http://www.nytimes.com/2011/01/01/us/01immig.html?_r=1&hp (accessed December 31, 2010).

———. 2010e. "Obama Signs Border Bill to Increase Surveillance." *New York Times*, August 5, 2010, p. A10. Available at: http://www.nytimes.com/2010/08/14/us/politics/14immig.html (accessed January 2011).

Raju, Manu. 2010. "Immigration Promise Hard to Keep." *Politico*, June 21, 2010. Available at: http://www.politico.com/news/stories/0610/38776.html (accessed June 21, 2010).

Rector, Robert. 2006. *Importing Poverty: Immigration and Poverty in the United States: A Book of Charts*. SR-9. Washington, D.C.: Heritage Foundation. Available at: http://www.heritage.org/Research/Reports/2006/10/Importing-Poverty-Immigration-and-Poverty-in-the-United-States-A-Book-of-Charts (accessed January 25, 2011).

Reimers, David M. 1985. *Still the Golden Door: The Third World Comes to America*. New York: Columbia University Press.

Reinhard, Beth. 2011. "Immigration Policy Bedevils GOP with Hispanics." *National Journal*, January 15, 2011. Available at: http://nationaljournal.com/politics/immigration-policy-bedevils-gop-with-hispanics-20110115 (accessed January 15, 2011).

Riccardi, Nicholas. 2011. "Utah Bucks Conservative Trend on Immigration." *Los Angeles Times*, March 19, 2011. Available at: http://www.latimes.com/news/nationworld/nation/la-na-utah-immigration-20110320,0,5307414.story (accessed April 18, 2011).

Rozell, Mark J., and Clyde Wilcox. 1996. "Second Coming: The Strategies of the New Christian Right." *Political Science Quarterly* 111(2): 271–94.

Schildkraut, Deborah J. 2009. "Amnesty, Guest Workers, Fences! Oh My! Public Opinion about 'Comprehensive Immigration Reform.'" Paper presented at the 2009 meeting of the American Political Science Association. Toronto (September 3, 2009).

Schuck, Peter H. 1992. "The Politics of Raid Legal Change: Immigration Policy in the 1980s." *Studies in American Political Development* 6(1992): 37–92.

———. 2007. "The Disconnect between Public Attitudes and Policy Outcomes on

Immigration." In *Debating Immigration*, edited by Carol M. Swain. New York: Cambridge University Press.

Schumer, Charles E., and Lindsey O. Graham. 2010. "The Right Way to Mend Immigration." *Washington Post*, March 19, 2010. Available at: http://www .washingtonpost.com/wp-dyn/content/article/2010/03/17/AR201003 1703115.html (accessed March 19, 2010).

Schumer, Charles E., with Daniel Squadron. 2007. *Positively American: Winning Back the Middle-Class Majority One Family at a Time*. Emmaus, Pa.: Rodale Books.

Shapiro, Robert, and Lawrence R. Jacobs. 2011. *The Oxford Handbook of American Public Opinion and the Media*. Oxford: Oxford University Press.

Shear, Michael D. 2010. "Republican Immigration Position Likely to Alienate Latinos, Democrats Say." *Washington Post*, July 20, 2010. Available at: http://www .washingtonpost.com/wp-dyn/content/article/2010/07/19/AR20100719 05351.html (accessed July 21, 2010).

Shihadeh, Edward S., and Raymond E. Barranco. 2010a. "Latino Employment and Black Violence: The Unintended Consequence of U.S. Immigration Policy." *Social Forces* 88(3)(March): 1393–420.

———. 2010b. "Latino Employment and Non-Latino Homicide in Rural Areas: The Implications of U.S. Immigration Policy." *Deviant Behavior* 31(5): 411–39.

Simon, Rita James. 1985. *Public Opinion and the Immigrant: Print Media Coverage, 1880–1980*. Lanham, Md.: Lexington Books.

Singer, Audrey. 2008. "Twenty-First Century Gateways: An Introduction." In *Twenty-First Century Gateways: Immigrant Incorporation in Suburban America*, edited by Audrey Singer, Susan W. Hardwick, and Caroline B. Brettell. Washington, D.C.: Brookings Institution Press.

Sisco, Jessica, and Jonathan Hicken. 2009. "Is U.S. Border Enforcement Working?" In *Four Generations of Norteños: New Research from the Cradle of Mexican Migration*, edited by Wayne A. Cornelius, David FitzGerald, and Scott Borger. Boulder, Colo.: Lynne Rienner Publishers; La Jolla, Calif.: Center for Comparative Immigration Studies.

Skocpol, Theda. 1992. *Protecting Soldiers and Mothers: The Political Origins of Social Policy in the United States*. Cambridge, Mass.: Belknap Press of Harvard University Press.

Skrentny, John D. 2001. "Republican Efforts to End Affirmative Action: Walking a Fine Line." In *Seeking the Center: Politics and Policymaking at the New Century*, edited by Marc Landy, Martin Levin, and Martin Shapiro. Washington, D.C.: Georgetown University Press.

———. 2002. *The Minority Rights Revolution*. Cambridge, Mass.: Belknap Press of Harvard University Press.

———. 2006. "Policy-Elite Perceptions and Social Movement Success: Understanding Variations in Group Inclusion in Affirmative Action." *American Journal of Sociology* 111(6): 1762–815.

————. 2007. "Are America's Civil Rights Laws Still Relevant?" *Du Bois Review* 4(1): 119–40.

Smith, Lamar. 2010. "The GOP's Other Election Day Victory." *Washington Post*, November 27, 2010. Available at: http://www.washingtonpost.com/wp-dyn/content/article/2010/11/19/AR2010111905213.html?hpid=opinionsbox1 (accessed November 27, 2010).

Solis, Hilda, and Gary Locke. 2009. "American Stories: Hilda L. Solis, Secretary of Labor, and Gary Locke, Secretary of Commerce on Immigration." *Center for American Progress*, December 16, 2009. Available at: http://www.american progress.org/events/2009/12/americanstories.html (accessed March 28, 2010).

Steensland, Brian. 2008. *The Failed Welfare Revolution: America's Struggle over Guaranteed Income Policy*. Princeton, N.J.: Princeton University Press.

Stewart, Martha. 2010. "Republican Suggests Immigration Reform Can Wait." *CNN Political Ticker*, April 25, 2010. Available at: http://politicalticker.blogs.cnn.com/2010/04/25/republican-suggests-immigration-reform-can-wait/?fbid=VLKpe3i03d3m (accessed April 25, 2010).

Tichenor, Daniel. 2002. *Dividing Lines: The Politics of Immigration Control in America*. Princeton, N.J.: Princeton University Press.

————. 2009. "Navigating an American Minefield: The Politics of Illegal Immigration." *The Forum* 7(3): Article 1.

United Nations. 2009. "International Migration, 2009." Wallchart, publication no. E.09.XIII.8. Department of Economic and Social Affairs, Population Division. Available at: http://www.un.org/esa/population/publications/2009 Migration_Chart/ittmig_wallchart09_table.xls (accessed October 4, 2010).

U.S. Chamber of Commerce. 2010. "Press Release: U.S. Chamber and ACIP Release Study on Importance of High-Skilled Immigration to American Competitiveness." August 11. Available at: http://www.uschamber.com/press/releases/2010/august/us-chamber-and-acip-release-study-importance-high-skilled-immigration-ame (accessed September 30, 2010).

U.S. Commission on Immigration Reform. 1995. *Legal Immigration: Setting Priorities*. Washington: Government Printing Office.

U.S. Department of Homeland Security. 2009. "Press Release: Secretary Napolitano Announces New Agreement for State and Local Immigration Enforcement Partnerships & Adds 11 New Agreements." Available at: http://www.dhs.gov/ynews/releases/pr_1247246453625.shtm (accessed October 2, 2010).

————. 2010. "Press Release: Secretary Napolitano Announces Secure Communities Deployment to All Southwest Border Counties, Facilitating Identification and Removal of Convicted Criminal Aliens." Available at: http://www.dhs.gov/ynews/releases/pr_1281457837494.shtm (accessed October 2, 2010).

U.S. Department of Justice. 2010. "Citing Conflict with Federal Law, Department of Justice Challenges Arizona Immigration Law." Press release, July 6, 2010.

Available at: http://www.justice.gov/opa/pr/2010/July/10-opa-776.html (accessed January 30 2011).

Waldinger, Roger. 2008. "Will the Followers Be Led? Where Union Members Stand on Immigration." *New Labor Forum* 17(2): 42–52.

Waldinger, Roger, and Michael Lichter. 2003. *How the Other Half Works.* Berkeley: University of California Press.

Washington Post Votes Database. 2010. "110th Congress, 1st session, Senate vote 200." Available at: http://projects.washingtonpost.com/congress/110/senate/1/votes/200/ (accessed September 21, 2009).

Waters, Mary C., and Tomás R. Jiménez. 2005. "Assessing Immigrant Assimilation: New Empirical and Theoretical Challenges." *Annual Review of Sociology* 31: 105–25.

Waters, Mary C., and Reed Ueda. 2007. *The New Americans: A Guide to Immigration since 1965.* Cambridge, Mass.: Harvard University Press.

Wilcox, Clyde, and Lee Sigelman. 2001. "Political Mobilization in the Pews: Religious Contacting and Electoral Turnout." *Social Science Quarterly* 82(3): 524–35.

Wilson, James Q. 1980. "The Politics of Regulation." In *The Politics of Regulation,* edited by James Q. Wilson. New York: Basic Books.

Wong, Carolyn. 2006. *Lobbying for Inclusion: Rights Politics and the Making of Immigration Policy.* Stanford, Calif.: Stanford University Press.

Wong, Scott. 2010. "Pols Profit from Immigration Impasse." *Politico,* July 26, 2010. Available at: http://www.politico.com/news/stories/0710/40210.html (accessed July 26, 2010).

Wroe, Andrew. 2008. *The Republican Party and Immigration Politics: From Proposition 187 to George W. Bush.* New York: Palgrave Macmillan.

Zolberg, Aristide R. 2006. *A Nation by Design: Immigration Policy in the Fashioning of America.* New York: Russell Sage Foundation; Cambridge, Mass.: Harvard University Press.

Chapter 8 | Cold Front: How the Recession Stalled Obama's Clean-Energy Agenda

Judith A. Layzer

IN JANUARY 2009 President Obama took office promising to restore prosperity and reduce American dependence on foreign oil by converting the United States from a fossil-fuel to a clean-energy economy. In many respects, the country appeared ripe for such a transformation: Obama was extraordinarily popular; public support for addressing energy and climate change was strong; environmentalists were unified; industry was divided and many prominent CEOs advocated limits on greenhouse-gas emissions; and the conservative opposition was beleaguered. Initially, at least, events seem to bear out the predictions of optimistic pundits: following a frenzied push by Speaker of the House Nancy Pelosi, as well as by Obama and his top aides, in June 2009 a comprehensive energy and climate-change bill narrowly passed the House of Representatives. But hopes were dashed in the summer of 2010, when a companion bill foundered in the Senate, derailed by the prolonged recession, as well as an extended and rancorous debate over health care and a resurgent conservative movement.

The president has not relied exclusively on legislation to achieve his goals, however; like his predecessors, he has employed an aggressive administrative strategy in pursuing his energy and environmental policy objectives. The White House used the stimulus package and a series of executive orders to transform the primary mission of the Department of Energy (DOE) from managing the cleanup of nuclear weapons sites to promoting energy efficiency and renewable fuels. More important, Obama's Environmental Protection Agency (EPA) has taken a series of steps toward curbing greenhouse-gas emissions under the Clean Air Act. These administrative actions may turn out to be the president's most effective weapon for getting a recalcitrant Congress to create a carbon-pricing structure—if only to avoid a more complex regulatory scheme.

This chapter tells the story of Obama's foray into the realm of energy and climate change. It begins by sketching out the policy and political context in which the administration sought to tackle the nation's overreliance on fossil fuels. (For a timeline, see appendix table 8A.1.)

CLIMATE-CHANGE CONUNDRUM

In the 1970s and 1980s meteorologists and atmospheric scientists around the world began to converge on the hypothesis that burning fossil fuels and extensive deforestation were raising the temperature of the earth's lower atmosphere, with potentially catastrophic consequences.[1] They implored the nations of the world to take action to prevent global warming and other impacts of climate change.[2] Although effective in Europe, scientists' increasingly urgent warnings generated little response in the United States until 1988, when National Aeronautics and Space Administration (NASA) physicist Jim Hansen testified before a Senate committee that human-induced global warming was imminent and that policymakers should take immediate measures to reduce emissions of greenhouse gases. Shortly after Hansen's speech, the United Nations' Environment Program and World Meteorological Organization jointly sponsored the creation of the Intergovernmental Panel on Climate Change (IPCC) to provide policymakers worldwide with a scientific foundation for international negotiations. In 1989, the United Nations (UN) called on its members to prepare a treaty spelling out steps they would take to address global climate change.

The prospect of an international treaty prompted a rapid and intense mobilization by members of the U.S. fossil-fuel industry and their allies in the conservative movement. Drawing on a storyline conservatives had been propagating for decades, this antiregulatory coalition claimed that extremist environmentalists, with the support of activist scientists, were exaggerating both the extent of humans' contribution to climate change and the hazards it posed, manipulating uncertain science to advance their primary agenda: control of the economy (Layzer, forthcoming). The real threat, they argued, was not global warming but government regulation of greenhouse-gas emissions, which would raise prices for consumers, send jobs overseas, and cripple the U.S. economy. To substantiate their arguments, antiregulatory activists challenged the science that supported global-warming claims: even as the scientific consensus grew that human activities were a primary cause of rising global temperatures and that the consequences of climate change—rising sea levels, more severe weather events, and widespread species extinctions—were likely to be serious, they continued to disparage the work of the IPCC and instead relied on the scientific claims made by a handful of climate contrarians. At the same time, they touted industry-sponsored studies suggesting the economic consequences of greenhouse-gas limits would be devastating, particularly if developing nations did not face similar constraints.

Such arguments resonated with conservatives in the George H. W. Bush administration, who persuaded the president not to promote domestic climate-change policies and obstructed international efforts to include specific timetables or goals in the emerging global climate convention. On the other hand, President Bush did sign—and Congress ratified—the 1992 Framework Convention on Climate Change, which established the goal of "stabiliz[ing] greenhouse-gas concentrations in the atmosphere at a level that would prevent dangerous anthropogenic [human] interference with the climate system." Moreover, the Bush administration allocated funds for climate-change research—thereby helping to build the scientific underpinnings that would eventually support arguments in favor of curbing emissions.

President Clinton took office in 1993 having vowed to reduce the nation's greenhouse-gas emissions, but he quickly retreated in the face of energetic opposition from antiregulatory activists and their allies in Congress. The most telling episode occurred when, at the behest of Vice President Al Gore, Clinton proposed a tax based on the heat content of energy, as measured in British thermal units (Btus), which he justified as a way to reduce the deficit. The Btu-tax proposal triggered a whirlwind of opposition from industry-financed groups that managed to derail it in the Senate.[3] Four years later, after another furious round of negative lobbying in anticipation of a meeting in July 1997 in Kyoto, Japan, the Senate resolved unanimously not to approve any treaty that failed to limit the emissions of developing countries or would impose serious harm on the U.S. economy.[4]

Stung, Clinton signed the Kyoto Protocol, which committed the United States to reducing its greenhouse-gas emissions by 7 percent below 1990 levels by 2012, but declined to submit it to the Senate for ratification. Furthermore, recollecting the defeat of the Btu tax, Clinton opted not to suggest a mandatory domestic emission-reduction plan for greenhouse gases. Instead, he proposed a $6.3 billion program of grants and incentives aimed at spurring the development of new energy-saving and alternative-energy technologies. Not surprisingly, although the carbon intensity of the rapidly growing U.S. economy fell, overall emissions continued to rise, increasing more than 10 percent between 1993 and the end of the Clinton administration in early 2001 (Energy Information Administration 2003a).

Like Clinton, as a presidential candidate George W. Bush pledged to limit U.S. greenhouse-gas emissions. Under pressure from his conservative allies, however, he reversed himself within months of taking office and subsequently shocked world leaders by pulling out of the Kyoto process altogether. The Bush EPA also firmly rejected a petition by states and environmental groups to regulate carbon dioxide, by far the most abundant greenhouse gas, under the Clean Air Act. As a sop to proponents of climate-change policy, in 2002 his administration instituted a program in which companies could voluntarily register their emissions and pledge to make reductions; it also created a package of incentives for the development of new technology. The goal of these initiatives was even more modest than Clinton's had been: to cut the nation's energy intensity by 18 percent by 2020—a target the United States was already on track to meet, and one that would put emissions at 30 percent above 1990 levels by 2020 (Eilperin 2008). Even as it took marginal steps to limit emissions, the Bush administration dramatically expanded access to domestic coal, oil, and gas reserves.

With the White House staunchly opposed and conservative Republicans in control of both the House and the Senate, efforts to address climate change legislatively made little headway during Bush's tenure. Senators John McCain (R-AZ) and Joseph Lieberman (D-CT) twice succeeded in bringing to the floor their Climate Stewardship Act, which would have rolled back greenhouse-gas emissions from three major economic sectors to 2000 levels by 2010 (for a list of major energy and climate-change legislation, see appendix table 8A.2). To do so, it relied on a market-based mechanism known as cap-and-trade, in which a limit that declines over time is placed on emissions, and polluters purchase or are given allowances that they can either use to cover their own emissions or sell to others. The idea is that those who can reduce their emissions at lowest cost will do so, and those for whom reductions are expensive can buy allowances; in this way, the overall cap is met most efficiently.

Its innovative policy mechanism notwithstanding, the Climate Stewardship Act failed both times, by substantial margins: in October 2003 the Senate rejected McCain-Lieberman by a vote of 55 to 43, with ten Democrats joining forty-five Republicans in opposition, and six Republicans joining thirty-six Democrats (and one Independent) in support; the second vote, in 2005, was an even more lopsided 60 to 38. Immediately after the 2005 vote, however, the Senate approved (53 to 44) a resolution officially acknowledging that greenhouse gases are contributing to global warming and urging Congress to "enact a comprehensive and effective national program of mandatory, market-based limits on emissions of greenhouse gases that slow, stop and reverse the growth of such emissions," albeit "in a manner that . . . will not significantly harm the United States economy."

The Senate resolution, though purely symbolic, reflected the changing political dynamics of climate change. For one thing, public opinion was shifting in favor of taking action. A *Time*/ABC/Stanford University poll taken in March 2006 found that 85 percent of respondents believed global warming was occurring, and 88 percent thought it threatened future generations (Greenwire 2006). A Gallup poll released a month later detected a marked rebound in concern about global warming between 2004 and 2006, reversing a decline that had begun in 2000: 36 percent of respondents said they worried "a great deal" about global warming, up from 26 percent in 2004 (Morello 2006). Other aspects of the political context were also becoming more hospitable to mandatory emission-reduction measures. The business community was increasingly fractured, and a handful of prominent CEOs had begun lobbying for greenhouse-gas emission limits. Demonstrating their seriousness, in 2004 some of the nation's largest companies had joined the newly created Chicago Climate Exchange, thereby making a binding commitment to reduce their greenhouse-gas emissions by 4 percent below the average of their 1998 to 2001 baseline by 2006. Some members of the evangelical community were advocating climate-change regulations as well, creating the potential for a schism within the Republican coalition.

At the same time, several of the country's biggest environmental groups were elevating climate change to the top of their agendas. The environmental movement is heterogeneous, and historically even the large, Beltway-based groups have pursued different legislative priorities. But in the mid-2000s, prodded by the urgency of scientific warnings, groups like the Environmental Defense Fund (EDF) and the Natural Resources Defense Council (NRDC) created climate-change offices and began redirecting personnel and resources to lobbying on the issue. Environmentalists also teamed up with members of the business community: in the summer of 2006, an alliance of ten Fortune 500 corporations and four Washington, D.C.–based environmental groups, including EDF and NRDC, began meeting behind closed doors to flesh out the elements of a climate-change bill they could all agree on. Calling themselves the U.S. Climate Action Partnership (USCAP), in early 2007 they issued a Call for Action on climate change.

Environmentalists made common cause with labor unions as well. In 2006, the Sierra Club and NRDC teamed up with the Steelworkers Union to form the Blue-Green Alliance; several mainstream environmental groups joined the Apollo Alliance, a coalition of labor, business, environmental, and community leaders whose aim was to advance a transition to a clean-energy economy. The National Wildlife Federation and other wildlife-conservation organizations forged relationships with blue-collar sportsmen's groups worried about the impact of climate change on sensitive habitats. And former Vice President Al Gore, who had rebounded from his defeat in 2000 to make the documentary *An Inconvenient Truth*, created the Alliance for Climate Protection, whose purpose was to deploy marketing techniques on behalf of the planet. In hopes of spurring concrete actions, Gore's We Can Solve It campaign focused not just on the magnitude and urgency of climate change but also on the tools available to address it.

A critical turning point for proponents of climate-change policy came in the spring of 2007, when the Supreme Court rejected the Bush administration's decision not to regulate emissions of carbon dioxide. In Massachusetts v. EPA the court ruled (5 to 4) that under the Clean Air Act, the EPA was not only authorized but obligated to determine whether carbon dioxide "may reasonably be anticipated to endanger public health or welfare." If the EPA did find that carbon dioxide posed a threat, the court added, the agency had a duty to regulate emissions of it.

Although environmentalists were elated by the Supreme Court decision, they were in for a rude awakening when, in June 2008, a third major legislative effort to limit greenhouse-gas emissions using cap-and-trade failed on a procedural vote in the Democrat-controlled Senate. A respectable forty-eight senators voted to break a Republican filibuster on what was known as the Lieberman-Warner bill, but nine Democrats who had voted yes promptly published a letter explaining why, although they opposed the filibuster, they did not support the legislation (Pooley 2010). In doing so, they sent an ominous signal about the challenges facing climate-change measures in the Senate: even when Democrats were in the majority, regional economic concerns superseded partisan loyalty.

The same regional divisions had impeded legislation to address acid rain during the 1980s, and it was a cap-and-trade system that had broken the logjam in the Senate. But there was a crucial difference: it was possible to reduce sulfur dioxide emissions relatively easily and cheaply by switching to low-sulfur fuel. By contrast, reducing carbon emissions promised to be more costly.[5] Those costs would also be distributed unevenly. Whereas the more populous states on the East Coast and the West Coast get much of their electricity from relatively clean energy sources—such as natural gas, nuclear, and hydropower—those in the Midwest, Great Plains, and Southeast rely heavily on coal-fired power plants. They also host the nation's coal mines, oil refineries, and manufacturing concerns. With so much to lose, senators from states whose economies depend on fossil fuel were hard-pressed to support a bill that would impose a price on carbon, whatever their party affiliations.

PRESIDENT OBAMA STAKES OUT
HIS POSITION

Although well aware of the political challenges, most environmentalists were hopeful that the election of Barack Obama, combined with Democratic majorities in the House and Senate, would enable the country to tackle climate change, both domestically and internationally. During the 2008 presidential campaign, candidate Obama had vowed to transform the United States into a clean-energy economy. The primary mechanism for accomplishing this goal, he argued, should be a cap-and-trade system for carbon-dioxide emissions. Obama made a host of other energy-related commitments as well: he pledged to double the fuel-economy standard for cars and trucks; boost to 25 percent the proportion of electricity Americans derive from renewable sources, including solar, wind, and geothermal; and spend $15 billion each year on the development of green technologies, such as biofuels, plug-in hybrids, and an advanced electricity-transmission grid.

At the same time, Obama was careful not to vilify conventional fuels. He cautiously supported nuclear power, as long as the waste could be disposed of safely. He also adopted the industry-favored term *clean coal* to demonstrate his support for the development of carbon capture and sequestration (CCS) technology. And in August 2008 he shifted from supporting a moratorium on new offshore oil and natural-gas development to accepting more offshore exploration if it was part of a broader energy package aimed at reducing dependence on foreign oil. This evolution was an early indication of Obama's willingness to make concessions proactively, in hopes of demonstrating reasonableness and flexibility.

On taking office, Obama made tackling climate change one of his top legislative priorities, along with economic stimulus and health care and financial regulatory reform. On the advice of pollsters, who noted that Americans were preoccupied with the country's economic woes, Obama characterized limiting carbon-dioxide emissions as a path to energy security and a revitalized economy. He focused on the jobs that would come out of renewable-energy generation, and typically mentioned averting climate change last in a string of benefits. For example, in his first major speech as president, Obama asserted that the country's economic recovery would start with energy. "To truly transform our economy, protect our security, and save the planet from the ravages of climate change," he said, "we need to ultimately make clean, renewable energy the profitable kind of energy. So I ask Congress to send me legislation that places a market-based cap on carbon pollution."

To help advance his energy and environmental agenda, Obama appointed a clutch of administrators who presented a stark contrast to the business-oriented Bush administration personnel.[6] He recruited Carol Browner, former EPA administrator under President Clinton, to coordinate the administration's climate-change initiatives as head of the newly formed White House Office of Energy and Climate Change Policy. To serve as EPA administrator, Obama named Lisa Jackson, former commissioner of the Department of Environmental Protection for the State of New Jersey and, before that, a sixteen-year EPA veteran. For energy secretary, he nominated Steven Chu, a Nobel Prize–winning physicist and outspoken advocate of reducing greenhouse-gas emissions. To head the Office of Science and Technology Policy, Obama chose John Holdren, a physicist and professor at Harvard's Kennedy School of Government and a longtime proponent of climate-change regulation. Finally, he selected a moderate Colorado senator, Ken Salazar, to head the Interior Department, where he would manage domestic fossil-fuel development and alternative-energy siting.

Just as Obama's appointees revealed a strong predilection for weaning the country off carbon-based fuels, so did his $3.55 trillion fiscal year 2010 budget, released in early February 2009. The budget assumed the enactment of a cap-and-trade system that would reduce greenhouse-gas emissions 14 percent below 2005 levels by 2020, and 83 percent by 2050. The new policy was forecast to raise $80 billion per year starting in 2012, based on a 100 percent auction of carbon-emission allowances, assuming a starting price of $20 per ton. To ensure that the new policy did not disproportionately harm the nation's poor and working class, of the $645 billion raised between 2012 and 2019, about $525 billion would be returned to "the people, especially vulnerable families, communities and businesses, to help the transition to a clean energy economy" through a refundable tax credit (known as Making Work Pay) of up to $400 for working individuals and $800 for working families. The rest, about $120 billion, would help pay for the development of low-carbon technologies.

Significantly, the budget also eliminated subsidies for fossil fuels, calling for new fees and taxes on oil companies that drill on federal land and for eliminating various tax credits—a step that would raise about $30 billion over a decade. Moreover, it included a 38 percent increase in the EPA's budget, from $7.6 billion to $10.5 billion, including $19 million to establish a greenhouse-gas inventory, and additional funding for greenhouse-gas regulation. In his budget message to Congress, Obama said, "If we lead the world in the research and development of clean-energy technology, we can create a whole new industry with high-paying jobs that cannot be shipped overseas" (Office of Management and Budget 2009, 21).

CONGRESS STRUGGLES WITH COMPREHENSIVE ENERGY AND CLIMATE-CHANGE LEGISLATION

Notwithstanding the president's apparent commitment and the auspicious political context, comprehensive energy and climate-change legislation faced long odds from the outset. It soon became clear that the issue was not Obama's top legislative priority. According to journalist Jonathan Alter (2010), Carol Browner had argued during the transition that climate change should come first, and senior White House advisor David Axelrod pointed early on to polls suggesting the public also favored moving forward on energy first because doing so might create jobs. Obama himself had stated during the campaign that energy was his top priority (Lizza 2010). But, once in office, the president—ignoring the trepidation of his advisors—was determined to pursue health care reform. There were other challenges as well. As earlier Senate votes had made clear, regional divisions on energy and climate change were at least as important as ideological ones, so having Democratic majorities in both the House and Senate did not guarantee legislative success.

Given these obstacles, drafters sought to assemble a set of provisions that would placate the conventional fuel industries and their allies without alienating environmentalists by completely gutting the bill's emission-curbing capabilities. To facilitate bargaining, legislative leaders once again began with a cap-and-trade mechanism. The preeminent issue in designing a trading system was the allocation of allowances, which could be used to soften the economic impact of a declining cap. Utilities, which are responsible for one-third of U.S. greenhouse-gas emissions, argued that they should get a sizable fraction of the allowances for nothing, so that they could insulate their customers from price increases. If allowances were distributed through an auction, they said, they would have to pay twice: once for the allowances and once to cut their emissions. By contrast, if they were given free allowances, they could avoid passing on the cost increases to their customers. Many environmentalists were aghast at the idea of dispensing free allowances; they argued that a strong price signal was essential to changing consumer behavior. But pragmatists like Fred Krupp of EDF insisted that not only were electricity rate increases a political nonstarter, they were unnecessary. What mattered, he said, was the overall cap on emissions (Pooley 2010).

A second issue was the impact of carbon regulation on energy-intensive industries. In addition to demanding free allowances that would keep their costs down, manufacturing industries wanted a "border adjustment mechanism" to insulate them from competition from countries without strong climate policies. Critics suggested that the World Trade Organization (WTO) would strike down such tariffs, but proponents pointed out that the WTO historically has allowed border measures that insulate countries from some competitive pressures, as long as those measures aim to conserve scarce resources or protect public health.[7]

A third issue was whether and how to incorporate offsets, mechanisms by which polluters can pay to sequester carbon dioxide—through reforestation, no-till farming, or other land-use practices—rather than reducing their own emissions. Offsets were particularly important to farm-state members and the agriculture lobby because they provide rural landowners with an additional source of revenue. Polluters also favored them because buying offsets is often simpler and cheaper than making process or equipment changes. Among environmentalists, however, offsets were controversial because they may reward landowners for practices they would have engaged in anyway, and because it is difficult to measure the carbon reductions attributable to a particular land-use practice. Critics also pointed out that offsets allow polluters to avoid curbing their own emissions and, because validation is so difficult, are ripe for abuse.

A fourth issue—and one that concerned not just industry but many economists as well—was the potential volatility of the carbon price. Three remedies for this were possible: a price collar establishing both a floor and a ceiling for prices; a safety valve releasing permits once the price hits a certain level; or a strategic reserve of excess allowances to be unleashed in the event of a sudden price increase. Environmentalists favored a strategic reserve because, whereas the price-collar and safety-valve mechanisms would weaken the cap, the strategic reserve could be taken from future allowances and so, in theory, need not violate it. Some worried, however, that drawing on a strategic reserve could undermine early emission-reduction targets.

The fifth major issue was whether the states or the EPA would be allowed to impose additional greenhouse-gas regulations once a federal cap-and-trade system was in place. Not surprisingly, industry interests across the board favored preempting both the EPA and the states because they wanted to have regulatory certainty at the federal level and avoid a patchwork of state regulations. Most environmentalists vehemently opposed preemption. Joining them were state regulators, who decried the notion of limiting states' prerogatives. The northeastern states were particularly adamant because in 2008 they had begun operating their own cap-and-trade system for utilities, and it was bringing in substantial revenue.

Beyond adding industry-friendly attributes to a cap-and-trade mechanism, legislators had several other ways of attracting the support of reluctant industry interests and their allies in Congress. The most important of these were measures to encourage offshore oil drilling, particularly revenue-sharing provisions for coastal states; loan guarantees and other inducements for the construction of nuclear-power plants; and generous subsidies for developing and installing carbon capture and sequestration technology.

Although such concessions were necessary to garner industry support, it was also essential to retain the support of environmentalists and their allies in Congress, who feared that offsets, free allowances, and other industry-friendly provisions would weaken the incentive to curb emissions. To appease environmentalists, bill writers had at their disposal a host of regulatory measures, such as a renewable electricity standard (RES), which mandates that a certain percentage of the nation's electricity must come from renewable fuels. An RES would ensure that utilities did not just rely on nuclear energy and natural gas to meet emission-reduction requirements. Other features that could be added were energy-efficiency standards for cars, trucks, buildings, appliances, and industry operations; subsidies for developing and installing alternative energy; and programs for updating the electricity-transmission grid to make it better able to incorporate renewable-energy sources.

In hopes of generating momentum for legislation in the 111th Congress, USCAP—which by January 2009 included thirty-one major corporations and five prominent environmental groups—developed a blueprint that could serve as a starting point for negotiations (USCAP 2009). Not all environmentalists were on board with the resulting approach, which endorsed emissions cuts of between 15 percent and 25 percent by 2020 and a large allocation of allowances to utilities. The National Wildlife Federation dropped out of USCAP to press for tougher targets; others, including Greenpeace and Friends of the Earth, derided the group's efforts as greenwashing. Nor were all of the country's top executives enamored of USCAP's scheme; for instance, the American Coalition for Clean Coal Electricity (ACCCE), a coal-industry group, disparaged the deal. Nevertheless, the USCAP bargain served as important evidence that there was a way forward that both industry and environmentalists could support.

For his part, Obama declined to offer Congress a White House blueprint. Instead, as he had opted to do with the stimulus and health care reform, he continued to talk publicly about the clean-energy economy and the importance of putting a price on carbon, letting legislative leaders broker the details. For example, although his budget conveyed his preference for a cap-and-trade system, Obama made clear early on that he was flexible on both the overall targets and the method of allocating allowances.

Carol Browner and other cabinet officials pressed for more specifics, but Chief of Staff Rahm Emanuel resisted, determined to husband the president's political capital and deploy it—to the extent possible—in service of legislative victories. Similarly, behind the scenes, Al Gore did everything he could to persuade the president and his political operatives that addressing climate change could be a win (Pooley 2010). But rather than going out on a limb for a controversial climate-change bill, the president opted to keep his distance until a bill stood a serious chance of passing, and then come in as a closer to clinch the deal.

The House Gets It Done

Encouraged by the apparent opportunity for long-deferred action on an issue he cared deeply about, Henry Waxman (D-CA), chair of the House Energy and Commerce Committee, declared that he would take up energy and climate change, regardless of the president's desire to move health care first (Alter 2010). On March 31, 2009, Democratic leaders of the House Energy and Commerce Committee unveiled a 648-page draft energy and climate-change bill, the American Clean Energy and Security Act of 2009 (HR 2454). Sponsored by Waxman and Ed Markey (D-MA), the bill established a cap-and-trade program for reducing carbon-dioxide emissions 20 percent below 2005 levels by 2020—a more ambitious near-term target than the president's—and 83 percent by 2050. To facilitate negotiations, Waxman-Markey left open the question of how emission allowances would be allocated. To hold down the cost of the program, the bill set up a strategic reserve of about 2.5 billion carbon allowances. To satisfy environmentalists, it included an RES that would reach 25 percent by 2025, as well as a variety of other regulatory measures.

Backers of Waxman-Markey echoed Obama's rhetoric in emphasizing the bill's threefold purpose. According to Waxman, "This legislation will create millions of clean energy jobs, put America on the path to energy independence, and cut global warming pollution. Our goal is to strengthen our economy by making America the world leader in new clean energy and energy efficiency technologies" (quoted in Samuelsohn and Geman 2009). House Republican leaders were not persuaded, however, and immediately denounced the bill. In an effort to intimidate Democrats likely to face tough reelection challenges in 2010, they pointed to polls showing declining public support for action on global warming, and charged that Democrats were insensitive to the plight of working people in the midst of a deep economic recession. They alleged that a cap-and-trade system (or, as they labeled it, cap-and-tax) would cause energy prices to skyrocket—although analyses by the Congressional Budget Office, the EPA, and the

Energy Information Agency all concluded that the costs to the average American household would be modest.[8]

In the face of Republican criticism, administration officials emphasized the bill's ostensible economic benefits. For example, in testimony before the House Energy and Commerce Committee in April, EPA administrator Lisa Jackson ventured: "I do believe this is a jobs bill. It is a bill that focuses on the growth of industries of the future. There are opportunities for us to create millions of jobs in the green energy industry." In an effort to rebut Republican claims, Jackson said, "Now, the 'No, we can't' crowd will spin out doomsday scenarios about runaway costs. I do not claim we can get something for nothing. But EPA's available economic modeling indicates that the investment Americans would make to implement the cap-and-trade program of the American Clean Energy and Security Act would be very modest compared to the benefits that science and plain common sense tell us a comprehensive energy and climate policy will deliver" (quoted in Samuelsohn 2009a). Waxman concurred, saying, "Some have said that true energy reform will undermine economic growth. They argue that there is a fundamental conflict between economic growth and clean energy. That is a false choice. Our economic future and clean energy are inextricably intertwined" (quoted in Samuelsohn 2009a).

Efforts to portray Waxman-Markey as economically benign were not directed solely at Republicans: although they held a thirty-six to twenty-three advantage in the Energy and Commerce Committee, the Democrats on the panel represented a diversity of regional economic interests. Negotiations aimed at winning over midwestern Democrats spanned much of the spring of 2009, with discussions focused primarily on the question of how emission allowances would be allocated. On this issue, a broad range of energy and utility groups lobbied furiously, spending record-breaking sums.[9] The White House sought to facilitate a legislative bargain by signaling its willingness to compromise on auctioning off emission allowances, as long as the larger goals of a clean-energy economy, job creation, and cutting oil imports were met. In early May the president convened a White House meeting with the Democrats on Waxman's committee at which he reiterated the urgency of addressing climate change before the Copenhagen meeting in December, where diplomats from around the world would hammer out a successor to the Kyoto Protocol.

To get the bill through committee, Waxman ultimately made concessions on three issues critical to the fossil-fuel-dependent industries and their legislative allies: the initial emission-reduction target was trimmed from 20 percent to 17 percent by 2020; the renewable electricity standard was cut from 25 percent by 2025 to 20 percent, of which utilities could meet 5 percent through energy-efficiency measures; and local-distribution utilities got 35 percent of total credits (Snyder 2009b). After a thirty-seven-hour markup and ninety-six amendments, Waxman succeeded in getting his committee to approve HR 2454 by a vote of 33 to 25 just before Congress adjourned for its Memorial Day recess.

When the House reconvened in June, Speaker Pelosi—for whom passing a climate-change bill was a legacy issue—took charge of preparing for a vote by the full chamber, bringing recalcitrant committee chairs into line and establishing a strict legislative calendar. Alarmed by the realization that Waxman-Markey was gathering steam, Republican opponents fanned out across the country holding rallies disparaging cap-and-trade. Centrists in the New Democrat Coalition, who feared that trying to address climate change in the middle of a recession was a losing proposition, urged Pelosi to focus on health care, without success; she not only rejected their suggestion, she rounded up votes relentlessly in the final weeks before the scheduled vote on Waxman-Markey. "It's the most extraordinary whip effort I've ever seen," said one veteran Democratic staffer (quoted in Allen 2009a).

Enhancing the bill's prospects, after two months in which the White House had focused almost exclusively on health care, high-level administration officials jumped into the fray during the week before the Waxman-Markey vote. Browner set up meetings with wavering lawmakers, as did Axelrod. Emanuel lobbied freshman Democrats in a session at the White House. In the final hours, both Emanuel and Obama called uncommitted members and tried to convince them that worries about rising utility rates were unfounded (Allen 2009a). In a short but widely publicized speech from the Rose Garden the day before the scheduled vote, the president reminded voters that Waxman-Markey was "a jobs bill" (quoted in Davenport 2009). At a White House luau that night, he interrogated members about their votes. And the following day he made another round of telephone calls during the debate leading up to the vote. Browner and Treasury Secretary Summers also made calls in which they explained the bill's benefits to individual members and brokered a final set of concessions.

Finally, on the evening of June 26, 2009, the House passed the American Clean Energy and Security Act by 219 to 212, with forty-four Democrats voting against the bill and eight Republicans voting for it. The vote marked the first time either chamber had passed a bill to address climate change. What's more, according to a Waxman aide, "It would not have passed without the White House" (quoted in Pooley 2010, 396).

Round One in the Senate

With the narrow passage of Waxman-Markey, attention shifted to the Senate, where comprehensive energy and climate-change legislation faced an even more uphill battle. Although by early July, after the swearing in of Al Franken in Minnesota, Democrats had a sixty-vote majority, not only were regional battle lines more sharply drawn in the Senate than in the House, but most of the eight newly elected Democratic senators were from relatively conservative states. Exacerbating the challenge, the fiscal year 2010 budget agreement included an amendment saying that Congress should not use the reconciliation process for cap-and-trade legislation, so the strategy ultimately used to pass health care reform with a simple majority was not a viable option for climate change.[10]

Making matters even more complicated, the Senate had opted to focus on health care as its main order of business, in accordance with White House wishes, and as it turned out the Senate health care debate was far more acrimonious and time-consuming than anyone had anticipated. Exploiting the extra time and capitalizing on the vitriol churned up by the anti–health care campaign, industry-funded antiregulatory groups ramped up their efforts to denounce the administration's efforts to impose a "nationwide energy tax." The recession, which showed no signs of abating, gave a boost to claims that pricing carbon would be an economic disaster and dampen public enthusiasm for aggressive action. Senators were clearly mindful of the preeminence of the economy for voters; the same day Waxman-Markey was released, the Senate passed a resolution 89 to 8 that any climate bill must achieve its goals "without increasing gasoline or energy prices"—a near impossibility (quoted in Pooley 2010, 349).

Despite these ominous signs, Senator Barbara Boxer (D-CA) was anxious to move the ball on climate change, and she announced that the Environment and Public Works Committee would begin holding hearings on climate change in early July. Hewing to the administration's formulation, Boxer said a cap-and-trade bill would "reduce our dependence on foreign oil, create millions of clean-energy jobs, and protect our children from pollution" (quoted in Snyder 2009d). Waxman made it clear that he was open to changes that the Senate needed to make to pass a companion bill; at this point, both he and Speaker Pelosi still held out hope of getting legislation signed by the president before the Copenhagen meeting (Allen 2009b). After the hard-fought battle in the House, Emanuel had doubts about the viability of an economy-wide cap-and-trade bill, and was already opening the door to a less ambitious approach (Pooley 2010). Nevertheless, Axelrod and other White House aides began meeting with Senate Democrats to hash out a legislative strategy.

Meanwhile, the opposition stepped up its efforts to mobilize the public. The U.S. Chamber of Commerce announced that it would launch a $100 million "campaign for free enterprise," whose aim was to "defend and advance America's free-enterprise values" in the face of the Obama administration's efforts to expand the size and scope of the federal government. Throughout the summer of 2009, the American Coalition for Clean Coal Electricity sent workers to 264 cities to attend state fairs and Kiwanis meetings, and set up tables at college campuses. The ACCCE also bought television ads featuring "real people" talking about the importance of coal as a source of low-cost electricity in their lives. The American Petroleum Institute funded what were called Energy Citizen rallies across the country in August and September in hopes of provoking phone calls, emails, and letters to lawmakers demanding that they oppose climate legislation. And Americans for Prosperity, backed by the Koch brothers, the oil magnates who had been prime movers behind the defeat of Clinton's Btu tax (Mayer 2010), held dozens of events targeting cap-and-trade legislation.

On the other hand, an unusually broad environmental coalition aggressively promoted the Senate effort. In addition to the usual suspects, there were newcomers to the climate issue; for example, the World Wildlife Federation, recognizing that climate change was one of the biggest threats to biodiversity, spent an unprecedented $2.2 million between March 2009 and March 2010 (Mulkern 2010). Clean Energy Works, a recently formed alliance of more than eighty labor, veterans, religious, and other groups, worked assiduously to demonstrate the diversity of support for comprehensive energy and climate-change legislation. Other backers weighed in as well: in early August a group of thirty-two former senators, cabinet officials, and other U.S. political leaders released a statement urging action on global warming and asking for a "clear, comprehensive, realistic and broadly bipartisan plan to address our role in the climate change crisis" (quoted in Samuelsohn 2009b). Also actively supporting cap-and-trade legislation were several business-environmentalist alliances, including USCAP; the Business for Innovative Climate and Energy Policy Coalition (BICEP), organized by Ceres, a network of investors focused on sustainability; and We Can Lead, a business coalition whose members included Exelon, Pacific Gas and Electric, and the Constellation Energy Group. The financial industry supported cap-and-trade as well but maintained a low profile in its lobbying, recognizing that its advocacy might not help the cause.

After a summer of passionately waged battles by interest groups to shape the legislative context, in late September Boxer and John Kerry (D-MA) released a first draft of their comprehensive energy and climate legislation (S 1733). President Obama praised the draft, which he said moved the country "one step closer to putting America in control of our energy future and making America more energy-independent. My administration," he added, "is deeply committed to passing a bill that creates new American jobs and the clean-energy incentives that foster innovation" (quoted in Snyder and Rushing 2009). In an effort to bolster the Senate negotiations, Obama again called on Congress to pass climate-change legislation to rehabilitate the economy. In a visit to MIT on October 22, he called out the bill's detractors, saying, "There are those who will suggest that moving toward clean energy will destroy our economy when it's the system we currently have that endangers our prosperity and prevents us from creating millions of new jobs" (quoted in Williamson 2009).

For proponents of policy change, however, Obama's speeches were not nearly enough; as the Copenhagen meeting drew near, allies both domestic and international urged Obama to throw more of his weight behind climate-change legislation (Eilperin and Shear 2009). The White House responded by pointing out that administration officials had met on energy and climate change with more than half of the senators, and had held more than fifty energy-related events in twenty-four states. Aides also noted that White House officials had reached out to hundreds of energy stakeholders and local lawmakers. They stressed that their aim in these engagements was to promote the need for a bill and to leave the details of fashioning legislation to Congress.

Despite the president's rhetorical efforts, climate-change legislation was clearly losing momentum during the fall of 2009, as health care continued to dominate the legislative agenda. Hoping to revitalize the issue, on October 23 Boxer kicked off three days of hearings with a 923-page chairman's mark of the Kerry-Boxer bill. In her usual uncompromising fashion, Boxer pressed for a vote over the protestations of her colleagues, and on November 5, after two days of markup, the Environment and Public Works Committee passed S 1733 by a vote of 11 to 1, without any Republicans present. Recognizing that Boxer's approach had alienated prospective Republican allies, the full Senate declined to take up the bill before the end of the 2009 legislative session, and U.S. negotiators were forced to go to the Copenhagen meeting in early December empty-handed.

Round Two in the Senate

Sure enough, in the absence of a strong positive signal from the U.S. Congress, the Copenhagen negotiations yielded little of substance. The president injected himself into the discussions on the summit's final day and managed to broker the Copenhagen Accord, a nonbinding agreement drafted in a meeting between the United States, China, Brazil, South Africa, and India. The accord pledged the United States and other developed countries to submit economy-wide emission targets by January 31, 2010. But the U.S. commitment was contingent on Congress passing legislation—an event that appeared increasingly unlikely.

With the disappointing results of Copenhagen fresh in everyone's minds, when the energy and climate-change debate resumed in January 2010, all eyes were on John Kerry, South Carolina Republican Lindsey Graham, and Connecticut Independent Joe Lieberman, who were trying to assemble a legislative package that could garner sixty votes in the Senate. Putting together a winning coalition would entail a delicate balancing act: as of early 2010 there appeared to be forty-one yes or probably yes votes, twenty-nine no or probably no votes, and thirty fence-sitters, of whom nineteen were Democrats and eleven were Republicans (Samuelsohn 2010a). Fortunately, some undecided senators seemed to have become more receptive to a comprehensive bill. Once staunch opponents, West Virginia Democrats Robert Byrd and Jay Rockefeller were meeting with Kerry, Graham, and Lieberman in hopes of ensuring the bill would protect the coal industry; similarly, Carl Levin and Debbie Stabenow, two Rust Belt senators from Michigan who previously had been reluctant to accept climate-change restrictions, were also engaged in the negotiations, as was Blanche Lincoln of Arkansas (Davenport 2010a).

The prospects for recruiting nineteen yes votes deteriorated, however, with the unexpected ascension of Republican Scott Brown of Massachusetts to Ted Kennedy's seat on January 20. Kerry, Graham, and Lieberman faced additional complications as well. Senators Maria Cantwell (D-WA) and Susan Collins (R-ME) were promoting an alternative bill that would require energy producers to participate in monthly auctions for carbon allowances, prohibit widespread trading of those allowances, and funnel 75 percent of the revenues back to consumers—a cap-and-dividend approach. Other Democratic senators—particularly New Mexico's Jeff Bingaman, Ben Nelson of Nebraska, and Kent Conrad and Byron Dorgan of North Dakota—expressed deep skepticism about any sort of climate-change legislation and instead were advocating an energy-only approach.

By March, Senate talks on climate change were intensifying because, with the 2010 elections already starting to loom, the window for action on climate change was closing. In its search for a sixty-vote majority, the Kerry-Graham-Lieberman trio began to vet the idea of imposing different types of carbon-emission limits on different sectors of the economy: the utility sector would face compliance with a cap-and-trade system in 2012, while the manufacturing sector would be allowed to delay its participation in the system until 2016; rather than operating under the cap, the transportation sector would pay a fee linked to the average price of carbon, an instrument that some big players in the oil industry supported. In hopes of garnering broad industry backing for this approach, in mid-March Kerry, Graham, and Lieberman met on Capitol Hill with representatives of the Chamber of Commerce, the American Petroleum Institute, the Edison Electric Institute, the Nuclear Energy Institute, the National

Association of Manufacturers, and nine other influential trade associations.

The White House engaged in the process as well. Obama's top aides—including Emanuel, Browner, senior advisor Valerie Jarrett, and White House legislative director Phil Schiliro—huddled with Reid and Democratic committee leaders to map out a strategy for assembling sixty votes. Economic advisor Larry Summers, who had become the White House point man on climate change, gave speeches warning of the long-term consequences of a failure to overhaul how the nation generates and uses energy, and emphasizing that an energy and climate-change bill could help the U.S. economy grow by creating jobs and reducing uncertainty for business (Samuelsohn 2010b). The president himself took a series of highly visible steps to demonstrate his willingness to accommodate holdouts—steps that infuriated some observers who thought he was giving away bargaining chips (Lizza 2010). In mid-February he pledged $8.3 billion in loan guarantees for two nuclear power plants in Georgia, shortly after releasing a budget that included $54.5 billion in such guarantees. Then, on March 31 he proffered a plan to allow oil and gas drilling for the first time in large tracts of water off the East Coast, in the eastern Gulf of Mexico, and off the Alaskan coast.

Although Kerry, Graham, and Lieberman had planned to introduce their long-awaited bill on April 22, Earth Day, they delayed its release after two unanticipated events in quick succession threatened to derail the process. First, on April 20, an offshore oil rig owned by Deepwater Horizon and operated by BP exploded, rupturing a pipe and sending thousands of gallons of oil into the Gulf of Mexico. The spill, which continued for months and consumed a tremendous amount of time that staff of the White House Energy and Climate Change Office might have spent working with legislators, complicated negotiations by making it more difficult to include in the bill generous offshore-oil provisions that were important to some senators but now anathema even to environmentalists who had once been willing to compromise. Two days later, Graham pulled out of sponsoring the bill, dealing a blow to hopes for attracting Republican support.[11] Graham told the press that he was withdrawing because immigration had vaulted to the top of Reid's agenda following the passage in Arizona of a controversial immigration law. But many observers speculated that Graham—facing pressure from Republican leaders on Capitol Hill and from conservatives at home—had been looking for an excuse to drop out of the energy and climate change debate, and the dimming prospects for expanded offshore oil drilling did not help matters.

Environmentalists, worried that these setbacks would enable Reid to opt for an energy-only bill rather than tackle the more fraught issue of climate change, did their best to keep the pressure on for a comprehensive bill. In addition to lobbying senators directly, they ran ads stressing that the United States was losing ground to other countries by delaying investments in green-energy jobs (Geman 2010b). Obama continued to promote a joint energy-and-climate agenda as well, telling an audience at a wind-turbine manufacturing facility in Iowa, "I believe that we can come together around this issue and pass comprehensive energy and climate legislation that will ignite new industries, spark new jobs in towns just like Fort Madison, make America more energy independent. Our security, our economy, the future of our planet all depend on it" (quoted in Kaplun 2010b). White House aides also continued to do their part: while Emanuel reached out to Graham, Browner was on the phone with Kerry and Lieberman helping devise a strategy to salvage their bill.

Finally, on May 12, after nearly eight months of negotiation, Kerry and Lieberman unveiled a 987-page draft, which they designated the American Power Act. They were surrounded by environmentalists and representatives of industry—including Tom Kuhn, president of the Edison Electric Institute, Marv Fertel of the Nuclear Energy Institute, and Duke Energy CEO Jim Rogers—but no Republicans. The Kerry-Lieberman bill called for a 17 percent cut in carbon-dioxide emissions from 2005 levels by 2020, 42 percent by 2030, and 83 percent by 2050. Those reductions would be achieved through participation in a cap-and-trade system by utilities and manufacturers, and the purchase of fixed-price allowances by the transportation and oil and gas sectors. The latter replaced the linked carbon fee, which conservative commentators had labeled a gas tax. To sweeten the pot, the Kerry-Lieberman bill included a host of additional industry-friendly provisions.[12]

The bill had the support of the president, who claimed in a prepared statement that it would "put America on the path to a clean energy economy that will create American jobs building the solar panels, wind blades and the car batteries of the future." He added, "It will strengthen our national security by beginning to break our dependence on foreign oil. And it will protect our environment for our children and grandchildren" (quoted in Samuelsohn 2010c). Kerry and Lieberman hoped that an EPA estimate suggesting it would cost the average U.S. household a mere $1 a day would further improve the fortunes of their bill.

What followed was a complicated dance, in which the president tried to display enough enthusiasm for climate-change legislation to keep it alive, and Reid insisted that he would bring a bill to the floor once supporters had rounded up sixty votes, but neither actually went to the mat for the bill. On the advice of his pollsters, Obama and his advisors tried—belatedly and in vain—to use the oil spill to galvanize support for action.

"We're not going to be able to sustain this kind of fossil fuel use. The planet can't support it," the president told an audience in California (quoted in Lee 2010). Having made the decision to bring oil and gas companies into negotiations on the bill, though, Obama was now constrained in his ability to vilify them. Moreover, a primary rationale for the bill all along had been reducing dependence on foreign oil, and it was hard to see how limiting domestic supply advanced that objective. At the same time, the disaster had hardened the resistance of many Democrats to including liberal drilling provisions in the law.

As time to pass a bill before the August recess wound down, the president and his advisors made clear that they were open to a climate bill that imposed a carbon cap just on utilities—an option Republican Senator Olympia Snowe seemed to welcome. But environmentalists were strongly opposed, and the utilities themselves were reluctant to make concessions given that neither Reid nor the president appeared committed to capping emissions (Lehmann 2010a); moreover, such a major shift in emphasis threatened to unravel the delicate agreements achieved among numerous industry sectors in months of talks. In any case, with the November elections in sight, Snowe was the only Republican even arguably in play, and at least four fence-sitting Democrats—Evan Bayh, Byron Dorgan, Blanche Lincoln, and Jay Rockefeller—were all but certain to defect. Carte Goodwin, the West Virginia Democrat who had replaced Robert Byrd in mid-July, made it clear that he would not support cap-and-trade in any form. In short, despite a series of last-minute negotiations on a narrower bill, the votes did not materialize, and by late July, Reid had abandoned the idea of a vote on climate change. He then tentatively embraced the idea of an energy-only bill, but quickly dropped that notion as well, and by the time the August recess rolled around no action had been taken on the issue. A flurry of energy-related bills were proposed in September, but none received serious consideration before the November elections or during the lame-duck session that followed.

Bitterly disappointed, environmentalists and their industry allies charged that more aggressive presidential leadership would have been required to move a bill through the Senate. They rued the president's decision not to offer his own plan; they complained that he failed to capitalize on the oil spill to rally the American public around reduced dependence on fossil fuels; and they pointed out that he did not make "a strong personal push" on the phone and behind the scenes on Capitol Hill" (Davenport 2010b).[13] They also noted that during the first Oval Office speech of his presidency, delivered in response to the Deepwater Horizon/BP debacle, the president's words appeared carefully chosen to lower expectations: he called for an overhaul in the nation's energy policy, but declined to refer specifically to the Kerry-Lieberman bill, mention its key concepts, or renew his demand for a price or cap on carbon; instead, he focused on Bingaman's RES and Republican Richard Lugar's energy-efficiency proposals (Bolton 2010).

It is not at all clear, however, that anything the president could have done in 2010 would have changed the outcome in the Senate. Once the conservative mobilization took hold, Republicans—including John McCain, who had once strongly supported action on climate change—were nowhere to be found. A handful of coal-state Democrats never budged on the issue, either, unconvinced by claims that the cost of cap-and-trade would be manageable. As Evan Bayh of Indiana explained, "Most of the people in my state get their electricity from coal. And so if we do something that dramatically increases the price of coal, we're going to increase their utility bills at a time when they're trying to make ends meet" (quoted in Marshall 2009).

More likely, the critical decision by the White House was to tackle health care first, while the president still had substantial political capital. By the time climate change resurfaced, much of the president's goodwill had been exhausted on the health care battle, and conservative activists had regrouped. The prolonged recession gave traction to antiregulatory slogans about the calamitous economic impacts of imposing a price on carbon (a "job killing, national energy tax"). By contrast, environmentalists' claims about green jobs felt speculative. Wavering members of Congress worried that the links between climate-change legislation and energy prices, and between energy prices and the state of the economy, were direct enough that they would risk punishment for their vote. It would be harder to claim credit for any green jobs that did materialize. Although he tried repeatedly to shift attention to the long-term costs of not addressing climate change, Obama felt the pinch of the recession as well: his political advisors probably calculated that for the president to extend himself for a bill whose short-term economic consequences could well be negative, and whose chances of passage were slim, would have been foolhardy. By contrast, deploying his political capital in service of reforming the financial regulatory system—where he had a storyline that featured clear villains and an undeniable crisis—was more likely to pay off.

MOVING FORWARD ADMINISTRATIVELY

Although President Obama made clear from the outset that comprehensive energy and climate-change legislation was preferable to regulation of carbon emissions by the executive branch, he nevertheless moved administratively to promote conservation, efficiency, and renewable-energy technologies, as well as to curb greenhouse-gas emissions under the Clean Air Act. His actions reflected a threefold motivation: first, he was genuinely determined to curb emissions and recognized that congressional support might not be forthcoming; second, he aimed to signal that the administration fully intended to proceed, in hopes of spurring Congress to legislate; and, third, he hoped to convey to the international community that the United States was serious and thereby revive negotiations on a global treaty. Using administrative means to accomplish environmental policy goals was nothing new; given the partisan polarization around environmental policymaking since the 1990s, both Clinton and George W. Bush had advanced most of their objectives in this area through administration as well (Layzer, forthcoming). Unfortunately, although such actions constitute a serious commitment to addressing climate change, they lack the symbolic appeal and democratic legitimacy of legislation. Moreover, they are subject to extensive delay if tied up in litigation and, because they can be reversed by subsequent administrations, do not provide regulatory certainty for business.

Promoting Energy Efficiency, Renewable Energy, and Emission Reductions

One vehicle Obama exploited to advance his energy and climate-change agenda was the $787 billion stimulus package, the American Recovery and Reinvestment Act (ARRA), passed in mid-February 2009. Eighty billion dollars of ARRA's total $787 billion constituted climate-related stimulus: $26 billion for low-carbon power, $27.5 billion for energy efficiency in buildings, $4 billion for low-carbon vehicles, $10 billion for rail, and $11 billion to upgrade the electricity grid. This infusion alone substantially altered the mix of DOE's responsibilities, from an emphasis on nuclear weapons cleanup and basic research to energy-efficiency projects, weatherization, and grid modernization. In addition to allocating new funds, in early February 2009, the president signed a memorandum ordering DOE to set new energy-efficiency standards for more than two dozen household appliances. Next, calling the development of a smart grid "an urgent national priority," in mid-May Obama unveiled standards to help ensure that new devices could send information to power suppliers (quoted in Pulizzi 2009). And in late June the administration announced tougher energy-efficiency requirements for certain types of fluorescent and incandescent lighting that it claimed would cut the amount of electricity used by affected lamps by 15 percent to 25 percent.

As DOE took steps to advance energy efficiency and alternative-fuel technology, the Interior Department slowed down or reversed many of the Bush administration's plans to open up more areas to coal, oil, and gas development. In early February 2009, Salazar angered oil industry officials by extending to 180 days the deadline for the public to comment on a Bush-era proposal to allow energy companies to drill for oil and gas in a half dozen areas off U.S. shores that previously had been off limits. Later that month, he put the brakes on plans to develop oil shale on federal land in the West. He also shelved Bush administration plans to lease Utah wilderness areas for oil and gas exploration. The EPA helped slow the development of conventional fuels as well with its more stringent reviews of mountaintop mining permits.

In addition to discouraging the pursuit of conventional fuels, Salazar promoted siting of alternative-energy projects. For example, in late June 2009, he unveiled measures that would expedite solar energy projects on federal lands. (Although nearly 200 solar projects had applied for leases, none had been processed, with many projects blocked at the local level.) And, in late April 2010, he announced his approval of the massive Cape Wind project off the coast of Massachusetts. In late November, the Interior Department announced it would begin environmental assessments for proposed wind energy areas in early January 2011, with the goal of issuing leases as early as 2012. Interior was also planning to accelerate the permit process for transmission lines.

Beyond taking actions to advance efficiency and renewables in the broader economy, the Obama administration took serious steps to control the greenhouse-gas emissions of the federal government, itself a major polluter.[14] In a speech in early January 2009, President-Elect Obama said he wanted to modernize 75 percent of existing federal buildings—mostly through energy-efficiency measures. Efforts to reduce energy consumption by the federal government preceded Obama's arrival in Washington, but Obama took them much further. In early October 2009, he signed an executive order requiring every federal agency to measure its greenhouse-gas emissions for the first time and to set targets to reduce those emissions by 2020. In late January 2010, he issued another order requiring the federal government to reduce its greenhouse-gas emissions by 28 percent by 2020.

Yet another step, taken by Obama's Council on Environmental Quality in February 2010, was to issue draft guidance requiring federal agencies to consider greenhouse-gas emissions and climate-change impacts when carrying out reviews under the National Environmental Policy Act (NEPA). The guidance encouraged agencies considering projects that would cause 25,000 metric tons or more of greenhouse-gas emissions annually to figure in the environmental impacts of those emissions before approving them. In addition, it urged agencies to consider the impacts of climate change on such projects. Such calculations might give pause to an agency considering infrastructure near the coast that would be threatened by rising sea levels, for example.[15]

Regulating Greenhouse-Gas Emissions under the Clean Air Act

Although Republicans decried the decision to broaden NEPA analysis, the administration's most contentious move by far involved regulating greenhouse-gas emissions. In April 2009, despite heavy lobbying from the U.S. Chamber of Commerce and the National Association of Manufacturers, the administration released a proposed endangerment finding for carbon dioxide and began to hold public hearings on the issue. After poring over 300,000 public comments gathered over the summer, the EPA finalized its endangerment finding in early December, thereby officially designating carbon dioxide as a pollutant that could be regulated under the Clean Air Act. Calling the EPA's actions "coercive," Senator Lisa Murkowski (R-AK) began organizing a drive to pass a "resolution of disapproval" under the Congressional Review Act that would veto the EPA's endangerment finding, and in early March of 2010 House Republicans—led by Representative Joe Barton (R-TX)—proposed a parallel resolution. The measure faced a certain presidential veto, however, and prompted environmentalists to launch an intense, three-day ad campaign that linked a vote with Murkowski to the Gulf of Mexico oil spill (Geman 2010a). On June 10, the Senate rejected the measure by a vote of 47 to 53—a victory for the White House, which had hoped to avoid exercising a veto.[16]

Even as the showdown over the endangerment finding was brewing, the administration moved in the spring of 2009 to regulate greenhouse-gas emissions from motor vehicles. In mid-May Obama unveiled the first national greenhouse-gas emission standards for cars and trucks, requiring automakers to increase fuel-economy standards for automobiles sold in the United States to 35.5 mpg by 2016—four years earlier than the 2007 energy law required. According to the administration, the new regulations will save 1.8 billion barrels of oil and reduce greenhouse-gas emissions by 950 million metric tons between 2016 and 2020, equivalent to shutting down 194 coal-fired power plants. In late June, the EPA granted a waiver, which had been denied by the Bush administration, allowing California and other states to set even more stringent fuel-economy standards.[17] In late September 2010 the administration was contemplating even more ambitious standards—possibly as high as 62 mpg by 2025. And in October the EPA announced it would propose the first mileage standards for heavy-duty vehicles that run on diesel fuel; the standards would yield a 20 percent reduction in greenhouse-gas emissions through improved engine efficiency and aerodynamics.

While it was working on mobile sources, the EPA was also moving to regulate greenhouse-gas emissions from stationary sources, such as power plants, refineries, and factories. In August 2009 the agency sent a final rule to OMB establishing a mandatory greenhouse-gas registry, as required by a 2007 spending bill. Even more significant, in September the EPA submitted a draft "tailoring" rule to OMB that would impose strict permitting requirements under the Clean Air Act on the largest industrial sources, those producing more than 25,000 tons of carbon dioxide each year.[18] The tailoring rule was part of the EPA's effort to keep the pressure on Congress without appearing overly zealous, as the rule shields millions of small businesses, households, and hospitals from new permit requirements; instead, it focuses the agency's regulatory efforts on the 13,000 sources that account for between 85 percent and 90 percent of U.S. emissions.

Under pressure from both Republicans and Democrats, Lisa Jackson assured Congress that no stationary sources would face greenhouse-gas regulations in 2010, and that the EPA was considering substantially raising the thresholds in its proposed tailoring rule. In response to a letter from eight moderate Senate Democrats—including Jay Rockefeller, Robert Byrd, and Alaskan Mark Begich—Jackson clarified that the EPA would phase in permitting requirements, focusing on fewer than 400 facilities in early 2011 and dealing with other large sources during the latter part of 2011. In early March 2010, Jackson authorized raising the tailoring rule threshold so that existing sources emitting less than 75,000 tons of greenhouse gases each year and new sources emitting less than 100,000 tons would not need a permit until 2012, after which the EPA would consider lowering the threshold to 50,000 tons per year (Bravender 2010b). The tailoring rule was finalized in mid-May 2010. A coalition of industry groups promptly sued.

Jackson's efforts to placate critics notwithstanding, the EPA's moves toward regulating greenhouse gases provoked a harsh reaction, and the agency became a favorite target of conservative blogs and Tea Party rallies. One petition, circulated by Americans for Prosperity, described the EPA as "an out-of-control bureaucracy attempting an unprecedented power grab, seeking to regulate every aspect of our lives and take control of the U.S. economy" (Kaplun 2010a). Representative Michelle Bachmann (R-MN) wrote in a blog post, "In an attempt by the Environmental Protection Agency to establish a national energy tax by circumventing the legislative process, the EPA (with the backing of the Obama Administration) is pushing emission regulations which will destroy jobs and further impact our already struggling economy" (2010). Some Democrats were irritated by the threat of EPA regulation as well: in early March 2010, four influential coal-state Democrats introduced companion bills in the House and Senate that would block the agency from implementing any sort of climate-related stationary-source rules for two years. In addition, Representative Earl Pomeroy (D-ND) introduced a bill to strip the EPA of its authority to regulate greenhouse-gas emissions altogether unless it received an explicit mandate from Congress. Undaunted by the mounting opposition in Congress and another round of rallies held by antiregulatory activists during the summer of 2010, the EPA forged ahead, and in January 2011 the EPA's Prevention of Significant Deterioration rules for stationary-source greenhouse-gas emissions took effect. With the exception of Texas, which refused to implement the new regulations, every state was prepared to either issue permits or allow the EPA to do so.

THE FATE OF OBAMA'S CLEAN-ENERGY ECONOMY

With comprehensive energy and climate legislation, as with the stimulus package and health care reform, the Obama administration sought to dictate the terms of the debate as Congress set the pace and worked out the details. The president consistently encouraged legislative efforts to find common ground, and his advisors testified, gave speeches, and met privately with members of Congress and stakeholders. But the administration's sporadic efforts to train the spotlight on energy and climate change, combined with its determination to characterize cap-and-trade as an economic boon, were not enough to overcome the inertia that has long plagued Congress on this issue. The poor economy, combined with efforts by Tea Party activists and other opponents to cast a carbon cap-and-trade system as a job killer and an energy tax created enough confusion among the public that, for fence-sitting senators, simply doing nothing appeared to be the most prudent course.

Even as comprehensive legislation stalled, however, the administration continued to take steps toward regulating greenhouse-gas emissions and promoting energy efficiency and the development of alternative-fuel technology. These less visible maneuvers may yet prove significant in terms of pushing a transformation in the U.S. economy. But they may not be enough to reassure the world's leaders, who are deeply pessimistic about the prospects for substantive change in U.S. policy. As Martin Khor noted in the U.K. *Guardian*, "Without the U.S. on board, the developed countries do not want to make final commitments . . . on how much they themselves will cut their emissions. So the world is waiting for America—and it could be a long wait" (2010).

There are several possible trajectories for energy and climate-change policy in the next two years. Obama is likely to continue pursuing a clean-energy transition through administrative action.[19] At the same time, opponents have vowed to derail the EPA's regulatory process. They hope to do so in court—the EPA's greenhouse-gas rules were facing more than ninety legal challenges as of January 2011—or by attaching provisions to appropriations bills that prohibit the EPA from spending money to issue or enforce regulations. That said, some of the more cynical Republicans must relish the prospect of EPA regulation: if they truly believe that carbon limits will cripple the economy, they will be anticipating a mighty backlash that could vault them back into power.

As for Congress, some legislators, such as Tennessee Republican Lamar Alexander, suggest that a narrower partisan balance may actually facilitate a deal that at least some Senate Republicans can abide (Bravender 2010a). But many of the newly elected Republicans reject the idea that human activities are linked to global warming (Eilperin 2010). Others, including Susan Collins of Maine, believe future efforts are likely to be smaller in scale. The president seems open to that suggestion. In September he told *Rolling Stone* magazine that one of his top priorities for 2011 was to have an energy policy that "begins to address all facets of our over-reliance on fossil fuels" (Obama 2010, 5). But he went on to acknowledge the possibility that such a policy might be made "in chunks, as opposed to some sort of comprehensive omnibus legislation" (Obama 2010).

In late October, Obama reiterated that he intended to pursue a "bite-sized" strategy, in collaboration with Republicans, on energy and climate-change issues (Ling 2010). One possibility under consideration is a Clean Energy Standard, which is similar to an RES except that it also promotes nuclear, natural gas, and coal with CCS. Another option being pushed by some policy entrepreneurs is new funding for the development of alternative-fuel technologies. All of these policy options will run into opposition from Republicans who have vowed to reject spending on new government programs. They are also unlikely to make a major dent in U.S. greenhouse-gas emissions.

Over time, however, President Obama may hold a trump card. With the issuance of additional greenhouse-gas regulations on stationary sources, the pressure from industry and conservative activists to enact legislation that strips the EPA of its authority to regulate carbon-dioxide emissions under the Clean Air Act is likely to be strong. The preferred mechanism for doing so is a rider on a must-pass bill. Because the president has vowed to veto such legislation, however, even conservative members of Congress eventually may perceive that the best way to provide regulatory relief for industry is by creating a system of allowance-trading that eases the transition. In the meantime, state and local governments—which have already taken the lead in addressing climate change—are likely to continue promoting policies and practices that reduce energy consumption and advance alternative energy.[20] With the ascension of GOP governors across the Midwest, some climate-change initiatives are threatened. But the most aggressive state action, California's AB 32, an emission-limiting law, withstood a challenge backed by the Koch brothers and other out-of-state oil interests at the ballot box in November. Local governments have been busy as well: since 2005 more than 1,000 mayors have signed the Mayors' Climate Pledge, and municipal officials are actively pursuing programs to enhance their cities' environmental sustainability. Although these initiatives are critical, the absence of a nationwide carbon price inhibits the most aggressive efforts to reduce emissions.

Thanks to Kate Dineen for research assistance and for assembling appendix table 8A.2, and to participants in the energy and climate debate who agreed to talk on condition of anonymity. Thanks also to Tom Hamburger, Robert Stavins, and the members of the Obama Project, all of whom provided helpful comments on chapter drafts.

APPENDIX

You will find additional information regarding energy and climate-change policy in these appendices.

Table 8A.1. Timeline of Energy and Climate-Related Activity

| January 1, 2008–December 31, 2008 | Energy is a key issue in the 2008 presidential campaign. Candidates Barack Obama and John McCain both vow to reduce U.S. reliance on foreign oil and fight global warming. Both support binding caps on greenhouse-gas emissions, advocate obtaining 25 percent of the nation's electricity from renewable sources by 2025, and endorse the expansion of nuclear power. Obama has a more aggressive plan for addressing global warming, however. He also advocates investing $150 billion over the next decade to foster the development of new technology and al- |

ternative fuels. Whereas McCain positions himself as a strong proponent of domestic drilling, Obama initially supports reinstating the moratorium on new offshore oil and gas drilling—a position that softens as the campaign wears on. In early August 2008, he says that he would support offshore drilling as part of a broader, bipartisan energy package to reduce dependence on foreign oil. Similarly, he becomes more enthusiastic about coal over the course of the campaign, eventually talking about clean coal and describing coal as "a very important way for us to meet our long-term energy needs."

January 2009

President Obama establishes addressing climate change and creating a clean-energy economy as a priority of his administration. He appoints Lisa Jackson as EPA administrator, Steven Chu as secretary of energy, John Holdren as director of the White House Office of Science and Technology Policy, and Ken Salazar as secretary of the interior. Carol Browner takes the position of climate czar.

A *Time*/CBS News poll demonstrates the impact of the economic downturn on public opinion: given a choice between stimulating the economy and protecting the environment, 58 percent choose the economy, and 33 percent choose protecting the environment. (Compare this with April 2007, when 36 percent said it was more important to stimulate the economy and 52 percent chose the environment.)

February 4, 2009

The president orders the Department of Energy (DOE) to set new energy-efficiency standards for a broad range of household appliances.

February 12, 2009

Congress passes the American Recovery and Reinvestment Act (ARRA, or the stimulus package) by votes of 246 to 283 in the House and 60 to 38 in the Senate. ARRA contains a total of $80 billion in energy-related spending. It gives the DOE some $40 billion, much of it for projects related to energy efficiency and conservation projects and the development of new technologies. Obama signs it on February 15.

February 24, 2009   Interior Secretary Salazar puts the brakes on plans initiated under the Bush administration to develop oil shale on federal land in the western United States.

February 26, 2009   The Obama administration releases its fiscal year 2010 budget, which is projected to raise about $80 billion per year, starting in 2012, from a cap-and-trade system for carbon emissions. It projects raising a total of $645 billion from the auction of emissions credits between 2012 and 2019. About $120 billion of that would be used to pay for low-carbon technologies; the rest—about $525 billion—would be returned to the "the people, especially vulnerable families, communities, and businesses, to help ease the transition to a clean energy economy."

March 2009   In early March, the House Energy and Commerce Committee's Energy and Environment Subcommittee begins holding hearings on comprehensive energy and climate-change legislation.

In late March, the Obama administration finalizes an 8 percent hike in the corporate average fuel-economy (CAFE) standards for 2011 models, requiring a combined CAFE of 27.3 mpg (a 2 mpg increase over 2010 models).

March 24, 2009   The Environmental Protection Agency (EPA) sends its proposed endangerment finding to the Office of Management and Budget (OMB). This finding, which was initiated under but suppressed by the Bush administration, sets the stage for the EPA to regulate greenhouse gases (GHG) under the Clean Air Act.

March 31, 2009   Democratic leaders of the House Energy and Commerce Committee unveil a 648-page draft energy and climate-change bill (HR 2454, the American Clean Energy and Security Act, known as Waxman-Markey) that would establish a cap-and-trade program for curbing U.S. greenhouse-gas emissions 20 percent below 2005 levels by 2020 and 83 percent below 2005 levels by 2050. The bill also creates a renewable-energy standard that would reach 25

	percent by 2025. And it includes a host of other programs as well, such as new energy-efficiency programs and limits on the carbon content of motor fuels.
April 2, 2009	On a court-ordered deadline, the Obama administration issues its endangerment finding linking manmade greenhouse gases to threats to public health and welfare. (It will take public comments and release a final document in September.)
April 22, 2009	On Earth Day 2009, President Obama warns that unless Congress acts, the job of regulating GHG emissions will fall largely to the EPA, which is limited in its ability to consider costs.
Late April 2009	Top Obama officials testify at hearings concerning Waxman-Markey on behalf of greenhouse-gas curbs, while repeatedly sidestepping questions about particular policy mechanisms. Lisa Jackson testifies that according to an EPA analysis, Waxman-Markey will cost the average American household between $98 and $140 per year, provided that most of the money raised by government is returned to households.
May 4, 2009	Obama summons Democrats on the House Energy and Commerce Committee to the White House in an attempt to break the impasses on Waxman-Markey. He reinforces the urgency of acting in advance of the Copenhagen meeting in December, and lays out four principles: lawmakers must acknowledge the cost of the bill and make sure everyone gets something back; the legislation must be predictable for business; regional needs must be taken into account; and the legislation should cooperate with other countries. He encourages lawmakers to come to consensus but does not suggest that he will become more directly involved in the negotiations.
Mid-May 2009	The U.S. Chamber of Commerce sharpens its critique of Waxman-Markey, saying it would create a complicated, expensive, regulation-heavy system that would ignore the emissions of developing countries. At the same time, the Chamber clearly re-

gards legislation as preferable to regulation by EPA under the Clean Air Act.

The Energy and Commerce Committee begins its markup of Waxman-Markey with the introduction of a 900-plus-page manager's amendment that includes "technical changes" to the underlying bill—reflecting additional deals the chair has struck with anxious Democrats.

May 17, 2009	Obama introduces a set of sixteen standards to help ensure that new devices can send information to power suppliers, as part of a push to develop a smart electric-power grid. The DOE boosts the maximum awards available for smart-grid programs under the stimulus bill.
May 19, 2009	Obama unveils new national fuel-economy standards that set the first national greenhouse-gas emissions standards on cars and trucks. The administration orders car-makers to increase fuel standards for vehicles sold in the United States to 35.5 mpg by 2016, four years earlier than current federal law requires.
May 20, 2009	Representative Collin Peterson (D-MN), chair of the Agriculture Committee, demands that House leaders give him a role in shaping climate-change legislation or risk losing every Democratic vote on his panel when the bill hits the floor.
May 21, 2009	Just before Congress departs for its Memorial Day recess, the Energy and Commerce Committee passes Waxman-Markey by a vote of 33 to 25.
June 1, 2009	Congress returns from its break, and Speaker Pelosi takes the reins on climate change. She meets with Agriculture Committee Chair Collin Peterson and Ways and Means Committee Chair Charles Rangel (D-NY), and tells them their panels will be allowed to mark up Waxman-Markey. (The other six committees with jurisdiction either decide or are told they do not need to hold their own markups.) She gives Peterson and Rangel until June 19 to complete their work or risk losing jurisdiction over the bill.

June 4, 2009	The Senate begins its markup of an energy bill sponsored by Senate Energy and Natural Resources Committee Chair Jeff Bingaman (D-NM) that does not include measures to curb greenhouse-gas emissions.
Early to mid-June 2009	Throughout early June, Peterson and Waxman negotiate, with Peterson complaining that the distribution of allowances in the bill favors populous over rural states. Lobbying on the bill is intense: a study by the Center for Public Integrity finds that 770 companies and public-interest groups have registered to lobby on the issue of climate change this year.
	As Pelosi struggles to line up votes, White House officials become involved: Carol Browner sets up meetings with lawmakers, and Chief of Staff Rahm Emanuel lobbies freshman Democrats in a session at the White House. (The freshmen are particularly vulnerable, since many come from conservative districts.)
	Peterson declares his support for Waxman-Markey after changes are made in the allocation of allowances, and Waxman agrees that the Department of Agriculture (USDA), rather than the EPA, will oversee the provisions dealing with carbon offsets (which concern agriculture and forested lands).
June 25, 2009	There is a massive, last-minute push for votes the day before the scheduled Friday vote. Carol Browner woos Republican centrists. Obama makes a short speech in the Rose Garden in which he says, "Make no mistake. This is a jobs bill." The White House reinforces the Democratic message all day, with phone calls from Emanuel and Obama himself. Wavering members are grilled (not literally) by the president at the White House luau that night.
June 26, 2009	The House passes Waxman-Markey by a vote of 219 to 212, after John Boehner (R-OH) spends more than an hour reading through the 300-page Democratic amendment that was filed at 3:00 a.m., sixteen hours before the vote. As passed, the bill requires a 17 per-

cent reduction in GHG emissions over 2005 levels by 2020 and an 83 percent reduction by 2050. The bill gives away 85 percent of the initial allowances, nearly 40 percent, to local distribution companies.

Late June 2009	Obama announces tougher energy-efficiency requirements for certain types of fluorescent and incandescent lighting. The new rule will take effect in 2012. Also in late June, Interior Secretary Salazar announces that his department will expedite solar energy projects on federal lands.
June 29, 2009	The Obama administration grants California a Clean Air Act waiver, allowing it to enforce its own GHG emissions standards for cars and trucks—and overturning a Bush administration decision to deny the waiver.
August 9, 2009	A group of thirty-two former senators, cabinet officials, and other U.S. leaders release a statement urging action on global warming and asking for a "clear, comprehensive, realistic, and broadly bipartisan plan to address our role in the climate change crisis."
Mid- to late August 2009	The American Coalition for Clean Coal Electricity sends workers to 264 cities to attend state fairs and Kiwanis meetings and set up tables at college campuses—all to provide positive public relations for coal. The American Petroleum Institute funds nineteen rallies across the country beginning in August and running through September, with the goal of stimulating phone calls, emails, and letters to lawmakers about climate legislation.
	The EPA sends a final rule to the OMB establishing a mandatory greenhouse-gas registry, as required under a 2007 spending bill signed by George W. Bush.
August 27, 2009	A *Washington Post*/CBS News poll suggests that there is still majority support among the public for changes to U.S. energy policy and for the way Obama is handling the issue. A majority (52 percent) also claim to support a cap-and-trade system, although support drops to 39 percent if it costs them

$25 per month. Large majorities favor requiring energy conservation from businesses and consumers, and 52 percent favor building more nuclear plants (up about 6 percent since 2001).

September 15, 2009   The Obama administration rolls out details of its strategy to reduce GHG emissions from cars, and Lisa Jackson says the proposal paves the way for regulating emissions from stationary sources.

September 22, 2009   Climate SOS stages nonviolent civil disobedience office occupations and protests in San Francisco, Boston, and New York in support of legislation to address climate change.

September 28, 2009   PNM Resources, a New Mexico utility, leaves the U.S. Chamber of Commerce over its position on climate change. Several other major companies have already left over this issue, or withdrawn from the organization's board, and more utilities follow PNM's lead in October.

September 30, 2009   The EPA launches a formal reconsideration of a Bush-era memo, authored by former EPA administrator Stephen Johnson, detailing when the government should regulate greenhouse-gas emissions from industrial facilities. (The Johnson memo said that facilities should be required to obtain permits only for pollutants controlled under the Clean Air Act.)

October 1, 2009   Senators John Kerry (D-MA) and Barbara Boxer (D-CA) introduce a comprehensive energy and climate-change bill (S 1733), a companion to Waxman-Markey. Kerry-Boxer would cut the nation's GHG emissions by 20 percent from 2005 levels by 2020 and create a "soft collar" (a ceiling and a floor on the carbon price, achieved through the release of emissions held in reserve or through automatic price increases) that curbs price volatility in the carbon market. The measure contains language preventing the EPA from regulating greenhouse gases as criteria pollutants under the Clean Air Act; it does not specify how allowances will be distributed, to allow for negotiations. Supporters of climate-change legislation rally outside the Capitol, and Obama says the release of the draft moves the country "one step closer to putting America in control of our energy future and making America more energy-independent." He adds, "My administration is deeply committed to passing a bill that creates new American jobs and clean-energy incentives that foster innovation."

October 5, 2009   President Obama signs an executive order requiring each federal agency to measure its GHG emissions for the first time and set targets to reduce them by 2020. The order launches the GreenGov Challenge, an effort to generate ideas from the 1.8 million federal employees on reducing emissions, conserving energy and water, minimizing waste, and generally becoming more sustainable.

October 11, 2009   A *New York Times* op-ed piece by Senators John Kerry and Lindsey Graham (R-SC) seems to open new avenues for a bipartisan compromise on energy and climate in the Senate. The senators link climate change and energy independence and emphasize their military service. They promise to take advantage of nuclear energy, clean coal, and offshore oil drilling. They conclude that legislation is preferable to EPA regulation: "Industry needs the certainty that comes with congressional action," they say. Observers believe the piece breathes new life into the Senate debate.

October 13, 2009   The U.S. Chamber of Commerce launches a five-year, $100 million "campaign for free enterprise" in response to sweeping climate-change, health care, and labor legislation. The campaign will involve national advertising, political lobbying, and grassroots education efforts.

October 14, 2009   CBO Director Douglas Elmendorf testifies before the Senate Energy and Natural Resources Committee that the development of new technologies and the growth of renewable energy will largely offset job losses in fossil fuel–based industries. He adds that a cap-and-trade system will impose some costs on the economy (on the order of 0.25 percent to 0.75

	percent of GDP in 2020 and 1 percent to 3.5 percent in 2050) and will affect regions differently.
Mid-October 2009	The Obama administration defends its efforts on behalf of energy and climate legislation in response to charges that the president is expending too little political capital on the issue. White House spokespeople note that administration officials have met with more than half the senators, made calls to 100 mayors in seventeen states, and held more than fifty energy-related events in twenty-four states. In addition, they say, the White House has reached out to "hundreds" of stakeholders and local lawmakers.
October 23, 2009	Obama asserts that a consensus is growing on Capitol Hill to pass comprehensive energy and global warming legislation, specifically mentioning the Kerry-Graham partnership.
October 26, 2009	Three days of Senate Environment and Public Works Committee hearings begin, after Senator Boxer releases a 923-page chairman's mark of the bill, complete with details on emission allocations that largely mirror Waxman-Markey. Along with the bill, Boxer releases an EPA analysis showing that it would cost the average U.S. household roughly $100 per year, about the same as the House bill. Boxer's bill incorporates provisions from Bingaman's energy-only bill, which he completed work on in the spring. Meanwhile, Maria Cantwell (D-WA) is working on legislation that would cap emissions but use a cap-and-dividend plan to curb carbon emissions rather than allow credits to be traded as a commodity.
Late October 2009	Obama travels around the country touting the job-creation promise of clean-energy projects. Meanwhile, a survey by the Pew Research Center for People and the Press shows a decline in the proportion of Americans who believe rising global temperatures are the result of human activity: 37 percent, down from 47 percent in 2008.
November 5, 2009	S 1733 passes the Senate Environment and Public Works Committee (11 to 1), with all seven commit-

tee Republicans boycotting the vote, as well as the three days of hearings that preceded it. The lone dissenter is Max Baucus (D-MT). After the vote, however, action on climate change grinds to a halt, as the Senate focuses on health care legislation. Lobbying moves to the EPA, which is preparing GHG regulations under the Clean Air Act.

November 19, 2009   Thousands of emails are released without authorization from the University of East Anglia's Climatic Research Unit. Conservative bloggers immediately seize on these emails as evidence that climate scientists are colluding to distort scientific evidence and suppress dissent about climate change. Within days, the U.S. media are calling the episode Climategate.

November 24, 2009   A *Washington Post*/ABC News poll finds that although fewer Americans believe global warming is a serious problem, a majority (53 percent) support cap-and-trade legislation. The increase in skepticism is largely driven by a shift within the GOP.

Mid-December 2009   House Republicans announce plans mirroring a Senate effort, led by Lisa Murkowski (R-AK), to introduce a formal resolution under the Congressional Review Act disapproving the EPA's endangerment finding.

December 18, 2009   The UN Framework Convention on Climate Change meeting in Copenhagen produces no global targets for cutting greenhouse-gas emissions. It does yield a three-page document, according to which each country needs to list its current domestic pledges for emissions reductions and promise to allow monitoring of their progress.

Late January 2010   A coalition of companies and environmental groups (USCAP) lobbies for climate legislation, portraying it as a job-creation engine. A separate business coalition, We Can Lead, whose members include Exelon, Entergy, and Constellation Energy Group, launches a $1 million ad campaign urging Congress to pass energy and climate legislation in 2010.

January 28, 2010   Obama issues an executive order requiring the federal government to reduce its greenhouse-gas emissions by 28 percent by 2020. The administration also submits its reduction targets to the UN Framework Convention on Climate Change, as required under the Copenhagen Accord. The administration pledges to cut GHG emissions by 17 percent from 2005 levels by 2020, consistent with the levels set in Waxman-Markey, as long as Congress passes legislation to do so.

February 1, 2010   The Obama administration releases its fiscal year 2011 budget, a $3.8 trillion spending plan that, once again, banks on Congress passing a "comprehensive, market-based climate change policy" that would curb greenhouse-gas emissions 17 percent below 2005 levels by 2020 and more than 80 percent by mid-century. In recognition of events in Congress, this budget does not assume a 100 percent auction of emissions credits, but it does assume the bill will be budget neutral and that "proceeds from emissions allowances will be used to compensate vulnerable families, communities, and businesses." The budget also eliminates subsidies for fossil fuels and increases investment in clean-energy projects. It gives the EPA $21 million to implement a reporting rule for greenhouse-gas emissions, plus another $43 million in new funding for regulations to curb emissions under the Clean Air Act. DOE gets $54.5 million for carbon capture and sequestration technologies (for coal), and the State Department gets $1.4 billion to help developing nations install U.S.-built technologies and increase land-based sequestration efforts.

Obama's State of the Union emphasizes the importance of passing a comprehensive energy and climate-change bill. Obama acknowledges the possibility that the Senate might pass an energy bill without a carbon cap, but says that doing so would be a bad idea. He continues to raise the specter of EPA regulation, saying, "And so the question then is: Does it make sense for us to start pricing in the fact that this thing is really bad for the environment? And if we do, then can we do it in a way that doesn't involve some big bureaucracy in a control-and-command system, but just says, look, we're going to—there's going to be a price to pollution. And then everybody can adapt and decide which are the—which are the best energies."

February 2, 2010   The Pentagon releases a long-term strategy that for the first time recognizes climate change as a direct threat to U.S. national security, noting that it could accelerate instability or conflict.

Mid-February 2010   The White House releases its first economic report by the Council of Economic Advisors. It says that the president's energy and environmental initiatives are necessary to reboot the U.S. economy and avert dangerous changes in the Earth's climate.

As Senators Kerry, Joseph Lieberman (I-CT), and Lindsey Graham (R-SC) flesh out the details of their energy-climate compromise, Senators Maria Cantwell and Susan Collins (R-ME) promote legislation that uses a cap-and-dividend mechanism to funnel 75 percent of the revenue raised back to consumers. The other 25 percent would go to renewable energy development.

Although the Environment and Public Works Committee has been silent on cap-and-trade since November's partisan meltdown on S 1733, Senator Boxer is back in the game, holding a hearing on the public-health warnings on climate change.

Polls continue to show that climate change is low on the public's list of priorities, and the conservative base is exercised about the issue—making it a political risk for Republicans and conservative-moderate Democrats. Meanwhile, Lisa Murkowski leads a charge by Republicans and conservative-moderate Democrats for a disapproval resolution under the Congressional Review Act. Environmentalists and faith-based activists launch radio ads on February 9 targeting some moderate Democrats—including Senators Evan Bayh (D-IN), Mark Pryor (D-AR), Mark Begich (D-AK), Claire McCaskill (D-MO), and others—who are considering supporting the resolution.

Hoping to draw out Climategate, Representatives James Sensenbrenner (R-WI) and Darrell Issa (R-CA) ask the National Science Foundation (NSF) to investigate the nearly $2.5 million in federal grants that have gone to Michael Mann, director of Penn State University's Earth System Science Center. Members of Congress also blast the SEC's position that publicly traded companies must disclose climate-related risks to shareholders—something it voted to require on January 27, 2010.

February 15, 2010   Touting nuclear energy as a key to dealing with climate change, Obama announces $8.3 billion in loan guarantees for Southern Company that will enable the utility to break ground on two nuclear power plants in Georgia.

February 21, 2010   Senator Jay Rockefeller (D-WV) and seven other Senate Democrats—many from coal states—send a letter to EPA administrator Lisa Jackson expressing concern about the impact of climate regulations. Rockefeller is considering proposing a suspension of EPA rule-making that would give the agency leeway to proceed if congressional action fails. Despite Jackson's reassurances that the EPA would phase in permitting requirements for industrial facilities, Senate Democrats are determined to move forward with their proposal, as is Murkowski, who has forty cosponsors by this point, three of them Democrats.

February 22, 2010   Lisa Jackson assures Congress that the EPA will phase in climate regulations for industrial sources gradually, focusing on fewer than 400 facilities in early 2011 and dealing with other large sources in the latter part of 2011. Furthermore, the EPA is considering "substantially" raising thresholds for its proposed "tailoring" rule from 100 to 250 tons of pollution per year to 25,000 tons of carbon-dioxide equivalent per year. The tailoring rule determines which facilities are regulated when.

Nevertheless, Lisa Murkowski plans to move forward with her bill; similarly, two top House Democrats—Collin Peterson and Ike Skelton (D-MO)—introduce a measure that would, like Murkowski's bill, use the Congressional Review Act to veto the EPA's endangerment finding. (The finding triggered a requirement to begin the regulation process by the end of March.) Everyone recognizes that such bills would face a presidential veto, but that doesn't deter Senator Rockefeller from introducing a bill to delay EPA's stationary source regulations for six to twelve months.

Early March 2010	The Kerry-Lieberman-Graham trio has assembled a short list of ideas they want to run by key blocs of Democratic and GOP senators. Each has meetings scheduled with key members of both parties. The draft nearly ready to be circulated seeks to reduce greenhouse-gas emissions around 17 percent from 2005 levels by 2020. But it does not rely on an economy-wide cap; instead, different sectors are to be governed by different mechanisms. The idea is to disable any coalition that could form to oppose the bill.
March 1, 2010	Five hundred and sixty-nine U.S. scientists send a letter to Congress urging lawmakers to oppose House and Senate resolutions that would veto the EPA's endangerment finding, which, they say, is based on solid science.
March 2, 2010	Lisa Jackson says that the EPA has revised its tailoring rule again, raising the threshold to 75,000 tons from 25,000 tons of carbon-dioxide equivalent. Sources emitting less than 75,000 tons will not need a permit until 2012.
March 4, 2010	The EPA sends its final reconsideration of the Johnson memo to OMB for review.
March 4, 2010	Four influential coal-state Democrats introduce companion bills in the House and Senate to block the EPA from implementing climate-related stationary source rules for two years. The measures draw little response from either powerful committee leaders or the White House.
March 9, 2010	Obama meets with fourteen key senators in a push to get stalled climate-change legislation moving

again. Moderate Democrats continue to promote an energy-only approach. Meanwhile, Kerry, Graham, and Lieberman meet with industry and trade association leaders. At this point, there are about forty-one yes or probably yes votes in the Senate, twenty-nine no votes, and thirty fence-sitters, including nineteen Democrats and eleven Republicans. There are about twenty coal-state senators in play; their demands include less aggressive emissions limits, allowances returned to consumers, the EPA's authority to regulate under the Clean Air Act stripped, and billions of dollars to promote carbon capture and storage. Some senators are particularly concerned about trade, and thirteen are preoccupied with oil and gas drilling.

March 10, 2010   A Gallup poll shows a sharp reversal in public attitudes about global warming: the percentage of Americans who believe climate change has been exaggerated has climbed dramatically between 2008 and 2010, according to the poll. Nevertheless, the majority (53 percent) still believe that climate change is real and its effects becoming evident, a steep drop from the 65 percent who felt that way in 2008.

March 11, 2010   More than 2,000 economists and climate scientists—including eight Nobel laureates, thirty-two NAS members, eleven MacArthur genius award winners, and three National Medal of Science recipients—deliver a letter to Capitol Hill highlighting the certainty that global warming is primarily due to human activities and the costs of waiting to deal with it.

At the same time, governors from eighteen U.S. states and two territories call on Congress to stop EPA regulations. A coalition of ninety-eight industry groups, mostly representing fossil fuel–related industries, send a separate letter urging senators to support Murkowski's resolution on the endangerment finding.

Mid-March 2010   Republicans continue to hammer away at Climategate and IPCC errors. Representative Joe Barton issues a letter questioning General Motor Company's and Chrysler LLC's membership in USCAP, an industry-environmental partnership, given that they have received billions in taxpayer bailout money. In February, Barton successfully pushed AIG to drop out of USCAP for the same reason.

March 31, 2010
Obama announces that his administration will open up several regions of the United States to offshore oil drilling, part of his effort to show good faith in energy and climate negotiations.

April 20, 2010
An offshore oil rig owned by Deepwater Horizon and operated by BP explodes, rupturing a pipe and sending thousands of gallons of oil into the Gulf of Mexico. The spill goes on for months before the well is finally capped in late August.

April 22, 2010
On Earth Day, the scheduled release of the Kerry-Graham-Lieberman bill, Senator Graham pulls out of sponsoring the bill, citing Democrats' focus on immigration.

April 28, 2010
Secretary Salazar announces the Interior Department's approval of Cape Wind, which—if built—would be the nation's first offshore wind farm.

May 12, 2010
Kerry and Lieberman unveil their 987-page American Power Act calling for a 17 percent cut in carbon-dioxide emissions from 2005 levels by 2020, 42 percent by 2030, and 83 percent by 2050. The bill includes a host of industry-friendly provisions.

May 13, 2010
The EPA issues its final tailoring rule. Industry groups promptly sue.

June 15, 2010
President Obama makes his first Oval Office address. Speaking for eighteen minutes, mostly about the Deepwater Horizon–BP oil spill in the Gulf of Mexico, he calls for an overhaul of the nation's energy policy in order to embrace a "clean energy future." He makes no mention of a carbon price or cap.

July 2010
After considering numerous options, Majority Leader Reid declines to take energy and climate-change (or energy-only) legislation to the floor before the

five-week August-September recess. The prospects for passing a bill before the November elections appear bleak.

Mid-August 2010   The EPA publishes its decision not to reconsider its endangerment finding (rejecting petitions to do so). The Chamber of Commerce and the Coalition for Responsible Regulation ask the Washington, D.C., Circuit Court of Appeals to review the agency's finding.

The EPA releases two proposals for implementing GHG regulations for stationary sources under the tailoring rule. States are required to revise their implementation plans; if a state fails to meet federal requirements, the EPA will establish a plan for it.

Late August 2010   The American Petroleum Institute (API) launches a major lobbying campaign tying the oil and gas sector to job creation. Clean Energy Works holds CarnivOil events in twenty-five cities; its goal is to depict the oil industry as too powerful in American politics.

The Natural Resources Defense Council (NRDC) runs ads attacking six moderate senators who do not support comprehensive energy and climate-change legislation.

September 1, 2010   The API kicks off another round of citizen rallies with events across Texas.

Late September 2010   The administration reveals that it is considering a fuel-economy standard of 62 mpg by 2025. It is also preparing the first mileage standards for heavy-duty vehicles that run on diesel fuel.

Early October 2010   Congress adjourns for the runup to the November elections.

Mid-November to December 2010   No energy or climate change proposals receive serious consideration during the lame-duck session of the 111th Congress. Jay Rockefeller abandons his effort to impose a two-year stay on EPA greenhouse-gas emission regulations.

January 2, 2011   EPA greenhouse-gas emission rules take effect for power plants and large industrial sources. Officials in all fifty states must now require large sources to install BACT (best available control technology) for greenhouse gases as a condition of permitting. Only one state, Texas, declines to implement the new rule.

Table 8A.2 Energy and Climate-Change Legislation, 2003 to 2010

Year	Bill	Sponsors	Key Provisions	Outcome
2003	Climate Steward-ship Act of 2003 (S 139)	*Sponsor:* Senator Joseph Lieberman (D-CT) *Cosponsors:* Senators John McCain (R-AZ), Daniel Akaka (D-HI), Maria Cantwell (D-WA), Richard Durbin (D-IL), Dianne Feinstein (D-CA), Frank Lautenberg (D-NJ), Patty Murray (D-WA), Bill Nelson (D-FL), Olympia Snowe (R-ME)	Summary: Proposes regulations to limit U.S. emissions of six greenhouse gases (GHG), including carbon dioxide, through a cap-and-trade system of tradable emission allowances and emissions reporting requirements. Would cap 2010 aggregate emissions from the commercial, industrial, transportation, and electric power sectors at the 2000 level. Also proposes a federal climate-change research program. Allocation of allowances: Each entity is given, without charge, a certain number of allowances. Entities can acquire additional allowances through trade or auction. The secretary of commerce determines the number of tradable allowances allocated to each sector, while the EPA determines the number of allowances allocated to each entity. Impact on energy-intensive industries (border adjustment mechanism-tariff): No explicit border adjustment. Carbon offsets: Entities would be allowed to fulfill 15 percent (during phase I), then 10 percent (during phase II) of allowance	Rejected on October 30, 2003, by a vote of 43 to 55

| 2005 | Climate Stewardship and Innovation Act of 2005 (S 1151) | Sponsor: Senator John McCain (R-AZ) Cosponsors: Senators Joseph Lieberman (D-CT), Barack Obama (D-IL), Olympia Snowe (R-ME) | requirements through various mechanisms, including carbon sequestration programs like agricultural and conservation practices and reforestation. Carbon volatility mechanism: Carbon prices to be determined by the market. Regulatory jurisdiction: EPA administrator would maintain a National Greenhouse Gas Database, and the Climate Change Credit Corporation would be established to manage tradable allowances. Summary: Slightly revised version of the Climate Stewardship Act of 2003. New proposals include renaming the Department of Commerce's Technology Administration the Innovation Administration and providing incentives for the development of various technologies, including nuclear. | Rejected on June 22, 2005, by a vote of 38 to 60 |

(Table continues on p. 370.)

Table 8A.2 *(Continued)*

Year	Bill	Sponsors	Key Provisions	Outcome
2008	Lieberman-Warner Climate Security Act of 2008 (S 3036)	*Sponsor*: Senator Barbara Boxer (D-CA) *Original version introduced in 2007 by sponsor Senator Joseph Lieberman (I-CT) and cosponsors John Warner (R-VA), Benjamin Cardin (D-MD), Robert Casey (D-PA), Norm Coleman (R-MN), Susan Collins (R-ME), Elisabeth Dole (R-NC), Thomas Harkin (D-IA), Amy Klobuchar (D-MN), Bill Nelson (D-FL), Charles Schumer (D-NY), Ron Wyden (D-OR)	Summary: Proposes regulations to limit U.S. GHG emissions through a cap-and-trade system. Covers entities using, producing, or importing a specified amount of fossil fuel. Would reduce GHG emissions from specified sectors by approximately 71 percent below 2005 levels by 2050. Allocation of allowances: Entities would be given a specified amount of allowances free of charge and could acquire additional allowances through trade or auction. Both the amount of total available allowances (the cap) and the percentage of total available allowances allotted free decrease annually. Impact on carbon-intensive industries: Provides a border adjustment mechanism requiring that importers of primary goods from countries without GHG reduction programs of "comparable stringency" purchase international reserve allowances. Smaller and less-developed nations are exempt, and proceeds are dedicated to climate-change mitigation in low-income communities overseas.	Dropped in June 2008 after failed cloture vote

Year	Act	Sponsor	Summary	Status
2009	American Clean Energy and Security Act of 2009 (HR 2454)	*Sponsor:* Representative Henry Waxman (D-CA) *Cosponsor:* Representative Edward Markey (D-MA)	Summary: Establishes a GHG cap-and-trade system designed to reduce emissions from specified sources to 83 percent below 2005 levels by 2050. Also mandates improving energy productivity and creating a combined energy-efficiency and renewable-electricity standard requiring electricity suppliers to meet 20 percent of their demand through renewable energy and conservation by Carbon offsets: Entities are permitted to satisfy up to 15 percent of the total allowance submission requirement through specified domestic and international carbon offset mechanisms, including agricultural and rangeland sequestration and management practices, land-use change and forestry activities, and manure management and disposal. Carbon volatility mechanism: Prices are to be determined by the market. Regulatory jurisdiction: The EPA would manage the national cap-and-trade system. Offsets from the Northeast's Regional Greenhouse Gas Initiative can be exchanged at a discount rate into the national system.	Passed as amended on June 26, 2009, by a vote of 219 to 212

(Table continues on p. 372.)

Table 8A.2 (Continued)

Year	Bill	Sponsors	Key Provisions	Outcome
			2020. Supports and encourages various research and development initiatives, including loan guarantees for nuclear energy.	
			Allocation of allowances: Entities are given a specified amount of allowances free of charge and can acquire additional allowances through trade or auction. Both the cap and the percentage of total available allowances allotted free decrease annually.	
			Impact on carbon-intensive industries: The president has the option of imposing a broader adjustment before June 30, 2017.	
			Carbon offsets: Entities can achieve compliance through approved offsets generally related to agriculture and forestry. Offsets may be domestic or international (generally 50 percent of total offsets) and must be limited to a collective 2 billion tons annually. The EPA administrator must establish regulations for an offset program, including a registry.	
			Carbon volatility mechanism: Sets an initial price floor of $10 per ton of carbon and creates a strategic allowance reserve to be auctioned when the average carbon price exceeds 60 percent of the historical three-year average.	

| 2009 | Clean Energy Jobs and American Power Act (S 1733) | *Sponsor:* Senator John Kerry (D-MA) *Cosponsors:* Senators Barbara Boxer (D-CA), Benjamin Cardin (D-MD), Paul Kirk (D-MA) | Regulatory jurisdiction: Emission allowances issued before December 31, 2011, by the State of California, the Regional Greenhouse Gas Initiative, or the Western Climate Initiative can be exchanged for federal allowances. Existing state or regional cap-and-trade programs would be suspended from 2012 to 2017.

Summary: Establishes a GHG cap-and-trade system designed to reduce emissions from specified sources to 20 percent below 2005 levels by 2020 and 83 percent by 2050. Also supports various research and development initiatives, including provisions to promote nuclear energy, natural gas, and carbon capture and storage.

Allocation of allowances: Entities are given a specified amount of allowances free of charge and can acquire additional allowances through trade or auction. Both the cap and the percentage of total available allowances allotted free decrease annually.

Impact on carbon-intensive industries: There is an International Trade placeholder where a border measure can be inserted. | Abandoned in favor of new proposal |

(Table continues on p. 374.)

Table 8A.2 *(Continued)*

Year	Bill	Sponsors	Key Provisions	Outcome
			Carbon offsets: Entities can achieve compliance through approved offsets generally related to agriculture and forestry. Offsets may be domestic or international (limited to 25 percent of total offsets) and must be limited to 2 billion tons annually. The EPA administrator must establish regulations for an offset program, including a registry.	
			Carbon volatility mechanism: The bill sets an initial price floor of $11 per ton of carbon and creates a strategic allowance reserve to be auctioned when the average carbon reaches $28 per ton in 2012, increasing thereafter.	
			Regulatory jurisdiction: Emission allowances issued before December 31, 2011, by the State of California, the Regional Greenhouse Gas Initiative, or the Western Climate Initiative can be exchanged for federal allowances. Existing state or regional cap-and-trade programs are suspended from 2012 to 2017.	

| 2009 | Carbon Limits and Energy for America's Renewal (CLEAR) Act (S 2877) | *Sponsor:* Senator Maria Cantwell (D-WA)

Cosponsor: Senator Susan Collins (R-ME) | Summary: Establishes a cap-and-refund carbon limitation program to reduce emissions from specified sources to 20 percent below 2005 levels by 2020 and 83 percent by 2050. Also provides direct funding for programs that reduce other GHG emissions.

Allocation of allowances: All carbon shares would be sold in monthly auctions run by the secretary of the Treasury and open only to first seller entities "in the business of producing or importing fossil carbon or production process carbon." Roughly one-quarter of carbon share auction proceeds would go toward the Clean Energy Reinvestment Fund. The remaining proceeds would be given back to U.S. residents in tax-free energy security dividends.

Impact on carbon-intensive industries: Specified imports would be charged a fee reflecting the intrinsic carbon share value of the product.

Carbon offsets: No offsets can be used to meet carbon caps. | No vote in 111th Congress |

(Table continues on p. 376.)

Table 8A.2 (Continued)

Year	Bill	Sponsors	Key Provisions	Outcome
			Carbon volatility mechanism: Initially, a price collar would be set between $7 and $21 per ton and would increase over time. A safety valve for carbon share demand would also be established.	
			Regulatory jurisdiction: Would protect voluntary state and regional renewable energy and carbon reduction credits, but impact on existing regional cap-and-trade programs is unclear.	
2010	American Power Act (discussion draft)	Sponsors: Senators John Kerry (D-MA) and Joseph Lieberman (I-CT)	Summary: Establishes a carbon cap-and-trade system to reduce emissions from specified sources to 17 percent below 2005 levels by 2020 and 83 percent by 2050. At least two-thirds of revenues would be directed to consumers through rebates and energy bill discounts. Supports domestic energy production, including offshore oil and gas drilling and the expansion of nuclear and clean-coal projects.	No vote in 111th Congress
			Allocation of allowances: Initially, approximately 75 percent of permits would be allocated free of charge; all permits auctioned by 2035. A cap on utilities would be instituted in 2012, and a cap on manufacturing would take effect in 2016.	

Impact on carbon-intensive industries: Establishes a carbon tariff on specified imports.

Carbon offsets: Entities can meet up to 15 percent of compliance obligation through approved domestic or international projects (generally limited to 25 percent of total offsets). Establishes a multi billion-dollar domestic carbon offset program to be managed by the Department of Agriculture.

Carbon volatility mechanism: Initially, a price collar would be set between $7 and $21 per ton of carbon, increasing over time. A strategic reserve would also be established.

Regulatory jurisdiction: Prohibits state and regional GHG cap-and-trade programs.

Source: Author's compilation based on information from THOMAS (Library of Congress, various years), GovTrack.us (2003, 2009), Pew Center on Global Climate Change (2003, 2005, 2008, 2009a, 2009b, 2009c, 2010), Energy Information Administration (2003b), U.S. Senate (2005), Kerry (2010), and Tutwiler (2010).

NOTES

1. The greenhouse gases that enter the atmosphere as a result of human activities are carbon dioxide, methane, nitrous oxide, and fluorinated gases. Of these, carbon dioxide is by far the most abundant, accounting for about 80 percent of greenhouse-gas emissions. Carbon dioxide lingers in the atmosphere for up to 100 years, so even if stringent emissions limits are enacted soon, some warming is inevitable. Nevertheless, scientists argue that rapid and immediate emission reductions are necessary to avert the worst impacts of climate change. The earth's average surface temperature has already risen 1.4 degree Fahrenheit over the last century, and most of that increase has been in recent decades. (The United States is home to only 4 percent of the world's population but responsible for 25 percent of the emissions that cause climate change.)

2. The phrase *global warming* refers to the rising surface temperature of the earth. The phrases *climate change* and *global climate change* refer to the many other impacts associated with higher levels of greenhouse gases in the atmosphere, including global warming but also changing patterns of precipitation and ocean acidification.

3. After the Btu-tax proposal passed in the House by a vote of 219 to 213, trade associations and antitax groups deployed public relations firms to wage a grassroots war against it. Citizens for a Sound Economy, an organization founded by the billionaire oil magnates David and Charles Koch, played a critical role in defeating the Btu tax (Mayer 2010). Intimidated, Clinton dropped his support for the tax, which was then drastically scaled back (to a four-cent gasoline tax) by Democrats in the Finance Committee, who were concerned about regional economic impacts (Cohen 1994). The Btu tax was one of several issues that conservatives used to take over Congress in the midterm elections of 1994.

4. According to journalist Eric Pooley, many senators who favored a binding commitment to reduce greenhouse gases believed that if the resolution was unanimous, its force would be blunted because observers couldn't possibly take it as a vote against the treaty (2010). Their reasoning was clearly flawed: the message sent was that Congress was monolithic in its opposition to any climate-change treaty.

5. The transition away from carbon-intensive energy production would involve switching from coal to natural gas and greatly increasing energy efficiency, and eventually shifting to low- or no-carbon fuels, including alternative fuels and nuclear energy.

6. In fact, the *Wall Street Journal* criticized Obama's lack of exposure to the corporate world and bemoaned the lack of prominent business leaders in his cabinet (Williamson and King 2009).

7. The gray area concerns the extent to which greenhouse-gas curbs constitute regulations on the means of production (on which the World Trade Organization has not allowed trade restrictions) versus the product itself.

8. The CBO estimated that Waxman-Markey would cost the average American household $175 in 2020, but that the poorest households would actually see a $40 benefit. The EPA calculated that the average American household would pay between $98 and $140 per year, as long as most of the money raised by the sale of allowances was returned to households. The Energy Information Administration (EIA) found that near-term impacts of the House bill would be modest: electric bills would increase 3 percent to 4 percent over what they would be otherwise by 2020. Longer term, though, after the period of free allowances ended, energy prices would increase more rapidly: by 2030, electricity prices could be 20 percent higher than they would be otherwise.

9. A study by the Center for Public Integrity found that 770 companies and public-interest groups registered to lobby on climate change in 2009 (Snyder 2009a). American Electric Power and Southern Company, two large utilities, spent $4.6 million and $6.3 million in the first half of 2009, compared to $3.3 million and $5.6 million, respectively, in the first half of 2008 (Snyder 2009c). Natural gas companies, which historically had not built a consensus around policy issues, joined forces with pipeline companies in March 2009 in their own effort to influence the legislative debate. With twenty-eight members and an anticipated budget of $800 million, America's Natural Gas Alliance dispatched lobbyists and took out ads in Washington publications in hopes of tilting the distribution of allowances in their favor. Major oil companies like ConocoPhillips and ExxonMobil also registered substantial increases in lobbying, although their main concern was trying to stop the bill: ConocoPhillips spent $9.3 million in the first six months of 2009, compared to $4.5 million during the same period in 2008 (Snyder 2009c). These figures do not cover money spent on grassroots organizing, which industry stepped up as well during this time.

10. Browner had pressed for the fast-track option for climate change. But twenty-eight senators—including eight Democrats—sent a strongly worded letter to Budget Committee leaders Kent Conrad and Judd Gregg warning them against such a tactic, and, on April 1, the Senate passed an amendment making it practically impossible to do so.

11. Beyond Graham, the Republicans ostensibly in play at that point were Senators Olympia Snowe and Susan Collins of Maine, Scott Brown of Massachusetts, and George Lemieux of Florida. More remote prospects included George Voinovich of Ohio, Richard Lugar of Indiana, Mel Martinez of Florida, Judd Gregg of New Hampshire, Lisa Murkowski of Alaska, and Bob Corker of Tennessee.

12. The bill's main industry-friendly provisions follow:

- It contained a hard price collar for carbon, with an introductory floor set at $12, increasing at 3 percent over inflation annually, and a ceiling of $25, increasing at 5 percent over inflation annually.

- It preempted the ability of states to implement mandatory greenhouse-gas reductions and provided compensation for those that must terminate existing programs; it also restricted the EPA's ability to regulate greenhouse gases under the Clean Air Act.

- In response to the Deepwater Horizon spill, it allowed states to opt out of drilling up to seventy-five miles from their shores and to veto drilling plans if threatened by significant adverse impacts from a spill; states that approved drilling would receive 37.5 percent of the royalty revenue. Just before the bill's release its sponsors rewrote the section on offshore-oil drilling, raising new hurdles for any future drilling off the Atlantic and Pacific coasts but allowing it to proceed off Louisiana, Texas, and Alabama.

- It allotted $2 billion per year for CCS R&D and created significant incentives for commercial deployment of the technology.

- For nuclear power, the package provided a set of financial incentives, including risk insurance for twelve projects, investment and manufacturing tax credits to promote construction of new facilities, and $54 billion in loan guarantees; it also promised to invest in R&D for small, modular reactors.

- It delayed the date that industrial sources would be regulated until 2016; before that date, they would get an allowance designed to offset increases in electricity costs. Starting in 2016, energy-intensive and trade-exposed industries would get allowances to help offset their compliance costs. Additionally, a border-protection mechanism shielded domestic manufacturers from foreign competition.

- It gave the Department of Agriculture the lead role in overseeing offsets, and exempted farmers from mandatory pollution-compliance obligations.

- Significantly, the Senate bill gave utilities more free allowances than did the House bill. It also shifted the emission-allocation formula: it distributed allowances seventy-five to twenty-five between companies based on their historic emissions and their retail sales, rather than the fifty-fifty split in the House bill. The shift was made to accommodate fourteen senators in states—mostly from the Midwest and Great Plains—whose utilities rely heavily on coal.

13. According to journalist Ryan Lizza (2010), White House aides were divided on the appropriate strategy. Phil Schiliro thought more engagement with Congress was required, whereas Axelrod believed that close engagement with legislative deal-making was tarnishing Obama's reputation as a change

agent. Lizza also argues that at times the White House's refusal to coordinate with Congress went beyond disengagement to outright subversion.

14. The federal government owns or leases more than 500,000 properties and accounts for nearly 1.5 percent of the nation's spending on fuel and electricity (Talley and Hughes 2010). Its actions therefore not only affect national emissions but also influence the cost of emissions-reducing technologies.

15. The administration's actions sparked a hostile reaction among Senate Republicans, who in mid-April introduced legislation, titled the NEPA Certainty Act, that would prohibit considering climate-change impacts in NEPA reviews. The bill's sponsors argued that the extended review would result in costly delays and litigation, and would hamper job creation. In May, House Republicans introduced a slightly weaker companion bill.

16. In late July 2010, Lisa Jackson rejected ten petitions, including two from the Texas and Virginia attorneys general, to reconsider the endangerment finding on the grounds that it was based on shoddy science. Seventeen states had also filed lawsuits challenging the endangerment finding, and eighteen filed in support; oral arguments were scheduled for the spring of 2011, and a final decision was expected in the summer.

17. The state of California had passed legislation that would cut vehicles' greenhouse-gas emissions by 30 percent between 2009 and 2016, but needed the EPA to waive less stringent requirements under the Clean Air Act in order to implement the law. More than a dozen states intended to follow California's lead. In late October 2009, the EPA moved to dismiss the legal challenge to the waiver from the U.S. Chamber of Commerce and the National Automobile Dealers Association in the D.C. court on the grounds that the organizations lacked the legal standing to sue. The car-makers ultimately lost the legal battle.

18. Pursuant to its New Source Review and Prevention of Significant Deterioration provisions, the Clean Air Act requires all new or substantially modified facilities that emit more than 250 tons of a criteria pollutant each year to install the best available pollution control technology. But that threshold is problematic for carbon dioxide, which is emitted in much greater quantities than the other so-called criteria pollutants. In the absence of a tailoring rule for greenhouse-gas emissions, as many as 6 million sources could require permits under the act.

19. In early August 2010, the Presidential Climate Project furnished the administration with a list of actions the president could take without congressional input, through executive orders (Lehmann 2010b). Among the recommended options are imposing a gasoline standard that cuts carbon intensity by 5 percent in five years and 10 percent in ten years, further increasing the fuel-efficiency of new cars, rolling back federal subsidies for the oil and gas industry (the group says oil and gas companies received $72 billion in such subsi-

dies between 2002 and 2008), and promoting state initiatives with additional funding.

20. Twenty-nine states have Renewable Electricity Standards, and about thirty have smart-meter programs that encourage demand reduction. The Regional Greenhouse Gas Initiative, a regional emission-trading program, has been operating since September 2008, and proposals are in the works to create a midwestern regional cap-and-trade system as well as a western system that includes Canadian provinces. Some states, like New York, were moving aggressively to add new climate-related policies. A study released in July 2010 by the Center for Climate Strategies found that if all states got on board with twenty-three policies already under way in more than a dozen of them, emissions could reach 27 percent below 1990 levels by 2020, even without a cap in place (Kahn 2010). As of the summer of 2010, however, the outlook for such widespread adoption of state-level policies was not good, and many existing state programs appeared vulnerable in the event of political turnover.

REFERENCES

Allen, Jared. 2009a. "Last-Minute Vote Push." *The Hill*, June 25, 2009. Available at: http://thehill.com/homenews/news/47985-last-minute-vote-push-on-climate-bill (accessed January 27, 2011).

———. 2009b. "Rep. Waxman Giving Senate Room to Work on Climate Change Bill." *The Hill*, July 9, 2009. Available at: http://thehill.com/homenews/news/49750-rep-waxman-giving-senate-room-to-work-on-climate-change-bill (accessed January 27, 2011).

Alter, Jonathan. 2010. *The Promise: President Obama, Year One.* New York: Simon and Schuster.

Bachmann, Michelle. 2010. "Keep Offshore Drilling in the U.S. Afloat." *The Bachman Blog*, Townhall.org. Available at: http://michelebachmann.townhall.com/blog/issue14 (accessed January 27, 2011).

Bolton, Alexander. 2010. "Climate Bill Teetering." *The Hill*, June 16, 2010. Available at: http://thehill.com/homenews/administration/103737-climate-bill-teetering (accessed January 27, 2011).

Bravender, Robin. 2010a. "'Comprehensive' Label Unlikely for Future Senate Energy Bills." *Greenwire*, September 23, 2010.

———. 2010b. "EPA to Revise GHG Permitting Limits, Will Focus on Larger Sources." *E&E News PM*, March 3, 2010.

Cohen, Richard. 1994. *Changing Course in Washington: Clinton and the New Congress.* New York: Macmillan.

Davenport, Coral. 2009. "A Landmark Climate Bill Passes." *CQ Weekly*, June 29, 2009.

———. 2010a. "Selling a Climate Change Bill to Coal Country." *CQ Weekly*, February 15, 2010.

———. 2010b. "Moment of Truth for Energy Bill." *Politico*, July 12, 2010.

Eilperin, Juliet. 2008. "Transition's Timing Hits Climate Talks." *Washington Post*, December 8, 2008.

———. 2010. "More Signs of Warming, but Legislative Climate Still Cold." *Washington Post*, September 24, 2010.

Eilperin, Juliet, and Michael D. Shear. 2009. "Obama Urged to Intensify Push for Climate Measure." *Washington Post*, October 12, 2009.

Energy Information Administration (EIA). 2003. "Emissions of Greenhouse Gases in the United States 2001, Executive Summary." Washington: U.S. Department of Energy. Available at: http://www.gcrio.org/OnLnDoc/pdf/usghg2001 summary.pdf (accessed January 27, 2011).

Energy Information Administration. 2003b. Analysis *of S. 139, the Climate Stewardship Act of 2003: Highlights and Summary.* Available at: http://www.eia.doe .gov/oiaf/servicerpt/ml/pdf/summary.pdf (accessed April 20, 2011).

Geman, Ben. 2010a. "Ad Ties BP Oil Spill to EPA Rule Resolution." *The Hill*, June 8, 2010.

———. 2010b. "Swing Senators Feel Pressure on Climate." *The Hill*, June 2, 2010.

GovTrack.us. 2003. *S.Amdt. 2028: To provide for a program of scientific research on abrupt climate . . .* Available at: http://www.govtrack.us/congress/amendment .xpd?session=108&amdt=s2028 (accessed April 20, 2011).

———. 2009. H.R.2454: American Clean Energy and Security Act of 2009. Available at: http://www.govtrack.us/congress/bill.xpd?bill=h111-2454 (accessed April 20, 2011).

Greenwire. 2006. "Public Opinion on Global Warming Echoing Studies, Media Attention." *Greenwire*, March 27, 2006. Available at: http://www.eenews.net/ Greenwire/2006/03/27/archive/7?terms=%22Public+Opinion+on+Global+ Warming+Echoing+Studies%2C+Media+Attention%22 (accessed January 28, 2011).

Kahn, Debra. 2010. "Study Estimates That States Together Could Cut Emissions by 27%." *ClimateWire*, July 26, 2010.

Kaplun, Alex. 2010a. "Looming Regulations Put EPA in Conservatives' Cross Hairs." *Greenwire*, March 5, 2010.

———. 2010b. "Obama Attempts to Sell Jobs, Energy Agenda on Midwest Swing." *E&E News PM*, April 27, 2010.

Kerry, John. 2010. *American Power Act.* Available at: http://kerry.senate.gov/work/ issues/issue/?id=7f6b4d4a-da4a-409e-a5e7-15567cc9e95c (accessed April 20, 2011).

Khor, Martin. 2010. "The Bonn Talks Were a Healing Process—But Stormy Meetings Lie Ahead." *The Guardian*, April 13, 2010. Available at: http://www.guardian .co.uk/environment/cif-green/2010/apr/13/bonn-talks-climate (accessed January 27, 2011).

Layzer, Judith A. Forthcoming. *Freedom, Efficiency, and Environmental Protection: Conservative Ideas and Their Consequences.* Cambridge, Mass.: MIT Press.

Lee, Carol E. 2010. "Obama Cites Spill in Climate Pitch." *Politico*, May 26, 2010.

Lehmann, Evan. 2010a. "Climate Talks Advance, but No Deal on the Table." *Environment & Energy Daily*, July 20, 2010.

———. 2010b. "Obama Gets a Menu of Climate Actions He Can Take without Congress." *ClimateWire*, August 6, 2010.

Library of Congress. Various years. THOMAS data. Available at: http://thomas .loc.gov (accessed April 20, 2011).

Ling, Katherine. 2010. "Obama to Address Emissions through 'Bite Sized' Energy Policy," *Greenwire*, October 25, 2010.

Lizza, Ryan. 2010. "As the World Burns." *The New Yorker*, October 11, 2010, pp. 70–83.

Marshall, Christa. 2009. "Coal Country Poses the Biggest Obstacle." *ClimateWire*, November 2, 2009.

Mayer, Jane. 2010. "Covert Operations." *The New Yorker*, August 30, 2010, pp. 45–55.

Morello, Lauren. 2006. "Polls Find Groundswell of Belief in, Concern about Global Warming." *Greenwire*, April 21, 2006.

Mulkern, Anne C. 2010. "WWF Emerges as Leading Lobbyist on Senate Emissions Bill." *Energy & Environment Daily*, May 18, 2010.

Obama, Barack. 2010. "Obama in Command: The Rolling Stone Interview." *Rolling Stone Magazine*, September 28, 2010. Available at: http://www.rollingstone .com/politics/news/obama-in-command-br-the-rolling-stone-interview-20100928 (accessed January 30, 2011).

Office of Management and Budget. 2009. *A New Era of Responsibility: Renewing America's Promise*. Washington: The White House. Available at: http://www .gpoaccess.gov/usbudget/fy10/pdf/fy10-newera.pdf (accessed January 27, 2011).

Pew Center on Global Climate Change. 2003. *Summary of The Lieberman-McCain Climate Stewardship Act of 2003*. Available at: http://www.pewclimate.org/ policy_center/analyses/s_139_summary.cfm (accessed April 20, 2011).

———. 2005. *Summary of McCain-Lieberman Climate Stewardship and Innovation Act of 2005*. Available at: http://www.pewclimate.org/federal/analysis/congress/ 108/summary-mccain-lieberman-climate-stewardship-and-innovation-act -2005 (accessed April 20, 2011).

———. 2008. *Analysis of the Lieberman-Warner Climate Security Act of 2008*. Available at: http://www.pewclimate.org/analysis/l-w (accessed April 20, 2011).

———. 2009a. *The American Clean Energy and Security Act (Waxman-Markey Bill)*. Available at: http://www.pewclimate.org/acesa (accessed April 20, 2011).

———. 2009b. *Summary of the Clean Energy Jobs and American Power Act (S. 1733) Chairman's Mark*. Available at: http://www.pewclimate.org/short-summary/ clean-energy-jobs-american-power-act-chairmans-mark (accessed April 20, 2011).

———. 2009c. *Summary of the CLEAR Act (Cantwell-Collins)*. Available at: http:// www.pewclimate.org/federal/congress/111/clear-act-cantwell-collins (accessed April 20, 2011).

———. 2010. *Kerry-Lieberman American Power Act.* Available at: http://www.pewcli mate.org/federal/congress/111/kerry-lieberman-american-power-act (accessed April 20, 2011).

Pooley, Eric. 2010. *The Climate War: True Believers, Power Brokers, and the Fight to Save the Earth.* New York: Hyperion.

Pulizzi, Henry J. 2009. "Obama Administration Unveils New Set of Smart-Grid Standards." *Wall Street Journal*, May 18, 2009.

Samuelsohn, Darren. 2009a. "Obama Administration Portrays House Emissions Bill as Economic Boon." *Greenwire*, April 22, 2009.

———. 2009b. "Letters on Cap and Trade Pour into Senate." *Greenwire*, September 8, 2009.

———. 2010a. "For Fence Sitters, Everything's in Play." *Environment & Energy Daily*, March 9, 2010.

———. 2010b. "White House Rhetoric May Signal Climate-Bill Surge." *Greenwire*, April 12, 2010.

———. 2010c. "Obama Renews Call to Pass Senate Bill." *E&E News PM*, May 12, 2010.

Samuelsohn, Darren, and Ben Geman. 2009. "House Democrats Release Draft Energy, Emissions Bill." *Greenwire*, March 31, 2009.

Snyder, Jim. 2009a. "Climate Lobbying Heats Up." *The Hill*, June 24, 2009.

———. 2009b. "Hoyer Says Climate Bill Is in Works." *The Hill*, May 14, 2009.

———. 2009c. "Millions Spent to Lobby Climate Bill." *The Hill*, July 22, 2009.

———. 2009d. "Senate Climate Debate Focuses on Economic Impact." *The Hill*, July 8, 2009.

Snyder, Jim, and J. Taylor Rushing. 2009. "Kerry and Boxer Launch Climate Debate." *The Hill*, October 1, 2009.

Talley, Ian, and Siobhan Hughes. 2010. "Obama Makes New Push to Cut Government Emissions." *Wall Street Journal*, January 29, 2010.

Tutwiler, Patrick. 2010. *Climate Change Legislation: Where Does It Stand?* Available at: http://www.govtrackinsider.com/articles/2010-04-27/climate-change (accessed April 20, 2011).

United States Climate Action Partnership (USCAP). 2009. "A Blueprint for Legislative Action: Consensus Recommendations for U.S. Climate Protection Legislation." Washington, D.C.: UNCAP. Available at: http://www.us-cap.org/pdf/ USCAP_Blueprint.pdf (accessed January 27, 2011).

U.S. Senate. 2005. "U.S. Senate Roll Call Votes 109th Congress—1st Session." Available at: http://www.senate.gov/legislative/LIS/roll_call_lists/roll_call_vote _cfm.cfm?congress=109&session=1&vote=00148 (accessed April 20, 2011).

Williamson, Elizabeth. 2009. "Obama Calls for Passage of Climate Bill, Touts Energy Initiatives." *Wall Street Journal*, October 23, 2009.

Williamson, Elizabeth, and Neil King Jr. 2009. "A Chilly Obama Dives into the Private Sector." *Wall Street Journal*, April 29, 2009.

Chapter 9 | Paying America's Way: The Fraught Politics of Taxes, Investments, and Budgetary Responsibility

Andrea Louise Campbell

CANDIDATE BARACK OBAMA made startling and politically courageous promises to reorient taxing and spending in the United States. He sought to turn Republican tax politics on its head, raising taxes on the politically powerful affluent and devoting the money to enhanced economic security for ordinary Americans, such as health care reform, and to greater investments in human and physical capital, such as education and infrastructure. And taxes were due on the agenda, thanks to the expiration of the Bush tax cuts. Between Obama's great popularity and apparent public support for raising taxes on the wealthy, the boldest plans in decades to change the tax burden and address economic inequality—indeed, to change the discourse of American politics—seemed poised for success.

But the Great Recession intervened, vastly complicating these carefully laid plans and raising questions in the public mind about whose side Obama was really on. The administration achieved a great deal, but its accomplishments either appeared to benefit the wrong people or lacked visibility. The financial sector rescue may have prevented worldwide economic collapse, but it also fanned a perception that those who caused the problems were saved first, and that the victims on Main Street paid the bill. The stimulus legislation may have averted a second Great Depression, but it largely backfilled huge cuts in state and local spending, and the saved jobs were difficult to appreciate in the face of double-digit unemployment. Many Americans believe the historic health care reform extended insurance coverage to the poor on their nickel. In the light of continuing economic pain, the benefits of these and other pieces of legislation were difficult to see. Indeed, the rapid succession of legislation and increased scope of government gave many ordinary Americans pause as they wondered how high future taxes might be and how large government might become.

In the meantime, Republicans capitalized on the downturn to pump new life into old arguments about taxes, spending, and deficits. They railed against Obama's plan to let the Bush tax cuts for the affluent expire, asserting that no one's taxes should increase during a recession. Most economists agreed that the large budget deficit that arose in 2009 was caused chiefly by declining revenues due to the recession and unfunded legacies of the Bush administration: two wars fought and a Medicare prescription drug benefit adopted without new revenues. But Republicans interpreted the deficit as a spending problem owing to Obama administration action and out-of-control entitlements, raising old complaints about Social Security, Medicare, and Medicaid. Such arguments conflated short-term economic conditions with long-term issues, distinctions that are lost on most Americans but that play into fears of big government and high taxes. Republicans rode such fears—and continuing economic distress—into significant gains in the 2010 midterm elections.

Despite these challenges Obama did achieve health care reform, financed in a progressive way that imposes new taxes on high-income households to expand insurance coverage to other less fortunate citizens. In his budgets he continued to propose additional changes to the tax code, repealing the Bush tax cuts for the affluent and expanding tax credits aimed at lower- and middle-income earners. However, deep divisions within the Democratic caucus as well as implacable resistance by an energized Republican Party undermined some of his most fervent goals. Most notably, the Bush tax cuts were extended for all for two years, into 2012, which may make future repeal of cuts for the wealthy that much more difficult. And the extension ensures that the issue will again come up in an election year. This may give Democrats an opportunity to expose Republican hypocrisy in desiring both tax cuts for the wealthy and lower budget deficits, but could also result in Democrats' yielding on tax relief for the rich yet again, given the party's historic vulnerability on tax-and-spend issues.

This chapter explores what happens when bold plans for redistribution encounter a historically deep recession. It also examines how inherited rules and policy legacies shape the possibilities for financing an ambitious agenda. It begins by describing Obama's campaign promises and early proposals on taxes and investment spending in a context in which conservatives have dominated the discussion of tax policy for thirty years. It reveals how the administration and congressional Democrats achieved progressive financing for health care. But it also shows how Republicans deployed their perennial antigovernment tropes, using the recession to argue for extended tax cuts for all, continuing high unemployment to argue that the stimulus was wasteful and government ineffective, and recession-driven deficits as an excuse to attack middle-class entitlement spending. In the short term, Republicans capitalized on Senate rules that advantage the minority in limiting further stimulus legislation and took advantage of the timing of the tax cut expiration to extend cuts for the wealthy. Most important, however, is what comes next as the country debates deficits, entitlements, and perhaps even the structure of the tax code itself leading up to the 2012 presidential election.

NO MORE TRICKLE-DOWN ECONOMICS: CAMPAIGN PROMISES

Barack Obama opened his campaign with a notably broad agenda of investment in America's people and infrastructure. His February 2007 announcement speech in Springfield, Illinois, emphasized higher educational standards, making college more affordable, ending poverty, easing retirement savings, and tackling the health care crisis (Obama 2007b). But if this agenda was unusual for its wide reach in confronting the insecurities felt by ordinary Americans, what was truly unprecedented was Obama's candor in saying that more revenues would be needed and that those revenues would come from the affluent—the very group most likely to resist higher taxes. In spring 2007 he made his redistributive agenda explicit in proposing to use expiring Bush tax cuts for the wealthy to fund health care reform and expand coverage to the uninsured (Obama 2007a, 2007d). At the same time expansions to the earned income tax credit (EITC) and child tax credit would ease tax burdens for lower- and middle-income earners.

In his rhetoric, Obama criticized the prevailing free-market and tax-cutting philosophy of conservative politicians: "They've told us [that] the market will correct all our misfortunes, and that there's no problem that can't be solved by another tax break that the wealthy didn't need and didn't ask for" (Obama 2007e). Throughout 2007, Obama excoriated the attitudes of "those who have benefited from the new global marketplace . . . [who] have not always concerned themselves with the losers in this new economy. There has been a tendency, during the boom times, to consider the casualties of a changing economy to be inevitable, and to justify outsized paydays or lower tax rates on Wall Street earnings as the natural order of things." These were trends that the Bush administration had accelerated "to the point where there is greater income inequality now than at any time since the Gilded Age" (2007c). He also pledged to simplify the tax code so that it was no longer "too complicated for ordinary folks to understand, but just complicated enough to work for someone who knows how to work the system," like "big business," which, when it "doesn't like something in the tax code [can] hire a lobbyist to get it changed" (2007f).

In his famous interaction with Joe the Plumber the month before the election, Obama further explained his philosophy, after declining to support a flat tax:

> And I do believe that for folks like me who are, you know, have worked hard but, frankly, also been lucky, I don't mind paying just a little bit more than the waitress who I just met over there, who's . . . things are slow and she can barely make the rent. Because my attitude is that if the economy's good for folks from the bottom up, it's gonna be good for everybody. If you've got a plumbing business, you're gonna be better off if you've got a whole bunch of customers who can afford to hire you. And right now, everybody's so pinched that business is bad for everybody. And I think when you spread the wealth around, it's good for everybody. (Obama 2008b)

The era of trickle-down economics was over; what mattered was investing in ordinary Americans, not giving further breaks to the affluent that served only to enrich them without enhancing economic growth more broadly.

Throughout the 2008 election year, Obama's proposals and rhetoric took further shape. Early in the year he began talking about providing a middle-class tax cut for "95 percent of Americans," and by summer 2008 started to iterate that taxes would not increase for those earning less than a quarter of a million dollars: "Let me be clear: if you're a family making less than $250,000, my plan will not raise your taxes—not your income taxes, not your payroll taxes, not your capital gains taxes, not any of your taxes. And unlike my opponent, I'll pay for my plan—by cutting wasteful spending, shutting corporate loopholes and tax havens, and rolling back the Bush tax cuts for the wealthiest Americans" (Obama 2008f). Stung by Republican accusations that ending the Bush cuts for the top two tax brackets would burden small business owners, he added to his stump speech the assertion that the under-$250,000 group included 98 percent of small business owners (Obama 2008d).

If Obama was intent on reducing taxes on most Americans and refocusing the tax system on the affluent, he also showed that he would not pander on taxes. With gas prices climbing above $4 per gallon, both Hillary

Clinton and John McCain supported a gas tax holiday for summer 2008, but Obama resisted the siren call of the easy tax cut. He argued that it would only save the average American thirty cents a day—a half tank of gas "altogether" (Obama 2008c)—and that prices would simply increase to fill the gap, enriching oil companies and depleting the federal highway fund (Obama 2008e). This kind of straight talk—supposedly McCain's MO—was something Americans had rarely heard on taxes.

Ultimately the Obama campaign pledges on revenues included a Making Work Pay refundable tax credit of $500 for workers and $1,000 for working couples (the main middle-class tax cut, intended as a partial rebate on payroll taxes); a universal home mortgage interest tax credit; a refundable college tuition tax credit of $4,000; elimination of federal income taxes for senior citizens making less than $50,000; an expansion of the earned income tax credit; an increase of the child and dependent tax credits; an expansion of the saver's credit for families earning under $75,000; and consumer tax credits for energy-efficient appliances and advanced technology vehicles.

Beyond these tax credits aimed primarily at lower- and middle-class earners, Obama also pledged to roll back the Bush tax cuts for the affluent, increasing the marginal income tax rates of families earning over $250,000 and individuals earning over $200,000 from 33 and 35 percent to the 36 and 39.6 percent levels of the Clinton administration. Personal exemption and itemized deduction phase-outs would also return to 1990s levels for taxpayers in these brackets. In addition, the capital gains and dividend tax rates would rise from 15 to 20 percent, and the estate tax would be frozen at 2009 parameters: a tax of 45 percent on estates over $3.5 million per individual or $7 million per couple, affecting 0.3 percent of all estates. In addition, Obama proposed adding a Social Security payroll tax of 2 to 4 percent, combined employer and employee contribution, on incomes over $250,000.[1] Although the focus in this chapter is on the individual income tax, Obama also proposed changes in the corporate income tax, including breaks for small firms and for firms engaging in research and development or starting new operations in the United States. He also proposed a $3,000 New American Jobs Tax Credit for each additional full-time employee businesses hired in 2009 and 2010.

In sum, Obama's campaign pledges sought to tilt the tax burden away from lower- and middle-class earners and toward the affluent, a politically risky proposal given the great influence of the wealthy on politics. For the vast majority of Americans, federal income taxes would be lower than they had been under Bush. By September 2008, Obama had even added a line to his stump speech asserting that for most taxpayers "under my plan, tax rates will actually be less than they were under Ronald Reagan" (Obama 2008a). His agenda turned the revenue strategies of the conservative movement on their head.

THE CONTEXT FOR THESE AMBITIONS: THE RISE OF THE CONSERVATIVE TAX AGENDA

The Reagan allusion was particularly apt, as the ascendance of the conservative arm of the Republican Party marked by Reagan's election, centered around a low-tax, antigovernment philosophy, had profoundly shaped the political economy of the United States over the previous three decades. During the 1950s and 1960s, taxes were a far less prominent issue on the national agenda than they became later, with both elite discourse about taxes and the salience of taxes to the public muted (Campbell 2009). Federal taxes rose rapidly during the postwar period, but real incomes grew even faster (Saulnier 1991). However, the 1970s were marked by a worldwide economic slowdown as well as rampant inflation and unemployment. Taxes became more painful, taking greater and greater bites out of Americans' flat or declining real wages. Frustration broke out with tax revolts in the states beginning in the late 1970s, and it became clear to Republican politicians such as Ronald Reagan that calls for tax cuts made for "good politics" (Martin 2008, 15). Taxes also served as an issue that united the various strands of the otherwise disparate Republican coalition (Morgan 2007) and that lined Republican candidates' coffers with corporate campaign contributions (Block 2009). It was also an issue that disproportionately helped the party of the right in a country with a stated ideological predilection for small government.

Cutting taxes became de rigueur for Republican politicians, and Democrats struggled to avoid the tax-and-spend label. Complicating the right's low-tax strategy, however, was the fact that Americans also liked much of what government did. They might assert a preference for small government in the abstract, but also supported spending on a variety of social programs, especially those that help the middle class such as Social Security and Medicare. They were, as public opinion researchers Lloyd Free and Hadley Cantril (1967) found, ideological conservatives but also operational liberals (see also Feldman and Zaller 1992; Page and Jacobs 2009; Page and Shapiro 1992). The public's appetite for social protections thwarted conservative efforts to trim the welfare state during the 1980s (Pierson 1994). Indeed, efforts to 'starve the left' by cutting taxes simply resulted in budget deficits, as revenues fell but spending continued during the 1980s. Reagan's famous 1981 tax cut was followed by a series of less publicized tax increases aimed at trimming the resultant deficits.

Thus the difficulty for elected politicians became how to raise taxes when necessary and how to satisfy the public's need for help in the face of life's vagaries. Overt tax increases were to be avoided, as several episodes seemed to indicate. George Bush the Elder was cast from office in part for raising federal income taxes in 1990—the top marginal rate climbing from Reagan's 28 percent to 31 percent—with an election-year recession finishing the job. Bill Clinton had to abandon a middle-class tax cut he promised during his campaign and was urged to tackle the budget deficit instead to satisfy the financial markets (Woodward 1994). He signed the 1993 Omnibus Budget Reconciliation Act (OBRA), which increased the top marginal income tax rate to 39.6 percent, which in turn, along with the failure of health care reform and other early mishaps, helped lead to the Republican takeover of Congress in 1994.

If raising taxes was difficult, so was the need to address societal needs while keeping the apparent size of government small. A common technique became the use of tax expenditures—issuing tax credits or breaks to subsidize a need or encourage a certain behavior. Americans needed help making ends meet, paying for day care, and providing a college education for their children, but the small government imperative meant direct spending programs were out of the question. Instead, Congress passed tax credits to assist with these needs, providing indirect help by excluding the money used to pay for them from federal taxation (Howard 1997, 2007). The problem with tax expenditures is that they greatly reduce federal revenues, and the recipients of such help do not credit government with providing help to the same extent as beneficiaries of direct spending programs do (Mettler 2009). Nonetheless, because they made government even smaller, tax credits were a mode of government provision even moderate and sometimes conservative politicians could support.

If the higher tax rate Clinton approved in 1993 was politically unpopular at the time, in combination with a booming economy, it produced the highest federal revenues in history and a budget surplus in the final years of his presidency. On assuming office, George W. Bush might have used the surplus for other goals—like financing a transition to Social Security individual accounts—but decided to prioritize tax cuts instead (Teles and Derthick 2009). The 2001 Bush tax cuts reduced rates across the board—from 15 percent at the bottom and 39.6 percent at the top, to 10 and 35 percent. It also increased child, child care, and education credits and reduced the marriage penalty. The estate tax was phased out, and would reach zero by 2010. To keep official cost estimates to a minimum and to allow the use of the reconciliation process requiring just fifty votes for passage in the Senate, these provisions were designed to sunset in 2011; if Congress took no further action, which it did for some provisions in 2004, the entire tax system would revert to its previous levels on January 1, 2011.

Further tax cut legislation in 2003 benefited mostly upper-income families by cutting the dividend and capital gains taxes to 15 percent and accelerating a number of the rate reductions, marriage penalty fixes, and child credits contained in the 2001 bill.

Distributionally, the 2001 and 2003 Bush tax cuts appeared to contain provisions for everyone—including lower- and middle-income taxpayers. However, the most significant cuts accrued to very high-income earners. The average cut resulting from the two rounds of legislation were $61 for the lowest quintile, $586 for the middle quintile, $2,907 for the ninety-fifth to ninety-ninth percentile, and $66,601 for the top percentile (Mishel, Bernstein, and Allegretto 2005, 85). Moreover, an analysis of the distribution of the tax cuts taking into account how they would ultimately be financed, because the cuts were funded with increased borrowing that eventually has to be paid off, shows that the cuts were "best seen" as net tax cuts for the top one-fifth to one-quarter of households, financed by net tax increases on the bottom 75 to 80 percent (Gale, Orszag, and Shapiro 2004, 2).

The rate reductions contained in the Bush tax cuts were a particular boon to the affluent, because they were taking home an increasing share of the nation's wealth. In 1970, the top 1 percent took home 9 percent of total income in the United States, including capital gains. By 2000 their share was 21.5 percent of total income, and in 2007 it was 23.5 percent (Piketty and Saez 2003, updated July 2010, table A3). The very wealthy were richer than ever before, but were also paying the lowest effective federal income tax rates in the postwar era (Brownlee 2000; Congressional Budget Office 2009).

Beyond slashing the tax burden of the affluent, the Bush tax cuts also quickly turned budget surpluses into budget deficits. Federal spending soared with the conflicts in Iraq and Afghanistan—the first wars in American history not accompanied by tax increases—and the addition of a prescription drug benefit for Medicare, a new entitlement passed on the eve of baby boomer retirement with virtually no financing attached to it. Billions of dollars of spending were put on the national credit card. Although future imbalances in Social Security and Medicare loomed, in 2007, when candidate Obama was formulating his spending and revenue plans, the budget deficit was still a manageable 1.2 percent of GDP. But all of that would change with the Great Recession that took hold by the next year.

THE NEW NEW DEAL MEETS THE GREAT RECESSION

The campaign year of 2008 was an economic hall of horrors, with one disaster following another as the housing bubble burst and the bad bets banks made on subprime mortgages and the esoteric financial instruments into which they had been rolled came to fruition: Bear Stearns went bankrupt in March; Merrill Lynch and insurance giant AIG were in trouble by early fall; the federal government seized control of Fannie Mae and Freddie Mac on September 7, 2008; Lehman Brothers filed for bankruptcy a week later. Fears that the nation's financial system could collapse, with unknown and inconceivable consequences, were real. The Bush administration scrambled to keep on top of the tsunami of events, piecing together the Troubled Asset Relief Program (TARP)—a financial-sector rescue plan—in October 2008. TARP authorized the U.S. Treasury to purchase up to $700 billion in troubled assets to stem the subprime mortgage crisis. The Bush administration also agreed to a $17 billion bailout of the automotive industry, with the money to be distributed by the next administration. In the meantime, unemployment, which had been below 5 percent throughout 2007, rose to 6.9 percent by election day (Bureau of Labor Statistics 2010). The Dow Jones Industrial Average, which had peaked above 14,000 in October 2007, had fallen below 9,000 by November 2008 (New York Stock Exchange 2010). Home foreclosures, typically below 100,000 per month in the middle of the decade, ticked above 200,000 by fall 2007 and above 250,000 by fall 2008.[2]

Obama in large part achieved his historic victory because of the Great Recession: his campaign's national polling shortly after the primaries showed that the economy was voters' main concern (Heilemann and Halperin 2010, 327; Wolffe 2009, 288); and his opponent was unable or unwilling to separate himself from Bush policies that seemed to many Americans to blame. Nor did some notable gaffes help the Republican candidate, such as McCain's insistence on the day Lehman collapsed that the "fundamentals of the economy are strong," and his failure to answer when asked how many homes he owned: "I'll have my staff get to you." Obama pounced: "If you don't know how many houses you have, then it's not surprising that you might think the economy was fundamentally strong" (Wolffe 2009, 295–96). Although the Republican Party had enjoyed many years of "issue ownership" over the economy—perceived as better stewards than tax-and-spend Democrats (Smith 2007; Bartels 2008; Petrocik 1996)—the Bush years and now the Great Recession took their toll. As Obama assumed office in January 2009, a CNN poll showed fully half of Americans thought the Republicans were "more responsible for the country's current economic problems," versus just 22 percent who blamed Democrats (CNN/Opinion Research Corporation 2009). Indeed, longer-running series of questions showed that the Republicans had lost much of the advantage on economic issues over time. Since 1984 the *New York Times*/CBS poll has asked, "Which party is more likely to ensure a strong economy?" Republicans held the clear advantage through the mid-1990s, when Democrats began to gain. During the Bush administration, the Republican image plunged further, and the percentage of Americans citing Democrats peaked at 56 percent in April 2008, higher even than the Republican peak of 52 percent in September 1984.[3]

But, in a cruelly ironic twist, if the recession helped Obama gain office, continuing economic pain also threatened to undermine his chief goals. During the late campaign and transition months, it became evident that the economy was in much worse shape than predicted. Bush left to Obama the politically messy tasks of lobbying Congress to release the second half of the TARP money (Alter 2010) and administering the automotive industry bailout, though Chrysler and General Motors would file for bankruptcy in spring 2009 anyway. And then there was the issue of economic stimulus, which dominated the transition and early days of the administration. If in Robert Reich's (1997) memory, every meeting in the early days of the Clinton administration was about the deficit, every meeting during the transition and early Obama administration was about the economy and the stimulus: how big should it be (confidential interview, August 2, 2010)?

Ultimately the American Recovery and Reinvestment Act of 2009 (ARRA) totaled $787 billion. Signed on February 17, 2009, the stimulus bill devoted about one-third each to tax cuts, infrastructure, and state relief and safety net programs (Office of Management and Budget 2010, 8). It included many of the redistributive elements of Obama's campaign promises, albeit on a temporary basis, including a $400 to $800 middle-class tax cut for 2009 and 2010, down from the $500 to $1,000 Obama had pledged; temporary expansions of the Child Tax Credit and EITC; and an expansion of the Hope Credit for college tuition for higher-income taxpayers, at $2,500 rather than the $4,000 of the campaign. The ARRA also included some provisions that were not among the Obama campaign pledges, including a one-time $250 payment to Social Security recipients, veterans, and railroad retirees; an $8,000 refundable first-time homebuyer credit[4]; a deduction for the taxes on new cars and trucks; an expansion of the Work Opportunity Tax Credit for early 2009 to cover new categories of workers (a credit for businesses for hiring persons in certain categories such as unemployed veterans, younger workers in certain communities, and the like); a nine-month, 65 percent COBRA subsidy for some unemployed; a provision deeming up to $2,400 in unemployment benefits for 2009 nontaxable; and some provisions for business.[5] The ARRA also extended the alternative minimum tax (AMT) relief through 2009.

The stimulus bill was an enormous and multifaceted bill. As Obama himself later remarked at an October 2009 gathering of the Democratic Senatorial and Congressional Campaign Committees:

Here's the thing about the Recovery Act people don't seem to remember. It wasn't just the most progressive tax cut policy in American history. It wasn't just emergency relief for states and individuals. It was also—people don't realize this—the single largest federal investment in education in our history. It was the largest investment in clean energy in our history. It was the largest boost to medical research and basic research in our history. It was the single largest investment in infrastructure since Eisenhower built the Interstate Highway System back in the 1950s. (Obama 2009)

Some observers thought Obama would have received more credit for the stimulus bill if it had been split into five bills, as its enormous investments in each of these areas would have been more visible. But Obama himself was afraid five separate bills could not get through the Congress (Alter 2010); better to get the necessary package through even if political credit suffered.

In a sign of what was to come, no House Republicans and only three Republican senators voted for the stimulus bill. Despite Obama's attempts at bipartisanship, the minority leaders in both chambers, Representative John Boehner and Senator Mitch McConnell, counseled complete obstruction. Some observers thought too much was devoted to the tax cut portion of the law—a sop to Republicans that utterly failed to attract support and that did undermine the bill's stimulative effect, given that the economic multiplier associated with tax cuts is thought to be lower than that of, say, direct aid to the unemployed.[6] With Republican votes, particularly in the Senate, unlikely, the pivot point moved to the Democratic Party, putting its internal factions on full display (Alter 2010, 116–30). Unseemly dealing to placate individual senators and to a lesser extent representatives— especially the conservative Blue Dogs—would characterize negotiations over each of Obama's major legislative efforts. This sausage-making, combined with the unprecedented amounts of money spent in very short order, made many members of the public nervous about the scope and reach of government. They may have been concerned about the magnitude of the recession, but soon many became focused instead on the government leviathan and what it might mean for future taxes. That the price tags attached to the stimulus and other legislative efforts were visible, but the saved jobs were not, added to the public's concerns, providing further basis for Republican obstructionism and putting wind behind the sails of antitax and antideficit forces.

If Obama's campaign promises were notable for pushing back on inequality, his first budget—released ten days after the stimulus bill signing—"flabbergasted" Washington types with its honesty and dearth of gimmicks (Herszenhorn 2009). Unlike Bush's budgets, Obama's included the costs of the Iraq and Afghanistan wars and a permanent AMT fix, and added $250 billion for additional bank bailouts, not to mention $10 billion for disaster relief, inevitable but rarely budgeted. He also set aside a ten-year $634 billion health care reform reserve to expand coverage and fund disease prevention, wellness programs, and research to reduce health spending. Beyond the accounting rectitude, the fiscal year 2010 budget included most of the redistributive promises from the campaign and sought to make permanent those that had been included on a temporary basis in the stimulus bill, such as the Making Work Pay middle-class tax credit and the EITC, child tax credit, and college tuition credit expansions. For the top two income brackets, the president's budget proposed rolling back the Bush tax cuts, that is, increasing marginal tax rates to 36 and 39.6 percent, increasing capital gains and dividend tax rates to 20 percent, and limiting the value of itemized deductions to 28 percent for 2011, when the recession would hopefully be over. In his budget message Obama reiterated his redistributive goals: "There is something wrong when we allow the playing field to be tilted so far in the favor of so few" (Office of Management and Budget 2009, 5).

The honest budgeting and redistributive goals notwithstanding, Obama had difficulty seeing his proposals put into practice. The congressional budget included the EITC, child tax credit, and education increases, but not the Making Work Pay tax credit beyond the 2010 end date stipulated in the stimulus bill. But that was to change with the health care reform, which not only extended coverage to the uninsured in an historic first for the United States but was also notably redistributive in its financing, with the haves paying for much of the new insurance coverage for the have-nots.

PROGRESSIVE FINANCING FOR HEALTH CARE

During the campaign, Obama had pledged not only to enhance the prospects of ordinary Americans by changing the distribution of the tax burden and making investments in areas like education, green energy, and innovation but also to engage in straightforward budgeting and fiscal rectitude. Each of his initiatives was carefully paid for. Investments in green energy and education would be financed by a cap-and-trade pollution system. Health care reform would be funded chiefly by rolling back the Bush tax cut for the affluent: each year's worth of expired tax cuts for the top two brackets would just about pay for a year's worth of expanded health coverage (confidential interview, August 2, 2010).

But the Great Recession thwarted these careful plans. The problem for health care reform was that the financial bailout and the stimulus bill—totaling an astonishing $1.5 trillion—had spent the next twenty years' worth of Bush tax cuts in one fell swoop. But tax receipts were plummeting, leaving the budget deficit for 2009 heading toward 11 percent of GDP or more. Several advisors urged Obama to put off health care in the face of the recession and a wary public (Alter 2010). But Obama insisted that they proceed, both because having watched his dying mother deal with insurance forms he thought it was the moral thing to do and because failure to reform health care would set the Democrats up for even more of a bloodbath in the 2010 midterm elections. Not to mention the fact that health care costs, which for years had risen faster than inflation, faster than the rest of the federal budget, and indeed faster than the growth rate of the economy itself, threatened to overtake first the federal budget and eventually the whole economy if unchecked (Congressional Budget Office 2007). The long-term fiscal health of the nation required health care reform, current conditions aside. Obama decided to go ahead with his health care initiative, but stipulated that the reform be deficit neutral.

But where to get the money? One way to achieve deficit neutral financing would be to use money from inside the health care system, such as reductions in reimbursements for doctors and hospitals. Another would be to use revenue sources that would bend the cost curve by providing incentives to reduce health care spending. Both kinds of sources emerged in the early proposals and were incorporated into the final bill.

All of the major bills—the House Tri-Committee bill of July 2009, the Senate Finance Committee bill of October 2009, and the November House and December Senate bills—financed reform from within the health care system with savings in future Medicare and Medicaid spending, including cutting payments for health-acquired conditions such as infections, reducing payments to disproportionate-share hospitals, and in most bills reducing the outsized subsidies that Medicare Advantage plans had been receiving since they were created in the 2003 Medicare Modernization Act.[7] Except for the House Tri-Committee bill, the proposals also scaled back some existing health-related tax credits, such as limiting the size of flexible spending accounts, increasing the tax on health savings account monies not used for medical expenses, and increasing the threshold for the itemized deduction for unreimbursed medical expenses.

Beyond these provisions, the bills varied more substantially. The most significant difference was in new sources of revenue. The House version sought additional revenues from outside of health care with new income tax surcharges on high earners: a 5.4 percent tax on individuals making over $500,000 and families over $1 million. In contrast, the Senate Finance Committee bill sought financing from within health care with an excise tax on high-cost insurance, the so-called Cadillac tax, designed to encourage people to select cheaper insurance plans. The Senate bill, which became the framework for the final legislation after the Scott Brown election, included both the excise tax and an increase in the Medicare payroll tax for higher earners: a 0.9 percent increase—from 1.45 percent to 2.35 percent—on incomes over $200,000 for individuals and $250,000 for families.

The differences in the bills' financing are in part due to general preferences of the respective chambers' members (confidential interview, August 4, 2010). The more liberal Democratic caucus in the House was more interested in taxing the incomes of the affluent. In contrast, the excise tax and increased Medicare payroll taxes were revenue sources from within health care, something that appealed to conservative Democrats in the Senate and possible Republican supporters like Senator Olympia Snowe.

The excise tax in particular became an important feature once other elements that might have changed consumer behaviors and bent the cost curve—such as a soda tax—were rejected, although a tanning tax was in the final bill: apparently more middle-class Americans drink soda than patronize tanning salons. That said, the excise tax on high-value health plans was wildly unpopular with the public and especially with unions. A majority of Americans supported many of the individual features of the health care reform, but the Cadillac tax, along with Medicare reductions and the individual mandate to purchase insurance, were the most disliked elements (Blendon and Benson 2010).[8] Unions objected to the tax as threatening the health care benefits they had so diligently achieved through collective bargaining over time; union leaders "scoffed" at some economists' assertions that they needn't worry because health care savings would be returned to workers in the form of higher wages (Greenhouse 2010). Over the course of months the tax took different forms as negotiators sought less politically repellant versions. Originally it taxed individuals on their health plans—a political nonstarter. Then the thought was to disallow the deduction for employers' premiums on such plans, also unpalatable. The final formulation taxes the health insurance plans themselves. Even though it is widely assumed the tax will get passed on to individuals through higher premiums or reduced benefits, the ability to say insurance companies are being taxed provided a modicum of political cover.

Unions did succeed in getting implementation of the excise tax pushed off until 2018. However, the tax—a 40 percent levy on the value of a plan that exceeds a threshold amount—is structured such that more and more plans will be taxed over time, as the 2010 thresholds of $10,200 for individual coverage and $27,500 for family coverage are indexed to the Consumer Price Index, which rises more slowly than medical inflation.[9] This was an intentional design: the tax affects a small number of plans at the outset in order to give people time to adjust, but over time becomes increasingly binding as more plans are taxed, encouraging people to move to less elaborate plans and spend less on health care. Similarly, the increased Medicare payroll tax on higher earners will hit growing numbers because its income thresholds are not indexed to inflation at all. Such mechanisms will raise increasing sums over time so that future Congresses can avoid blame and the necessity of taking explicit action to raise revenues (see Weaver 1988).

An additional new revenue source is a new tax on health care–related industries beginning in 2012 and 2014. The legislation stipulates a fee on each sector, such as the $2.8 billion charge on pharmaceutical manufacturers for 2012 and 2013, that individual firms pay according to market share (Kaiser Family Foundation 2010, 4). Given the health industry lobby's muscle, such fees may seem like an extraordinary provision: why would these industries agree? Basically they were told: you're going to benefit from this reform, and you should help finance it. In part, Obama's health care reform passed and other efforts over the past century failed because most of the major health-care interest groups stood to benefit and supported the reform, or at least muted their opposition. With the reform imposing a mandate that all Americans must have insurance, and the government subsidizing those who would have trouble purchasing insurance on their own, both insurers and providers (particularly hospitals) stood to fare quite well. In the absence of reform, their revenue would have declined, given concerns that the long-term budget deficit is driven chiefly by health care costs. With reform they instead will garner millions of new customers and billions in new revenue; the industry fees were a way to claw some of that back to help pay for the reform while still leaving insurers, hospitals, device makers, and pharmaceutical manufacturers better off.[10]

In sum, the revenue provisions of the health care reform, along with its promise to bring health insurance coverage to millions of Americans, were a key achievement in Obama's agenda to address the growing economic inequality of the previous three decades. Those who could not afford insurance now would be able to, with the affluent footing much of the bill. For years high-income households had been pulling away from the rest of society; now they would share their spoils, and at least one major driver of economic insecurity among ordinary Americans would be defeated.

LOOMING ISSUES: THE DEFICIT AND TAX POLICY

If with the health care reform Obama achieved what so many of his predecessors had failed to do, all the while battling the worst economic conditions in seven decades, the rest of his agenda was now threatened.

Although the president had been elected on a pledge of change, many Americans felt the changes were coming far too quickly and that the scope of federal government was growing far broader than they ever anticipated, between the bailouts, the health care reform, and the rest of the dizzying activity of the president's first year. Never mind that most of the TARP money would be repaid by the banks or that market mechanisms—private insurers rather than Medicare for all—were used for the health care reform. The government leviathan was growing too fast. Epitomizing these concerns was the federal budget deficit, which had risen above $9 trillion for the decade, triggering a debate about the need to shore up a fragile recovery in the short term with addressing the long-term mismatch between revenues and spending obligations. And on top of that difficult set of issues was the looming expiration of the Bush tax cuts. At the end of 2010, the 2001 and 2003 tax cuts would expire. Obama had long pledged to keep the cuts in place for the vast majority of Americans, letting only the income taxes of the top 2 percent revert to Clinton-era levels. But Republicans, newly emboldened by the president's sliding popularity and anticipating big gains in the 2010 midterm elections, argued that no one's taxes should be raised during a recession. In their eyes, the deficit was caused by excess spending, and skirmishes about offsetting further spending with reductions elsewhere in the budget dominated policymaking during the spring and summer of 2010.

The Long Shadow of the Deficit

The Obama administration could argue that two-thirds of the long-term deficit was due to problems it inherited from the tax-and-spend policies of the Bush administration and the long-term liabilities in Social Security and Medicare. Liberal economists, led by Paul Krugman, could argue that more stimulus was needed. But the sheer size of the number brought a salience that the deficit and national debt had not enjoyed since Ross Perot's presidential run in 1992. Multiple academic and think tank conferences were convened about the deficit; the $1 billion Peter G. Peterson Foundation worked inside and outside the Beltway to call attention to what it called "the real national debt"—both known liabilities and promised future entitlement payments.[11] Polls showed concern about the deficit rising.[12] The Tea Party movement began in summer 2009, with concerns about the deficit paramount in the group's antigovernment rhetoric. In Washington, bills extending unemployment insurance and providing fiscal relief for state and local governments were held up over deficit concerns. The administration may have saved the financial system from collapse, counteracted some of the recession's worst economic damage, and achieved victories of historic proportion such as the health care reform, but deficit concerns would shape debate and constrain the administration's agenda henceforth.

By fall 2009 the size of the deficit was apparent and beginning to sway arguments about further stimulus. Some economists argued that a second stimulus should be enacted, as the first was too small and its effects were waning. Republicans argued that the first stimulus did not produce more jobs; why enact a second round of a failed policy? Even the public was lukewarm at best, a July 2010 *Time* magazine poll finding two-thirds of Americans opposed to a second stimulus, as had been two-thirds of respondents in an August 2009 Gallup/*USA Today* poll (*Time* Magazine/Abt SBRI 2010, Gallup/*USA Today* 2009). The administration also felt a second stimulus was unnecessary, in part because spending from the first bill was still rolling out, with many projects, especially in infrastructure, slated for 2010 and even 2011 (Calmes 2009). But it also continued to get hammered on the economy, with the unemployment rate over 9 percent by May 2009 and over 10 percent for the last three months of the year (Bureau of Labor Statistics 2010), and long-term unemployment reaching levels not seen since the Great Depression.

Deficit concerns were on full display in Obama's first State of the Union address in January 2010 (2010b). The president used the address as a platform to defend his actions thus far in rescuing the economy from depression, arguing that the bank bailout was "necessary" if unpopular, that the stimulus had saved 2 million jobs, and that he had cut taxes for millions of middle-class families: "We extended or increased unemployment benefits for more than 18 million Americans; made health insurance 65 percent cheaper for families who get their coverage through COBRA; and passed 25 different tax cuts. Now, let me repeat: We cut taxes. We cut taxes for 95 percent of working families. We cut taxes for small businesses. We cut taxes for first-time homebuyers. We cut taxes for parents trying to care for their children. We cut taxes for 8 million Americans paying for college" (2010b). He tried to rally Congress to pass health care. But he also acknowledged deficit concerns by proposing a three-year freeze on discretionary domestic spending, although by exempting the Defense, Homeland Security, and Veterans Administration budgets as well as the big three entitlement programs, Medicare, Medicaid, and Social Security, such a freeze would constitute only a tiny percentage of the total deficit reduction needed. To the consternation of many progressives, he also pledged to create a bipartisan commission to address the deficit if Congress failed to do so.

Progressives could take heart from Obama's fiscal year 2011 budget, released days later, which reiterated many of the redistributive proposals from his first budget: in addition to some provisions for business,[13] it sought to extend the Making Work Pay tax credit for one year, extend the American Opportunity college tax credit expansion for ten years, expand the EITC and child and dependent care tax credits, expand the saver's credit, and require automatic enrollment in individual retirement accounts (IRAs). For high-income households, the budget yet again called for a rollback of the Bush tax cuts for the top two brackets, increasing their tax rates, limiting the value of itemized deductions to 28 percent, and raising the capital gains and dividend tax rates to 20 percent. The budget would make permanent the 2009 estate tax parameters.

However, as of late summer 2010, Congress had declined to pass a budget resolution, in part because of the sensitivities of an election year, in part because Washington was in limbo awaiting the recommendations of the deficit commission, due December 1, 2010. Such recommendations could set the agenda for the rest of the Obama administration.

The Deficit Commission

Talk of a deficit commission to address the long-term shortfall between revenues and spending had heated up by fall 2009. With Democrats opposed to cutting entitlements and Republicans opposed to raising taxes, normal lawmaking procedures seemed destined for deadlock. After all, with the Bush tax cuts expiring at the end of 2010, Congress should probably have addressed the tax issue during 2010, but by late summer had not. Certainly many observers thought the disappearance of the estate tax in 2010 for one year would have forced action in 2009, but Congress demurred on this as well.[14] The House did pass a permanent extension of the 2009 estate tax parameters in December 2009, with no Republican votes, but that was the end of estate tax action. A permanent extension was deemed too great a measure and a one-year extension was contemplated instead, but even that failed, caught up in a House-Senate dispute about budget rules (Maggs 2010).

The idea behind a deficit commission was that an independent body might be able to construct a package of proposals to address this contentious set of issues that Congress wanted to avoid, much in the way that the Greenspan Commission rescued Social Security in 1983, when the program's trust fund was exhausted. North Dakota Democrat Kent Conrad, chair of the Senate Budget Committee, and New Hampshire Senator Judd Gregg, the senior Republican on the committee, proposed a deficit commission whose recommendations would be voted on up-or-down, much like the successful military base–closing commission. However, the proposal's prospects appeared to flag as congressional leaders such as Speaker Nancy Pelosi and Senate Finance Committee Chairman Max Baucus opposed the idea as giving up too much congressional power (Hulse 2009a, 2009b).

The issue reached a head when several senators agreed to raise the U.S. debt limit in December 2009 only if they were promised a debate about a commission in January (Hulse 2009b). Vice President Biden negotiated with the Senate on an eighteen-member commission, which Obama would create by executive order if the Senate failed to approve the Conrad-Gregg proposal to establish the commission by law. Indeed, the Senate did reject the proposal, and Obama signed the executive order in February.

The deficit commission—officially named the Bipartisan Commission on Fiscal Responsibility and Reform—was charged with devising a package of proposals that would lead to a balanced budget by fiscal year 2015, outside of interest on the national debt, and was due to report December 1, 2010, after the midterm elections. Cochaired by Republican Alan Simpson, the former senator from Wyoming, and Democrat Erskine Bowles, Bill Clinton's chief of staff, the commission consisted of ten Democrats and eight Republicans.[15] Fourteen of the eighteen members had to support any recommendations, giving Republicans a veto.

In November 2010, chairmen Simpson and Bowles issued a preliminary report that, on the one hand, challenged the conservative view that the federal budget could be balanced with spending cuts only, but, on the other, prompted fury from progressives for focusing more on the spending side, with $2 in spending cuts for every $1 in increased revenue. The plan set revenues at 21 percent of GDP and spending at 22 percent of GDP at first, moving down to 21 percent—a level in keeping with postwar averages but one that did not acknowledge an aging population, allow for investment, or contain realistic assumptions about growth in health care spending. Indeed, in its February 2010 report, an earlier deficit panel convened by the National Academy of Sciences and the National Academy of Public Administration created four paths to a stable long-term debt ratio. The lowest spending pathway required truly draconian cuts in Social Security, Medicare, and Medicaid, as well as a 20 percent cut in funding for all other federal programs. This pathway was intended to illustrate a politically unviable extreme to contrast with two centrist pathways: it held spending to 21 percent of GDP, exactly the level of the Simpson-Bowles proposal (see Horney, Van de Water, and Greenstein 2010; NRC-NAPA 2010).

Specifically, the chairmen's preliminary plan included both military and domestic spending cuts; a higher federal gas tax; an income tax reform that would eliminate or trim various tax breaks such as the home mortgage interest deduction, child tax credit, and earned income tax credit in exchange for lower rates (8 to 23 percent on individuals, down from the existing 10 to 35 percent, and 26 percent on corporations, down from the existing 35 percent); a higher Social Security retirement age (with exemption for physical laborers); imposition of the Social Security payroll tax on higher income levels; and reductions in Medicare and Medicaid spending. The commission chairmen tweaked the plan slightly and met with each member individually in the hopes of garnering the fourteen votes needed to send the package to Congress. Ultimately, only eleven members supported the plan (see Fiscal Commission 2010a, 2010b).

Also in November, the Bipartisan Policy Center issued the recommendations of a nineteen-member commission headed by former Clinton budget director Alice Rivlin and former Republican senator Pete Domenici. Their plan sought to reduce the budget deficit over a slightly longer time frame—2012 through 2020—and with a more even split between spending decreases and revenue increases than the Deficit Commission chairs' proposal—about fifty-fifty, compared to the two-thirds spending cuts and one-third revenue increase mix in the Deficit Commission plan. Recommendations included a one-year Social Security tax holiday to encourage hiring; new individual tax rates of 15 and 27 percent and a corporate rate of 27 percent in exchange for turning the deductions for home mortgage interest and charitable contributions into 15 percent refundable tax credits; an increased Social Security payroll tax on high earners and a reduction in future program benefits except for low-income retirees; a new soda tax; four- and five-year freezes on domestic discretionary and military spending; a reduction in Medicaid growth; and perhaps most radically, the transformation of Medicare into a voucher program and a new national sales tax for debt reduction.

The recommendations of both the president's deficit commission and the Rivlin-Domenici panel were middle grounds between two other sets of plans offered, including, on the right, Representative Paul Ryan's Roadmap for America's Future, which would slash entitlement spending and taxes on the very rich, and from the left, plans from liberal groups that delayed action until 2015, fixed Social Security's ills through tax increases without benefit cuts, and eliminated tax expenditures to address the deficit without lowering tax rates.

Without approval by fourteen members, the Deficit Commission's recommendations did not go to Congress for a vote, but its proposals, along with those of the other groups, gave Obama a menu of options as he developed his fiscal year 2012 budget. Although they take very different approaches to looming tax and spending questions, these reports suggest the parameters around which a conversation about the nation's fiscal future must revolve.

The Midterm Elections and a
Reenergized Republican Party

As that conversation takes place, it will do so in the context of divided government. Democrats lost party control of the House and therefore unified control of government as the 2010 midterm election pitted an energized Republican electorate against a demoralized and diminished Democratic constituency. Many of those who turned out in heavy numbers in 2008, such as youth and minority voters, stayed home in 2010, and Democratic candidates lost ground among suburban residents, college graduates, women, and independents as well (Calmes and Thee-Brenan 2010). Along with control of the House, Republicans gained seats in the Senate, greatly complicating the second half of Obama's term.

During the lame-duck session, Democrats did pass an extraordinary number of measures: repeal of the "don't ask don't tell" policy on gays in the military, a 9/11 workers' health bill, a food safety bill, and a New Start arms control treaty with Russia, among others. But if Democrats were able to prevail in important ways on those measures, Republicans left their mark on the repeal of the Bush tax cuts, feeling that the elections had given them a mandate on tax-and-spend issues and free rein to extend tax cuts for the wealthy.

The Expiring Bush Tax Cuts

When they were passed in 2001 and 2003, the Bush tax cuts were designed to expire at the end of 2010, both to hold down the estimates of their cost and to tap the reconciliation process, given that Republicans lacked the sixty votes needed to get the legislation through the Senate without threat of filibuster. Reconciliation was devised in 1974 to facilitate the budget process, but has come to be used for many controversial measures because it limits debate and thus circumvents the filibuster, and only fifty votes are needed for passage. The Bush tax cuts had to expire after ten years to comply with the Byrd rules, passed in 1985 and modified in 1990, which further stipulate that a bill cannot be passed under reconciliation if it affects federal revenues for more than ten years (Tax Foundation 2010).

The expiration date had an agenda-setting effect: no matter what was happening, Congress would have to take action before the cuts expired December 31, 2010, to prevent reversion to higher tax rates (Hacker and Pierson 2005). As President Obama said in his weekly address in early November, "None of us want [middle-class Americans] to wake up on January 1st with a higher tax bill" (Obama 2010c). Obama's plan all along had been to use the tax cuts' expiration to decouple the cuts for the middle class and those for high incomes, continuing the former and letting the latter expire. Indeed, among the public raising taxes on the rich remained very popular, particularly compared with raising taxes on the middle class. A March 2010 Bloomberg poll found that the most popular options to "decrease the deficit" were to "allow the tax rate for the highest income earners to go back up to where it was ten years ago" and to remove the wage cap on the Social Security tax. Dead last was "raising the income tax rate on middle-class Americans by 2%" (2010a). To carry out Obama's strategy, the Democrats should have taken care of this issue before the election, but were divided. Some within the party felt Democrats were on the winning side of the issue. But others thought that the party was vulnerable to the tax-and-spend label and bought into Republican arguments against tax increases during a recession, even on the rich. Several vulnerable incumbents "implored" Senate Majority Leader Harry Reid not to force a vote before the election (Calmes 2010).

Because of their inaction, Democrats were forced to deal with the tax issue during the lame-duck session, during which they still controlled both houses of Congress but also had to negotiate with a Republican Party emboldened by the election results. Republicans insisted on an extension of cuts for the wealthy, deaf to accusations of hypocrisy that such an extension would make the budget deficit worse. Senator Chuck Schumer pushed a fallback position for Democrats—a so-called millionaire's tax repealing the Bush tax cuts for those earning over $1 million rather than over $250,000—but Republicans countered that the Democrats were trying to foment class warfare (Steinhauer 2010).

Ultimately, Obama forged a deal with Republicans in which they achieved a two-year extension of the Bush tax cuts for everyone including the wealthy, in exchange for several economic stimulus provisions that Democrats wanted: chiefly a thirteen-month extension of unemployment benefits and a one-year payroll tax reduction on workers. The price tag for the two-year package was $858 billion, $57 billion for the unemployment insurance extension and $801 billion for tax cuts, all added to the deficit.

Many on the left were furious with Obama's deal, and the president was angry with them in return. "This is the public option debate all over again," Obama complained at a December 7 press conference, purists angry about failing to achieve the ideal when they should be celebrating achieving the politically possible. Obama added, "I think it's tempting not to negotiate with hostage takers, unless the hostage gets harmed" (2010a). In truth, Obama did give way on two signature pledges from the campaign, most notably letting tax cuts for the wealthy continue, failing to achieve the decoupling he desired, and having to trade a continuation of his Making Work Pay tax credit for the one-year payroll tax reduction.

Republicans also succeeded in securing a two-year deal on the estate tax at a lower rate than Obama had pledged.[16] The deal contained many elements helping the middle class and upper middle class—the payroll tax deduction, another AMT adjustment, a temporary repeal of the limit on itemized deductions, and repeal of a phase-out for personal exemptions. Distributionally, however, the wealthy accrued most of the benefits— lower income tax rates, the estate tax provisions, and the continuation of capital gains and dividend taxes at a 15 percent rate—and the top 1 percent of earners got at least 25 percent of the total tax savings. And taxes on low-income workers will actually increase, because the payroll tax reduction is less valuable to them than the Making Work Pay tax credit had been (Kocieniewski 2010; see also Tax Policy Center 2010).

In sum, the first two years of the Obama administration included both victories and defeats in the president's efforts to reorient taxing and spending in the United States. Robust financing for the health care bill not only helped secure its passage, by giving important interest groups like providers substantial new revenue flows, but also increased taxes on the wealthy to pay for coverage expansions to the uninsured. Temporary features of the stimulus bill and other pieces of legislation also helped ordinary Americans. But the political impacts of the recession, along with Republican recalcitrance, made it difficult for Obama to achieve more. And the inconvenient timing of the expiring Bush tax cuts thwarted Obama's plans to increase taxes on the wealthy and shift the distributional impact of the income tax. Obama opened the conversation on economic inequality and redistribution, but two years in, the conversation is far from over.

LOOKING FORWARD: WHAT DIFFERENT PATHS MEAN

Tax policymaking in the near future will be dominated by two policy issues: the expiration (again) of the Bush tax cuts in 2012, and the need for comprehensive tax reform. Both will offer another opportunity for Obama to realize his vision of altering the trend toward economic inequality by tilting the tax system to rest more heavily on the affluent. But both will be negotiated in the context of a weak economy and the policy legacies of the conservative assault on taxes.

The deal Obama forged with congressional Republicans in December 2010 ensures that the Bush tax cuts will come onto the agenda yet again during an election year. Some Democrats see this as a political boon, an additional opportunity to expose Republican hypocrisy on tax cuts and the deficit. Others fear, however, that the extension of tax cuts for the wealthy may make rollback in a couple of years even more difficult. Moreover, the economist Paul Krugman argues that the tax deal is politically problematic because popular provisions for the middle class, such as the payroll tax reduction and unemployment benefits extension, will expire at the beginning of 2012, precisely the moment Obama needs the economy to be as strong as possible to aid his reelection bid. Obama and the Democrats may yet again be left in the position of begging Republicans for extensions. Jonathan Chait of *The New Republic* characterizes the likely Republican position on tax cuts: "First you extend them into 2012. Then, in 2012, if the economy is still weak, that weakness becomes the reason to extend the tax cuts once more. If the economy has recovered, you credit the tax cuts with sparking the recovery" (2010). A potent legacy of the Bush tax cuts is in generating a perennial political problem for the Democrats.

One way to get out of this cycle would be comprehensive tax reform. A two-year extension may buy time for tax reform before the middle-class tax cuts expire once more. What all of the deficit proposals agree on—from the center to center-right Deficit Commission and Rivlin-Domenici recommendations, to the more ideological plans of Paul Ryan on one end and the liberal groups on the other—is the need for comprehensive tax reform. The proliferation of tax expenditures is often cited as a problem—federal revenues lost to tax breaks now exceed those collected from the individual income tax—but more fundamentally, the enormous complexity of the tax code undermines faith in the system.

What is also necessary, however, is a national conversation about the distribution of the tax burden and the scope of government. Americans have become accustomed to low federal taxes. But the 21 percent of GDP they are used to paying cannot support the continued spending on Social Security, Medicare, education, infrastructure, defense, and other areas they also say they want. Surveys show they are also not prepared to give up cherished and expensive tax breaks like the deductions for home mortgage interest and employer-provided pensions and health care (Pew Research Center for the People and the Press 2010b). The various commissions and reports make these mismatches between revenue and spending preferences clear, but real decisions about paths to take must be made soon. The distribution of taxation is just as important: the top 1 percent of earners have accrued much of the nation's total economic growth over the last thirty years, yet now pay nearly the lowest effective tax rates in history. A conversation about these matters could provide a powerful opportunity for Obama to reassert his vision, but one which would be politically fraught, due to two contextual factors.

First is the continuing impact of the Great Recession. Officially the recession ended in June 2009 (National Bureau of Economic Research 2011), but most Americans in early 2011 believe the recession continues. GDP may be growing, but haltingly and unevenly. The stock market may be rising, but unemployment remains high. The economy feels like it is in a recession and will for some time, coloring public opinion. The United States is in a very deep hole, the rate of job growth for the foreseeable future lagging the growth needed to keep up with population growth, much less that needed to put millions of unemployed Americans back to work.

The economic downturn makes conversations about taxing, spending, and the role of government difficult for several reasons. It puts into sharp relief the contradictory strands of public opinion. Americans were hit hard by the downturn, with a Pew Research Center study (2010) showing that two and a half years into the recession, 55 percent of all adults in the labor force had experienced some work-related hardship such as unemployment, reduced pay or hours, or an involuntary switch from full- to part-time work. And yet such pronounced hardship does not necessarily translate into desire for government help. After all, Obama assumed office not only under the worst economic conditions in seventy years but also at an historic low in trust in government (Pew Research Center for the People and the Press 2010a). Moreover, Obama's efforts on behalf of ordinary people were overshadowed by the continuing pain of the recession and the great deal of publicity garnered by efforts to bail out the financial sector. Among the major bills enacted by the 111th Congress were new protections from wage discrimination, expansion of the Children's Health Insurance Program, new prohibitions on credit card abuses, the cash for clunkers program, home-buyer credits, and a major student-loan overhaul, not to mention the health care reform. But when asked whether Obama had "paid more attention" to the problems of banks and other financial institutions or those of middle-class Americans, 60 percent of respondents in a January 2010 CNN poll said the banks and only 28 percent said the middle class. And it seemed difficult for Americans to see redistributive policies at work. A July 2010 Pew/*National Journal* poll found that 53 percent of respondents thought large banks and financial institutions had been helped "a great deal" by the "federal government's economic policies since the recession began in 2008," unsurprising given similar results on other polls. However, 31 percent thought the wealthy had been helped a great deal, 7 percent thought the poor had, and just 2 percent thought the middle class had.

It is apparently difficult for ordinary citizens to appreciate such action—probably the most legislation helping lower- and middle-class Americans since the Great Society—when unemployment remains above 10 percent and underemployment a good deal higher. Or when one believes that one's taxes are going to go up in the future: the modal answer when respondents are asked whether their taxes or taxes for most Americans have gone up under Obama is that they have "stayed the same,"[17] but two-thirds say their taxes will go up in the future (Gallup 2010) and three-quarters say health care reform will increase the taxes they pay (Quinnipiac University 2010). It's hard to sell tax rate hikes on the wealthy to a middle class that thinks they are next in line. CBO scoring may have concluded that the health care reform would reduce the deficit, but 70 percent of Americans say it will make the deficit worse (Blendon and Benson 2010). And reflecting in part polarization at the elite level, but also perceptions of who benefits and who will pay, opinion is more negative among higher-income, white, independent, and of course Republican individuals (Pew Research Center 2010). They are also less likely to approve of the health care reform (Blendon and Benson 2010). Thus the recession and continuing poor economic conditions—and perceptions that government has done little to improve the lot of many—leave Americans feeling vulnerable and anxious around issues like taxation as well as skeptical about the ability of government to help them.

The second contextual condition that will complicate debates about the nation's fiscal future is the continuing legacy of the conservative antitax agenda. We see this in the fiscal legacy left by the Bush administration, with the creation of a medium-term deficit due to the prescription drug benefit, Iraq and Afghanistan wars, and tax cuts having two effects. There is confusion between the shorter-term deficit and the long-term shortfalls in the major entitlement programs, enhancing arguments for cutting the latter; and the existence of the medium-term deficit lends credence to deficit hawk arguments against stimulus needed to relieve the effects of the economic downturn. The antitax agenda has also created a perceptual legacy, delimiting what fiscal policy parameters are viewed as possible. We see this in the emphasis on spending cuts over revenue increases even in supposedly centrist deficit proposals. We also see it in the recommended structure of the individual income tax. An enduring legacy of the Reagan-era tax reforms was not just that top tax rates should be so low, but that the number of brackets should be so small. During the 1980s, the top marginal income tax rate fell from 70 percent to 28 percent. Critically also, the 1986 reform collapsed more than a dozen tax brackets into just two, which since has expanded to six, the top rate kicking in at just under $380,000 in 2011. What is remarkable is that twenty-five years later, when the income of the top 1 percent has increased so enormously, the individual income tax recommendation of the centrist Rivlin-Domenici deficit commission is again just two brackets. That a millionaire's tax cannot get on the agenda—that a $20 million CEO pays the same marginal tax rate as his $250,000 dentist—is telling of the political influence of the rich and of the legacy of the conservative low-tax agenda.

OBAMA AND THE POLITICS OF TAXING AND SPENDING

Barack Obama came into office with audacious plans to tackle growing income inequality and make the wealthy contribute more to the society that had so richly rewarded them. But a tragedy of the Obama presidency was how quickly the economic collapse became his. In the failed politics of the stimulus, Americans could not see the relief the government was pumping into the economy. Wall Street got rescued before Main Street, and the gamble that such structural fixes would lead to more jobs failed. With millions out of work, homes in foreclosure, and consumers tackling old debts rather than spending anew, Obama's accomplishments in other areas—areas that ironically would help the middle class in unprecedented ways—were utterly overshadowed by continuing economic woes. With impunity, Republicans used the budget deficit—owing in large part to the policies of the previous Republican administration—as an excuse to refuse further stimulus measures. Tax cuts for the rich could continue, however.

With the health care reform and other legislative accomplishments benefiting lower- and middle-class Americans, Obama has begun to change the national debate about inequality and the role of government. But how far the conservative mindset has infiltrated is illustrated in something else Obama pledged, which is to continue the Bush tax cuts for the bottom 98 percent of the income distribution—at a cost of $3.2 trillion over a decade compared with $700 billion for continued cuts for the top 2 percent. On the one hand, many in this broad swath have seen their real incomes fall over time, so tax relief has some merit. On the other, keeping their taxes low— indeed cutting them further with the Making Work Pay credits and payroll tax reduction—plays into the Republican trope that taxes are bad and that one should not have to pay for government, or even one's Social Security benefits. Thirty years of conservative rhetoric has delegitimized taxes and promoted the view that "public services aren't worth paying for" and that the "correct answer is to get someone else to pay for them" (Yglesias 2009). Getting Americans to agree that government is worthwhile would be truly transformational.

I am indebted to Mike Sances for his invaluable research assistance and to the individuals I interviewed during the summer of 2010. I also thank Mo

Fiorina, Desmond King, Sarah Binder, Tom Hamburger, Theda Skocpol, Larry Jacobs, and my fellow participants in the Obama Agenda Project for their helpful comments.

NOTES

1. Hence there would be no Social Security tax between the wage cap—$102,000 in 2008—and $250,000 in earnings.
2. RealtyTrac data, available at: http://www.recharts.com/rt/RT_1.html.
3. Responses to a *New York Times*/CBS survey item: "Regardless of how you usually vote, do you think the Republican party or the Democratic party is more likely to ensure a strong economy?" as compiled from the Roper Center's iPoll database.
4. This credit was an enhancement of the first-time homebuyers' tax credit established in the Housing and Economic Recovery Act of 2008, which gave a credit of up to $7,500 for homes purchased in 2008 that had to be paid back in fifteen equal annual installments beginning in 2010.
5. The ARRA business provisions include extending through 2009 increased Section 179 expensing; 50 percent bonus depreciation for 2009; and increased net operating loss carryback period to five years (Altshuler, Lim, and Williams 2009).
6. For example, in testimony before the U.S. House Committee on Small Business on July 24, 2008, economist Mark Zandi of Moody's Economy.com said that the multiplier effect—the associated gain in GDP—was $1.73 for each dollar of increased food stamp benefits but only 29 cents for making the Bush income tax permanent (U.S. Congress 2008).
7. The Senate bill restructured Medicare Advantage payments rather than cut them outright.
8. Only 24 to 34 percent of Americans supported the excise tax, 28 percent supported an individual mandate with penalties, and 19 percent supported reductions in Medicare spending. In contrast, 64 percent approved increased taxes on families earning $250,000 or more, 69 percent approved the employer mandate, 79 percent supported filling in the Medicare prescription drug "doughnut hole," 81 percent supported the new insurance exchanges, and 90 percent approved tax breaks for small employers to provide coverage for their employees (Blendon and Benson 2010).
9. The thresholds are higher for those in high-risk professions and retired individuals age fifty-five and older who are not eligible for Medicare (Kaiser Family Foundation 2010).
10. Indeed, the only major interest group that was not happy with the reform were physicians. Although in a historic move the American Medical Association did endorse the legislation, physicians did not get the Medicare payment

system fix they wanted—the so-called sustainable growth rate (SGR) problem. The difficulty was that there wasn't enough revenue to cover the $300 billion cost of a SGR fix and still keep the reform deficit neutral.

11. The foundation asserted that these liabilities totaled $56.4 trillion (Peter G. Peterson Foundation 2009).

12. An increasing share of *New York Times*/CBS News poll respondents had heard "a lot" about the deficit, increasing from 30 percent in July 2009 to 42 percent in February 2010 (2009, 2010). The percentage of ABC News/*Washington Post* poll respondents saying they were very concerned about the size of the federal budget deficit increased from 49 percent in December 2008 to 59 percent in April 2009 and 56 percent in June 2009 (2008, 2009a, 2009b).

13. Eliminating capital gains taxes for small businesses, making the R&D credit permanent, reforming the international tax system, among other provisions.

14. In the absence of congressional action, there was no estate tax for the 2010 calendar year. As of January 1, 2011, the tax would revert to a 55 percent tax on the value of estates over $1 million.

15. Six members each were chosen by Republican and Democratic leaders and by Obama—that is, after Simpson and Bowles, Obama selected one more Republican and three more Democrats.

16. Rather than restoring the 2009 parameters of a 45 percent tax on estates over $7 million per couple, Republicans achieved a 35 percent tax above $5 million.

17. A February 2010 CBS/*New York Times* poll found that 53 percent of respondents said the Obama administration has kept "taxes for most Americans" about the same, 24 percent said they were higher, and 12 percent said they were lower. In this poll, 44 percent of Tea Party identifiers said their taxes were higher, 46 percent said they were the same, and 2 percent said they were lower (2010a). An April 2010 CBS/*New York Times* poll found that 48 percent said their taxes were about the same, 34 percent said higher, and 10 percent said lower (2010b). And a July 2010 Bloomberg poll found that 65 percent said their "federal income taxes" were about the same as under the Bush administration, 20 percent said higher, and 7 percent said lower (2010b).

REFERENCES

ABC News/*Washington Post*. 2008. U.S. National Opinion Survey. iPoll Database Item No. USABCWP.121708.R11 (December 11–14, 2008). Storrs: Roper Center for Public Opinion Research, University of Connecticut. Available at: http://www.ropercenter.uconn.edu/data_access/ipoll/ipoll.html (accessed January 28, 2011).

———. 2009a. U.S. National Opinion Survey. iPoll Database Item No. USABCWP .042609.R15 (April 21–24, 2009). Storrs: Roper Center for Public Opinion Re-

search, University of Connecticut. Available at: http://www.ropercenter.uconn
.edu/data_access/ipoll/ipoll.html (accessed January 28, 2011).

———. 2009b. U.S. National Opinion Survey. iPoll Database Item No. USABCWP
.062209.R31 (June 18–21, 2009). Storrs: Roper Center for Public Opinion Research, University of Connecticut. Available at: http://www.ropercenter.uconn
.edu/data_access/ipoll/ipoll.html (accessed January 28, 2011).

Alter, Jonathan. 2010. *The Promise: President Obama, Year One.* New York: Simon and
Schuster.

Altshuler, Rosanne, Katherine Lim, and Roberton Williams. 2010. "Desperately
Seeking Revenue." Paper prepared by Tax Policy Center for "Train Wreck: A
Conference on America's Looming Fiscal Crisis." USC Gould School of Law,
Los Angeles (January 15, 2010).

Bartels, Larry M. 2008. *Unequal Democracy: The Political Economy of the New Gilded
Age.* New York: Russell Sage Foundation; Princeton, N.J.: Princeton University
Press.

Blendon, Robert J., and John M. Benson. 2010. "Public Opinion at the Time of the
Vote on Health Care Reform." *New England Journal of Medicine* 362(16): e55.

Block, Fred. 2009. "Read Their Lips: Taxation and the Right-Wing Agenda." In *The
New Fiscal Sociology: Taxation in Comparative and Historical Perspective,* edited by
Isaac William Martin, Ajay K. Mehrotra, and Monica Prasad. New York: Cam-
bridge University Press.

Bloomberg. 2010a. U.S. National Opinion Survey. iPoll Database Item Nos.
USSELZER.032410.R11D, USSELZER.032410.R11A, and USSELZER.032410
.R11E (March 19–22, 2010). Storrs: Roper Center for Public Opinion Research,
University of Connecticut. Available at: http://www.ropercenter.uconn.edu/
data_access/ipoll/ipoll.html (accessed January 28, 2011).

———. 2010b. U.S. National Public Opinion Survey. iPoll Database Item No.
USSELZER071410A.R11 (July 14, 2010). Storrs: Roper Center for Public Opinion
Research, University of Connecticut. Available at: http://www.ropercenter
.uconn.edu/data_access/ipoll/ipoll.html (accessed January 28, 2011).

Brownlee, W. Elliot. 2000. "Historical Perspective on U.S. Tax Policy toward the
Rich." In *Does Atlas Shrug? The Economic Consequences of Taxing the Rich,* edited
by Joel B. Slemrod. New York: Russell Sage Foundation.

Bureau of Labor Statistics. 2010. "Employment Status of the Civilian Population by
Sex and Age." Labor Force Statistics. Household Data, Table A-1. Washington:
U.S. Department of Labor. Available at: http://www.bls.gov/webapps/legacy/
cpsatab1.htm (accessed January 27, 2011).

Calmes, Jackie. 2009. "Debate on Creating Jobs, without Raising Deficit." *New York
Times,* November 30, 2009, p. A20.

———. 2010. "Tax Cut Timing Is Proving Problematic for Democrats." *New York
Times,* November 9, 2010, p. A24.

Calmes, Jackie, and Megan Thee-Brenan. 2010. "New Support from Independents Fueled G.O.P. Gains, Exit Polls Show." *New York Times*, November 3, 2010, p. P8.

Campbell, Andrea L. 2009. "What Americans Think about Taxes: Opinion and the American Fiscal State." Unpublished manuscript. Cambridge, Mass.: Massachusetts Institute of Technology.

CBS/*New York Times*. 2010a. U.S. National Opinion Survey. iPoll Database Item No. USCBSNYT.021110A.R067 (February 11, 2010). Storrs: Roper Center for Public Opinion Research, University of Connecticut. Available at: http://www.ropercenter.uconn.edu/data_access/ipoll/ipoll.html (accessed January 28, 2011).

———. 2010b. U.S. National Opinion Survey. iPoll Database Item No. USCBSNYT.041410A.R053 (April 14, 2010). Storrs: Roper Center for Public Opinion Research, University of Connecticut. Available at: http://www.roper center.uconn.edu/data_access/ipoll/ipoll.html (accessed January 28, 2011).

Chait, Jonathan. 2010. "Save Donald Trump! Is Now a Really Bad Time to Soak the Rich?" *The New Republic*, September 22, 2010. Available at: http://www.tnr .com/article/politics/magazine/77847/shall-we-soak-the-rich-now-magazine-donald-trump-jonathan-chait (accessed February 7, 2011).

CNN/Opinion Research Corporation. 2009. U.S. National Opinion Survey. iPoll Database Item No. USORC.011609.R23 (January 12–15, 2009). Storrs: Roper Center for Public Opinion Research. University of Connecticut. Available at: http://www.ropercenter.uconn.edu/data_access/ipoll/ipoll.html (accessed January 28, 2011).

Congressional Budget Office. 2007. "The Long-Term Budget Outlook." Washington: Government Printing Office, December. Available at: http://www.cbo .gov/ftpdocs/88xx/doc8877/12-13-LTBO.pdf (accessed January 27, 2011).

———. 2009. "Historical Effective Federal Tax Rates: 1979 to 2006." Washington: Government Printing Office, April. Available at: http://www.cbo.gov/ ftpdocs/100xx/doc10068/effective_tax_rates_2006.pdf (accessed January 27, 2011).

Feldman, Stanley, and John Zaller. 1992. "Political Culture of Ambivalence: Ideological Responses to the Welfare State." *American Journal of Political Science* 36(February): 268–307.

FiscalCommission.gov. 2010a. "CoChairs Report." Washington, D.C.: National Commission on Fiscal Responsibility and Reform, November 10, 2010. Available at: http://www.fiscalcommission.gov/news/cochairs-proposal (accessed January 27, 2011).

———. 2010b. "The Moment of Truth." Washington, D.C.: National Commission on Fiscal Responsibility and Reform. Available at: http://www.fiscalcommis sion.gov/sites/fiscalcommission.gov/files/documents/TheMomentof Truth12_1_2010.pdf (accessed January 27, 2011).

Free, Lloyd A., and Hadley Cantril. 1967. *The Political Beliefs of Americans.* New Brunswick, N.J.: Rutgers University Press.

Gale, William G., Peter R. Orszag, and Isaac Shapiro. 2004. "Distributional Effects of the 2001 and 2003 Tax Cuts and Their Financing." Washington, D.C.: Tax Policy Center. Available at: http://www.taxpolicycenter.org/UploadedPDF/411018_tax_cuts.pdf.

Gallup. 2010. U.S. National Public Opinion Survey. iPoll Database Item No. USGALLUP.041410A.R1 (April 8-11, 2010). Storrs: Roper Center for Public Opinion Research, University of Connecticut. Available at: http://www.roper center.uconn.edu/data_access/ipoll/ipoll.html (accessed January 28, 2011).

Gallup/*USA Today.* 2009. Gallup News Service Poll: Social Series–Work and Education. iPoll Database item no. USGALLUP.09AUT06.R30 (August 6–9, 2009). Storrs: Roper Center for Public Opinion Research, University of Connecticut. Available at: http//www.ropercenter.uconn.edu/data_access/ipoll/ipoll.html (accessed April 27, 2011).

Greenhouse, Steven. 2010. "Unions Rally to Oppose a Proposed Tax on Health Benefits." *New York Times*, January 9, 2010, p. B1.

Hacker, Jacob S., and Paul Pierson. 2005. "Abandoning the Middle: The Bush Tax Cuts and the Limits of Democratic Control." *Perspectives on Politics* 3(1): 33–53.

Heilemann, John, and Mark Halperin. 2010. *Game Change: Obama and the Clintons, McCain and Palin, and the Race of a Lifetime.* New York: HarperCollins.

Herszenhorn, David M. 2009. "High-Minded Budget Goals Yield to Reality." *New York Times*, March 28, 2009, p. A10.

Horney, James R., Paul N. Van de Water, and Robert Greenstein. 2010. "Bowles-Simpson Plan Commendably Puts Everything on the Table but Has Major Deficiencies Because It Lacks Appropriate Balance between Program Cuts and Revenue Increases Plan Needs Substantial Improvement in Key Areas." November 16, 2010. Washington, D.C.: Center on Budget and Policy Priorities. Available at: http://www.cbpp.org/files/11-16-10bud.pdf (accessed January 27, 2011).

Howard, Christopher. 1997. *The Hidden Welfare State: Tax Expenditures and Social Policy in the United States.* Princteon, N.J.: Princeton University Press.

———. 2007. *The Welfare State Nobody Knows: Debunking Myths about U.S. Social Policy.* Princeton, N.J.: Princeton University Press.

Hulse, Carl. 2009a. "Senate Passes an Increase in Debt Limit." *New York Times*, December 25, 2009, p. B2.

———. 2009b. "Senate Passes Spending Bill amid Debate on Raising Debt Limit." *New York Times*, December 14, 2009, p. A22.

Kaiser Family Foundation. 2010. "Summary of New Health Reform Law." Available at: http://www.kff.org/healthreform/upload/8061.pdf (accessed January 27, 2011).

Kocieniewski, David. 2010. "Tax Package Will Aid Nearly All, with the Highest Earners Benefiting Most." *New York Times*, December 8, 2010, p. A22.

Maggs, John. 2010. "Tax Snafu Déjà Vu." *National Journal*, April 30, 2010.

Martin, Isaac William. 2008. *The Permanent Tax Revolt: How the Property Tax Transformed American Politics*. Stanford, Calif.: Stanford University Press.

Mettler, Suzanne. 2009. "From Shifting Modes of Governance to Transformed Civic Attitudes? Exploring Social Program Effects, 1970–2008." Paper presented at the annual conference of the American Political Science Association. Toronto (September 3–6, 2009).

Mishel, Lawrence, Jared Bernstein, and Sylvia Allegretto. 2005. *The State of Working America: 2004–2005*. Ithaca, N.Y.: Cornell University Press and Economic Policy Institute.

Morgan, Kimberly J. 2007. "Constricting the Welfare State: Tax Policy and the Political Movement against Government." In *Remaking America: Democracy and Public Policy in an Age of Inequality*, edited by Joe Soss, Jacob S. Hacker, and Suzanne Mettler. New York: Russell Sage Foundation.

National Bureau of Economic Research. 2011. "U.S. Business Cycle Expansions and Contractions." Available at: http://www.nber.org/cycles/cyclesmain.html (accessed January 27, 2011).

National Research Council and National Academy of Public Administration (NRC-NAPA). 2010. *Choosing the Nation's Fiscal Future. Committee on the Fiscal Future of the United States*. Washington, D.C.: National Academies Press. Available at: http://www.ourfiscalfuture.org/wp-content/uploads/fiscalfuture _full_report.pdf (accessed January 28, 2011).

New York Stock Exchange. 2010. "Dow Jones Industrial Average History." Available at: http://www.nyse.tv/dow-jones-industrial-average-history-djia.htm (accessed January 27, 2011).

New York Times/CBS News. 2009. U.S. National Opinion Survey. iPoll Database Item No. USCBSNYT.072909B.R29 (July 24–28, 2009). Storrs: Roper Center for Public Opinion Research, University of Connecticut. Available at: http://www .ropercenter.uconn.edu/data_access/ipoll/ipoll.html (accessed January 28, 2011).

———. 2010. U.S. National Opinion Survey. iPoll Database Item No. USCBSNYT.021110B.R032 (February 5–10, 2010). Storrs: Roper Center for Public Opinion Research, University of Connecticut. Available at: http://www .ropercenter.uconn.edu/data_access/ipoll/ipoll.html (accessed January 28, 2011).

Obama, Barack. 2007a. "Cutting Costs and Covering America: A 21st Century Health Care System." Speech in Iowa City, Iowa. (May 29, 2007). Available at: http://www.barackobama.com/2007/05/29/cutting_costs_and_covering _ame.php (accessed January 30, 2011).

———. 2007b. "Full Text of Senator Barack Obama's Announcement for Presi-

dent." Speech in Springfield, Ill. (February 10, 2007). Available at: http://www
.barackobama.com/2007/02/10/remarks_of_senator_barack_obam_11.php
(accessed January 30, 2011).

———. 2007c. "Our Common Stake in America's Prosperity." Speech in New York,
N.Y. (September 17, 2007). Available at: http://www.barackobama.com/
2007/09/17/remarks_of_senator_barack_obam_24.php (accessed January 30,
2011).

———. 2007d. "Remarks of Senator Barack Obama to the National Conference of
Black Mayors." Speech in Baton Rouge, La. (May 5, 2005). Available at: http://
www.barackobama.com/2007/05/05/remarks_of_senator_barack_obam_13
.php (accessed January 30, 2011).

———. 2007e. "Strengthening Families in a New Economy." Speech in Spartan-
burg, S.C. (June 15, 2007). Available at: http://www.barackobama.com/2007/
06/15/remarks_of_senator_barack_obam_15.php.

———. 2007f. "Tax Fairness for the Middle Class." Speech in Washington, D.C.
(September 18, 2007). Available at: http://www.barackobama.com/2007/
09/18/remarks_of_senator_barack_obam_25.php (accessed January 30, 2011).

———. 2008a. "Confronting an Economic Crisis." Speech in Golden, Colo. (September 16, 2008). Available at: http://www.barackobama.com/2008/09/16/
remarks_of_senator_barack_obam_113.php (accessed January 30, 2011).

———. 2008b. "Joe the Plumber: A Transcript." *St. Petersburg Times*, October 19,
2008. Available at: http://www.tampabay.com/news/perspective/article858
299.ece (accessed January 28, 2011).

———. 2008c. "Plan to Fight for Working Families and Take on Special Interests in
Washington." Speech in Indianapolis, Ind. (May 3, 2008). Available at: http://
www.barackobama.com/2008/05/03/remarks_of_senator_barack_obam_61
.php (accessed January 30, 2011).

———. 2008d. "Remarks of Senator Barack Obama." Speech in Tampa, Fla. (October 20, 2008). Available at: http://www.barackobama.com/2008/10/20/
remarks_of_senator_barack_obam_140.php (accessed January 30, 2011).

———. 2008e. "Remarks of Senator Barack Obama: A Secure Energy Future."
Speech in Dayton, Ohio (July 11, 2008). Available at: http://www.barack
obama.com/2008/07/11/remarks_of_senator_barack_obam_90.php (accessed
January 30, 2011).

———. 2008f. "Remarks of Senator Barack Obama: Town Hall Meeting on the
Economy." Speech in Springfield, Mo. (July 30, 2008). Available at: http://
www.barackobama.com/2008/07/30/remarks_of_senator_barack_obam_98
.php (accessed January 30, 2011).

———. 2009. "Remarks to the Democratic Senatorial and Congressional Campaign Committees." Speech in Miami Beach, Fla. (October 26, 2009). Available
at: http://www.whitehouse.gov/the-press-office/remarks-president-dsccdccc
-reception (accessed May 10, 2011).

———. 2010a. "Dec. 7, 2010—Washington, D.C.: Obama Holds a News Conference." *Washington Post*, December 7, 2010. Available at: http://projects.washingtonpost.com/obama-speeches/speech/520 (accessed January 27, 2011).

———. 2010b. "Remarks by the President in State of the Union Address." January 27, 2010. Washington: The White House, Office of the Press Secretary. Available at: http://www.whitehouse.gov/the-press-office/remarks-president-state-union-address (accessed January 30, 2011).

———. 2010c. "Weekly Address: President Obama Calls for Compromise and Explains His Priorities on Taxes." November 6, 2010. Washington: The White House, Office of the Press Secretary. Available at: http://www.whitehouse.gov/the-press-office/2010/11/06/weekly-address-president-obama-calls-compromise-and-explains-his-priorit (accessed January 27, 2011).

Office of Management and Budget. 2009. "Fiscal Year 2010 Budget of the United States Government." Washington: Government Printing Office. Available at: http://www.gpoaccess.gov/usbudget/fy10/browse.html (accessed January 27, 2011).

———. 2010. "Fiscal Year 2011 Budget of the United States Government." Washington: Government Printing Office. Available at: http://www.gpoaccess.gov/usbudget/fy11/index.html (accessed January 27, 2011).

Page, Benjamin I., and Lawrence R. Jacobs. 2009. *Class War? What Americans Really Think about Economic Inequality.* Chicago: University of Chicago Press.

Page, Benjamin I., and Robert Y. Shapiro. 1992. *The Rational Public: Fifty Years of Trends in Americans' Policy Preferences.* Chicago: University of Chicago Press.

Peter G. Peterson Foundation. 2009. "State of the Union's Finances: A Citizen's Guide." March. Available at: http://www.pgpf.org/~/media/PGPF/Media/PDF/2009/04/01/PGPF_CitizensGuide_2009.ashx (accessed March 2, 2011).

Petrocik, John R. 1996. "Issue Ownership in Presidential Elections, with a 1980 Case Study." *American Journal of Political Science* 40(3): 825–50.

Pew Research Center. 2010. "A Balance Sheet at 30 Months: How the Great Recession Has Changed Life in America." A Social and Demographic Trends Report, June 30, 2010. Washington, D.C.: Pew Research Center. Available at: http://pewsocialtrends.org/assets/pdf/759-recession.pdf (accessed January 27, 2011).

Pew Research Center for the People and the Press. 2010a. "Public Trust in Government: 1958–2010." Available at: http://people-press.org/trust (accessed January 27, 2011).

———. 2010b. "Deficit Solutions Meet with Public Skepticism: Consensus in Principle, Resistance in Practice." December 9, 2010. Available at: http://people-press.org/report/683 (accessed January 27, 2011).

Pierson, Paul. 1994. *Dismantling the Welfare State? Reagan, Thatcher, and the Politics of Retrenchment.* New York: Cambridge University Press.

Piketty, Thomas, and Emanual Saez. 2003. "Income Inequality in the United States, 1913–1998." *Quarterly Journal of Economics* 118(1): 1–39.

Quinnipiac University. 2010. U.S. National Public Opinion Survey. iPoll Database Item No. USQUINN.032510.R43 (March 16–21, 2010). Storrs: Roper Center for Public Opinion Research, University of Connecticut. Available at: http://www.ropercenter.uconn.edu/data_access/ipoll/ipoll.html (accessed January 28, 2011).

Reich, Robert B. 1997. *Locked in the Cabinet.* New York: Vintage.

Saulnier, Raymond J. 1991. *Constructive Years: The U.S. Economy under Eisenhower.* Lanham, Md.: University Press of America.

Smith, Mark A. 2007. *The Right Talk: How Conservatives Transformed the Great Society into the Economic Society.* Princeton, N.J.: Princeton University Press.

Steinhauer, Jennifer. 2010. "Some Democrats Count on 'Millionaires' Strategy on Tax Cuts." *New York Times,* December 3, 2010, p. A22.

Tax Foundation. 2010. "Why Are the Bush Tax Cuts Expiring?" May 26, 2010. Available at: http://www.taxfoundation.org/news/show/26312.html (accessed January 27, 2011).

Tax Policy Center. 2010. "Compromise Agreement on Taxes." Available at: http://www.taxpolicycenter.org/taxtopics/Compromise_Agreement_Taxes.cfm (accessed January 27, 2011).

Teles, Steven M., and Martha Derthick. 2009. "Social Security from 1980 to the Present: From Third Rail to Presidential Commitment—and Back?" In *Conservatism and American Political Development,* edited by Brian J. Glenn and Steven M. Teles. New York: Oxford University Press.

Time Magazine / Abt SBRI. 2010. Time/Abt SRI Poll: Economy. iPoll Database item no. USSRBI.071510.R23 (July 12–13, 2010). Storrs: Roper Center for Public Opinion Research, University of Connecticut. Available at: http//www.ropercenter.uconn.edu/data_access/ipoll/ipoll.html (accessed April 27, 2011).

U.S. Congress. House of Representatives. Committee on Small Business. 2008. "Economic Stimulus for Small Business: A Look Back and Assessing Need for Additional Relief." 110th Cong., 2nd sess., July 24, 2008. Serial No. 110-108. Washington: Government Printing Office. Available at: http://www.gpo.gov/fdsys/pkg/CHRG-110hhrg40870/pdf/CHRG-110hhrg40870.pdf (accessed January 28, 2011).

Weaver, L. Kent. 1988. *Automatic Government: The Politics of Indexation.* Washington, D.C.: Brookings Institution.

Wolffe, Richard 2009. *Renegade: The Making of a President.* New York: Crown Publishers.

Woodward, Bob. 1994. *The Agenda: Inside the Clinton White House.* New York: Simon and Schuster.

Yglesias, Mathew. 2009. "The Next Tax Revolt." *The American Prospect* 20(5): 38. Available at: http://www.prospect.org/cs/articles?article=the_next_tax_revolt (accessed January 27, 2011)

Index

Boldface numbers refer to figures and tables.